BOOKS BY R. TURNER WILCOX
The Dictionary of Costume
Folk and Festival Costume of the World
Five Centuries of American Costume
The Mode in Furs
The Mode in Footwear
The Mode in Hats and Headdress
The Mode in Costume

THE DICTIONARY
OF COSTUME

THE DICTIONARY
OF COSTUME

R. Turner Wilcox

B. T. BATSFORD LTD

London

to RAY WILCOX
and RUTH WILCOX

First published 1969 by Charles Scribner's Sons, New York

First published 1970 in Great Britain by

B. T. Batsford Ltd, 4 Fitzhardinge Street, London W1H 0AH

Reprinted 1973

Reprinted 1979

First paperback edition 1989

ISBN 0 7134 0856 1 (*hardcover*)

ISBN 0 7134 6277 9 (*paperback*)

Printed in Great Britain by Courier International Ltd., Tiptree, Essex

PREFACE

A dictionary, according to one definition given by Webster, is "a reference book listing alphabetically terms or names important to a particular subject . . . along with discussion of their meanings and applications." In the present case, the subject pertains to historic costume and its many branches. No longer will it suffice to recount only the Ancient, Medieval, Renaissance and Western periods to provide the researcher of today with the foundation upon which to build. For build he must, as our world grows ever smaller while peoples increase in undreamed-of numbers and distances decrease as airtravel carries men to the farthest corners of the earth.

In costume, such words as aba, agal, amout, bürka, caften, chadar, chogā, dhoti, djellaba, kaffiyeh and hundreds more, are becoming everyday words in the language of the mode. And at the same time, the aborigines are intrigued into adopting and wearing clothes of Western make. In this day and age, we, the Westerners, have learned to manufacture textiles not from the age-old staples such as cotton, linen, silk, wool and fur but to produce beautiful fabrics from air, gasses, chemicals and what not! All of which creates words and more words to be recorded in the language of costume and fashion.

To dig in and record this vast subject, I found to be a task of unusual proportions. In fact, I discovered that it was almost impossible for a lone individual to both write and illustrate such a work in a given length of time and without assistance. I am deeply indebted to my editor, Miss Elinor Parker, for her checking and rechecking of the many, many items in the manuscript and for her long hours of work that went into alphabetical arrangement.

R. T. W.

THE DICTIONARY
OF COSTUME

A

aal Hindustani name of the East Indian morinda bush of the madder family which yields a red dye.

aba, abba, abayeh a primitive Moslem garment of Africa, Turkey and Persia which serves as cloak and blanket, a square of cloth with openings for head and arms. Usually of wool, plain or striped; camel's or goat's hair for travelers, or silk for upper classes. The woolen cloth itself is called aba.

abaca Filipino name for manila hemp from the banana stalk native to the Philippine Islands, and the most important of cordages. Used for fabrics and straw hats.

abalone a shellfish lined with mother-of-pearl, which is used for inlaying ornaments, buttons, beads, etc.

abaya the silk scarf of fallahs, or peasant women, in Egypt, Syria and other Arabic countries.

abbé's cape the three-tiered shoulder cape of the abbé's cloak.

abbot cloth a canvaslike, coarse cotton fabric in basket-weave similar to monk's cloth.

abnet a long scarf or sash worn by a Jewish high priest or officer. Of fine linen or wool with embroidery.

abolla a Roman military cloak similar to the Greek chlamys, fastened at the neck. Worn by ancient soldiers on parade. see *birrus; byrrus; pœnula; Oxford gown.*

aba
or abayeh

abolla

academic gown a full-length black gown with long flowing sleeves. Accompanied by a cap or mortarboard and perhaps a hood, which is draped over the shoulders. Worn by faculty, students and graduates of colleges and universities and by honored celebrities upon official academic occasions. Slight variations in design indicate the rank of undergraduate, bachelor, master and doctor.

abbés
Cape

academic Gown

Adonis Wig

acton or
aketon

acus-
pin
for cloak
or hair

accessories   a term which covers all items that complete a costume and if not carefully chosen, such hat, shoes, gloves, handbag or whatever, can mar a costume.

accordion pleating   see *pleating.*

acetate   one of the first man-made fibers produced in America, by the Celanese Corporation of America in 1925.

acorn   an ornamental knob attached to men's hat cords. Also, a small military motif on the cap or collar of a uniform, representing the rank and corps of the wearer.

acrilan   trademark of a liquid derivative of natural gas and air. It is used alone in lightweight fabrics such as challis and is combined with other fibers for children's clothes, blouses, skirts, uniforms and work clothes and pillows.

acton   see *gambeson, pourpoint, doublet.*

acus   an ancient Roman hairpin or bodkin of copper, bone or silver. The Saxons, who also used such a pin, called it a hair-needle and fastened their mantles with it.

adati   a fine light cotton fabric imported from Bengal, India.

Adolpho   see *couture, haute*

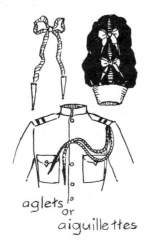

aglets
or
aiguillettes

Adonis wig   see *wig, Adonis.*

African capes   see *lamb shearlings.*

agabanee   a Syrian-made cotton fabric embroidered in silk.

agal   the hoop or fillet of thick cords of wool or goat's hair which holds the

agal

kaffiyeh or cloth of the African headdress in place. The agal is often wound around with gold and silver threads. see *kaffiyeh.*

agate   a stone, chalcedony of variegated colors, cloudy and striped, used in ornaments and costume jewelry. Moss agate is white or gray, with black or green flecks.

agbada   the Nigerian man's cape, worn over pajama-like breeches, both of cotton. Of brilliant, dazzling colors with printed motifs. see *iro.*

agilon   the trademark for stretch nylon yarn, the original yarn used for stretch seamless stockings. Also used in sweaters, other sportswear and carpets.

aglet, aiglet, aiguillette   a metal point or tag attached to a ribbon, cord or lacing for tying dress accessories in the fifteenth, sixteenth and seventeenth centuries. Sleeves were so tied to the armholes. Also called points. Aglets were replaced by buttons and hooks in the mid-seventeenth century. Aiguillettes survive today in an ornamental festoon worn with military officers' full dress uniforms.

Agnès, Mme.   see *couture, haute.*

agraffe, agrafe   a fastening for clothing originally devised for armor in the form of a hook, clasp or buckle, which lasted into the eighteenth century.

aiglet   see *aglet.*

aigrette   plume or tuft of plumes, used for woman's hairdress, etc.; the feather aigrettes of commerce were formed of the plumes of various egrets. see *egret; Audubon plumage law.*

aigrettes

aiguillette   see *aglet.*

airplane cloth   a plainweave pima-yarn cloth, water-repellent, with a mercerized, highly lustered finish which was used for covering lightweight airplanes and gliders. Later, much in use for sports and work shirts.

aketon   see *acton.*

akwaba doll   young women of Ghana wear a doll tied around the waist as part of their draped toga-like cotton clothes, which are in brilliant designs and colors. The akwaba doll is a sign that the wearer is unmarried.

alabaster   as a color, resembling alabaster, a mineral of fine texture, usually white and translucent and carved into small works of art.

à la mode   a surah type of silk, a popular fabric from Surat, India. Soft, lightweight, twilled cloth. The lustrous quality was called surah and the heavier grade, silk serge. Used for dresses and blouses. Nineteenth and early twentieth centuries.

Alaska or **American sable**   see *skunk* or *raccoon.*

Alaska sealskin   see *seal.*

alb, alba   a Latin secular garment worn up to the ninth century. It was white and embroidered, a long-sleeved full-length vestment put on over the cassock and girdle. Now worn by priests at mass.

albatross   a soft, fuzzy and loosely woven material used principally for warm nightgowns, negligées and infants' wear, and for nuns' habits. Usually woolen, but can be cotton.

Albert cloth   an overcoating of double cloth construction, all wool and reversible, each side a different color and requiring no lining.

Alençon lace   made in Alençon, France, and has been called "the queen" of French handmade needlepoint laces. It dates from the early seventeenth century. On a fine net ground, the design, usually floral, is worked and outlined by a heavy thread or cordonnet. The early pieces were copies of Italian lace, the art having been taught by Italian lacemakers, since the wearing of lace not made in France was prohibited by royal edict. It was used for altar hangings, ecclesiastical garments, gentlemen's cravats and for adornment of court ladies' dresses. Often used today in bridal dresses and veils.

alépine   a silk and wool cloth used for

akwaba doll
of Ghana

alb
or
alba

alicula

"all-in-one made possible by stretch nylon and the slide fastener— 1940's

men's apparel in the early eighteenth century.

Algerian stripe   an imitation of Moorish cloth woven in rough, knotted cotton and silk in alternating colored stripes on a cream ground.

alicula   a Roman traveling and hunting cloak with sleeves and cowl, worn over the tunica. Greek for red, because it was usually red. see *byrrus; birrus*.

A-line, trapeze silhouette   dress or coat style, flaring slightly from shoulders to hemline without a break. Launched by the youthful Yves Saint Laurent in his first collection shown at Dior's, 1958, after the sudden death of the maestro. It brought him great acclaim. see *trapeze line*.

alizarin, alizarine   a purplish-red dye, formerly obtained from madder root, first discovered in 1831. In 1869, a method of manufacturing the dye from coal tar was produced. The first synthetic or artificial dye.

alligator   the tanned hide of a water reptile from the United States and India, with square boxlike markings. Belly and shanks only, of baby alligators, are used for shoes, handbags, luggage, etc. Imitation alligator leather is stamped with hot rollers to produce the square alligator markings. see *leather*.

all-in-one   a corselet, or combination brassière and corset for the heavy figure, which first appeared in the 1920's, with steel replacing whalebone. In the 1930's an all-in-one which obliterated the "debutante slouch" was introduced. It was made of lastex, a two-way stretch fabric in a one-piece body garment, which held the body firm without the aid of gores and stays.

alloutienne   a French silk which has a slight slub in the weave and is sturdy

enough not to pull at the seams. Used principally for formal evening gowns.

allover   a term applied to a pattern or design which is repeated or covers the whole surface of the material.

amuce·aumusse

almuce, aumuce   a cloth hood lined with fur or a fur hood with cloth lining worn by the clergy in the thirteenth, fourteenth and fifteenth centuries, in cold weather. Attached to the cowl, it could be dropped in back and was called a monk's hood.

alnage   an ell, or forty-five inches, the former English measurement of cloth, now little used. Of varying measure in different countries.

aloe hemp or fiber   any species of Agave, an important genus of plants which give a hemplike fiber used for lace, cloth, embroidery, musical instruments, etc.

aloe lace   a fragile lace made of aloe fibers.

aloha shirt   a brilliantly colored printed silk shirt, a copy of the Hawaiian man's garment, generally worn outside the trousers. Its breezy comfort made it

aloha Shirt

alpargata-Spanish

American Indian with roach and war paint

smokers' articles and in blending certain perfumes.

amber, black   see *jet*.

American cloth   the name given by the British to American oilcloth, used occasionally for waterproofing caps, jackets and traveling cases.

American Indian costume   When the explorers first came, Indian dress consisted of skins and furs beautifully dyed, feathers, and the soft bark of trees and grasses. New England Indian women wore a short wraparound skirt of skin, and men a breechclout of skin. If needed, men and women might wear a short, sleeveless type of skin poncho. In New England and Virginia, an Indian woman's dress was sometimes made of two elkskins fringed, beaded and tied with thongs at the sides and over the arms, belted by a thong. *Footwear*, from Virginia northward moccasins were worn, but southern Indians, as a rule, went barefoot. Along with moccasins, in New England and the upper Mississippi valley, leggings of tanned deerskin were worn by both sexes. They were decorated with red, yellow and blue motifs. *Headband*, worn by both sexes, of dyed black cloth sewn with porcupine quills, beads, wampum, feathers and small stones. *Headdress*, masculine, a natural cut or artificial roach of deer hair was worn by Indian men of New York and New England. Southern Indians wore a topknot and Indians of the Great Lakes braided long hair. Indian women wore long, braided hair and, occasionally, cut a fringe over the forehead. *Mantle*, when needed, a robe or cloak was worn by both sexes; it was made of moose, deer, elkskin, fox or squirrel. Indians fashioned beautiful cloaks of iridescent turkey feathers woven with self-made twine.

American sable   see *skunk*.

American shoulders   known in France as *épaules Américaines*, because most male American tourists wore broad, straight, padded shoulders from the late

a fad, beginning in the 1930's and continuing to the present.

alpaca   long hair of the Peruvian alpaca, a species of llama. Used principally for women's suits and sportswear, the cloth woven of hair alone or combined with wool. see *vicuña; llama*.

alpargata   sandal of woven hemp or rope in shaped sole with attached straps. Worn by Spanish, Italian and French. see *espadrilla*.

aluta laxor   heavy leather boots of ancient Rome made of aluta leather softened and made pliable by alum.

amazon   a woolen dress goods in a satin or twill weave with the nap raised and shorn for softness. Amazon, from the Greek signifying a female warrior. The word passed into the European languages to designate a horsewoman, later a tall, strong woman. In French, it is applied either to a horsewoman or her long riding skirt.

amber   a brittle fossil resin similar to vegetable resins ranging in color from pale yellow or light brown. Found by the ancients, as it still is, on the coasts of the Baltic sea. It may be cloudy, opaque or transparent. Sicilian amber is reddish brown. Baltic amber is yellow and Burmese amber honey-toned, and occasionally black. Often used for jewelry and

American shoulders-1905

amice

Mennonite woman in two tones of gray homespun wool or cotton—black neckerchief, shoes and stockings

amout

nineteenth and early twentieth centuries up to World War II.

American tiger   see *jaguar* under cat.

amethyst   a crystallized quartz of violet to purple, the finest specimens from India, Ceylon and Brazil. Used in jewelry as a semiprecious stone; the deeper the hue, the more valuable.

amice   a liturgical hood of fine white linen, a rectangular piece folded diagonally with strings tying over the chest. Up to the thirteenth century, a priest covered his face with a hood upon mounting the altar.

amictus   the general term for apparel in ancient Rome.

Amish

Amish dress   the plain black costume of the Christian Mennonites, or "Plain People." Both sexes wear black or a muted, dark color in public. Garments are fastened by hooks and eyes, and have no buttons or ornamentation, for which reason in earlier days the Amish were called hookers.

amout   see *parka.*

amulet   a piece of jewelry worn around the neck to ward off enchantments, accident or any ill luck.

anadem   a poetic term for a chaplet or wreath of flowers worn upon the head.

anadem or Chaplet

anamite   string color or the color of unbleached twine.

androsmane,   Kevenhüller,   continental   a Swiss military hat, popular to both civilian and military men. To the French it was *androsmane*, and to English and Americans, the *Kevenhüller*, named after the famous Austrian field marshal. Really a bicorne, it was built high in front and back with a spoutlike crease in the center front. Worn by General Washington, it was also called the *continental hat*. see *hat, cocked.*

Androsmane-
Kevenhüller-
Continental

angel skin or **peau d'ange** a modern finish—waxy, smooth and dull—applied to satin. Popular in the early twentieth century.

angel sleeve see *sleeve, angel.*

Angelus cap see *cap, Angelus.*

anglesea early twentieth century trade name for the slightly curling curve in men's hat brims.

Angleterre, English edging small needlepoint loops of cord or braid, worked to an edge.

Anglo-Saxon embroidery an ancient embroidery, the design outlined with long stitches and couched with silk or metal thread.

angora an overcoating of twill-woven cloth, soft and woolly, made of angora cat, rabbit or goat hair. The cloth originated in Turkey.

Angora cat

angora goat, mohair the wiry, lustrous and strong hair or wool of the angora goat of central Asia Minor, usually pure white and four to seven inches long. Formerly used as fur for the large nineteenth-century muffs, now imported for weaving with other fibers and called mohair.

Angora Goat

Angora rabbit

angora rabbit hair originally from the Madeira Islands, the animal was successfully raised in England and as a sideline by American farmers, rapidly becoming one of the important small industries in the United States. The fur is spun into yarn for sweaters, gloves and scarfs and sometimes mixed with wool. The hair is clipped or plucked, the plucked bringing a higher price.

aniline, anilin the product of dry distillation of indigo, discovered in 1826, becoming eventually the source of hundreds of dyes. In modern manufacture, anilin is derived from benzine, which is obtained from coal. Some anilin colors are fuchsia, magenta, aniline red, malachite green, Martino yellow and Victoria green.

animal fiber fibers taken from animals such as sheep, goats, camels, vicuña, etc. for the purpose of weaving, felting or knitting into fabric.

animal skins or **peltries** *Furs* are from fur bearers of both wild and domestic animals. *Pelts* are from sheep and lamb families. *Skins* are from goat and kid families. *Hides* are from cattle and horse families.

anklet a short sock, generally with a cuff, worn by children or for sports. An ankle bracelet, sometimes adorned with tiny nameplate or with jewels.

Annette
Kellerman
1920's

Anne Boleyn costume   named for one of Henry VIII's queens (1533–1536). A tight bodice with square décolletage and wide flaring sleeves; a bell-shaped canvas underskirt, forerunner of the hoop or farthingale.

Annette Kellerman   a swimsuit which was practically sleeveless and which ended a good two inches above the knee, named for a famous swimmer who wore such a shocking garment as early as 1909. The first rib-knit, elasticized wool swimsuit, a one piece tank suit was made by Jantzen in 1920 for American women, and from then on it became more abbreviated.

anorak   see *parka*.

antelope   soft, velvety, light leather dressed with suede finish on the flesh side. The antelope gazelle, the best-known species from Africa, Arabia and Persia. A small graceful animal, usually brownish or silver-tan.

anteri   a short white undervest quite generally worn by both sexes in the Balkans.

anti-crease   a process whereby cotton, linen, rayon fabrics are rendered crease-resistant by synthetic resin.

antique finish   a "weathered" or satin finish of wax and oil applied to shoes and leather goods.

antique satin   see *satin, antique*.

Antwerp lace   a rare bobbin lace, the original design representing the angel's Annunciation to the Virgin Mary. The surviving motif is a basket or pot of flowers.

apodesme, stethodesme   bosom band of wool, linen or chamoised leather which was either tied with tape or pinned with fibulae. With it was worn a wide stomach band called the *zona*. see *bosom band*.

apparel   clothing or garments. Also, the embroideries on the liturgical alb, amice or almuce.

Appenzell embroidery   point d'Alençon embroidery which originated in the Swiss Canton of Appenzell. It is very fine drawnwork embroidery on very sheer white linen or lawn; used for kerchiefs, handkerchiefs and aprons.

appliqué embroidery   French, meaning "applied to." A style of embroidery used on fabrics, lace, net, leather, etc., in which cutout motifs are sewn on by hand.

apron   a shield or protection for the wearer's dress, and most often secured by strings or ties. The earliest European apron was worn by the blacksmith, gardener and stone mason, and was of leather. Farm women and housekeepers wore the long apron of homespun or white linen. In the sixteenth and seventeenth centuries fashionable ladies adapted the apron. It was then made of fine sheer linen or lawn, embroidered, lace-trimmed, beruffled and finished with colored ribbons and bowknots. This dainty piece in the nineteenth century became the small "tea apron," pinned on and therefore called a pinner. see *Hoover apron.*

aquamarine   a beryl or semiprecious stone of clear light blue or blue-green.

arabesque   a type of ornamentation used in textile design, employing flower, foliage and fruit. The intricate, interlaced pattern of lines is founded basically on the acanthus and palmetto designs of the early Roman Empire.

aralac   a fiber resembling wool but of casein base, used for clothing and sometimes as a substitute for wool and some other fabrics in the millinery trade.

Aran sweater   see *fisherman sweater.*

araneous lace   thin, delicate, cobweb-like lace using the long, straight lines of the spider's web as the pattern. The term in the Middle Ages was used for embroidery in general.

Arctic fox   see *fox, Arctic.*

Arctic half-boot   see *mukluk.*

Arctic hare   heavy, long-haired animal from Russia and Siberia processed to simulate white fox. Blue fur fiber with white, tan or bluish-gray guard hair, the white peltries most desirable to the fur trade.

Also some from Arctic North America but not in demand.

arctics, galoshes   waterproofed, heavy black cloth overshoes with rubber soles, fastened by buckles. Worn by men, women and children. see *galoshes.*

argentan lace   also called point de France, an edging, insertion or banding. A needlepoint originally of Alençon, later made with a bolder floral pattern and a more open mesh.

Argyle, Argyll   a multicolored diamond pattern in woolen socks, sweaters and scarfs. Formerly hand-knitted in Great Britain, now mostly machine-made in England and America. Also, a sock having this pattern. Argyll is the name of the clan whose tartan is imitated in this kind of knitting.

arisard   the mantle or plaid worn by Scottish women to the mid-eighteenth century. It was long enough to cover the head down to the ankles, being draped at the waist.

armband   a band worn around the arm as identification or, when black, as a sign of mourning. *see mourning band, brassard.*

Armenian cloak   a fashionable gentleman's cloak of the 1850's and 1860's. With the exception of the deep velvet collar, the cloth was all in one piece with no inserted sleeves, but with side seams forming very loose arm coverings.

Armenian lace   a handmade narrow edging in tiny pointed scallops, used for infants' wear, handkerchiefs, lingerie, collars and cuffs.

Armenian rat   the Greek term for ermine because imported from Armenia. see *ermine.*

armet   a helmet of the fifteenth and sixteenth centuries.

Arctic Hare

arisard-Scottish plaid wrap-around cloak to mid 18th C.

Armenian cloak

armilla-gold-
Roman

armhole the opening left in the garment for attaching the sleeves. see *armscye.*

armilausa a short cloak or cape of cloth or silk, worn over armor in the medieval period.

armilla, armil, armlet bracelets of antiquity in bronze, silver and gold. Worn by Greek ladies and by Roman men, conferred upon the latter for heroic deeds. A pair of armillas is part of the English regalia used at the Coronation.

armlet a very short, plain sleeve sewn into the armhole or armscye.

armlets see *armilla.*

armor, armour as protective body covering in battle, has been in use from ancient times to the Renaissance. It was made principally of metal and cuirbouilli, or boiled and hardened leather. European armor dates from about the twelfth to the fourteenth century, in mixed mail and plate, and complete plate armor from the fifteenth to the seventeenth centuries. Decorative armor dates from after 1600, with partial plate lasting to 1700. The advent of the sturdy buffcoat and the cuirass of buff leather in the sixteenth and seventeenth centuries spelled the doom of heavy metal armor. see *buffcoat, cuirass.*

armozeen, armozine a heavy corded silk, usually black, formerly used for waistcoats but now for scholastic and clerical robes.

armscye a tailor's term for the armhole; also, the shape or outline of the armscye.

armure in medieval times a fabric woven with a small pattern resembling link-chain armor, hence its name. Still woven with small design in several colors on rep or twill ground in silk, wool, cotton and synthetics. Used for men's scarfs, waistcoats, formal costume and also drapery. see *barathea.*

Arnel trademark for synthetic fabric of cellulose triacetate.

arras the European tapestry which originated in the medieval Flemish town of northern France, Arras. The people also produced beautiful patterned leathers which rivaled those of Spain. They wove cloth from English and Scottish wools which was used by the other European countries and also sent to the East in exchange for Oriental luxuries.

arras lace bobbin lace made in Arras, France, and similar to that of Lille.

arrasene embroidery stitching worked with a chenille cord having wool or silk pile which produces a velvety effect.

arrowhead an embroidered triangle placed at the ends of seams of tailored garments, pleats or pocket joinings, as a stay.

artificial silk An eminent British scientist writing a book in 1664, foresaw the possibility of spinning out fiber-like silk. Commercial development delayed until 1910 when it was established by the American Viscose Company. Since the new fabric was not identical with pure silk, being produced from varied raw materials such as wood pulp, corn protein and chemical compounds, it was given the name of *rayon.* A fine synthetic fabric, it not only possesses the good qualities of the natural fiber but also is endowed with many advantageous features that pure silk can never have. Gabrielle Chanel first displayed a collection of models made of rayon at Deauville in 1915. In the United States, any metallic weighting in a silk fabric must be so labeled. Pure silk should be labeled "silk," "all silk," or "pure dye." see *rayon.*

artois   a fashionable garment of the late eighteenth and early nineteenth centuries, worn by both sexes. It was a cloak named for the Count of Artois, brother of Louis XVI, and later Charles X of France. The style, a long cloth coat with three or four short capes ending at the waist, lasted a long time as the coachman's box-coat.

Artois cloaks

asbestos   a non-inflammable, non-metallic mineral fiber which is woven into fabrics used where flame-proof protection is required in such as a theater curtain. Cotton with asbestos is sometimes used in covers for ironing boards.

ascot   a double-knot cravat with wide square ends folded over and held in place by a plain or jeweled scarfpin. Worn with a cutaway coat, especially to the fashionable English Ascot Heath horse races held early in June. The Ascot tie appeared first in the 1850's and was the origin of the Ascot puff of the 1870's. Its distinctive feature was its very wide puffed ends. Used periodically to the present by men and women as a wide kerchief or stock.

Asiatic cat   see *caracal.*

Assisi embroidery   a form of cross-stitch where the design itself is left plain or perhaps outlined.

astrakhan   formerly a general name for broadtail or karakul lambs from Astrakhan in Russia. A type of lambskin now called *caracul.* see *caracul,* under lamb.

astrakhan cloth   a manufactured cloth made to resemble astrakhan fur.

atef   crown of Egypt about 3000 B.C. When the victorious King Narmer united Upper and Lower Egypt, he added the red wicker crown of Lower Egypt to the white felt crown of Upper Egypt, placing it on top of the felt crown. Crowns were ornamented with the royal asp or uraeus.

athletic underwear   general name for the light, loose lisle underwear adopted by athletic men in the early twentieth century. Drawers were cut knee-length, shirts low-necked and sleeveless, with deep armholes. Undershirt and cotton briefs of today.

attar of roses   an essential oil, fragrant and volatile, obtained by distillation from rose petals, especially the damask rose. Used pure or as a base for many other perfumes.

attifet   bonnet and coiffure; a heart-shaped style with a point dipping over the forehead, the bonnet held in shape by wire frames. Worn by Catherine de' Medici in black, and Mary, Queen of Scots in white, mid-sixteenth century. The fashion survived as the widow's peak and cap to our times. see *barbette.*

auburn   usually pertains to hair color, a dark brown with reddish or copper-colored tinge.

ascot or puff-scarf

atef-Egyptian crown

attifet Coiffure

aumônière for
carrying alms

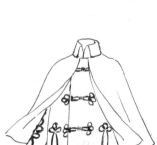

Austrian knots

automobile togs

Aubusson   a shade of red, rather like brick red.

Aubusson stitch   a vertical canvas stitch founded upon that used in the wall tapestries made at Aubusson, France.

Audubon plumage law   passed in 1905 to prevent the slaughter of native birds and the importation or merchandising of bird of paradise or egret feathers in the United States. In 1941, an agreement was reached between the Audubon Society and the Feathers Industries of America Inc. whereby the use of wild bird plumage for millinery and decorative purposes ended.

aumônière   a small bag carried in the Middle Ages by men and women. Originally of fabric or leather with a drawstring, it hung from belt or girdle, and was called a hanging pocket. During the Renaissance as men acquired pockets in their dress, they gave up the bag. Women continued its use, making it of silk or velvet and covering it with handsome embroidery and beadwork. see *reticule; pockets.*

aumuse   see *almuce.*

aune   the old French fabric measure of forty-five inches, or one and a quarter yards.

Australian wool   a fine type of wool raised in Australia from Spanish merino stock.

Austrian knots   heavy, black silk braid ornamentation on military uniforms appliquéd in looped designs. It decorated Austrian military dress, was copied by the Napoleonic and European armies, and adopted by the American armies in the nineteenth century.

automobile togs   necessary motoring attire in the early twentieth century. Cap and goggles were worn by men and women, with a long linen or silk coat or "duster"; women tied a long chiffon scarf over their hats, large and small, and, very often, over the face. see *veil, motoring.*

Ave Maria lace   a type of Valenciennes bobbin lace made at Dieppe, France, in the sixteenth and seventeenth centuries.

aventurine   a form of quartz, usually green but sometimes brown and yellow, containing a mass of tiny mica flakes which give the stone a speckled sheen. Used in jewelry.

avocado   a light greenish yellow, fashionable in dress and house-furnishing fabrics, named for a West Indian fruit with flesh of this shade.

awning   cloth or heavy, brightly striped canvas copied in narrower-striped cotton for summer sports clothes such as women's skirts and men's blazers.

Ayrshire embroidery   a dainty, popular Scottish embroidery on linen and cotton. Small floral patterns worked in eyelets. Used on dresses and linens.

azür   a Hungarian greatcoat made of black or white felt, or sheepskin with the fur to the inside in winter. The full-length broad lapels turn into a wide collar in back and the enormous sleeves are rarely used, being sewn closed to carry things. The coat is elaborately decorated on the skin side with variegated color appliqué of cut-out motifs accented with silk embroidery. It is a contemporary cloak.

azure   a term covering many hues of blue ranging from sky-blue to lapis lazuli.

B

babiche   an Algonquinian word meaning cord or thong of rawhide, sinew, etc.

babouche   the ancient Moslem slipper made without heel or quarters, often of leather embroidered in gold and silver.

babushka; shale   the Russian peasant head-scarf of wool, called the *shale*, is tied under the chin. The silk, summer scarf, *platok*, is tied at the nape. Because the older women refused to discard the head-kerchief it came to be called *babushka*, the Russian word for grandmother.

baby bunting   a flannel swaddling bag, with gown, hood, and sleeves made all-in-one and ribbon-tied at the neck, wrists and lower end. see *barrow coat*.

baby lace   usually Valenciennes, a very narrow lace made for baptismal dresses, layettes, etc.

baby pins   tiny gold bar pins usually in pairs and sometimes joined by a fine chain, set with semiprecious stones or pearls.

baby ribbon   a very narrow ribbon about a quarter of an inch wide, usually white, pink or blue. Much used in the late nineteenth and early twentieth centuries for threading and bowknots on fine hand-made lingerie of white nainsook, lawn and batiste; used also on infants' wear.

baby seal   see *seal, baby*.

Baby Stuart cap   see *cap, Baby Stuart*.

Babylonian work   the name by which Babylonian embroideries were known.

Linen was used but the principal fabric was wool elaborately embroidered with separate motifs founded upon the design of the rosette. Garments were always trimmed with fringe and tassels. The Babylonians were fond of brilliant colors, reds, blues, greens and purples. The purple kandys embroidered with gold was reserved for the king. see *kandys; kaunace*.

bachlik, bachelik   a short cape with hood finished with a fat tassel. A return to an ancient garment, worn since the beginning of the present century in France and the Balkans.

backstitch   a stitch used for strength in hand-sewing and embroidery, made by setting the needle back half the length of the last stitch on the under side, coming out on top, a half-stitch length ahead, making a continuous line of stitches on both sides, like machine-stitching.

badger   a heavily furred mammal allied to the skunk and weasel family, with coarse, durable hair of black mixed with white, gray or tawny; American badger the best. Badger hairs are important for pointing long-haired furs. Used for collars, cuffs and trimming.

badger whiskers   prescribed for the navy by the Honorable George E. Badger, Secretary of the United States Navy, 1841, "sailors' whiskers not to descend lower than one inch below the ear and on a line with the mouth."

bag   see *aumonière; handbag; musette bag; pouch; purse; reticule; shoulder bag*.

bag sleeve   see *sleeve, bag*.

babushka hood

Babylonian-
Assyrian-ancient

badger

badger whiskers-
American-1860's

Baju-Malaysian jacket

Balaclava

Balagnie cloak-17th C.

bag wig   see *wig, bag.*

bagheera   see *velvet.*

baishan   sleeveless coat worn by Chinese men as everyday costume.

baize   a coarse woolen cloth used for servants' clothes. In the time of Queen Elizabeth I, it was made at Colchester, England, but first made in Baza, Spain.

baju   a short, loose white cotton jacket with simple collar, breast pocket and short sleeves. Worn with short or long cotton breeches in Malaysian countries.

Bakelite   trade name of a synthetic resin formed by the condensation of chemicals producing a high electrical and chemical resistance resembling hard rubber and celluloid. Used for costume accessories such as buttons, buckles, pendants, etc.

baku, bakou   a fine straw of dull finish made from the unopened leaf stalks of the talipot palm of Malabar and Ceylon.

bal   a convertible collar.

bal, bicycle   see *bicycle bal.*

balaclava   a heavy woolen helmet crocheted or knitted by British and American women for the soldiers in World Wars I and II. Of khaki-colored yarn, it had a cuff around the neck that could be drawn up over the chin. It was also a winter cap for younger boys. The name comes from Balaklava, a seaport village on the Crimean coast of Russia, the scene of the memorable Charge of the Light Brigade in 1854.

balagnie cloak   an elegant garment of the seventeenth century in the reign of Louis XIII. A cape with deep collar draped over both or only one shoulder,

and held in place by cords attached under the collar.

balandrana, over-all, supertotus   a traveler's coat; a raincoat cloak of the sixteenth and seventeenth centuries which had a hood and enveloping sleeves and was worn by men and women.

balandrana or raincoat- 17th C.

balayeuse   French for sweeper, or a dust ruffle which was sewn to the under side of the long, trailing skirts of fashionable women in the late nineteenth and early twentieth centuries, to protect the skirt fabric. see *dust ruffle.*

balbriggan   first made in Balbriggan, Ireland, an unbleached cotton fabric with fleeced back manufactured in variations of tan and gray. It was used especially for men's winter underwear, which came to be known as balbriggans. Also used for hosiery, sweaters and such.

baldric   a wide silk sash or leather belt, often richly decorated. Worn over

baldric of silk-
English-Restoration-
1660's

the right shoulder and fastened on the left hip to carry sword, bugle, powder horn, etc. see *balteus*.

Balenciaga, Cristobal   see *couture, haute*.

baline   a coarse woolen or cotton fabric used for packing. Also, a hemp or jute fabric used for stiffening in handbags or upholstery.

Balkan blouse   a long-waisted blouse shirred into a wide hip-band with long, full sleeves gathered into tight wrist cuffs. Made of fine linen, lawn or voile and colorfully embroidered in combinations of red, blue, or black cotton thread in cross-stitch. A Western fashion during the Balkan War in 1913 and after, for several decades.

ball gown   a formal, full-length gown, usually with décolleté corsage.

ballerina   the toe-dancer's traditional dress of tight bodice and the tutu, a very short full skirt of layers of tulle or gauze that stand away from the body. Worn over tights. see *tutu*.

ballerina dress   the short dinner or evening dress was an origination of Valentina, an American couturière of

Russian extraction. The length proved a happy solution in the postwar years, filling a woman's need of an informal but dressy look when her escort was in business suit. see *Valentina*, under *couture, haute*.

ballet or **chorus shirt**   a garment worn by members of the corps de ballet for rehearsals; a plain white cotton shirt with turned-down collar.

ballet slippers   soft, low, flat slippers with a well-boxed toe to support toe-dancing, laced with ribbons. The style copied in comfortable bedroom slippers, 1940's.

ballibuntl, balibuntal   a hat of light-weight woven straw manufactured in Luzon, Philippine Islands.

ballibuntl, baliluk, ballybuntals, bally-wags   all are straws from the unopened palm leaf stems.

balloon sleeve   see *sleeve, balloon*.

balmacaan   a loose, flaring coat of Scottish origin, with flaring sleeves, usually of tweed, gabardine or raincoat fabric with military standing collar and slashed pockets.

Balkan blouse

ballet tutu-19th & 20thC.

balmacaan overcoat.
similar to the raglan-
1850's

Balmain, Pierre   see *couture, haute.*

balmoral   a laced-up shoe or half-boot with closed throat, introduced by Prince Albert about 1853. Everything new and smart at that time was named Balmoral, after the royal castle in Aberdeenshire, Scotland, built by the Prince and Queen Victoria. Also, a tennis shoe, 1890's. see *tennis dress.*

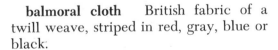

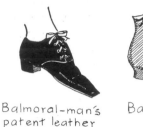
Balmoral-man's patent leather

Balmoral-feminine

Balmoral petticoat

balmoral cap   see *bluebonnet.*

balmoral cloth   British fabric of a twill weave, striped in red, gray, blue or black.

balmoral petticoat   a red woolen underskirt striped in black and worn under a long dress looped up for walking, popular in the 1860's and 1870's.

balteus   a form of the baldric worn in ancient Rome. Also, a leather girdle worn by soldiers and ecclesiastics.

bambino hat   a large-brimmed hat framing the face in halo fashion. Named after the famous round plaques of the Christ Child by the fifteenth century Florentine sculptor, Luca della Robbia.

band   in American colonial days, the neckband which finished that part of the white linen chemise next to the face. The simple collar of the Puritans was a plain band. The wider collar edged with lace which lay upon the shoulders was a falling band, as were the linen strips or tabs of the clerical and academical collars, still worn by clergymen.

bambino hat of the 1930's

bandeau concealed under bird

band strings   used in the sixteenth and seventeenth centuries to tie bands, collars and ruffs. Band strings ended in tassels or crochet-covered balls and often jewels.

bandanna, bandana   from the Hindu bāndhnū, the East Indian word for tie-dyeing. A large silk or cotton headkerchief dyed in brilliant colored spots on a dark ground.

bandbox   small, round, lightweight boxes originally for holding bands or collars. Charmingly decorated or covered with pretty wallpaper, they held various accessories, including hats.

bandeau   a narrow brassière, formerly worn to support the breasts. A narrow buckram band covered with silk or velvet to tilt a hat on the head. Also, a narrow fillet of jewelry, ribbon or wreath of flowers encircling the head.

banditti   a small panache of feathers on a feminine bonnet in the early 1800's.

band or falling band with band strings

band and strings-Pilgrim

band-plain-Puritan

bandle   in Scottish and English dialect, a word meaning two feet wide. Also Irish linen, coarse, homemade and two feet wide.

bandoleer, bandolier   see *baldric;* also, coarse, woven fabric belting for military and sportwear use.

bandore   the widow's black-veiled headdress of the eighteenth century.

Bangkok   a fine lightweight straw woven into a hood from fibers of a palm tree which grows in the vicinity of Bangkok. The finished hat is also known as a bangkok.

bangle bracelet   a ring bracelet or anklet from which dangle tiny tinkling charms.

bangs   fringe of hair covering forehead; has occurred as a coiffure fashion some time in every century for both men and women.

banian   see *banyan.*

Ban-Lon   the trademark of a crimped knit yarn, permanently set, of an attractive texture which is imparted to fabric and garments made from it.

Bannockburn   a cloth made in Bannockburn, Scotland, a tweed center. A typical British tweed and one of the best used for suitings and topcoatings.

banyan, banian   a luxurious negligée wrap worn by men and women in the seventeenth and eighteenth centuries, especially in the American South. Usually of bright color in silk, velvet or wool striped and lined to be worn either side out. see *Indian gown.*

bar pin   a long, narrow brooch or breast pin, a design in jewelry much worn in the first half of the twentieth century.

About 3 inches long, of platinum or gold, it was sometimes set with a row of gems, usually diamonds.

bar tacks   stitches forming a bar to reinforce the edges of seams, tucks, pleats, buttonholes, pockets, etc.; commonly used in tailoring.

barathea   a more general name for armure, so called because of the pebbly weave which resembles chain armor. Ribbed, plain or striped, woven in silk, cotton, combined with synthetics and often in two colors. Used for suits, dresses and scarfs. see *armure.*

barbette   a mourning headdress of widows in the sixteenth century. Of white linen worn over or under the chin, it has survived to modern times in nuns' dress.

barbette

barbute   a helmet of the fourteenth century, Italian origin, first with a high pointed crown and later round. The face was almost entirely covered with large cheek pieces. Also, a variety of the fifteenth century sallet.

barcelona   the kerchief in Spanish dress worn around head or throat or carried in the hand. Of twilled black silk and also in solid colors, gay patterns and checks.

bare midriff   a style first used in beachwear and briefly incorporated into

banditti
plume-1800

banyan

bangs

barong tagalog

barrister's Wig

evening dress in 1939, when the naked section between short bodice and belt was exposed. Modest females filled in the space with flesh-colored chiffon.

barège   a gauze-like fabric originally made in Barègas, France. Of wool, silk and wool, or cotton and wool, and used for veils, dresses, etc.

Barentzen, Patrick de   see *couture, haute.*

Bargello work   see *Florentine* or *Flame stitch embroidery.*

barmcloth, barmskin   From barm, the English word for both lap and the apron of leather. Worn by workmen.

Baronette   trade name for rayon fabric with high luster in satin weave and cotton back.

barong tagalog   the Filipino shirt or blouse worn in place of a dinner jacket. Often made of banana fiber cloth and embroidered.

baroque period   of extravagant ornamentation as from the fifteenth and sixteenth centuries to late nineteenth, equivalent to rococo. Of irregular form, as a baroque pearl.

barracan, barragan   a camel's hair or goat's hair cloth for menswear. Also, a kind of moleskin cloth in England. Used for cloaks and mantles in Eastern countries.

barracano   a Bedouin cloth blanket of coarse camlet carried by travelers or cavalry troops.

barré   silk or cloth, barred or striped from selvedge to selvedge. Used in costume and interior decoration according to weight and quality.

barretino   Italian for bonnet, a long stocking cap of knitted wool, or of felt in red or black. Worn in various shapes, folded or hanging, by Italian fishermen, Portuguese fishermen and farmers. It is used for carrying small possessions, even lunch.

barrette   a bar-shaped clip of varied length for holding women's hair in place. Much used in the late nineteenth and twentieth centuries when the coiffure was dressed up off the nape. Made of metal or shell, later of plastic.

barrister's wig   see *wig, full-bottomed, professional.*

barrow coat   a baby-bunting or pinning blanket, a flannel or knitted wrap for an infant. Usually a baglike garment with cap attached, folded and pinned and ribbon-tied at neck, wrists and lower end. Today the zipper has replaced such fastenings.

barracan - draped red and white barracanos of the spani police corps-worn over the kamis

barracan-a length of striped silk worn by a Moslem woman of Palestine

barretino

barrow-coat

Basque knitted shirt

bateau neck-line-1920's

Basquine

Lady's fishing costume-see Basque bodice 1870's

basil   sheepskin tanned by various processes. Used for shoe linings, less often now than formerly.

basinet, bacinet   a light helmet of a single piece of steel, the conical point was the special feature. A chain-mail hood worn over the camail in the thirteenth century.

basket weave   a style of weave resembling a plaited basket, produced by the interweaving of double threads.

basque   a short, skirt-like termination of an upper garment, formerly on a man's doublet, now on a woman's bodice. The same general effect was created by a woman's wearing a man's fishing jersey over the tightly corseted figure of the latter nineteenth century. The Princess of Wales, wearing such a jersey on an impromptu fishing expedition, created a vogue for the form-fitting Basque bodice in the 1870's.

basque belt, masculine corset   a confining girdlelike garment to give the desired small waist and corseted look; worn by many men in the 1830's and '40's.

basque shirt   originally the shirt of Basque fishermen of Spain and France. Of knitted wool and cotton with horizontal strips of contrasting colors, crew-neck, and half-sleeves.

basquine, vasquine   a fitted, boned hip-length garment with petticoat. A bolster was tied around the waist over the petticoat to produce the drum-shaped silhouette seen in the Velázquez portraits.

The masculine basquine was a fitted, padded doublet fastened down center front. Both sexes wore a heavy canvas corset shaped with steel busks and tightly laced.

bassanet   see *basinet.*

bassarisk   see *sable, mountain* or *rock sable.*

basting   temporary stitching.

basting cotton   thread used in long stitches to hold the fabric in place for final stitching. The thread is thin, soft and easily broken.

bateau neck   a boat-shaped straight neckline reaching from shoulder to shoulder, equally high front and back.

bathing dress, feminine   The custom of resort or surf bathing dates from the mid-nineteenth century when body-concealing suits were worn by both sexes. Women wore a real dress with short sleeves and a short skirt over pantalets or bloomers and black stockings. The fabric was flannel, alpaca or perhaps plaid

Basque Bodice

worsted, usually dark blue, brown or black with braid trim. After World War I the clinging one-piece, knitted maillot from France became fashionable and about 1935, again from France, the two-piece silk suit of top and shorts. In 1947 came the bikini comprising bosom-band and cache-sexe. see *bikini; Annette Kellerman; maillot.*

bathing dress, masculine   The popularity of seashore bathing was linked up to railroad building, the trains enabling people to reach shore points on vacation trips. The earliest outfits were of flannel, alpaca and worsted in navy blue, brown, black or a mixed gray cloth which later in the period changed to a machine-knitted fabric called jersey. At first it was a one-piece garment, usually sleeveless and reaching to the ankles or just below the knees, eventually shaping into knee breeches and a sleeveless "jumper top." In the early twentieth century, young men especially, doffed the top and simply wore shorts. see *jersey.*

bathrobe   a full or knee length garment, often of Turkish toweling or terry cloth, worn by men and women before and after bathing. Also, a dressing gown.

batik   an ancient method of resist-dye coloring which originated in Java. A design is planned, and some parts of the fabric are coated with wax, leaving only the uncoated parts to absorb the dye. The process is repeated for each new color.

batiste   a sheer, finely woven cloth of linen, wool lighter than challis, silk or spun rayon. Named for the inventor Baptiste Chambrai, a French weaver of the thirteenth century. see *wool batiste.*

Battenberg lace   a coarse form of Renaissance lace handmade or machine-made of linen thread, braid or tape and varied in design. The handmade is used for dress trimming and the machine-made for draperies.

batting   felt, cotton or wool in sheets prepared for interlining or padding.

battlemented stitching   see *castellated.*

battle jacket   waist-length, single-breasted jacket used by the United States Army in World War II. Adapted to sportswear later. see *Eisenhower jacket.*

batts   the popular women's shoe of the seventeenth century, resembling the heavy masculine shoe of black leather with medium heel and latchets tied over the tongue. Batts were shipped to the American colonies as early as 1636, and worn with home-knitted cotton or wool stockings.

batwing   a popular name for a man's bow tie. Also a feminine sleeve, see *sleeve, batwing.*

bauble   any trifling, cheap ornament.

baudequin   a tissue of silk and gold thread originally from Baghdad and later from Cyprus and Palermo. Brought back by the Crusaders and used by European royalty for throne drapery and robes from the twelfth to the sixteenth centuries.

bautta   an Italian cloak of black cloth with a hood which may be arranged to conceal the face.

Bavarian lace   also known as peasant's or beggar's lace. Bobbin-made of heavy linen or cotton thread, the coarse lace is used in fancy work and the fine in clothing. see *torchon lace.*

bavolet   a woman's headdress worn in the sixteenth century by European bourgeoisie and peasantry. The wearer was called a bavolette. Called a tovaglia, it is still worn in Italy. The bavolet was a towel-like piece of white linen, about two yards long and eighteen inches wide

battle or
Eisenhower
jacket-W.W.II

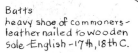

Batts
heavy shoe of commoners-
leather nailed to wooden
sole-English-17th, 18th C.

with fringed ends, folded and pinned to the cap. The deep back-ruffle on any bonnet was called a bavolet, a style revived in the nineteenth century.

bayadere   fabrics and ribbons striped horizontally in brilliant colors. Also the name of a female dancer and singer of an East Indian temple.

Bayeux lace   see *black lace*.

bazna sash   the silk sash of an Algerian woman's dress.

beachwear   garments designed for wear on the beach and while swimming.

bead embroidery   tiny, sparkling, variegated glass or metal ornaments which are sewn to fabric by hand following a design. see *paillettes; sequins; spangles*.

beading; entre-deux   a very narrow insertion resembling hemstitching, used in seam-joining of fine handmade lingerie in white batiste, lawn and nainsook. It is also made wide enough for threading narrow baby ribbon.

beads   probably the oldest form of adornment, aside from berries. They have been found in the most ancient Egyptian tombs and have been made of bone, metal, wood, pottery, ivory, amber, coral and jet. Modern glass beads are accredited to the Venetians in the fourteenth century.

beanie, beany   a twentieth century American name for the calotte.

beany or calotte-1930's

bear-white-black-Himalayan-Isabelline

bear, black   a durable fur used for coat trimmings and, in Great Britain, for the tall cap of Guard Regiments. General in North America, best from Canada. The animals have fine, dark-brown under fur, guard hair long and bright black. Brown, whitish-brown and cinnamon are color phases of the bear shipped to European and Asiatic markets.

bear, Himalayan or **Isabelline**   a heavier and more lustrous fur than that of the American black bear, from the large black bear of Eastern Asia. This fur was popular for the large muffs of the eighteenth century.

beard   The masculine beard has been an object of attention in all ages and all lands. The manner of wearing it has changed with each epoch, and has even been banned. In some periods it has proven a costly vanity what with cuttings, trimmings, shavings and even perfumes. In the seventeenth century the gentleman wore a pasteboard box to protect his well-groomed beard while asleep. In the nineteenth century whiskers were very popular. Dundreary whiskers were those separated by a shaven chin. The cathedral beard was a broad square-cut beard, so named because it was worn principally by academics and churchmen. After the middle of the nineteenth century appeared the imperial, as worn by Napoleon III, a pointed tuft on the chin accompanied by a small mustache. Beards and whiskers disappeared in the 1880's but the mustache retained its popularity; in the twentieth century the clean-shaven face has generally been favored. see *sidewhiskers, sideburns*.

bavolet-16th century

bavolet or fanchon bonnet-1857

beard-Roman

beard-Greek

beard after Napoléon III-Imperial

beard Dundrearies, sideburns or mutton-chops

Egyptian

Beards

Babylonian

Greek

Persian

Roman

Moorish

Etruscan

Byzantine
16th C.

Frankish
9th C.

Cavalier or
Van Dyck
1622

1831
Polish

Italian-
early
16th C.

1643-
Swedish

English-
1536

Van Dyck or
or Cavalier
1630's

19th C.
moustache - imperial-
side whiskers or muttonchops

German
1519

22

bearskin   the tall fur shako of black bearskin worn by the five foot regiments of the British Household Brigade of Guards.

bearskin pants   characteristic white bearskin pants worn by the men of Thule at the most northern end of Greenland, the pants known as the "trademark" of the men of Thule.

bearskin pants, white, of the men of Thule, Greenland

bear's paw   see *solleret.*

Beatles   four young British entertainers in 1960's who grew longish coiffures and adopted Mod, or Edwardian clothes, styles quickly taken up by many young men. see *Mod.*

Beatle haircuts 1960's

Beau Brummell   George Bryan Brummell (1778–1840), an English dandy and a friend of the Prince of Wales, later George IV. He was arbiter in the details of dress and famed for his skill in tying a cravat. It was he who first wore black or dark blue evening pantaloons instead of breeches, thereby making trousers popular.

beau-catcher, spit curl   the coquettish curl in the middle of a woman's forehead, popular at the turn of the century.

Beau Feilding   Robert Feilding, the first of the great English dandies who exercised an influence over fashion. He was known at the Court of Charles II as Handsome Feilding. He died in 1712.

Beau Nash   Richard Nash (1674–1761), a dandy and leader of English society and fashion. The king appointed him master of ceremonies at the resort town of Bath, where he ruled in matters of deportment and dress.

beauty patches   worn in ancient Rome not only by women but by men and we are reminded that the mole was considered a beauty mark. From Italy in the sixteenth century came the fashion of patches, or as the English said, "patching the face." Also worn in the seventeenth century, of black velvet, taffeta or court plaster, they were carried in tiny jeweled boxes. Patches were placed near the eyes, on the cheeks, the throat and breasts. And there were gallants who wore them too. see *mouches.*

beaver   see *bevor.*

beaver   *castor* in French. Found widely in North America and Canada, in the Rocky Mountain States to the Pacific and some protected colonies east of the Mississippi. The best comes from the Province of Quebec, and some from western Russia and eastern Siberia. The fur

black bearskin– Coldstream Guards

Beau-catcher or Spit-curl–1890s

beauty patches

beaver or castor

is soft, warm and durable; a rich brown, from light to dark with long, black or reddish-brown guard hair; used for coats, jackets and trimmings. Beaver imitations, all noted as beaver-dyed, are Australian opossum, coney (rabbit), mouton (lamb), raccoon and skunk. Beaver-dyed coney is an old English name for rabbit processed to simulate beaver. Sheared beaver is a fashion developed in the second half of the twentieth century in which the de-haired, thick underfur is trimmed short, making a less bulky fur and removing the tendency to curl when wet. Russian beaver is sometimes dyed and pointed to simulate sea otter.

beaver cloth   fur imitation, thick-napped woolen cloth sheared to produce a close, dense surface like the fur; originally made in England. A wide range of finishes suitable for overcoats, uniforms, hats, etc.

beaver fustian   a coarse, rough over-coating fabric made in and around Philadelphia since the early nineteenth century. It is dark blue and similar to kersey.

beaver hat   fur hat which was the fashionable headpiece of American men and women of the seventeenth century. A costly item, it was so valuable that it was often left as a bequest in a will. In the nineteenth and twentieth centuries, men and women wore hats of nappy felt for general wear.

beaver
Cavalier hat

bed jacket, bed sacque   a short, flattering, feminine jacket of any favored material or weight, to wear over the nightgown when sitting up in bed.

bed socks   ankle-high, knitted, warm socks for winter bed-wear.

Bedford cord   first made in New Bedford, Massachusetts. A worsted fabric made with raised, rounded cords or ribs running lengthwise; may be in combination fibers, rayon, cotton, silk or wool.

Favored for riding habits, livery wear, suits and children's coats.

beech martin   see *marten, stone* or *beech*.

Bedouin sheik's costume - KIBR of plaided white cotton - white kaffiyeh with black agal - ba bouches, red or yellow

Bedouin - desert - mounted police force under French flag - Berber, Moorish and Tuareg - white cotton with black accessories

Beefeater's hat a black beaver hat with red, black and white ribbon cockards around the crown, of sixteenth century origin, worn by the British Yeomen of the Guard and the Warders of the Tower of London.

beehive bonnet see *bonnet, beehive.*

beehive coiffure hair worn piled very high over a back-combed base, 1950's.

Beene, Geoffrey see *couture, haute.*

Beer see *couture, haute.*

beer jacket a twentieth century college fashion. A simple straight jacket of flannel, cotton or linen which male students originally wore to beer parties in the twenties and thirties.

beetling a finish for cotton and linen fabrics achieved by hammering the fabric flat over rollers. The process produces an increased luster.

beggar's lace known as *torchon lace.*

beguin, biggon, biggin a headcovering for men, women and children from the twelfth century on. Worn in Byzantium and later by the Béguines, women of religious orders, hence its common name. A three-piece cap, it was of finest linen for elegant folk and of coarse weave for commoners. It was worn by the clergy, under nobles' crowns, and of leather or felt under the helmet. In the fifteenth century the white linen coif was replaced by felt or velvet, often red. In the eighteenth century it was worn under the wig and was retained in the nineteenth century under the wig of the British barrister.

Belgian laces see *Antwerp; Brussels; Mechlin; Valenciennes.*

bell skirt see *skirt, bell.*

bell-bottoms the flaring trousers worn by sailors for four centuries. A seaman's breeches had to be roomy enough to permit the acrobatic movement necessary aboard a sailing ship. Today's breeches have but slight flare to the bottoms.

bellboy's cap a small round hat of stiffened fabric and color matching the hotel bellboy's uniform. see *pillbox.*

bellows pocket see *pocket, bellows.*

bellows tongue a man's work or sports shoe with a broad folding tongue stitched to either side of the quarter to keep out water when laced.

bells, silver small tinkling bells in fashion in the fourteenth and early fifteenth centuries. They were suspended from leather belts, jeweled girdles, and around the neck of men and women. Particularly used for the jester's costume of particolored clothes, hood and short cape with castellated edges, all tinkling with bells.

belt a band to encircle waist or hips, male or female. It may be of leather, cloth, chain links or decorative cord, and plain or jeweled. It may serve to carry gun, sword, money bag or purse, and may be tied, hooked or buckled; according to the mode, it may tightly shape the waist or loosely hold the folds of robe or cloak.

belt, Basque see *Basque belt.*

belt, Sam Browne a wide leather belt supported by a narrow strap passing over the right shoulder, worn by army officers. A sword belt designed by the British General Sir Samuel Browne (1824–1901).

Bemberg trademark owned by American Bemberg Corp. for the rayon yarn

Beefeater's or Warder's hat—London

beer Jacket

Sam Browne belt— designed by British Gen. Sir Samuel Browne worn in World War I

Beguin, biggin or coif

béret

two berets

plumed béret
1530's

béret of
British General
Montgomery - W W II

made by a process called cuprammonium composed principally of cotton linters.

bench-made   a British term for "bespoke" or custom handmade shoes. So called because the workmen, before the days of machinery, sat on benches along the wall, each workman making a complete shoe.

Bengal stripes   a cotton gingham cloth originally from Bengal, India, woven in colored stripes. This cloth was the origin of the multicolored striped silks popular in men's neckwear.

bengaline   a general term applied to silk and wool fabrics with a corded or rep effect. The heavy, soft-spun woolen weft is covered closely in the weaving with silk or wool. Used for coats, dresses and draperies. Made first in Bengal, India.

béret   a very simple form of headgear; a round piece of woolen cloth or felt drawn up at the edge with a thong to fit the head. The history of the béret goes back to ancient Greece and Rome, reaching the Basque country by way of the traders. The modern béret of dark blue felt is shrunk to shape and size in the dyeing. The tiny spike, or tontarra, is sewn on last to cover the "eye" of the weave. The béret is worn today by men and women of many lands.

beretta   see *biretta*.

Berlin or **German wool**   a fancy-work yarn made from wool of Merino sheep mostly of Saxony. Generally dyed very bright, strong colors.

Berlin work   embroidery done on "Berlin canvas" using various stitches, but principally cross-stitch, worked in Berlin wool. Popular handiwork in the nineteenth century.

Bermuda shorts   feminine, knee-length for sports. see *pant lengths*.

Bersagliere   a distinctive hat named for the Italian army corps of riflemen and sharpshooters whose uniform it is. Of black glazed felt with cock plumage.

Bersagliere - infantry corps of riflemen in the Italian army. Hat of black glazed felt with cock plume

Bertha of lace

bertha   a capelike collar of varying length and generally made of lace, which recalled the Palatine capes. see *Palatine*.

Bertin, Rose   see *couture, haute.*

beryl   a stone of beryllium aluminum silicate, of great beauty and hardness when transparent. In colors, bluish-green, yellow, pink, and white. Emerald and aquamarine are varieties.

bespangled   decorated with sparkling spangles, tiny disks of gold, silver, or steel, extensively used in the late nineteenth century for formal evening gowns.

bespoke tailoring   the British term for custom-made clothes. The only ready-to-wear worn by the well-dressed English-man is confined to certain overcoats and raincoats or utility sports coats of out-standing tailoring.

Bethlehem headdress   an ancient Moslem headdress worn by women of Bethlehem, Jerusalem and Nazareth; a tarboosh, red or green, to which are sewn gold and silver coins representing the dowry. A chain is often attached to the cap, hanging below the chin, from which dangle more coins. The married woman wears a large white veil draped over the cap.

Bethlehem headdress

Betsie or **cherusse**   a small ruff or collarette of several rows of fluted Brabant lace or mull. The fashion orig-inated in England where it was named for Queen Elizabeth I; carried to Paris by the famous tailor Leroy and renamed cherusse. It became popular with the low-necked gowns of the First Empire. By 1807 the collarettes had acquired six or seven falls of lace.

bevor, beaver   a movable piece of armor attached to the armet, a helmet of the fifteenth and sixteenth centuries. When lowered, it protected the lower part of the face.

biagga gallas   see *Lapland bonnet.*

bias   a line running diagonally across warp and woof threads. Bias-cut bindings are easier to apply to curved edges, and lingerie cut on the bias may have better fit and wear.

bib   a small pad, plain or fancy, fastened around the neck of an infant to protect its clothing. Also, the upper part of an apron, above the waist. Decorative deep-front collars are sometimes called bibs.

bicorne, chapeau bras   an evolution of the tricorne; supplanted the three-cornered hat in the 1790's. It folded flat for carrying under the arm, hence the name. It became the ceremonial dress hat worn to the present day in the American, British and French navies.

bicycle bal   a leather or canvas ankle shoe with low heel and front lacing nearly to the toe. Worn for bicycling. Bal, short for balmoral, late nineteenth century.

Biedermeier   a German style of furni-ture and furnishings, less ornate than the preceding French Empire, of the period from 1825 to 1860. The term includes the German version of dress similar to the Second Empire mode in France.

bietle   a jacket of deerskin worn by Apache Indian women.

bietta   meaning bright; a red cloth that American Indians coveted and made efforts to procure either by trade or war. The Spanish, who used it for uniforms, brought it to America first. The Indians used it sparingly and effectively on their deerskin garments.

Betsie or cherusse

bib

bicycle bal

Bikini

biliment
headdress

Billycock
or melon-
1862

biggon, biggin   see *beguin.*

bikini   the most abbreviated form of feminine bathing dress, originally created by the House of Heim, Paris. It consists of two separate pieces: a band covering the breasts and the *cache-sexe*. Though it first appeared on French beaches in 1947–48, a late Roman mosaic of 406 A.D., recently uncovered in central Italy, reveals several ladies wearing the identical garb.

biliment   an elaborate but delicate headdress of the sixteenth century, usually of a lace of gold threads worked with beads, jewels, ribbons, gauze, and even sometimes a single feather.

billicock, billycock   a Briticism for the hard felt hat with round crown; the derby, bowler or melon. "Billycock" was derived from William Coke, Earl of Norfolk, who made the hat popular. see *derby; bowler.*

Binche lace   one of the earliest of Flemish laces, bobbin-made at Binche. It has floral scrolls spreading over the ground, sprinkled with spots like snowflakes.

binding   tape cut on the bias used to bind edges. It is available in single or double fold, in several widths and many colors. Seam binding is a narrow ribbonlike tape, about a half inch wide, formerly of silk, now of rayon, in all colors.

bird of paradise   any one of the beautiful birds of the Paradise family of New Guinea and adjacent islands. Noted for brilliant and elegant plumes, the importation of which was banned in the United States in 1905. see *Audubon plumage law.*

birdseye   a small geometric pattern woven with a dot in the center resembling a bird's eye. Birdseye pattern is used in cotton, linen, silks and synthetic fabrics

bird of paradise feathers

and there is also a diamond weave in piqué cotton for gentlemen's evening wear accessories, such as waistcoat and bow tie.

biretta   a stiff square cap with three or four projections rising above the crown, radiating from the center and often finished with a pompon. Originally a choir skullcap, it became a headdress for the clergy about the fifteenth century, being worn by secular academicians as well as the clergy. Today the birettas worn by cardinals are red, bishops wear purple, priests black, and some canons and abbots, white.

biretta of
universities
and professions

biretta of a
Venetian general

biretta of
cardinal

birrus   see *byrrus*.

bishop's or **Victoria lawn**   a fine lawn made for clerical vestments, especially the bishop's full sleeves.

bishop's sleeve   see *sleeve, bishop's*.

bison   see *buffalo*.

bi-swing   a sportswear jacket which, by an inverted pleat or gusset from shoulder to waistline in center back, gives a play of extra material when the wearer is in action.

black   an absence of color.

black amber   see *jet*.

black fox   see *fox, silver*.

black lace   made in the seventeenth century at Bayeux, France, and sometimes called Bayeux lace. The fashion for wearing it was brought to France by the Spanish Infanta who married Louis XIV in 1660.

black tie   a popular term denoting men's semiformal evening wear consisting

black tie-
semi-formal,
single-breasted
dinner jacket
cummerbund-
contemporary

of a dinner jacket (tuxedo), a black waistcoat or cummerbund, and a black bow tie worn with a soft white shirt. The term is often used on invitations to indicate that semiformal dress will be worn, as opposed to formal dress or "white tie." see *dinner jacket, tuxedo*.

blackwork   black counted thread embroidery on white fabric, principally linen and cotton. English sixteenth and seventeenth centuries. see *Spanish blackwork*.

blanket coat   same as Hudson Bay coat, worn with a woolen sash. Copied from the cloth peasant coats of Normandy and introduced by the early French settlers of Canada.

Blass, Bill   see *couture, haute*.

blazer   a lightweight jacket, usually of flannel, in solid color or brilliant regimental or club stripes. Originally, the scarlet jacket of the English Cambridge University students for cricket or tennis. The jacket was taken up later for informal country wear by British army and navy men.

bleeding   the running of color when a fabric is immersed in water. A characteristic of madras.

blends   combinations of certain synthetic fibers. A blend can change a texture to smooth or coarse, make the weight heavy or light, soft or more wrinkle-proof.

bliaud, bliaus   a medieval shirt which was the origin of the linen blouse or smock worn by European peasants of both sexes today. The bliaud was worn over the chainse, or chemise, and slit up the sides to allow freedom for the legs when riding horseback. Today's shirt, blouse or shirtwaist is simply a form of the original bliaus. Similar to the *gertrude*.

block printing   a process where a design is carved on wooden blocks, coated

blazer

with coloring matter and then pressed onto fabric by hand; practiced in China and Japan for many centuries.

blond, blonde   hair, flaxen or golden-hued.

blonde lace   a very fine silk bobbin-lace, closely woven, originally in cream color but now bleached white or dyed black.

bloomer dress   a style of play dress with matching bloomers for little girls.

Bloomer dress 1851

bloomers   in general, any knee-length leg garment worn by women and girls. Originally long, loose pantaloons gathered at the ankles, showing below full skirts. Designed by Mrs. Amelia Jenks Bloomer, an American social reformer who appeared publicly in the costume about 1850. Worn by schoolgirls in the 1910's and '20's with a middy blouse, for athletic uniform.

blouse   a sleeved or sleeveless garment generally reaching below the waist, but of varying lengths. It evolved from the bliaud. see *Balkan blouse; middy blouse; over blouse; Russian blouse; sash blouse.*

Balmoral or Blue bonnet

blouse, middy   see *middy blouse.*

blouse, Russian   see *Russian blouse.*

blouse, step-in   see *step-in blouse.*

Blücher   a shoe or half-boot invented by Field Marshall von Blücher (1742–1819), commander of the Prussian forces at Waterloo. A laced shoe in which the quarters reached to the front over the instep and were laced together over the tongue.

Blücher- front lacing over a leather tongue- early 19th C.

blue   one of the three primary colors blue, red, and yellow. Blue mixed with red gives the secondary color purple, and mixed with yellow, the secondary color green. Blue plus purple gives the tertiary color blue-purple; blue plus green, the tertiary color blue-green. The blue-purples include such names as periwinkle and hyacinth; the blue-greens include aqua, teal and peacock. The palest blues are sky blue and baby blue; the bright medium shades are cornflower and royal; with black added the tones deepen to navy and midnight. Grayed blues include powder, Wedgwood and horizon.

blue fox   see *fox, blue.*

blue jeans   see *levis.*

blue jeans or Levis

bluebonnet, balmoral   the traditional cap worn by shepherd, soldier and gentleman in Scotland, woven in one piece without seam or binding, of dark blue wool with either a red or blue tuft on top. A ribbon cockade, a sprig of native evergreen and feather signified the wearer's rank in his clan. Three feathers were permitted the chief or head of the clan, two for the gentleman and one for the clansman. The cap was named after Balmoral Castle, Queen Victoria's summer home. see *cap, Glengarry.*

bluff edge   a braid-bound hand-felled edge on a cloth coat.

boa   a long, cylindrical neckpiece of

feathers, fur, tulle or lace, according to season; a graceful fashion of the late nineteenth century. The boa was very long, usually six to eight feet, so that a lady could wrap it around her neck with floating ends that hung below her knees. Revived in the 1930's and 1960's.

boarded calf   see *calf, boarded.*

boater or **hard hat**   a man's sennit straw sailor coated with shellac from India, popular in the late nineteenth century. The English wore it punting, hence the name. In America it was worn almost universally from June first to September first. The name "sennit" comes from the nautical term "seven-knit," a method of braiding rope.

boating wear   functional sports clothes developed before World War II. Both men and women wear lightweight slacks, shorts and T-shirts or sweaters in mild weather and for poor weather lined waterproof nylon. Lined nylon trousers have elastic at waist and ankles and lined nylon anoraks are high-necked and have drainage vents in pockets in case of a ducking. The nylon used is available in several different colors, white being avoided because sea water turns it yellow.

bob wig   see *wig, bob.*

bobbed hair   Small boys were the first to wear bobbed hair following the Dutch style, cut straight around covering the back and straight-cut bangs over the forehead. In the second decade of the twentieth century some of Paul Poiret's mannequins adopted the coiffure as did some of the dancers of Isadora Duncan's troupe. First made fashionable in America by the ballroom dancer Irene Castle, bobbed hair did not become an established fashion until the 1920's when a mannish haircut was necessitated by the fashion of the head-hugging felt cloche of the same period. During the vogue of the bob, fruitless efforts to revive long tresses succeeded only in establishing a still

shorter cut. The boyish bob or shingle was clipped very close in back and trimmed to a V at the nape. The windblown bob was a style with the hair cut short and tousled. The page boy bob was a style of the 1930's favored by young women. This coiffure was founded upon the medieval page-boy style, the hair cut shoulder-length with the ends rolled under. The same shape was given the bangs rolled under on the forehead. see *windblown bob.*

bobbin   a spool-like device used on a lock-stitch sewing machine which feeds the thread for the under side of the stitching; also a small pin or cylinder which is used in the making of bobbin lace.

bobbin lace, bone lace, pillow lace   lace made on a pillow with the design marked out by pins, and the bobbins or bones worked back and forth over the pins. The name distinguishes it from needle lace.

bobbinet   a net made with a hexagonal mesh. Of twisted cotton or silk yarn, it was originally made by hand with bobbins. It is used for lace grounds and dresses.

bobby pin   a style of clip hairpin which appeared with the fashion of bobbed hair in the nineteen-twenties and resembles the cotter pin of modern machinery.

bodice   the part of a woman's dress above the waist. In medieval times it meant two "bodies" of boiled leather or canvas which were boned. Front and back were first hooked together to shape a small waist. Next, the bodies were whaleboned and laced tightly together, forming an underbodice or corset.

bodice, Basque surplice   see *surplice bodice.*

bodkin   a long, pointed pin of bone or bronze used as a hairpin by the ancient

boa of fur —
1800

bobbed
hair —1920

bobbed hair
Dutch cut —
early 20th C.

Greeks and Romans. It was called a hair-needle by the Saxons and was used for fastening the mantle, see *acus.* also, a large-eyed, blunt-ended needle used for drawing elastic, ribbon, etc., through a hem or row of eyelets.

bodkin cloth   of the seventeenth century, a rich cloth woven of silk and gold. The name is a corruption of Baghdad.

body garments   those worn next to the body such as lingerie, sleeping apparel, underwear.

body paint   see *tattooing.*

body stocking   a finely knit body garment of stretch nylon backless to the waist and low-necked in front with the narrowest of shoulder straps; a step-in which eliminates brassiere and girdle. 1960's. see *leotard; tights.*

Bohan, Marc   see *couture, haute.*

Bohemian lace   a coarse net with a design worked in a braid effect.

boiled leather   see *leather, boiled.*

boiled shirt   a former inelegant colloquialism in the United States for a man's white shirt with stiffly starched bosom.

bolero   a tailored short Spanish jacket reaching to the waistline, ornamented with braid. Worn open over a fine white shirt and a wide crushed silk sash of brilliant color.

bolero hat   see *hat, bolero.*

bolero, Scanderbeg   see *Scanderbeg bolero.*

Bolivar hat   see *hat, Bolivar.*

Bolivia   a woolen cloth with a soft, plushlike surface, light to heavy quality, with pile tufts in either vertical or diagonal rows. Used for suits and coats.

body
stocking-
1960's

bolero hat-
bolero jacket-
bullfighter's
frilled shirt-
Spanish

bombachas   long, full pantaloon breeches gathered at the ankles and held at the waist by a silver-studded leather belt. Worn by some gauchos of Uruguay.

bombachas-
gaucho of
Uruguay

bombast or peasecod-
bellied fashion-
Spanish-16th C.

bombast, bombace   a type of cotton stuffing and padding, originally French. Used by the Spanish in the peasecod-bellied doublet shaped of buckram and busks, which influenced the fashions of the European courts. The period from 1545 to 1620 was known as Spanish bombast.

bombazine   a plain, twilled English fabric, made of cotton in the Middle Ages, later of cotton and wool and later of silk and wool. Generally dyed black for mourning use. In the eighteenth century the name was given to a silk made in France and Milan.

Bonaparte helmet   a gathered white silk bonnet with a forehead band of black velvet embroidered with gilt laurel leaves and mounted with a panache of white ostrich, early nineteenth century.

bonded fabrics   laminated fabrics employed principally as interfacings. Fibers are pressed into thin sheets held together by plastic and adhesive. In the latest process, fabrics are bonded back to back, as for instance, a silk sheet applied to a woolen cloth, eliminating the need of a lining.

bone or **ivory**   a warm, creamy white sometimes designated as parchment color or antique white. Most often used for feminine accessories.

bone lace   of linen thread, lace made over bobbins of bone instead of wooden ones.

bonet, bonaid   Scotch forms of the word *bonnet*.

bongrace   a short headdress of silk, velvet or chiffon which hung free in back but dipped over the forehead in a peak, sometimes weighted with a pearl or other jewel. Also called an attifet headdress, sixteenth century.

bonnaz   a type of embroidery made on a sewing machine supposedly invented by a Monsieur Bonnaz.

bonnet, bonet   any soft head covering with strings tied under the chin. The same pattern as the medieval three-piece white cap but later made of coarse woolen green cloth called bonet. The cap was called bonnet to the sixteenth century.

bonnet   in the nineteenth century became a frivolous feminine headpiece, the wearing of which was not permitted a young woman before her debut in society or her marriage. She wore a hat. The widow wore a black crêpe bonnet draped with a heavy veil.

bonnet, American Indian   a headdress of upstanding feathers attached to a headband, with two feathered streamers hanging down the back. Imitated in a British colonial army fashion, early nineteenth century, with a shallow black velvet cap with upstanding ostrich plumes and bead earrings.

bonnet, beehive   a lady's simple straw bonnet of the early nineteenth century made in the shape of a beehive and trimmed with a ribbon which tied under the chin.

bonnet, coal scuttle, poke bonnet, capote   of straw with crown and a coal-scuttle-shaped brim. Worn over a lingerie cap and tied with ribbons. English late eighteenth century.

bonnet, conversation   with turned-up brim of red-and-yellow-striped silk. French, early nineteenth century.

bonnet, cottage   a fashion for summer wear. Of straw with squarish crown and a brim faced with silk or velvet, turned up in front and down in back; ornamented with moss roses and worn over a frilled lingerie cap, ribbon-tied under the chin.

bonnet, ducal   see *corno*.

bonnet, Easter   the feminine, usually brand new spring hat, flower-trimmed, that is worn to church on Easter Sunday. Late nineteenth and early twentieth centuries.

bonnet, Hardanger   a four-piece square bonnet for children and young girls of Norway. Fashioned of scarlet velvet or woolen cloth, it is edged with black velvet and embroidered with motifs of fine beadwork.

bonnet, Lapland   see *Lapland bonnet*.

bonnet, Pamela   a yellow straw bon-

bongrace of black velvet - pearl earrings - French - late 16th C.

bongrace - white satin with pearls and aigrettes - Italian - 16th C.

beehive or cottage bonnet

bonnet - American Indian - British Army Captain - son of Joseph Brant - 1812

ducal bonnet or Corno of the doge - Venetian - 15th C.

"bonet" of green felt - Medieval

bonnet with bird - English - 1880's

bonnet or mobcap - kate Greenaway 1883

bonnet - poke with ostrich plumes - 1833

bonnet - b lace - Frer

bonnet with frills - 1797

cottage bonnet with cap - 1804

Fanchon bonnet - 1865

Pamela bonnet - 1865

Bibi bonnet with ostrich - French - 1847

bonnet Thérèse spotted gauze - French - 1780's

poke bonnet - straw - 19th C.

calash - bonnet

bonnet capote - poke or coal scuttle - English - 1797

bonnet - cabriolet - French - 1844

widow's bonnet of crepe - 1880's

net, having a very tall crown, with daffodils and rose-colored ribbons which tied under the chin. French second decade, nineteenth century.

bonnet, Phrygian   the ancient Greek cap or bonnet of felt or leather with chin strap. When the masters of Rome freed a slave, they placed the Phrygian bonnet upon his head. Later, Rome made it an emblem of liberty to be worn by manumitted slaves. In the eighteenth century it was again adopted as *le bonnet rouge* of the French Revolutionists. The female figure personifying Liberty wears such a cap.

bonnet, Quaker or **Friends**   a version of the Directoire mode, in gray or brown cloth, felt or straw in cabriolet or wagon-top style. The fashion of the day was followed, but the bonnet was shorn of trimming except for the bavolet or ruffle in back which was usually of the fabric of the dress.

bonnet, Salvation Army Lassie   the original bonnet of the Army's uniform lasted well into the twentieth century. Of black straw or felt according to season, it was lined with dark blue silk and tied with silk brides. The contemporary bonnet is smaller and jauntier, though still dark blue with the edge piped with red. The bonnet is secured by a chinstrap of dark blue silk finished with a large bowknot at the left side and the silk band lettered Salvation Army.

bonnet, slat bonnet or **sunbonnet**   of cotton fabric, plain or figured and fashioned with a brim or poke held in shape by stitched slots holding thin wooden slats. In general, the sunbonnet was a peasant type of headdress with a bavolet. It had a wide brim of straw or stiffened, starched fabric and a gathered full crown with chin ties.

bonnet, sugar-loaf   a man's high cap worn with bobbed hair; French midfifteenth century.

bonnet, Watteau   see *Watteau bonnet.*

Bonnie and Clyde   the name of a contemporary suit for young men and women inspired by a popular movie. Of dark gray or dark blue cloth pin-striped with white and with flaring trousers.

book linen   a firm, sized linen used in men's wear to stiffen collars and belts.

boot, ankle   a lumberman's ankle-high boot of thick leather for wear over heavy boots.

boot, carriage   worn by women in the days of carriages, over dainty slippers to keep the feet warm. Made of cloth or velvet, they continued to be used in the automobile and for evening wear in winter.

boot, chukka   see *jodhpur.*

boot, cavalier; boothose, French   seventeenth century; leather boots with bucket or funnel tops wide enough to crush down, often worn over lace-edged boot hose which flared over the cuffs. Completed with wide quatrefoil spur leathers and jungling rowels.

boot, Courrèges   a mid-twentieth century fashion, first designed for warmth, which developed from lined and often fur-topped galoshes. As skirts grew shorter the boot became longer and, by the sixties an almost indispensible part of winter dress. Principally white, of real or imitation leather.

boot, cowboy   a type of boot worn by the western horseman, a calf-high boot with a high slanting Cuban heel to hold the foot in the stirrup. The tops are usually of fancy cut with appliquéd motifs.

Watteau hat-straw or felt-ostrich and ribbon-powdered hair in puffs and cadogan-French-1770's

bonnet-Quaker or Friend-19thC.

bonnet of the Salvation Army

Phrygian bonnet-red-French-1790's

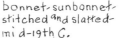

bonnet-sunbonnet-stitched and slatted-mid-19th C.

Boots

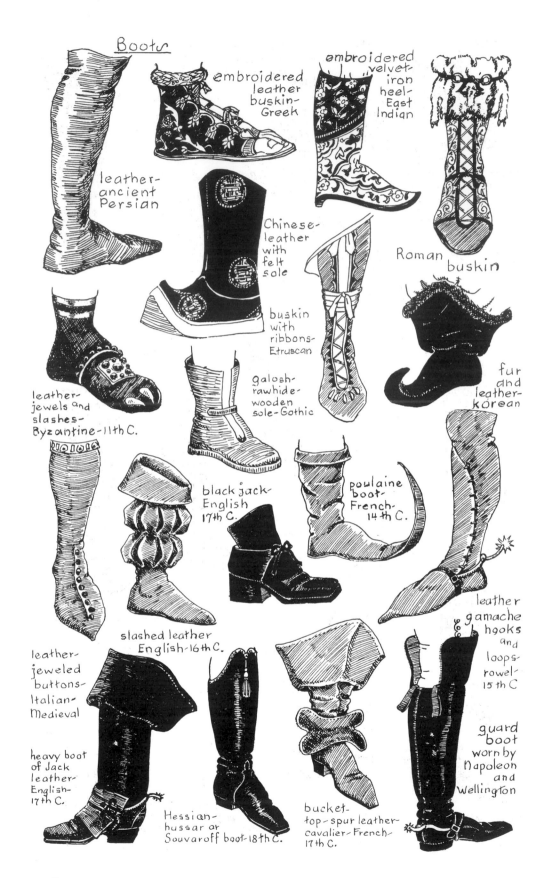

embroidered leather buskin - Greek

embroidered velvet - iron heel - East Indian

leather - ancient Persian

Chinese - leather with felt sole

Roman buskin

buskin with ribbons - Etruscan

leather - jewels and slashes - Byzantine - 11th C.

galosh - rawhide - wooden sole - Gothic

fur and leather - Korean

black jack - English 17th C.

poulaine boot - French - 14th C.

leather gamache hooks and loops - rowel - 15th C

slashed leather English - 16th C.

leather - jeweled buttons - Italian - Medieval

heavy boot of Jack leather English - 17th C.

Hessian - hussar or Souvaroff boot - 18th C.

bucket - top - spur leather cavalier - French - 17th C.

guard boot worn by Napoleon and Wellington

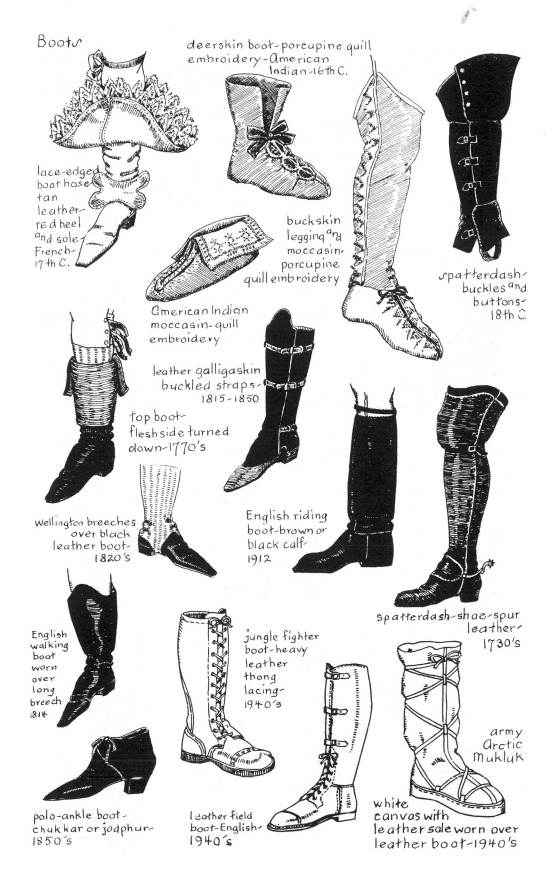

Boots

deerskin boot-porcupine quill embroidery-American Indian-16th C.

lace-edged boot hose tan leather-red heel and sole. French-17th C.

American Indian moccasin-quill embroidery

buckskin legging and moccasin-porcupine quill embroidery

spatterdash-buckles and buttons-18th C.

leather galligaskin buckled straps-1815-1850

top boot-flesh side turned down-1770's

Wellington breeches over black leather boot-1820's

English riding boot-brown or black calf-1912

spatterdash-shoe-spur leather-1730's

English walking boot worn over long breech 1814

jungle fighter boot-heavy leather thong lacing-1940's

army Arctic Mukluk

polo-ankle boot-chukkar or jodphur-1850's

leather field boot-English-1940's

white canvas with leather sole worn over leather boot-1940's

37

Boots-feminine

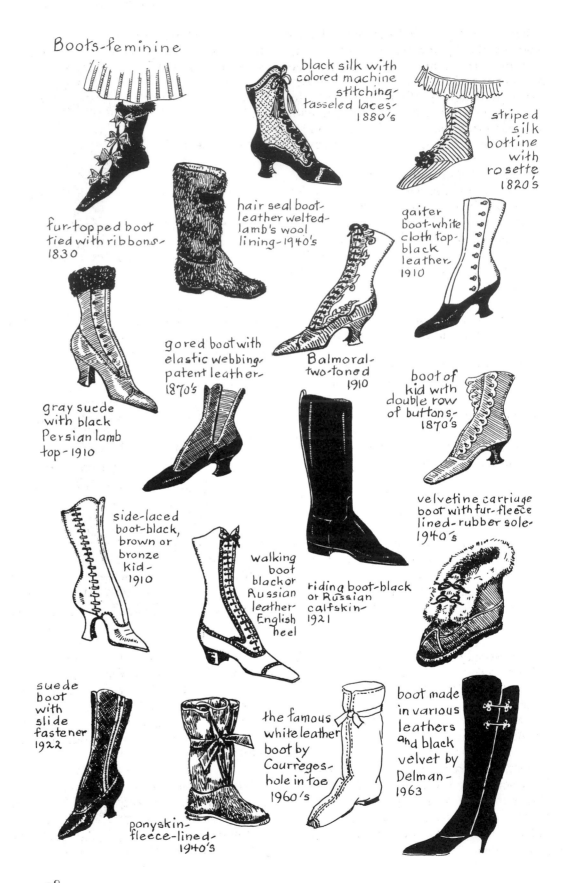

black silk with colored machine stitching- tasseled laces- 1880's

striped silk bottine with rosette 1820's

fur-topped boot tied with ribbons- 1830

hair seal boot- leather welted- lamb's wool lining- 1940's

gaiter boot-white cloth top- black leather- 1910

gray suede with black Persian lamb top- 1910

gored boot with elastic webbing- patent leather- 1870's

Balmoral- two-toned 1910

boot of kid with double row of buttons- 1870's

side-laced boot-black, brown or bronze kid- 1910

walking boot black or Russian leather- English heel

riding boot-black or Russian calfskin- 1921

velvetine carriage boot with fur-fleece lined-rubber sole- 1940's

suede boot with slide fastener 1922

ponyskin- fleece-lined- 1940's

the famous white leather boot by Courrèges- hole in toe 1960's

boot made in various leathers and black velvet by Delman- 1963

boot, flight   a chukkar type of boot worn by the "plane pushers" of the big aircraft carriers in World War II. The former high boot with hooks was discarded as dangerous. Of natural color, the flight boot was made flesh-side-out with a nonskid traction sole. It became official equipment on all United States carriers.

boot, Hessian, Souvaroff, or Hussar   boot worn by the Hessian mercenaries hired to fight the American colonists. To the Americans and English it was the Hessian boot, and to the French the Hussar boot. A tassel swung from a dip in the top just below the knee. The boot was adopted for civilian wear in the late 1790's.

boot, hip or **wading**   of rubber, reaching to the hips and used for fishing.

boot hose   were of sheer white linen with wide lace frills worn to protect the cavalier's costly silk hose worn underneath. The lace frill hung over the leather top of the boot. Especially smart in the mid-seventeenth century and worn even by some dressy Puritans in the Colonies.

boot, jack   the generally-worn boot of the seventeenth and eighteenth centuries, large enough to wear a shoe or slipper inside it. It was lined with pockets enabling the wearer to carry papers and small objects. It was made of jack leather, a wax leather coated with tar or pitch, the same leather employed for the huge tankard which held beer and ale.

boot, jungle fighter or **paratrooper**   a Blücher-style boot of oiled, stout brown leather, water-resistant and laced with leather thongs. In World War II, because of the dangerous hooks, it was replaced by the chukkar style of laced boot.

boot, Napoleon   also worn by Wellington, a military guard or army officer's boot, of heavy black leather, chamois-lined and a square top cut out in back. Worn by the officers of the European armies.

boot, Oxford half-boot   the first Oxford, a shoe of heavy jack leather. English, seventeenth century.

boot, paratrooper   see *boot, jungle fighter*.

boot, pegged   a boot having soles fastened on by wooden pegs.

boot, Souvaroff   see *boot, Hessian*.

boot, top   of the 1780's and 1790's. Of black grain leather with flesh side turned down and a strap around the knee. Used for such sports as riding, hunting, fishing.

boot, Wellington   guard or officer's boot, also worn by Napoleon. Heavy black leather, chamois-lined with square top cut out in back.

boot, Wellington half-   worn up to the 1860's under the trousers, which were fastened under the sole with strap or gaiter.

bootee   any low boot made of leather, fabric, especially knitted yarn or fabric for infants.

bootjack   a V-shaped device for pulling off boots.

Borgana   trademark for a deep-furred pile fabric used exclusively for women's coats. A blend of Orlon, Darlan, and Dynel.

borsalino   a hat of Italian make, supposedly the finest of men's felt hats. Of natural fur which has been aged for three years; the felted body is aged for another year. All detailing is done by hand. The hats have been made in Alessandria for over a century.

bosom band   a band of wool, linen or chamoised leather worn by Greek women next to the body. It was tied with strings or pinned with fibulae, the Greek safety pins. see *apodesme*.

bosom or **breast knot**   a scented bow-knot or rosette of colored satin ribbon of the eighteenth century, a vogue from about 1730 on. Its particular name was "perfect contentment."

Botany   trademark of fine wools, worsteds, yarns and fabrics manufactured by Botany Mills, Inc. and licensed for woven woolens in men's, women's and children's manufacture.

bottine or **jemima**   a lady's gored boot of beige fabric with black leather tip and elastic inserts. It was first designed for Queen Victoria, in 1836. The first elastic cloth or webbing woven with rubber was invented by T. Hancock of Middlesex, England. The shoe was designed by J. Sparkes Hall, bootmaker to the queen. It had either cloth or leather uppers with elastic gussets at the sides and was a style worn by men and women. "Jemima" was the British term.

bottles   as used in feminine dress of the late eighteenth century, a small slim bottle holding water and fresh flowers which was tucked into the bosom of the stomacher. Also, a small flat bottle holding water and fresh flowers tucked into the elaborate headdress.

bouclé, boucle   French for looped or curled. A rugged-looking but soft fabric for sportswear woven or knitted with tiny loops. It may be of any knitted fiber but is executed principally in wool. Also, a wool knitting yarn with a silk thread that gives it an uneven texture. Used for sweaters and sports suits.

boudoir cap   a flattering head covering worn to cover a lady's undressed hair. It was a dainty, softly shirred cap with a pretty lace ruffle. Today called a curler cap, its purpose being to cover a head done up in pincurls and rollers.

boudoir slipper   see *mule.*

bouffant   French for puffed, puffy. Generally applied to full, stiff skirts.

bouffant, bouffants   from the French for puffing in costume. Bouffants appear in the mode from time to time, sometimes in panniers, sleeves or breeches and often in the coiffure. The eighteenth century was decidedly an era of bouffant dress.

Bourbon lace   a net ground with design and edge worked with cording.

bourette, bourrette   a yarn of silk, cotton or linen with a rough uneven appearance made by nubs and knots. Also, the fabric woven of it.

boutique   French word for shop. The advantages of shopping in the boutique are many, the greatest of all being able to browse over the copies of ready-made clothes, including accessories and gadgets, which are much less expensive. Usually copied in the finest fabrics, they cost less because of no fittings. Priced $150. to $500, while a second degree boutique may be $50. to $150, at the same time, building a splendid clientelle.

boutonnière   from the French for buttonhole. In France under Louis XV a gentleman wore a boutonnière of artificial flowers. The fashion returned in the early twentieth century, men wearing a single fresh flower or very small spray, a fad of about a half century.

bow tie   a man's small tie in a bow-knot having two loops and two short ends for daywear. Also a small tie in a bowknot for evening wear, white with tail coat and black with dinner jacket. see *neckwear, masculine.*

bowknot   a flat, black ribbon which secured the looped-up cadogan of the eighteenth century coiffure. Also, a flat black bow which ornamented the black leather slippers or pumps.

lady's black satin bottine—black net stocking over pink cashmere—1830's

lady's bottine elastic webbing—fabric and leather tip

bowler   a British name for the hard, dome-shaped felt hat which appeared in 1850, designed by the English hatter, William Bowler. The Americans called it a derby because the Earl of Derby always wore the bowler to the races at Epsom Downs. see *derby.*

box coat   a coachman's overcoat new in the 1830's, straight and loose-fitting, of heavy beige cloth with or without cape. Single or double breasted. Worn by the driver sitting on the box of the coach, hence its name.

box pleats   see *pleats.*

boyish form, debutante slouch   a fashionable stance in the second decade of the twentieth century. A pose of hands on the hips, the pelvis thrown forward to produce the desired flattening of the bosom, By the 1920's the stance had developed into a pencil-straight, low-waisted figure aided by a Poiret-designed flattening brassière and an unboned knitted elastic girdle.

braccae   All Asiatics, barbarians and the northern Europeans wore braccae in the form of a piece of fabric wrapped around the hips and legs as is worn today in many Eastern countries. When the Roman legionnaires invaded the country of the Franks, Gauls, and British Celts, they adopted the braccae of the "panted people" or "breeched people" as a protection against cold. Upon returning home, they divested themselves of the forbidden garment before entering Rome. Their own leg-covering was short, made of wool or coarse linen and cross-gartered with strips of cloth or leather. In time, the northerners copied the short woolen tunic of the Romans. see *drawers.*

bracelet   an arm or wrist ornament which may be in ring or chain form, of gold, silver or other metals, plain or set with jewels. see *bangle bracelet; charm bracelet; slave bracelet.*

bracelet sleeve   see *sleeve, bracelet.*

braces   British for suspenders which hold up trousers. see *bretelles; gallowses; suspenders.*

braconnière   a part of late fourteenth and fifteenth century armor; hip-length skirt formed of hoop-shaped steel plates overlapping one another, hinged on one side and fastened on the other side by leather straps and buckles. It gradually shortened, finally disappearing in the seventeenth century.

braconnière late 14th C.

bragou-braz of the Breton peasant leather belt

bragou-braz   the very full knee breeches of the French Breton peasant worn with a wide sash or vest and short jacket. Of coarse dark blue linen shirred to self belt. Worn at the hips, ending with tight knee cuffs. Worn to modern times.

braguette   French word for codpiece.

braid   a narrow flat strip of woven, pleated or interlaced wool, cotton, silk, linen or metallic thread. Used for trimming, binding or appliqué work on apparel. *Coronation braid,* a round braid alternating thick and thin evenly, used to outline a design. *Military braid,* a flat, silk

bowler- American 1879

box coat of tan covert cloth- 1899

boyish form- 1920's

braid of diagonal basket weave. *Rickrack braid,* a flat woven braid in an even zigzag pattern. Made in cotton, silk and wool in many colors and used for trimming. *Soutache,* a very narrow, flat cord with uses such as finishing an edge, or a seam, or for decorative motifs. On men's clothes braid came into fashion about 1850 as edging or binding on jackets, coats and capes, or stitched down the side seams of trousers, a decoration which survives today on trousers worn with tailcoats.

braid   verb or noun in *headdress.* to plait or "braid" strands of hair together, usually three in number, making a "braid."

braid, middy   a narrow ribbed braid in various colors used especially for trimming navy middy blouses, hence its name.

braids, straw   see *straw braids.*

Brandenburg   decorative fasteners on outer garments in braided loops and buttons. They were termed *Brandenburgs* by the French after contact with the Brandenburg troops of Prussia in 1674 whose cassocks were so ornamented. The long loops and buttons or "frogs" which covered the whole front of the Hussar dolman date from 1812.

brassard, brassart   medieval armor for the arm; today, a badge worn on the arm such as a mourning band of black crêpe, or the fringed white satin ribbon tied on the arm of a young first communicant of the Roman Catholic Church. see *mourning band.*

brassière, bra, brasserole   The brasserole of medieval days was a type of camisole worn by little girls, also by women in childbed. The brassière, which was shorter and without sleeves, was a night garment for both sexes from the fourteenth to the seventeenth centuries. Fur-lined, it was a winter piece. A short

quilted jacket popular from 1600 to 1670 was called a brassière by Molière. From the Middle Ages to the twentieth century, the feminine bosom was firmly held by a high boned corset. Finally, Paul Poiret, in 1912, designed the modern brassière or bra to wear with a low-cut, soft girdle. see *uplift.*

Brazilian mink   see *marmot.*

breacan-feile   the older form of Scottish Highland dress, worn until 1746. The piece of cloth, some two yards wide and four to six yards long, was folded in half and pleated and fastened around the hips by a leather belt. The lower part formed the kilt, the upper half being fastened over the left shoulder by a brooch, with the end hanging in back forming the plaid. The right side, which was longest, was tucked into the belt and could also be drawn up over the head in inclement weather. The plaid or tartan of the wearer's family colors was a cloak by day and blanket by night. During the English Prohibition Act of 1746–1782 the breacan-feile hung from the shoulders in back to conceal the wearer's Scottish garb. see *Scottish Highland dress.*

breast knot   see *bosom knot.*

breastpin   former name for a jeweled brooch. see *pin; brooch.*

breechclout, breechcloth   a cloth worn round the body.

breeches, Hussar   very tight breeches of the French Directoire period. The favored colors for the breeches were canary yellow and bottle-green with the frock coat usually brown.

breeches, petticoat or **Rhinegrave** came to France on the person of Count Salm Rheingraf in the mid-seventeenth century. The garment was kiltlike or in divided skirt style and ornamented with ruffles, lace and ribbons. A small apron

breeches-
Roman
drawers
and tunic

breeches-canions with codpiece-English-16th C.

breeches-Venetians-with picadills-1572

breeches-Spanish Slops-1623

breeches-trunk hose and canions-English-1624

breeches-petticoat or Rhinegrave 1660

masculine "habit à la française" of coat, waistcoat and breeches-1770's and 1780's

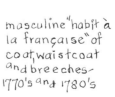

breeches of buckskin-fob seals-Hessian boots-1797

43

Breton Sailor

of ribbon loops concealed the front closure. Canions were worn under the petticoat breeches in Louis XIV's day, the canions being tubes of white linen, lace and bowknots tied around the knees.

breeches, Spanish   see *Spanish slops.*

breitschwantz   from the German for broadtail.

breloque   an ornament, charm or seal which formerly hung from a man's watch chain.

bretelles   French term for suspenders which hold up trousers or a skirt.

Breton sailor   a straw, felt or fabric hat with wide brim turned up evenly all around, originally worn by the peasants of Brittany. Also the name of the shape.

Bretonne lace   a net ground worked with an embroidered design in heavy colored thread.

bridal dress   In ancient Rome the pagan bride's dress for several centuries was of white wool, symbolizing virginity. The white wool cord girdle tied in a Hercules knot was to be untied only by the husband. The bride wore her hair long and flowing, covered with a flame-colored veil and with a chaplet of vervain or myrtle. The white dress of present-day custom dates to about 1800. see *wedding gown; orange blossoms; train.*

bridal or **carnival lace**   see *reticella lace.*

bridge trousers   see *pantalons à pont.*

brigandine   the first corset, fifteenth century; a piece of armor worn by a soldier knight, consisting of overlapping metal plates and scales sewn between layers of canvas, linen and leather. Such soldiers were called "brigands" and the companies, brigades.

brigandine- 14 th C.

brilliantine   a plain or twill-woven fabric of cotton and mohair with a lustrous surface used for men's jacket lining. In toiletry, an oil for dressing the hair.

British warm   the short warm, or car coat of suburban living. Also called duffer, duffel or tow coat, it came into use on the ski lift after World War II when surplus English Navy coats were made available to civilians. Worn by men, women and children, often of Tyrolean cloth with wooden toggles and hemp loops.

Brittany work   the embroidery of Breton peasants, geometric and floral patterns worked in chainstitch.

broadcloth   formerly, cloth made wider than twenty-nine inches. A high grade woolen cloth used especially for men's wear, a lighter fabric being made for women's wear. Woven of the finest felting wool, usually dyed in the raw, but always made in a wide width, thus its name. see *cotton broadcloth.*

broadsilk   silk made wider than 18 inches.

broadtail   see *karakul.*

broadtail, American   South American lamb processed to simulate broadtail. Pelts of animals one day to nine months old, sheared very close.

broadtail, Persian   pelts of very young or prematurely born Persian lamb. Lustrous, flat pelts with beautiful moiré design, delicate, costly and fragile.

brocade   a luxurious fabric woven on a jacquard loom in an allover pattern of flowers and figures with contrasting colors and gold and silver on a background of satin or twill weave. Originally, a rich silk cloth embroidered in gold and silver; then silk embroidered in arabesques; and, finally, made without metal threads.

brocatelle, brocatel   a brocade made in combination of yarns. The design is in high relief of silk or linen upon a plain or satin ground. Used for upholstery and draperies especially in the eighteenth century.

brodequin   see *buskin.*

brogue, brogan   a sturdy low shoe, of Irish-Scotch origin, for country wear. Originally hobnailed.

brolly   a British colloquialism for a tightly furled umbrella.

brooch   feminine and masculine, an ornamental piece of jewelry which is fastened to a garment or hat by means of a spiked pin hinged to the back. The brooch may be of simple design or set with jewels and of great beauty and value. see *Celtic brooch; pin.*

brooch   masculine, a large, jeweled pin or clasp worn by gentlemen on their velvet or beaver hats in the sixteenth and seventeenth centuries.

Brooks, Donald   see *couture, haute.*

brown   a color in the red-yellow group; with white added, the shades vary from tan to beige. The darker shades, with black added, deepen to chocolate.

brown, Devonshire   see *Devonshire brown.*

Bruges lace   a coarse Belgian bobbin-made lace in a weave resembling guipure tape. Coarse weaves are used for table linen and the fine for dresses.

brummaggem   old local name of Birmingham, England. The name applied to a counterfeit coin made there and later, to the cheap, tawdy jewelry manufactured there.

brushed wool   a knit or woven cloth made of long fibers which have been brushed or teaseled. A fabric appropriate for sweaters, scarfs and trimmings.

Brussels lace   any lace made in Brussels. A bobbin-made lace with the ground executed first, the threads following the curves of the pattern. A ground of hexagonal mesh is put in later.

buck   see *buckskin.*

Buckinghamshire lace   made in England since the sixteenth century. A fine bobbin-made lace with simple accented design.

buckle   a fastening device in use since antiquity for leather belts and armor. In the medieval period, buckles held up the long hose and fastened all parts of dress including footwear. Pumps with buckles of brass, steel and silver, some set with pearls and diamonds, either real or false, appeared in the 1650's. Round and oval shapes came in the eighteenth century and by the nineteenth century buckles became fashionable accessories on women's shoes.

bucko, reversed calf   see *calf, reversed.*

buckram   a coarse open weave of linen or cotton sized with glue and used as far back as the sixteenth century for stiffening parts of dress. It was much used in the period of bombast. It was first made as a floor covering under fine rugs in Bukhara, from which derived the term *buckram.*

buckskin, buck   formerly made of deer and elk, but calves and sheep now included. The skin of the buck, yellowish or grayish-white, made strong, soft and pliable. Genuine buckskin is made from small deer of Mexico and South American countries. In the nineteenth century, buckskin was the popular name for a tan-colored leather riding gaiter.

brogue-rawhide with single thong-British Celt

brogue or cuaran-waxed rawhide-Scotch-1632

modern calfskin version of the Highland rawhide cuaran or brogue-origin, of the modern ghillie-Scotch

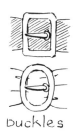

buckles

budge   an old English term for lamb-skin dressed with its wool and used as lining and trimming edge.

buff, buffskin   buffalo skin given oil tanning like chamois, turning it into a stout, velvety, brownish-yellow leather. Elk, deer and oxen are dressed the same way.

buffalo   The American bison is the largest of American animals, has dark-brown, long shaggy hair over head, shoulders and forelegs. Both European and American species are now nearly extinct. Formerly used for buff leather or buffskin and buffalo robes.

buffalo or
American bison

buffalo cloth   a cloth with considerable nap which was popular in cold-winter territory. Now replaced by mackinac or mackinaw.

buffcoat   the military coat of the sixteenth and seventeenth centuries made of buffalo hide and worn with buff gauntlets. The body was formed of four pieces with deep skirts, some thong-laced in front. Those of the officers were richly embroidered, the sleeves trimmed and edged with lace, buttons and loops, often in gold and silver.

buffonts   a scarf of gauze worn with a low-necked gown and puffed over the bosom in "pouter-pigeon" effect. A fashion of the late eighteenth century, advertised in the New England papers of the 1770's.

buffskin   see *buff*.

Bulgarian embroidery   worked in strong, bright colors on coarse linen for peasant garments. Solidly stitched in silk, gold and silver in flat stitches.

buffcoat or
or cassock-
16th and
17th C.

bulgha   slipper shoes of soft, yellow-colored leather worn by the village people of Egypt.

bull leather   see *leather, bull* or *cow*.

bullion embroidery   gold wire embroidery, originating with the Phrygians.

bullion lace   a lace of gold or silver thread used in robes of state or church vestments. Also, a braid or heavy twisted fringe of gold or silver thread.

buntal   a fine white fiber of the Philippine talipot palm, used in the making of straw hats.

bunting, baby   see *baby bunting*.

bur'a'   modern name for the Egyptian yashmak or face veil of crocheted silk yarn.

Burano lace   Italian needlepoint lace with square mesh and cordonnet design made on the island of Burano, Venice. Most of it was a coarser version of Venetian point lace.

burberry cloth   a mercerized, waterproofed cloth. Also, a staple cheviot, twill-woven overcoating, topcoating and suiting. A similar cloth of lighter weight is called roseberry cloth.

bure   a loosely woven, heavy, brown woolen cloth worn by Roman slaves and the peasants of Gaul. It also served as a chest or table cover and eventually was called bureau, the name of the chest. Used until the seventeenth century.

burgonet, burganet, bourquinotte   a bonnetlike helmet or casque similar to an armet with cheek pieces and sometimes a nosepiece. Its distinctive feature was the browpiece or umbril to shade the eyes. First worn by the Burgundians in the fifteenth century, and lasting to the end of the seventeenth century. One of the last types of helmet, which was in use to about 1670.

buriti, burity   leaf fiber of the Brazilian palm, used in making straw hats.

burka, burkha, bourkha   the traditional cover-all with which a Moslem woman drapes herself when she appears in public. It conceals her from head to foot except for a bit of lace over her eyes to see through. Many women now forego the burka.

Burmese man- holiday dress- sarong-like skirt-white cotton jacket- plaid pillbox-

Burmese- sarong-like skirt-white cotton shift- two hats-straw and turban-

burkä or Haïk of the Moslem woman when in public

burl   see *slubs*.

Burmese costume   see *tamehn; longi*.

burnous, burnoose   a long, circular mantle with hood and neck opening worn by Arabian men and women when traveling. With it the men sometimes wear straw hats and the women, veils. The caid or tribal magistrate of Algeria wears a burnous of vermilion cloth with a separate white hood topped by a varicolored wide straw hat. European, mid-nineteenth century, also a hooded cloak of cloth, the hood weighted with silk tassel.

burnous-red cloth with white hood- straw hat-worn by Algerian caid

burnous- traditional Moslem circular cloak for men and women

burnous- French- 1850's

burnous- European version- 1850's

bush safari jacket-
wind and water-proof
cotton-1950's

burnsides   see *side whiskers.*

burunduki   see *chipmunk, Siberian.*

busby   a tall fur shako originally worn in the eighteenth century by the Hungarian hussars, artillerymen and engineers. A colored cloth bag hangs from the top on the right side, originally designed to be fastened to the shoulder to ward off sword thrusts. Also another name for the bearskin worn by the English Brigade of Guards.

bush jacket   a traditional jacket for the African bush safari, or beach. Made of water-repellent corduroy, heavy linen or cotton, suede-finished and waterproofed. It is furnished with game and shell pockets, breast and hand-warming pockets.

bushel   a tailor's thimble. Also, to alter or repair a garment.

bushelman   a tailor who repairs or alters a garment.

buskin, brodequin, cothurnus, kothornos   first worn in Greek drama, thus "tragic kothornos." Over the centuries, there followed many variations, the distinct feature of boot and sandal being a thick sole of three or four inches which added to the actor's height on the stage. The Roman cothurnus was strapped up the calf of the leg and decorated with an animal paw, tail and perhaps a snout swinging from the top. As the brodequin of the Middle Ages, it was fashioned of soft dyed leathers or costly fabrics brocaded and embroidered.

bust forms   pads separately molded of foam rubber and worn inside the brassière to round out a flat bosom, 1930's. Popularly known as "falsies." Less popular in the 1950's and 1960's because replaced by the padded or contour brassière.

bust forms
of foam rubber-
20th C.

Buster Brown   a small boy character of a New York City Sunday newspaper at the beginning of the present century. He was created by artist R. F. Outcault, who was also the originator of the "Yellow Kid." The serial ran for years and years, his dress and Dutch hairdo being copied by many of his admirers. His style of collar is still known as the Buster Brown collar.

Buster Brown
and his collar-
early 20th C.

Buster Brown collar   see *collar, Buster Brown.*

bustle or **tournure,** (French) originally a crinoline, which it replaced in 1869, but with rows of whalebone placed

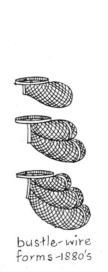

bustle-wire
forms-1880's

bustle gown-1870's

only from the sides around the back. The wide flare of the hemline disappeared and a bunched-up tunic or polonaise in back created the bustle look of the 1870's, called "tied-back time." In the 1880's the bustle was fashioned of one, two or three rolls of braided wire or perhaps a stuffed cushion tied around the waist by tapes, all of which disappeared in the 1890's. see *crinoletta*.

butcher's linen   a coarse homespun linen formerly used for butchers' jackets and aprons. Also, a white linen, strong and coarse, formerly used for backing men's shirt bosoms.

butterfly sleeves   see *patadyong; terno*.

butternut   homespun, strong, twilled cotton cloths, woven prior to and during the Civil War; called butternut because they were colored brown with a dye from the butternut tree.

button   It is recorded that buttons were worn in the reign of Edward III, 1327–1377. They became very fashionable during the period of Charles I, 1625–1649. Jeweled and sewn to handkerchiefs, they were known as handkerchief buttons. From 1860 buttons were used lavishly on the vest, cuffs and pockets of the male costume. Made of wood, bone, metal or passementerie over a form, the shapes varied from flat, round, ball, olive, to tiny mirrors in the eighteenth century. Hand-painted miniatures on ivory framed with chip diamonds were not rare. Button-making began in the American colonies in 1706, and has been a prosperous manu-facturing business ever since. Horn buttons appeared in the nineteenth century. By the middle of the century dyed vegeta-ble ivory became most popular, continu-ing to the present. In Birmingham, Eng-land, 1807, B. Sanders invented the metal button of two discs locked together by turning the edges, and the shell button with metal shank. In the United States in

1827 Samuel Williston of East Hampton, Massachusetts, patented the invention of a machine to produce cloth-covered but-tons. The vogue of buttons for fastening and trimming continues in varied shape and size. They are sewn on or attached to garments by shank or holes and are made in bone, plastic, glass, metal and other compositions. Cloth-covered but-tons often match suit and coat. Hoop and knot are early words for the button. The Chinese and Japanese use knots of silk or cotton as buttons. see *mother-of-pearl; temple jewelry*.

buttoned-down collar   see *collar, but-toned-down*.

buttonhole   In a handmade button-hole, the cut edges are first overcast with a plain stitch and then worked over with a close stitch and a firm looped or single purled edge. It is similar to a blanket stitch, which is much larger and broadly spaced.

buttonhole, bound   a slit cut for but-ton-entry, bound with braid or fabric instead of being finished with buttonhole stitchery.

buttonhook   an implement for draw-ing buttons through buttonholes of shoes, spats and gloves, used in the late nine-teenth and early twentieth centuries.

Byrd cloth   cotton cloth made to the specifications of Admiral Richard E. Byrd for his Polar expeditions; a lightweight fabric, strong and water-repellent, wind-resistant and porous, designed to take the place of the fur parka.

byrnie   a coat of chain or linked mail used as body armor by northern Euro-peans. see *hauberk*.

byrrus, birrus   similar to the heavy woolen cloak with cowl of the ancient Romans. Worn all through the Middle Ages by commoners. see *alicula*.

byrnie–
coat of linked or chain mail–
and linen tunic–13th C.–
Gothic and Celtic

Byzantine

cloth hose
with garters-
leather shoes-
9th c.

cloth hose
with garters-
leather boots-
9th c.

the white linen camisia-
cloth hose with garters-
leather boots-
4th and 5th c.

empress in
embroidered
silk stola over
long tunic-
6th c.

leather or wooden
soles with
linen or leather
bandelettes-
9th c.

emperor wearing
metal lorica
over long sleeve
tunic- white
braccae-
jewel sewn
leather boots-
11th c.

woolen tunic
over linen camisia-
embroidered braccae-
footless hose-
leather shoes-
11th c.

Byzantine

boy in camisia
with colored
bands-fabric or
leather hose-
4th c.

the linen
camisia or
undershirt-
boots of soft
leather (calcei)

empress wearing
white linen or
silk camisia
under stola of
heavy colored
silk-4th c.

soldier wearing
braccae and
linen camisia-
woolen tunic-
4th c.

emperor in white
camisia worn
under woolen
tunic and metal
lorica-leather
boots-
4th c.

early Christian
wearing linen
camisia under
embroidered
woolen
dalmatic-
5th c.

emperor in
white camisia
under tunic of
brocaded silk-
4th c.

byssus   a name applied to linen, cotton and silk. It is also thought to have meant, more properly, a yellowish flax from which linen was made for mummy cloths.

Byzantine embroidery motifs

Byzantine   The Byzantine period runs from about 400 to 1100 A.D. when Byzantium, later called Constantinople and now Istanbul, was the capital of the Roman Empire, Rome itself having fallen to the barbarians. From Constantinople emanated the prevailing mode worn by the upper classes. The making of clothes became an intricate and very important craft for which exorbitant prices were charged. The Emperor Diocletian in 301 A.D. finally settled on a maximum selling price for every article. At the same time he divided the industry into two classes: the workmen who fashioned the outer draped garments, and the artisans who produced, cut and fitted pieces. Those who made the elaborately embroidered flowing robes and cloaks were dress-

Byzantine juppe or tunic- 12th C.

makers, while the group who made tunics and braccae and were called bracarü or breechmakers, were actually the tailors. The undertunic, the shirt or camisia, was long-sleeved, knee-or ankle-length for men and full-length for women. It was visible at neck, sleeves and hem and usually adorned with strips of embroidery similar to that on the priest's chasuble. For ordinary folk the garment was made of very coarse linen or canvas and worn under the outer woolen tunic. The wearing of two tunics now became common. The Christian Church advocated a covered body in contrast to the sinful exposure of the pagan. Therefore hose were worn, along with shirt and underdrawers. Fascia or tibiale, strips of leather or cloth were wound round the legs, or in winter, there were leggings of cloth, cut, and sewn. Knitting in the round was known then as is revealed by a tube-shaped sock which belonged to an abbé of the seventh century. Fine linen, silk and velvet went into the making of hose for the wealthy, while linen, canvas or a heavy blanket cloth was used for the hose of the commoners. Rich hose were enhanced with colored silk and gold thread embroidery. Breeches and hose were gartered with bandelettes of linen and leather. Beginning with the fourth century the Byzantine mode became more and more sumptuous, and its influence is evident throughout medieval and Renaissance Europe. It was the foundation of Russia's costume, lasting into the twentieth century in the vestments of the church. See illustrations on preceding pages.

C

cabasset an open-faced helmet shaped like a high-crowned hat with a narrow, straight brim, a small sized morion. see *morion*.

cable stitch an overlapping link stitch, by machine or hand, in a serpentine pattern alternating with straight lock stitch to form a raised design.

cabretta a species of Brazilian haired sheep which produces a fine-grained leather like kid which is used for gloves and shoe linings.

cabriolet a bonnet shaped like the cabriolet carriage top and tied under the chin. It was collapsible too; eighteenth century.

caddie, caddy Australian term for the slouch hat.

caddis a plain, thin woolen fabric made since medieval days. When woven of fine wool, the product is similar to flannel.

cadogan a club-shaped knot into which men and women dressed their hair at the nape in the late eighteenth century. A cadogan wig of the 1770's, named after the Earl of Cadogan of earlier date, was worn by the Macaronies. It was looped up and tied by string or the black solitaire and was sometimes held in place by a small comb or, like the ladies' hair, confined in a net.

café au lait a light, creamy brown color.

caffa, kaffa a rich silk made in the Arabic town of Al Kufa in the sixteenth

to eighteenth centuries. Also the name of a painted cotton made in India during the sixteenth and seventeenth centuries.

caftan, kaftan a long, coatlike Oriental garment with long sleeves covering the hands, worn by both sexes throughout the Levant. Often worn under an outer cloak. Usually of handsome cloth in striped or brocaded silk, velvet or cotton, held by a cummerbund or hizaam wrapped around the waist. Worn by members of the Mohammedan priesthood, in Turkey, Arabia, Egypt, etc. see *djellaba; litham; gallibaya; jelab; haik; mandeel; djubbeh; yasmak, etc.*

cai-ao a long tunic of rich silk worn by both sexes in Vietnam, with standing collar and long sleeves, buttoned on the right side. The woman's tunic is slit from hip to hem.

caiquan Vietnamese trousers, men's of white linen, women's of black silk or velvet.

cairngorm a quartz crystal, grayish yellow to smoky brown, found especially in the Cairngorm Mountains of Scotland. Formerly considered the gem of Scotland.

calamanco, calimanco a European woolen cloth of satin weave in an imitation of camel's hair. Used for coats and popular until the late eighteenth century. Also a glazed, shiny woolen used for garments as well as quilts. Also the name of a cap made from the cloth.

calash, calèche, Thérèse a cage for the huge eighteenth century coiffures; of black silk sewn on reed or whalebone

cadogan held by combin wig - 1795

caftan worn by man of Uzbek, Russia - 19th C.

caftan - traditional Oriental robe of the Levant

53

felt calotte
and hat-cord with bead

calotte or
skullcap-
ancient Greece

calpac of
astrakhan-
Cossack
officer-1830

hoops which could be raised or like a carriage hood. A bonnet worn in the eighteenth and nineteenth centuries.

caleçons   see *underdrawers.*

Caledonian silk   having a small checked pattern of color on a white ground, new in 1817.

calendering   a process of finishing cloth to produce a smooth, glazed or watered (moiré) surface.

calf, calfskin   a fine-grained leather from cattle a few days to a few weeks old. It is finished in high polish, suede and patent leather, dyed all colors, and especially used for gloves and shoes.

calf, boarded or **box**   a novelty leather of the late nineteenth century, calfskin tanned with chrome salts. Rolling it cross-wise, then lengthwise, produced square markings on the grain, thus the term *box calf.*

calf, reverse   finished heavyweight calfskin dressed on the flesh side. It has a napped surface. Also called bucko because of its resemblance to buckskin.

calf, veal   upper leather from large-size or partly grown calf. A soft, heavy, durable, waterproofed leather used principally for ski and woodsmen's boots.

calfskin   see *calf.*

calico   a cotton textile printed on one side. Used for dresses, aprons etc. It came from Calicut, India, where printed cottons originated in the mid-nineteenth century. At the same time it filled a great need in clothing for families traveling and settling in the American West.

California embroidery   the braiding and stitching on leather garments done by the California Indian women of the pre-Spanish period.

California sports shirt   a fashion for men of cotton velours, in plain colors, light or dark or striped, with short sleeves, and round, crew or collared necks. The cloth is washable and requires no ironing.

caliga   the shoe or sandal of the Roman soldier up to and including the centurion, varying in design according to rank. It was a heavy-soled leather sandal, often hobnailed with iron or bronze nails. Characteristic was the gartering, or ligulae, which involved an elaborate manner of tying above the ankle.

calimanco   see *calamanco.*

Callot Soeurs   see *couture, haute.*

calotte, calot, zucchetto   headgear of ancient Greek origin commonly worn by all classes, the fabric varying according to the wearer's means and position. A small round skullcap covering the tonsure, it was often worn under the hood or crown and gradually acquired significance in color, especially among churchmen. The scarlet zucchetto was a skullcap worn by the clergy at all times to cover the tonsure; fifteenth century.

calpac, calpack, shapka, Cossack cap   the Cossack officer's traditional cap of astrakhan.

camail   a chain mail hood with buckled fastening worn over an iron skullcap with steel circlet; English, thirteenth century.

camblet   see *camlet.*

Cambodian costume   see *sampot.*

cambric   of linen but also a fine white cotton; a fancy costume fabric glazed on one side, made in Cambrai, France, but originally made in Camerike, Flanders.

Cambridge mixture   see *Oxford cloth.*

camel's hair, camel hair   There are three types of camel hair, a down type next to the hide, short, soft and silky in beautiful beige shades which may be used natural or dyed; a shorter, moderately coarse fleece between the outer hair and the down; the outer hair, coarse, tough and wiry, reddish-brown to brownish-black. The camel is not shorn or plucked but sheds its hair in clumps which are gathered by the caravan end man. Camels are native to all the desert regions of Asia and Africa, but the finest fiber comes from Mongolia.

camel's hair coat, polo coat   of natural-color camel's hair cloth, worn by both men and women. It appeared in the first decade of the twentieth century evolving from the British *wait coat* thrown over the shoulders between periods of play at polo matches.

camel suede   a cotton fabric resembling camel's hair cloth.

cameo   a gem carved in relief, usually of two colors with the design carved in one color and a second color serving as a background. Of Oriental origin, it may be of shell, onyx or sardonyx. During the reign of Augustus, first Roman emperor 27 B.C.–14 A.D., little cameo portraits became the rage.

camicia rossa   see *Garibaldi shirt.*

camisa   the Spanish word for the Philippine overbodice made of rengue, a native pineapple cloth. Wide-arched butterfly sleeves with fine embroidery.

camisia   in ancient Greece, a short tunic or sleeping garment; the root of the word, in the Byzantine era, an undergarment to protect the robe from body wear. The robes were of heavy, sumptuous fabrics lavishly embroidered and bejeweled. Though two millennia have come and gone since the Ionian camisia was first worn, it still exists as the basic white linen shirt, smock or blouse. *Camisia* in Italian,

camisa in Spanish, and *kami* to the Orientals.

camisole   an underbodice and formerly a corset cover. *Camisole top,* the upper part of a slip, snug over the bosom and held by shoulder straps. *Camisole neckline,* an evening neckline cut straight across the bosom and held by shoulder straps.

camlet, chamlet   a closely woven fabric originally made in Turkey of camel's hair and later imitated in Europe; made mostly of Angora wool with silk, linen or cotton. The name came from the place of manufacture in England on the River Camlet. Used in the seventeenth and eighteenth centuries by the American colonists for petticoats, cloaks and hoods. see *paragon.*

camoca, kamaka   a rich, figured silk of the Middle Ages. Originally from China but later imported from Persia and elsewhere in Asia.

campaign wig   see *wig, campaign.*

Canadian embroidery   the name given the primitive and artistic work created by the Indians of Canada. A unique decoration of animal skins with cut and dyed porcupine quills combined with colorful beads.

candy stripe   an imitation in fabric of striped candy. bright-colored stripes of varying widths on silks and ribbons.

candys, Persian   a shaped and sewn garment of linen or wool with flowing sleeves which fell into set pleats in back of the arm. This was the first appearance of a set-in sleeve. There were carefully arranged pleats in the skirt.

cane, walking stick   a costume accessory in vogue in various periods down the centuries, doubtless a follow-up of carrying a sword. In the eleventh century

camisa—traditional overbodice of embroidered gauze—of the Philippines

sticks of applewood are recorded as a French fashion. Dandies of the Italian Renaissance carried small canes like the modern swagger stick. Henry IV of France (1589–1610) is noted as the first owner of a specially designed walking stick. Spaniards in the sixteenth century wore sword, dagger and rapier attached to the belt. In the seventeenth and eighteenth centuries, tall sticks with ivory tops and tasseled cords were à la mode, and the cane often concealed a sword. The tall lady's stick of the last quarter of the eighteenth century was usually of scented wood, tortoise shell or ivory, with a gold or silver top which held powder and perfume. In the nineteenth century the man's stick was cut shorter, to measure from the hand of his slightly bent arm to the ground. The handsome gold-headed cane was carried all through the nineteenth century. During the Prohibition Period in America, a cane concealing a slim bottle was popular, but since the Depression the smart walking stick has virtually disappeared. In the 1920's there was a fad of swagger sticks for women.

canepin   fine leather made of lambs', kids' and chamois' skins were used for gloves and hairpieces.

canezou- shoulder cape with belted ends- 1830's

canezou   a lady's short cape of the 1830's, of sheer muslin with embroidery, worn over the bodice. A false canezou was simply a deep ruffle or bretelle with long ends.

caniche   from the French for poodle, a cloth with curly, tufted surface in imitation of the French poodle's coat. Used for baby caps and tiny jackets.

canions with codpiece   canions or canons of the sixteenth century were shaped, short breeches. These were of silk and paned or slashed, the codpiece of silk with embroidery. see *codpiece.*

cap of shirred lace- Baby Stuart- English 1634

cannelé   a style of weaving producing a channeled or fluted surface; a taffeta-type fabric resembling rep.

cannetille   a very fine gold and silver thread twisted spirally, used in embroidery. Also a lace made of the same thread.

cannons, canions   tubes of white linen and lace ruffles with bowknots tied around the knees, worn under French petticoat breeches; seventeenth century. see *canions with codpiece.*

canotier   French for the straw sailor worn by a sailor of a *canot,* or small boat.

Canton crêpe   originally from China and made of silk, today also of rayon. A durable fabric with pebbly surface. Used for dresses and linings.

Canton flannel   see *flannel, canton.*

Cantrece   the trademark of a kind of nylon yarn with the sheerness and resiliency necessary to the fit and look of a stocking.

canvas   a coarse fabric with square mesh, plain-woven and strong, with soft finish or sized. Of linen, cotton, flax, tow or jute, bleached or unbleached. Used for tropical clothing, shoes, stiffening material and other items, such as embroidery canvas.

canvas, Java   see *Java canvas.*

cap, Angelus   the tied headkerchief peasant cap shown in *The Angelus,* a famous painting of the nineteenth century by the French artist, Jean François Millet.

cap, Balmoral   see *bluebonnet.*

cap, Baby Stuart   cap of shirred lace with baby lace edging. English, 1634; from the portrait of an infant Stuart prince painted by Van Dyck.

cap, bellboy's   see *bellboy's cap.*

cap of
cloth for
country wear-
German-1830's

Jockey cap-
black velvet-
tasseled ribbon
bowknot-French-
1790

trembling cap of
gold cord-pearl
band-Italian-18th C.

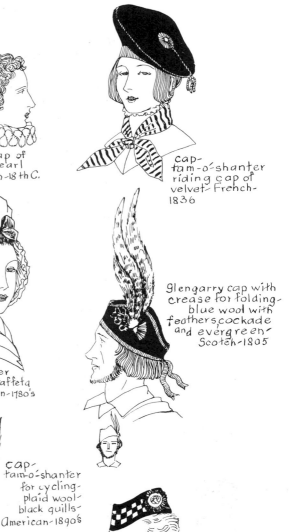

cap-
tam-o'-shanter
riding cap of
velvet-French-
1836

cap or
képi of red
cloth-blue
leather-white
braid-silver
buttons-
Italian-1848

Windsor cap
of straw-
velvet ribbon
and ostrich-
French-1864

mobcap of sheer
white lawn and taffeta
ribbon-American-1780's

Glengarry cap with
crease for folding-
blue wool with
feathers,cockade
and evergreen-
Scotch-1805

sailor cap-
"Pie-Pan or
Pie-Plate"-
dark blue
cloth with
black ribbon band-U.S.Navy

Gob
or "white cap"-
machine-stitched
cotton-U.S.Navy

cap-
tam-o'-shanter
for cycling-
plaid wool-
black quills-
American-1890's

Glengarry cap-
modern-blue wool-
red and white diced
band-black ribbon
cockade and lappets-
Scotch

cap-
boy's tam-o'-shanter-
plaid woolen cloth with
pompon-English-1890's

blue cloth cap-earflaps-
black leather visor-
cockade-black cock
brush-Austrian Tyrolese
soldier-1940's

helmet-formal hunt cap-
black velvet
reinforced
crown-black
bowknot
denotes
gentleman
rider-
20th C.

overseas cap-
khaki woolen
cloth-officer
U.S.Army-1940's

Gandhi cap of
white undyed
homespun-1940's

Jinnah cap
of karakul-
the tarboosh
worn by men
of Pakistan

boy's military
cloth cap-
leather visor and
chinstrap-French-1860's

cap, boudoir   see *boudoir cap.*

cap, calotte   see *calotte.*

cap, Cossack   see *calpac.*

cap, curler   see *boudoir cap.*

Deerstalker cap-visor front and back-earlaps and reversible scarlet crown

cap, deerstalker   a cloth cap with visor back and front, usually having turn-under earflaps and a reversible crown of scarlet poplin. The style is popularly associated with the character of Sherlock Holmes.

cap, duckbill or **jockey cap**   an extreme style of cap of straw or felt with a very long peak or visor worn by the merveilleuse of the French Directoire period.

city flat-cap of black wool- English-16th C.

cap, flat   English, after 1565; the hat of city folk, merchants, professional and elderly men, also apprentices and servants; the "city flatcap" or "status cap." Queen Elizabeth I passed a law compelling every person over seven years of age in the middle class to wear the cap on Sundays and holidays upon pain of fine. Made of wool, felt or black yarn, it was an important commercial item.

cap, forage, képi   in the mid-nineteenth century the military shako was replaced by the cap. French troops in Algeria adopted the German kappi, or cap, which was copied in 1857 during the American Civil War and called a forage cap.

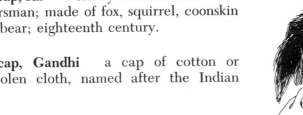

cap- "fore and aft"- earflaps-travel and sports-English-19th C.

cap, fore and aft   for traveling and sports, of plaid woolen cloth with earflaps; English, 1870's.

cap, fur   worn by the American frontiersman; made of fox, squirrel, coonskin or bear; eighteenth century.

cap, Gandhi   a cap of cotton or woolen cloth, named after the Indian

cap or shako of leather-Russian-1813

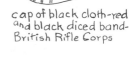

cap of black cloth-red and black diced band- British Rifle Corps

cap of the frontiersman-American-19 th C.

cap- escoffion of brocade- with wimple-Italian-14th C.

fur cap-American frontiersman-18 th C.

jeweled
Juliet cap at
back of head-
Italian-15th C.

jockey cap of
japanned leather-
buck's tails-
silver braid-
Philadelphia
Cavalry-1775

cap of red cloth-
blue tassel
and braid-
U.S. Army-1860's

cap of Jester with
bells-medieval

cap like the képi-
plaid woolen
cloth-New York-
1880's

cap under hat-worn
by peasant-Medieval

cap, montero-
cloth faced
with fur-
1858

political leader, Mahatma Gandhi (1869–1948). A cap he wore constantly.

cap, Glengarry not as old as the bluebonnet, dating only from 1805. It was named for Glengarry, Invernessshire, Scotland, the members of the Glengarry Clan being the first wearers. A flat cap with center crease. It has a red checkered tartan band of the Stuarts finished with a black ribbon ending in lappets. The tuft or boss on top is either red or blue. The wearer's clan brooch is worn pinned on the left side.

cap, gob worn by the enlisted men of the United States Navy. Of white cotton twill with four-pieced round crown and full-stitched brim. "Shall be worn squarely on the head and shall not be crushed or bent in the middle."

cap, horned see *cornet.*

cap, jinnah the karakul tarboosh worn by men of Pakistan, named in honor of Mohammed Ali Jinnah, Pakistan's founder and first governor general.

cap, jockey a close-fitting cap with a rounded peak, worn by jockeys in horse races and displaying the owner's stable colors.

cap, Juliet an evening cap of wide, open mesh sewn with pearls and jewels. A tiny calotte usually worn by Juliet in Shakespeare's tragedy. Both renaissance and modern.

cap, Liberty see *bonnet, Phrygian.*

cap, Monmouth originally made in the town of Monmouth, England, a knitted, close-fitting cap with turned-up band and hanging crown, a stocking cap, as it is known. It was used by sailors and workmen in the Colonies.

cap, montero a man's cap, popular in Europe and the American colonies for

cap or
roundlet-
black velvet-
gilt embroidery-
Italian-16th C.

cap-hunting-of
japanned leather-
French-1833

mortar-shaped
cap of felt or
velvet-gauze
veil-frontlet-
French-14th C.

cap-pillbox
over chignon
Venetian-
1500

cap-pilos, Greek-
pileus, Etruscan
or Roman-
athlete's
cap

cap of
red felt-wig
or frizzed
natural hair-
Venetian-1510

cap with attached beaded
béret-ostrich plume-
English prince-16th C.

jeweled steeple
hennin or cap over
wimple-
Italian-11th C.

sleeping cap-"dormeuse"-
sheer lawn, lace and ribbon-
English-1770's

cap of
varnished
leather-
metal
shield and
ostrich-
American
rifleman-
1770

satin
negligée
cap-
shaved head-
English-18th C.

Queen
Victoria's
military cap-
wide gold braid
black visor-1840

cap-sports-
red and green
wool plaid-
tiny feathers-
French-1844

Princeton
cap-orange
and black-
college
cricket
1870's

Yale cap-
blue felt-
college
cricket
1870's

polo cap-Piping
Rock Club-1870's

Windsor cap-
worn with the
Beatty Tilt-
1920's

cap pillbox-
black velvet-
jeweled buckle-
black silk fringe-
French-1940's

negligée, hunting and riding. Of cloth or felt with flaps usually of fur which could be turned down; seventeenth century. It is worn today by farmers and hunters. see *Eugénie's wigs.*

cap, negligée   see *negligée cap*

cap, overseas   World War I; fashioned along Glengarry-cap lines with center crease, of olive drab wool cloth.

cap, ski   with flaps to let down and tie under the chin. Has a long, squarish peak or visor.

cap, stocking   see *Monmouth cap.*

cap, swordfisherman's   of water-repellent cotton with a very long visor of plastic or leather.

cap, toboggan   the long, knitted, woolen, pointed stocking cap ending in a tassel or pompon and worn when tobogganing. The same cap was also worn as a nightcap.

cap, trembling   see *trembling cap.*

cap, trencher   see *mortarboard cap.*

cap, watch   a knitted cap of dark blue yarn with turned-up cuff worn by the United States sailors in bad weather.

cap, Windsor   of straw with ostrich tips and velvet ribbon; French, 1864.

cap and bells   refers to the jester's costume. The jester originated in Byzantium to amuse royalty and reached European courts after the Crusades. His costume included a fool's cap with ass's ears and a petal-scalloped shoulder cape. IIis scepter was a rattle with miniature head, cap, cape and bells. The custom of having a court jester disappeared in the seventeenth century. see *motley; bells, silver.*

cape, cloak or **mantle**   masculine or feminine, a sleeveless outer garment which may be of shoulder length or reach to the ankles. In shape, it may be circular and flaring, or cut and seamed to hang in straight silhouette. Capes became fashionable in men's dress in the eighteenth century when worn with or attached to loose cloth overcoats called wrap-rascals. Since then the cape has been worn by all classes of both sexes and by the military.

cape seal   see *seal.*

cape sleeve   see *sleeve, cape.*

capeline   see *skimmer.*

capes   see *lamb shearlings.*

capeskin   a washable, glacé-finished, soft leather. Formerly from the Cape of Good Hope in Africa, it now comes from other countries as well.

capibara   see *capybara.*

capishaw   a hood on a child's winter coat. A Canadian corruption of the French *capuchin.*

capoc   see *kapoc.*

capote   a long, full military overcoat. In the Levant, a coat of shaggy cloth; also, a medieval cloak worn by women and also a bonnet of the mid-Victorian period with strings and a bavelot or deep ruffle at the back of the head. see *fanchon; coal scuttle bonnet.*

cappa, capa   Spanish for cape or cloak. A long cape or cloak, ecclesiastic or academic. Also the scarlet cape of the Spanish toreador.

cappa magna   the long, trailing, luxurious cape or cloak, a ceremonial vestment hooded in ermine or silk; red for bishops or cardinals, violet for some other prelates.

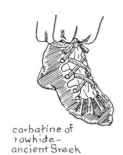

carbatine of
rawhide-
ancient Greek

capulet - worn by women
of the Pyrenees-early
17th C.

caraco-long basque with
peplum-French-
1780's

cappadine   silk floss or the waste obtained after the silk has been reeled off the cocoon.

capri pants   same as pedal-pushers but loose and tapered and ending at mid-calf. see *pant lengths, feminine.*

capuchin   see *hood, French; capuchine.*

capuchon   in medieval times a hooded cape, short or long, worn by men, women and churchmen. The pointed hood developed into the chaperon, a hood with a long tail called a liripipe. see *chaperon.*

capucine   French for nasturtium, a fashionable flower at the beginning of the nineteenth century. In hues known as capucine buff, lake, orange, red and yellow.

capulet   a feminine short cape and hood with tasseled end worn in the Pyrenees and copied into the mode. Early nineteenth century.

capybara   the fur or pelt of the largest living rodent, of South American origin and related to the guinea pig. The skin is similar to pigskin, elastic and soft; used for gloves and leather goods.

car coat   see *British warm; cardigan.*

caracal   local name for Asiatic cat; a Turkish word meaning black ear, a species of lynx from India, the warm sections of Asia and northern Africa. Reddish brown with black ears tipped with long black hairs, a poor fur, seldom imported. see *wildcat, lynx.*

caraco   a gown of the 1780's; a long-waisted, long-sleeved, tight-fitting basque finished with a peplum. Sometimes called à la Créole. Also, a woman's short coat or jacket, usually about waist length; from Turkish alpaca coat called kerrake.

caracul   see *karakul.*

carbatine, karbatine   the shoe of the earliest Greeks and Romans and primitive Europeans. The British name was "es-cid," meaning protection from hurt, and "brogue" was the Scotch name. Made of one piece of rawhide drawn up by thongs through self-loops of the leather, quite like the modern gillies, the shoe was worn to recent times by the Scotch and Irish and was akin to that of the early American Indians.

carbuncle   formerly any polished red stone; now, specifically, a garnet.

carcan   French for the iron collar of a criminal, a punishment suppressed in 1832.

carcanet   a high jewcled or pcarl-beaded collar, often called a dog collar; a necklace or chain of precious stones, late nineteenth and early twentieth centuries. see *carcan.*

cardigan   originally a short military jacket or dolman of knit worsted designed and worn by the Earl of Cardigan, a British general in the Crimean War. It was trimmed with fur, braid and buttons. As such, it was worn to World War I. Today, a sweater with or without sleeves and buttoned center front.

carcanet-
evening necklace-
pearls and jeweled
bars   1890's

cardigan jacket
was suggested by
the Hussar jacket

Cardin, Pierre   see *couture, haute.*

cardinal   a feminine shoulder cape with hood resembling the bishop's mozetta of scarlet cloth. Seventeenth and eighteenth centuries. see *French hood.*

cardinal or French hood- silk, cloth or velvet, worn by all women of all nations- 17th and 18th centuries

cardinal red   the color of vestments worn by cardinals, a bright yellowish-red.

cardinal's red hat   originated in the black-brimmed hat commonly worn by clergy and laity. Tied under the chin by a cord, it was slung in back when off the head. In 1245 Pope Innocent IV granted the red hat to cardinals. The rank of the wearer is designated by the number of tassels which terminate the cords.

cardinal's red calotte or zucchetto- 1630's

caribou; reindeer   caribou is the American Indian name. A wild and domestic animal found in northern Canada, United States, Europe and Asia. The animal, along with food and transportation, furnishes fur and leather for clothes and boots. Grayish-brown with white neck, under and hind quarters.

carmagnole   a short vest or jacket worn by the French Revolutionists; originally worn by Piedmont workers who came from Carmagnole in Italy. The deputies of Marseilles took the garment to Paris in the 1790's where it was adopted by the Revolutionaries. It buttoned down the front, had pockets, revers and a turned-down collar.

carnelian   an orange-red, brown and wax-yellow chalcedony quartz, uniform in texture, of a waxlike surface. Used for jewelry.

carnival, or **bridal lace**   see *bridal lace; reticella.*

Caroline spencer   a revival of the short jacket invented by Lord Spencer in the 1790's. It was named for Caroline, queen and wife of the British George IV (1820–1830). It was of white kerseymere or black velvet and lined with pale blue satin. see *spencer.*

carriage boot   see *boot, carriage.*

cardinal's red biretta-Spanish- 17th C.

cardinal's red hat with cords, beads and tassels- 14th C.

Carmargnole jacket of the French revolutionists- 1790's

Caroline spencer jacket of velvet- English- 1820's

carrick-topcoat for driving-1830

cassock-cloth, velvet or buffskin 18th C.

carrick   a gentleman's greatcoat for driving. Of heavy fawn-colored cloth, double-breasted and with deep collar. It had one, two or three shoulder capes. Of the 1850's and popular to the end of the century. The coach was called carrick, named for a Britisher, John Carrick.

Carrickmacross lace   a lace which originated in Ireland. The design is cut from sheer fabric, the edges whipped and then applied to the net with buttonhole stitch. Also, *Carrickmacross guipure* made without net.

carroting   a process used in preparing hat furs for felting. It consists of a treatment of nitric acid and quicksilver before the skin is defurred.

cartridge pleats   in military dress, small round pleats to hold cartridges; simulated in civilian dress as ornamentation.

cartwheel ruff   see *ruff, cartwheel.*

cartwheel ruff of lawn and lace-wire supportasse-Spanish-16th C.

Carven, Mme. Carmen Mollet   see *couture, haute.*

casaque   originally a sleeveless short jacket worn over armor and also worn by civilians. Today's term designates the short silk jacket of brilliant colors worn by jockeys in France.

casaquin   a short negligée or dressing sacque with full flaring back worn with petticoats at home; eighteenth century.

cascade   a fall, frill or ruffle of lace or soft fabric hanging vertically to cascade from neck, waist or skirt. see *jabot.*

Cashin, Bonnie   see *couture, haute.*

cashmere   the soft wool found under the hair of goats raised in Kashmir, Tibet and the Himalayas. Such goats are now raised in America. The fine, soft wool is mixed with sheeps' wool. Overcoatings, suitings, vestings and sweaters are of Indian commercial cashmere. The famous cashmere shawls are made of the under coat hair of the cashmere goat.

cashmere work   a beautiful, elaborate appliqué embroidery of patterned cashmere cutout motifs which practically covered the large fringed shawls of India, and became a Western fashion in the nineteenth century.

casque   a helmet or defensive headpiece in ancient and medieval armor.

casquetel   a light open helmet without beaver or visor.

cassimere, kerseymere   a soft-textured cloth of medium weight, coarse and fine, plain and twill-woven, in checks, plaids and stripes. Usually made of wool, the name is a variant of cashmere.

Cassini, Oleg   see *couture, haute.*

cassock   originally the outer coat of the European foot soldiers and horsemen of the seventeenth century; a flaring, knee-length coat of cloth buttoned down the front; also of buff leather and worn by the mousquetaires. The cassock of the clergy is of cloth with a standing collar;

a straight, full-length garment buttoned from neck to hem, worn indoors and out, and sometimes with a sash. Worn under a surplice for church services. Also worn by acolytes and members of vested choirs under a cotta. see *soutane*.

castellated, battlemented the ornamental slashings of the edges of garments into square-cut edges like the crenellated parapets of castle towers; stitching in that style, a fashion of the Middle Ages. see *dagged*.

Castilian red a brilliant red with a yellowish hue, also called Dutch scarlet.

cat, civet see *civet*.

cat, house a tamed member of the Felidae family. The best fur from wild or semiwild animal. It has thicker fur than the domestic cat and is raised all over the globe. The best peltries come from Holland and Belgium, the American grade is poor. Colors are white, black and bluish-gray, used for trimming and children's fur sets.

cat, leopard from China, India and Africa. The best peltries are small and from Somaliland, with very short hair shading from white or pale yellow to tawny and orange with black rosette markings; a durable pelt used for coats, jackets and trimmings.

battlemented

catercap or mortarboard worn by university men

catercap see *mortarboard*.

Catherine wheel see *farthingale*.

Catherine or St. Catherine's wheel-farthingale or hoop-English and French-1530 to 1630

caracal or Asiatic cat

genet or spotted cat

cat-lynx

cat-leopard

civet cat or spotted skunk

cheetah

house cat

cat-ocelot

cat-jaguar

golden net caul over silk-jewels and wimple-English-14th C.

caul and crown of jewels and pearls-German-15th C.

caul-golden net with jewels-French-1377

golden net caul over silk cap-jeweled crown-English queen-15th C.

cerevis-flat visorless cap of German student corps-1815

caul   a medieval headdress known also as crepin, crestine, crespinette, tressure, tressour. The hair was concealed in silken cases and covered with a heavy net of reticulated gold or silver cord interspersed with pearls, beads or spangles.

caushets   an early American and now obsolete word for corsets.

cavalier   one of the party loyal to Charles I of England. Their elegant costume included handmade boots with spur leathers and falling tops showing boot hose of sheer white linen, lace-edged, worn to protect costly silk hose inside.

cavalry twill, tricotine   a stout twill weave with a decided diagonal cord of wool, cotton or rayon. Used for sportswear and uniforms.

Celanese   trademark owned by the Celanese Corporation of America, which produces fashion fibers of Celanese acetate and rayon. see *acetate*.

Celtic brooch   Among the many fine pieces of pure gold jewelry unearthed in Ireland during the past few centuries were brooches which fastened an animal skin or a woolen shawl. The characteristic Celtic brooch was formed of a long pin hinged to an open circle; the pin was

inserted through the fabric and the end snapped through the circle opening, which was generally finished with two decorative knobs.

cendal   a fabric of the Middle Ages, possibly from China, often mentioned. It was still worn in the seventeenth century. It was made very sheer and also heavy and was used for the dress of nobles and ecclesiastics. It could be painted upon and was used for banners.

cepken   a richly embroidered bolero-like jacket worn by Turkish men over a fine white shirt and with a sash.

cerevis   a visorless type of pillbox cap worn by German university students.

cestus   the magic girdle of Venus, a beautifully embroidered sash worn outside the chiton. It encircled the waist and hung down in front. In Greek and Roman mythology, the wearing of it made the lady irresistible to any man she set her heart upon having. Also, a boxer's glove of leather bands loaded with pieces of iron; ancient Rome.

Ceylon native dress   see *comboy*.

chadar, chuddar   an enveloping black mantle which Persian women always

chadar of modern flowered cotton-Iran

wore in public. Banned in the 1920's in favor of Western dress, it is still worn by many women in winter. In summer it is now seen in light colors and gay flowered prints, often over Western dress.

chain mail the first form of protective armor, of flexible meshlike metal links and rings.

chainse the body garment of man and woman, noble and peasant, which later became the shirt or chemise. It was made of hemp, linen, sheer wool or even precious silk, the fabric varying in quality according to the wearer's station and means. see *chemise*.

chainse-sherte or chemise-Flemish 12th C.

chalcedony a translucent variety of quartz usually pale blue or gray tinge with waxlike luster. Varieties in other colors are known as carnelian, agate, onyx and chrysoprase. Used for jewelry.

chalk stripe cloth with stripes that appear to have been marked with white chalk.

challis, challie formerly a wool and silk fabric, lightweight, now made of fine wool, or wool with rayon or cotton. Usually printed with a delicate floral pattern

and used for negligées, dresses, infant's wear and nightgowns. The Anglo-Indian name is *shalee*.

chalwar-pantaloons worn by Turkish and Balkan women

chalwar (pantaloons) worn by an Algerian dancer

chalwar the very loose, baggy trousers with long drapery that all Persian women wore until the 1890's. The baggy pantaloons of the Turkish and Balkan women reach to the ankles. When spread out, the pantaloons resemble a pillow case open at either end. A blouse is worn with the chalwar and over the blouse the eték or jacket, and very often over that the beautifully embroidered caftan. Albanian pantaloons, when fully draped, require for either man or woman a piece of fabric measuring about ten yards or ninety square feet of material thirty-six inches wide. Persian women were ordered to change this dress to short skirts in 1890, following a trip of their ruler to Paris where he saw the short skirts worn by dancers in the ballet.

chambord a woolen mourning cloth with ribbed surface which may contain silk, rayon or cotton.

chambray a fine-quality gingham with colored warp and white filling with a linen finish. Named after Cambrai, France, where it originated and was first used, for sunbonnets.

chamma-toga-like piece about 4 yards long. The man's right arm left free - the woman's left arm free - Ethiopia

chamma the principal outer garment for Ethiopian men and women, a white cotton toga-like scarf about four yards long. A difference lies in the manner of draping, the man leaving the right arm free while the woman leaves the left arm free. The wearer's rank and position is indicated also by the manner of wearing. The women's chamma is often bordered with a wide band of brilliantly colored embroidery. The traditional Ethiopian robe, it continues to be worn.

chamois a very soft, strong and pliable leather from the skin of the chamois goat; or the skin of sheep or goat with the grain removed. Of a deep yellow color. Used for gloves, garment interlining, pockets.

chamois cloth a yellow-dyed thick cotton fabric napped and sheared to simulate the leather. Used for sportswear and gloves.

champagne color the pale golden color of the sparkling wine, a delicate amber hue.

chandelier earrings very long earrings, sometimes reaching to the shoulders, worn with evening dress. Of delicate design, articulated and set with sparkling gems; early 1960's.

Chanel, Gabrielle one of the most influential of French twentieth century couturieres. A pioneer in the use of fabrics which have later been universally adopted; in 1915 she introduced rayon or artificial silk into fashion and in the 1920's, wool jersey. Shortly after World War I she presented the elegant and casual tailleur, a skirt with hip-length boxy jacket which has been worn for decades and has become the "Chanel suit, an American classic."

chang-fu the long, plain Chinese robe with standing collar of the Ch'ing Dynasty (1644–1912), the basic dress for several centuries.

Chaps or chaparajos of deerskin with hair left on sides and front. U.S. cowboy

chang shan a long gown worn by Chinese men for formal dress, sometimes with a black outer jacket.

Chantilly lace a delicate silk or linen bobbin lace on a simple ground, mostly black but sometimes white. Made formerly at Chantilly but now chiefly at Bayeux.

chaparajos, chaps batwing cowhide overalls open in back and worn over riding trousers as a protection against brush and thorns. California leggings of deerskin with the hair left on the front and sides for warmth and protection.

chaparajos chaps-batw style- cow

chaps of angora goat hide-American cowboy-19th C.

chapeau bras see *bicorne*.

chapel de fer, helmet, iron hat worn over the camail or hood of chain mail; early thirteenth and fourteenth centuries. Reappeared as the montauban in the seventeenth century.

chaperon hood and shoulder cape in one, worn by churchmen, nobility and commoners from the twelfth to the sixteenth centuries. The hood acquired a

chaperon with liripipe- Medieval

chaperon- black velvet with fur-jeweled silk caul- French-1330

chaperon or hood worn by all classes- men and women- 13th C.

chaperon- French-14th C.

chaperon- turban with liripipe- Flemish 15th C.

chaperon turban- roundlet over coif- chaperon and liripipe pleated and draped- French- 15th C.

long tail, or liripipe, which was arranged in all manner of styles. see *liripipe*.

chaplet   a wreath or garland of leaves or leaves and flowers worn upon the head, bestowed as a mark of honor or symbol of esteem. Also, a necklace of beads.

chaps   see *chaparajos*.

chaqueta   Spanish name of a heavy cloth or leather jacket worn by Texas cowboys.

charcoal gray   a rich, grayed black produced by weaving together black and gray yarn or fiber.

charm bracelet   a feminine bracelet usually of flexible links to which bangles or charms are attached, each charm supposedly a gift of remembrance. A contemporary fad.

charm string   a necklace of the 1880's composed of small fashionable buttons strung together combining pearl, gilt, silver, cut steel, enameled and others.

charmeuse   a formal dress satin new in the early twentieth century. A semilustrous surface with dull back and fine draping quality.

chartreuse   a luminous yellowish-green, the color of the liqueur made by the Carthusian monks in France.

charvet   elegant silks of irregular twill weaves formerly called Régence but better known as Charvet et Fils de Paris.

Used for gentlemen's accessories such as neckwear, mufflers and waistcoats.

chasuble   the outer garment of Roman Catholic, Greek and Anglican priests at Mass. Formerly a long, sleeveless cloak, with an opening for the head. *Planeta* in Latin and *pianeta* in modern Italian.

chatelaine, troussoire   sixteenth and seventeenth centuries and later, a long gold or silver chain or chains fastened around the waist and pinned to the skirt. It carried keys, mirror, scent box, smelling salts, handkerchief and sewing things, including a pincushion.

chatelaine watch   a ladies' watch, often with a hunting case, worn on a long chain and tucked into the waistband. 1890's and 1900's. see *watch, hunting case.*

chatta   from Hindu *chata;* East Indian word for umbrella.

chausettes   French for socks or anklets. Stockings are called *bas.*

chechia   a name for the Berber tashashit or cap with tassel in the same

chechia, red with white scarf and tassel -French Zouave-1830's

chechia or Zouave cap- red cloth with blue tassel- French-1854

category as the fez and tarboosh. A deep-crowned, flat-topped cap of felt, it is the headgear of the Zouaves and Spahis of Africa, with tassels of varied colors for the different regimental companies.

checks   small squares or plaids woven or printed on cloth. see *glen checks; gun club checks; hound's-tooth* and *shepherd's checks*.

cheesecloth   unsized cotton of plain weave, thin, soft, bleached or unbleached. Used for garment interlining, covering of padding and in many other ways.

cheetah   sometimes sold as leopard, which the fur resembles. It is not adaptable to costume use.

chemise   the body garment of medieval times was a chainse which, by the thirteenth century became the sherte or chemise, made of soft wool or linen in a saffron color. A new fabric for the chemise appeared in the thirteenth century, closely woven and sheer, made of fine linen thread. By the nineteenth century the chemise had become a knee-length garment worn next to the body under the corset, the beginning of modern lingerie. Handmade, embroidered, lace-trimmed, it was of soft, white cotton or silk; today, mostly of fine nylon.

chemise, shift, sack, sheath   a recurring classic one-piece silhouette in women's fashions dating from ancient Greece and Rome to the French Consulate and First Empire, 1799–1815. It returned in 1914 and was generally worn by 1925. The chemise hangs straight from the shoulders to the hem, with no tuck at the waist, though it may be loosely fitted or sashed. In 1950 *Vogue* magazine displayed a knitted T-shirt dress, forerunner of a revival in 1954. Paris designers presented their versions, and in 1958 Saint Laurent sponsored the Trapeze or A-line with a slight flare in the side seams. see *cheongsam; shift.*

chemise à la reine   a popular style from 1781, worn by Marie Antoinette. A comparatively simple dress of sheer cotton or light silk but noteworthy as being the introduction of the lingerie frock into Europe. It was nevertheless a luxury, as cottons and prints were imported from India. Late eighteenth and early nineteenth centuries.

chemisette   an underbodice of lawn and lace with short or long sleeves. Worn to supply sleeves and cover the cutaway neck of a jumper frock. A style for women and girls of the late nineteenth and early twentieth centuries. see *guimpe.*

chenille   French for caterpillar. A yarn with protruding fibers like the caterpillar's tufts. It is used for embroideries and fringes and woven into luxurious carpets. Also used for knitted or crocheted accessories.

chenille embroidery   originated in France; the design is worked with fine chenille yarn of various colors in flat stitches producing a velvety texture.

chenille lace   a French needlepoint of the eighteenth century, a six-sided mesh ground net with the design outlined in white chenille.

cheongsam   the modern Chinese sheath, popularly known as the Hong Kong sheath. It is straight, high-collared, short-sleeved, of silk or cotton with a slit on one side of the skirt. The length of the slit prescribed by Chinese stylists is eight to ten inches, and not extending more than four or five inches above the knee.

cherusse or **Betsie**   see *Betsie.*

chesterfield   a classic knee-length overcoat of the late nineteenth and early twentieth centuries, named after the Earl of Chesterfield. A single-chested fly-front coat of black cloth with velvet collar and plain back.

cheongsam or Hong Kong sheath of flowered silk

Chesterfield overcoat-black cloth-velvet collar-fly front-silk top hat-1890's

cheviot a woolen or worsted fabric used for suits and overcoats. Twill-woven from the coarse, shaggy wool of the sheep of the Cheviot Hills on the border between England and Scotland. Also the name of a shirting, a plain or twilled heavy cotton with soft finish.

chevron an inverted V device or motif used on heraldic shields. Also one or more V-shaped bars worn on the sleeve of noncommissioned officers to indicate rank. Chevron, broken twill, herringbone, zigzag fishbone pattern, all similar, of woven cloth. Used for top-coats, suits and sports.

chicken skin used formerly for fans and gloves. The gloves, worn overnight by both men and women as a beauty aid for the hands, proved effective, but in 1778, a perfumer wrote that these gloves were really made of a strong, thin leather dressed with almonds and spermaceti.

chiffon a lightweight transparent fabric, dyed or printed. Of silk, rayon or cotton, and durable despite its flimsiness.

chiffon velvet see *velvet, chiffon.*

chignon hair twisted into a knot at the nape or top of the head, a coif copied down the ages. see *Psyche knot.*

Chignon—the classic coiffure of Venus de Milo

chimere a sleeveless robe of black or red satin worn by Anglican or Episcopal bishops over the rochette.

chimneypot a name applied to the tall top hat when of black felt.

China mink see *mink, China.*

China silk originally a pure silk fabric made in China. Now a plain-woven, lightweight, lustrous fabric of silk or rayon, used for slips and dress linings.

chinchilla a very soft, beautiful fur of delicate bluish-gray with black markings; fragile, costly and scarce. A squirrel-like beautiful fur of delicate bluish-gray with black markings; fragile, costly, and scarce. The fashion craze of the late nineteenth century practically exterminated the chinchilla, a squirrel-like rodent native to the Andes of Peru and Bolivia. Now being bred in the United States and Canada, but still rare. Used by the Incas for mantles and also woven into cloth. The fur is used today for coats, jackets and trimming.

chinchilla cloth a heavy double-woven fabric with a napped surface of tufts and nubs, similar to petersham but softer and finer. Not an imitation of chinchilla fur. Used for children's coats, bonnets and trimming.

chinchilla rabbit or **coney** the result of a French experiment with a black-and-white hare now raised in California. A feathery salt-and-pepper fur, fairly durable and used for jackets. see *rabbit.*

chinchilla rat see *rat.*

chinchilla squirrel processed to simulate chinchilla.

chiné French for the Chinese technique of coloring the warp threads before weaving, thereby producing a silk of variegated or mottled effect. Also, a fabric with a chiné design.

Chinese damask see *damask, Chinese.*

Chinese dress see *balshan; cheongsam; koo; shan.*

chinchilla-length, 9"—tail, 5"

Chinese-blouse-pantaloons and apron

Chinese everyday dress-same for men and women—

Chinese woman's field-dress

Chinese embroidery originally, painted designs worked over in satin stitch with floss and metal threads. Embroidered on silk and velvet for garments, screens, hangings and many other objects.

Chinese sable see *marten, Himalayan.*

chin piece a piece of armor to protect the chin.

chin scarf or **medieval headdress** a stiff linen toque-shaped cap, often without top, the scarf or barbette passing under the cap and under the chin. From the twelfth century on. see *barbette.*

chin strap a leather strap to hold cap, hat or helmet on the head; a strap worn at night to prevent a sagging chin.

chino a twilled cotton fabric of stout texture for uniforms, riding togs, work clothes, sports, etc. In the nineteenth century the British in India dyed their white uniforms with coffee, curry powder, mulberry juice, etc., calling them by the Hindu name khaki or dust-color. The Americans in the Philippines followed suit and named the cloth chino.

chintz originally, in the twelfth century, a printed or stained calico from India. Now, cotton cloth printed with colorful bird motifs and flowers, and usually glazed. Used for both costume and interior decoration.

chipmunk-
length 8" - tail, 3¼"

chipmunk a short-haired, silky fur popular for coat linings; from the North American ground squirrel, smaller than the gray species, reddish-brown and gray with black-and-white striped back and short-haired silky fur.

chipmunk, Siberian burunduki a striped ground squirrel with more stripes than the American rodent, usually four white and five black. A fragile skin used

for lining, trimming and jackets. Also from China.

chirinka a former Russian feminine accessory, a square of silk or muslin embroidered in metallic threads and fringed with tassels. An elaborate kerchief, it was held in the hand when going to church, a party or any ceremony.

chiripa the South American gaucho's skirt worn over very full long pantaloons. It is formed of a large, square, colored woolen blanket with the center cut out for the waist and held up by a heavy silver belt of chains and buckle.

chirapa over
pantaloons-
S.A. gaucho

chiton the basic garment of ancient Greece worn by both sexes with or without belt. There were two distinct styles, the feminine version reaching to the ankles and the masculine to the knees. The rectangular piece of woolen or linen cloth was sewn partway up the sides and fastened on the shoulders by fibulae. Usually purple, red, blue or saffron. Roman and Athenian women wore a full-length chiton which could be girded up short for sports or let down for housewear. The fold above the belt was a rectangle of woolen cloth of variable size worn over the

chiton and himation
ancient Greece

chiton, unsewn and fastened on the shoulders. The bloused section was called the kolpos or deploidion and was carefully arranged in artistic folds and weighted with lead pellets.

chitterlings linen frills which appeared on the gentleman's shirt front in the late eighteenth century and were worn through the nineteenth.

chivarras a colloquialism for leggings in southwestern United States and Mexico.

chlamys in ancient Greece a light summer mantle worn chiefly by young people on horseback. Of woolen cloth, it was a rectangle about one by two yards with weights at the four corners to prevent its blowing. It also served as a protection against rain and as a blanket when sleeping. In ancient Rome the chlamys was a cape of woolen cloth semicircular in shape fastened on the right shoulder or in front by buckle or fibula. It passed into Byzantine dress and was worn for centuries more in Europe as a sports and traveling piece.

choga Nehru tunic, a Mohammedan tailored coat slightly fitted, worn by East Indian men, principally in Kashmir and the Punjab. Presently in the Western mode. Brought out in London, 1967, and followed by the Paris-made suit for women. Usually of black silk crepe, a tunic-length jacket, most often buttoned down center front with a standing collar. Also called guru, Mao, oriental, meditation or mandarin. Of woolen cloth, cotton, heavy linen, velvet or handsome silk, it is knee-length, has side slits, a standing collar and is buttoned down the center front.

choker a woman's high, snug collar in fabric, fur or jeweled form such as one or more rows of pearls. A fashion of the late nineteenth century continuing into the twentieth.

choker collar see *collar, choker.*

chola derby see *derby, chola.*

choga-Moslem
outer coat of white
linen or brocade
for formal wear

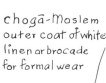

chitterlings-
shirt front
frills-French-
1804

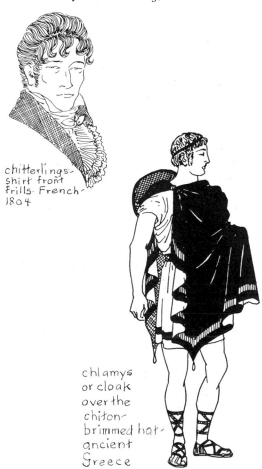

chlamys
or cloak
over the
chiton-
brimmed hat-
ancient
Greece

cholee or choli-
blouse worn
under the sari-
Hindu

chopine of wood-
jeweled strap-
Turkish-
16th C.

chukker or
polo shirt-
fine white
cotton knit-
20th C.

choli, cholee   the short-waisted cotton blouse with V-neck and short sleeves that the Hindu woman wears with the sari. In the north and central part of India a short, full skirt, the ihenga, is usually worn with the choli.

chopines   originally from Turkey, reaching Europe by way of Venice in the sixteenth century. "Chapineys", the European name, were high wooden stilts designed for sand and mud and suited the Venetian ladies, who traveled by gondola. Chopines were popular in Italy and Spain, but seen only occasionally in northern Europe.

chorus shirt   see *ballet* or *chorus shirt*.

chou   French for cabbage; in fashion, a cabbage-shaped soft rosette of tulls, lace, velvet and ribbon used as a feminine dress ornament at the neck or on hats. Late nineteenth century.

chrisom   a veil, robe or mantle signifying innocence, thrown over an infant at a christening ceremony.

chrome leather   see *leather, chrome*.

chromo embroidery   work in which the design to be embroidered is printed on a paper pattern laid on the fabric and worked over in satin stitches.

chrysoberyl   a semiprecious stone; varieties are *chrysolite*, pale yellow to green yellow; *alexandrite*, green in daylight, red in artificial light; *cymophane*, a chrysoberyl cat's-eye.

chrysoprase   a green form of chalcedony quartz, used for jewelry.

chuddar   a form of the Hindu word *cadar*, the name for bright green, the color of billiard cloth; in Anglo-Indian usage, a square of fine wool worn as a shawl. see *chador*.

chukka-
of East Indian
origin for polo
play-20th C.

chukka   a two-eyelet, ankle-high boot of suede or smooth leather with rubber or leather soles. The low jodhpur boot fastens with a strap. The two names are of East Indian origin, chukka being a period of play in polo and jodhpurs the riding breeches with which the boot is worn. see *jodhpurs; riding breeches*.

chukker   a man's pull-over sports shirt, round-necked, short-sleeved, of knitted soft white cotton. see *polo shirt*.

church or **laid embroidery**   work in which the design in silk or metal threads is laid on the fabric and held in place by tiny couching stitches.

cidaris   the tiara of ancient Persian kings and Jewish high priests.

cigar case   a gentleman's pocket case of leather or metal, made to hold cigars.

cigarette case   a small case to hold cigarettes, often of silver or gold and jeweled, carried by fashionable men and women in the first half of the twentieth century. Ladies also carried jeweled cigarette holders of amber or ivory.

cilice   a haircloth shirt formerly worn by monks as a penance.

cimier   an ornament forming the apex or crest atop the helmet worn in ancient times and down the centuries. Its forms have ranged from the floating lambrequin, plumage, horses' tails, carved birds and fantastic animals, most of which were movable when the wearer was in action. see *cointoise*.

circassienne   a fabric of wool and cotton mixture with a diagonal weave.

circassienne gown   a bell-shaped var-

Circassienne gown with three panniers— French—1780

woven or sewn to the toga and tunic, a wide one for a senator and narrow ones for knights. Also, narrow decorated panels used vertically.

claw-hammer coat   evening dress coat in the swallow-tail fashion of two long tapering skirts falling in back. see *tails*.

claw-hammer tails-riding habit— 1811

iation of the polonaise, with three bouffant panniers drawn up on silk cords. Made of two different-colored silks, the underskirt of ankle length.

circingle   see *surcingle*.

circular skirt   see *skirt, circular*.

civet   the popular name for the so-called North American civet cat, really little spotted skunk, a species of skunk but without the disagreeable odor. The under-wool is short, thick and dark, with irregular markings. Used for coats, jackets and trimmings. Also bleached and dyed to simulate fitch and marten.

civetta   a native cat of Africa and used more for its secretion than fur. It is two or three feet long and brownish-gray with black bands and spots on body and tail. It produces most of the commercial civet used as a perfume base.

clavi   purple stripes or badges which told the wearer's rank and profession in ancient Rome. The stripes were either

clay-worsted   serges, diagonals and worsteds woven after the process of Clay, Huddersfield, England, and so named. Fabrics used for men's and women's suits.

clip, clip brooch   a twentieth century decorative jeweled ornament that is fastened by a strong clip to an edge of a garment, such as collar, lapel or neckline.

cloak   following the mantles of the ancient Greeks, Romans and Byzantines, a shorter, bell-shaped outer garment developed as a wrap or coat during the Middle Ages. The name is from cloke or cloche, French for bell, finally becoming cloak in English.

cloak, Armenian   see *Armenian cloak*.

cloak, balagnie   see *balagnie cloak*.

cloak, Inverness   see *Inverness cloak.*

cloak, Kerry   see *Kerry cloak*

cloak, opera   see *opera cloak.*

cloche   a small and tight hat with the narrowest of brims, became popular as the bobbed head of the 1920's evolved into the shingle. Of felt, both for summer and winter, it enveloped the head to the neck in back and came to the eyes in front. Reboux of Paris produced this hat with no decoration but the ornamental shaping of the felt. This was relieved occasionally by a grosgrain ribbon band or a jeweled pin. Frequently revived but popular into the mid-thirties.

clock   a decorative line of colored silk embroidery which eliminated the former ankle-shaping machine work on stockings.

clogs   see *pattens.*

cloisonné   bracelets, necklaces, rings, buttons and bric-a-brac inlaid with enamel. Formerly applied to precious metal but today mostly on brass.

cloister cloth   a drapery fabric in a rough, canvaslike weave similar to monk's cloth.

cloqué or **cloquet**   French for blistered or swelling; thus, silk or other cloth in a blistered effect. The cloth is backed with a very thin lining and then machine- or hand-stitched in an allover pattern to give the blistered surface. An Americanism for the French word is "cloky."

cloth   see specific terms of *cloth; airplane, Albert, American, Astrakan, bodkin, Balmoral, beaver, buffalo, burberry, chamois, chinchilla, coronation, convent, druids, forestry, Granada, grass, hair, honeycomb, moleskin, monk's, Moorish, mummy, Orleans, Palm Beach, parashute, peasant, pilot, pima, polo, Saxony,*

Shetland, Sicilian, suede, tapa, Tibet, tinsel, Venetian, waffle, west of England.

clothes   a general term for pieces of attire worn by men and women.

clothes horse   a stand or frame of wood or iron, upon which to hang garments while the wearer lounged.

cloud   a light, fluffy, three-cornered head scarf of lace, net or loosely knitted silk or yarn, worn in the evening, especially in winter. The seventeenth century spelling was clout. Other names in use to the end of the nineteenth century were opera hood and Molly hood.

clown costume   a masquerade dress in cotton cloth with neck, wrist and ankle ruffs, and a peaked hat with a pompon which evolved from the traditional Pierrot costume of the Italian commedia dell'arte.

club bow tie   a straight-cut bow tie for evening wear, white with tailcoat and black with dinner coat.

Cluny lace   a lace of Cluny, France, of heavy colored linen or cotton thread. Originally a meshed net with a darned design of wheels, triangles, etc. A coarse, bobbin lace.

cnemis, greaves   leggings of bronze, brass or hard leather worn with sandals by the Greek and Roman military man as a protection to the left from knee to ankle. Those of metal were leather-lined.

coal scuttle bonnet   see *bonnet, coal scuttle.*

coal tar colors   mauve was the first obtained, in the manufacture of coal gas, separated into fractions which upon further refining yielded many compounds. These yielded dyes such as aniline, phthaliens, indigo and alizarin for modern manufacture. The process was discovered by Sir W. H. Perkin, English chemist (1838–1907).

cloche of straw with velvet band—1920's

clown's costume n black and white—red pompons—

coat   an outer garment for the upper part of the body, but lengths vary: floor length; full length to the hemline; three-quarter length; above or below the knee, depending on the fashion. see *cote*.

coat, all-purpose   a coat for all kinds of weather and temperatures, made of water-repellent and stain resistant fabrics, often reversible.

coat, barrow   see *barrow coat*.

coat, blanket   see *blanket coat*.

coat, box   see *carrick*.

coat, British lounge   often worn instead of the cutaway or morning coat. Black cheviot with braid-bound or bluff edge and waistcoat to match, heavy silk four-in-hand scarf and gray striped trousers. Worn with a homburg or derby.

coat, camel's hair   see *camel's hair coat*.

coatee   a single-chested coat buttoned to the waist in front but with skirts in back, as in the West Point dress uniform.

coat, car   see *British warm*.

coat, coolie   see *coolie coat*.

coat, English or Prince Albert   see *frockcoat*.

coat, guard's   see *guard's coat*.

coat, polo   see *polo coat*.

coat, raccoon   see *raccoon coat*.

coat, Red River   see *Red River coat*.

coat, sleep   see *sleep coat*.

coat, swallowtail   see *tails*.

coat, tow   see *British warm*.

coat, toggle   see *toggle coat*.

coat, trench   see *veldt coat*.

coat, walking   see *frock coat*.

coat of mail   a hauberk or tunic of metal scales or chain mail worn by the medieval soldier.

coat-tails   the skirts of a man's frock-coat, cutaway or swallowtail coat. see *cutaway coat*.

cobra   any of several very venomous snakes of the genus naja (serpent of the hood). The largest length is five feet, variable in color. Used for women's shoes and handbags.

coburg   a lightweight cloth, originally from Germany, worsted, silk or cotton; often used for mourning apparel.

cockade, French cocarde   a rosette of pleated ribbon, originally a military insignia, of a different color for each nation. Eighteenth and early nineteenth centuries.

cocked hat   see *hat, cocked*.

cockers, cokers, cocours   old English for untanned leather half-boots and gaiters and for knitted woolen leggings without feet, worn by country men. The term was still used in the nineteenth century.

cocktail dress   a fashion which originated in the late 1940's, a semiformal dress for late afternoon and evening.

codpiece   a small bag or box that concealed the front opening of men's breeches. It was of fabric, usually of silk and often elaborately decorated. Codpiece and trunk hose were secured to the doublet by points and lacings. A fashion of the European courts, of Spanish origin. It was popular in the fifteenth and sixteenth centuries. Considered a sign of virility, the container really served to hold

British lounge coat often worn instead of cutaway-contemporary

coatee of the cadet-American

coif - Norman and English - 9th C.

coif - French bob - circa 1468

coif Zazzera - yellow silk wig - Italian - 15th C.

coiffure over wire frame - pearls and jewels - pearl earrings - French - late 16th C.

atiifet coiffure - hair dressed over wire frame - bandeau of gold enamel and jewels - French - 1585

coiffure with love lock - Swedish - 1643

widow's coif - black silk with pearls - heartbreaker curls - French - 1663

coiffure - wired ringlets tied with pearl-weighted bowknots - spotted breast feathers - Spanish - 1650's

coiffure à la moutonne (lamb) chignon in back - Dutch - 1632

coiffure fontange - bonnet à la Fontanges - framework, commode or palisade - 1680's

coiffure "tête de chou" - cabbage head - French - 1680's

coiffure in cadogan style worn by Josephine - 1798

coiffure - hedgehog with falls sides and back - 1780's

coiffure Titus - velvet ribbon filet - French - 1802

coiffure - Byronesque hairdo of the period - English - 1820

coiffure - "waterfall" - tiny ribbon hat - 1860's

money, handkerchief and sometimes, bonbons.

coiffure any style or method of dressing the hair. see *bob, curls;* illustrations, for specific types.

coin dots an all-over pattern of dots usually about five eighths of an inch in diameter.

cointise, quintise the scarf or favor either worn over a lady's headdress or presented to a knight who wore it floating from his jousting helmet in the tournament. The scarf was also called mantling or lambrequin in heraldry. see *cimier; heaume.*

cokers see *cockers.*

colberteen, colbertine a coarse French lace resembling net named for Jean-Baptiste Colbert, one of the ministers of Louis XIV.

cold wave see *permanent wave.*

collar originally and for centuries part of a linen shirt or chemise. It then became an extra fabric piece finishing the neck of the garment, growing to an extravagant addition of yards of sheer lawn and costly lace in falling bands and ruffs. The French Revolution did away with frills and laces, and in the nineteenth century the man's collar became a simple, starched, detached white linen. In the twentieth century it again was joined to the shirt. see *falling band; ruff; gallila.*

collar, Buster Brown the stiffly starched lay-down collar with soft bow popularized by the newspaper serial character, a small boy, in the 1900's.

collar, buttoned-down a style in which the two collar points are held in place by small buttons.

collar, choker the fashionable high collar of the 1890's which lasted into the

coiffure- "spit curl"-American colloquialism 1880's

coiffure with jeweled tiara- evening dress- 1870's

coiffure pompadour with tortoise shell comb- pearl and diamond choker- 1890's

coiffure- pompadour- Marcel wave- French-1901

Page boy bob with rolled-under ends- 1937

coiffure- wind-blown bob-1922

Coiffure- shingle clip- 1923

coiffure- page-boy bob- 1930's

notch collar

bal or convertible

peak lapel

shawl collar

collarette framing
a ruched collar-
Dutch-mid 16th C.

collarette wired-worn
by the Medici women-
Italian-late 16th-early 17th C.

collar-gallila or
whisk-Spanish
1630's

collar or ruff-
velvet-faced felt
hat over lace cap-
Dutch-1610

collar of wired lace-1616-
beaver hat with galloon band-
Princess Powhatan Pocahontas

collar or rabat
tied with strings-
felt hat with band-
Pilgrim-1650's

collar-"plain band"
hair worn with love-
lock over shoulder-
Puritan-1650's

collar and cap
of white linen-
beaver hat-
English Puritan-1650's

collar, white
linen or lawn-
heartbreaker
curls wired-
Dutch-
1660's

first decade of the twentieth century. A woman's collar of tucked or crushed fabric, often boned to the ear tips.

collar, clerical or **Roman**   a stiff standing collar buttoned in back, with attached tabs. see *rabbi*.

collar, coat   for various types, see illustrations.

collar, dog   during the time when the very high dress or shirtwaist collar was in fashion, a tight necklace of several rows of pearls held in line by tiny bars studded with diamonds or other stones, was worn with evening dress.

collar, Dutch   a simple, lay-down collar with round or pointed ends.

collar, Eton   a starched white linen, folded, lay-down, rather wide collar with round corners worn with four-in-hand scarf. The Etonian uniform dates from 1820 when the boys were ordered to wear mourning clothes at the funeral of George III.

collar, fused   a collar in which wilting and shrinking have been eliminated by the use of a specially prepared interlining which is laminated to the outer layers. circa 1920's.

collar, Gladstone   a comfortable standing collar with flaring points worn with a silk scarf in a bowknot. Worn in the 1850's by William Ewart Gladstone, Prime Minister of Great Britain.

collar, mandarin, Nehru or **Johnny** a standing collar about one and one half inches high attached to a close-fitting neckline of coat, jacket, dress or blouse. Nehru was the name given the jaunty collar in 1967. see *Mao suit*.

collar, Medici   shaped like the falling band but pleated and wired, rising from a low décolletage and standing high in back. Originating in Italy, it was worn by the Medici women, including Queen Marie of France, 1573–1642.

collar, moat an upstanding narrow collar, bateau neckline; English, thirteenth century.

collar, mourning of black velvet on a light-colored coat, worn by the refugee aristocrat on his return to France as a sign of mourning for Louis XVI. The Revolutionist wore a red collar on his coat, giving rise to many street quarrels between the Blacks and the Reds.

collar, mousquetaire turned-down collar or whisk of starched linen with points; the style revived in feminine fashion in the eighteenth, nineteenth and twentieth centuries. see *bertha; palatine.*

collar, Napoléon a high-standing, folded-down collar with wide revers and black satin cravat.

collar, Peter Pan a lay-down round collar about two or three inches wide, attached to a round neck, closing in front with rounded ends. Named for the hero of the play "Peter Pan" by Sir James Barrie, 1904.

collar, Piccadilly see *wing collar.*

collar, poet's from the Ossianic or Romantic period; the soft, unstarched collar of a shirt or blouse, preferred to a bulky cravat, especially among writers and artists. It was notably worn by three contemporary English poets; Lord Byron (1788–1824), Percy Bysshe Shelley (1792–1822), and John Keats (1795–1821).

collar, poke a stiff standing collar with slight front opening and points softly bent forward. Early twentieth century.

collar, Robespierre a high-standing coat collar with deep fold and broad pointed revers filled in with a softly falling lawn jabot.

collar, roll a long collar without peak or notch. Also called shawl collar.

collar, Roman see *collar, clerical.*

collar, sailor part of the sailor's uniform; two thicknesses of cloth, broad and square in back, narrowing to a V-pointed neckline in front.

collar, shawl see *roll collar.*

collar, slotted a man's soft shirt collar with slots on the under side to hold tiny plastic stays which keep the collar in shape.

collar, surplice see *surplice collar.*

collar, tuxedo on a woman's coat, a long straight fold forming the collar going around the neck and down the front edges to the ends of jacket or coat.

collar, Van Dyck see *falling band.*

collar, Windsor the early nineteen-thirties, widespread, cutaway collar adopted by the popular Prince of Wales, later the Duke of Windsor. Worn with a tie arrayed in a fairly large and intricately tied knot, called the Windsor knot.

high coat collar worn by Robespierre – French – 1794

high collar – black satin cravat – habit, red with gold embroidery – Napoleon

collar – black velvet – mourning for Louis XVI of France – 1805

collar worn by poets – Byron, Shelley, Keats – 1830's

collar worn by Gladstone – Prime Minister of Britain – mid-19th C.

choker collar of the late 19th and early 20th C's

collar worn with Eton jacket and top hat by boys of Eton College

Collar – narrow and standing – 20th C.

Collars

white linen and white scarf-French 1814

collar attached to shirt-English-1830

starched white linen and black silk-French-1808

collar attached to shirt-long silk tie-English-1830's

collar attached to shirt-plaid silk tie-French-1840's

white linen collar-silk tie-French-1820's

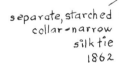
collar attached to shirt-black silk tie-worn by Abraham Lincoln-1862

collar attached to shirt-silk scarf-New York-1868

separate, starched collar-narrow silk tie 1862

separate starched collar-silk cravat-1870's

starched collar-striped muslin-silk cravat-French-1870's

high collar and silk scarf-English-1890's

high starched collar-silk cravat-American-1890's

formal dress-wing collar with bow tie of fine white piqué-English-1890's

wing collar-bow tie-American-1890's

linen collar-round corners-silk cravat-1913

soft buttoned-down collar-attached to shirt-1930's

collar, wing, white wings, Piccadilly a standing collar with pointed turned-back tabs. Worn for formal day or evening dress, beginning in the 1880's.

collarette a high-ruched feminine collar of the sixteenth century worn inside any outer flaring collar.

colletin a piece of plate armor in combination standing collar and shoulder piece which protected neck and shoulders; Middle Ages.

cologne see *eau de cologne.*

color *Hue* is the name of a color or color family whether light or dark, dull or bright, such as the blue-greens; *value* refers to the darkness or lightness of a color, *intensity* to the dullness or brightness. Colors in fashion are constantly changing and different names, generally self-descriptive, appear each season. The relationship of colors can be easily determined by referring to a color wheel.

comb a toothed toilet article for cleaning and dressing the hair which dates back to antiquity. Made of ivory in Egypt and of boxwood by Greeks, Romans and Germans. Bone and horn combs have been found in Swiss lake-dwellings and have come to light in early Christian tombs. Modern machinery has added rubber, celluloid and plastic to the list of usable materials.

combination see *teddy.*

combing an advanced form of carding, separating the choice fibers from the poor, which is called noil. Combing removes all foreign matter from the fiber. Only the best grades of cotton, wool and other important fibers may be combed.

combing jacket see *rayle.*

comboy a skirtlike garment, part of Ceylon national dress, worn by both sexes. The man's is wrapped around the figure and gathered into the belt in front. Above the belt or sash he is naked or wears a short-sleeved bolero jacket. The woman often adds a sari, bringing it over her left shoulder and tucking it into the belt. The length and width of the comboy indicates the wearer's class. Those of the lowest may not wear one below the knee.

commode, palisade from about 1675 into the early eighteenth century, the hair was dressed high off the forehead in clusters of curls arranged over a silk-covered wire frame called a commode or palisade. Occasionally the hair was powdered. see *fontanges.*

compact, vanity case a small case of gold, silver, metal or plastic containing powder and puff, a mirror in the cover, and sometimes a lipstick.

conch a woman's enveloping, full-length cloak worn in most European countries from the sixteenth century on. Of black woolen cloth or crepe, it was boned

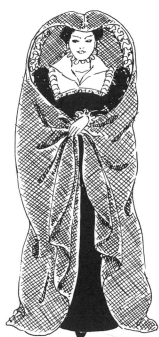
conch or huke mounted on a wooden frame - Flemish - 16th C.

comboy - national Singalese dress wrap-around worn by man - woman and child

Comboy as worn by women, half draped with sari - Ceylon

comboy - worn by small Ceylon boy

conch, sheer black with wired wings-mourning dress-Catherine de Medici 16th C.

coquard bonnet worn by German and Swiss knights-16th C.

or hooped into a conch-shell shape from the waist up, covering head and shoulders. Used especially as a mourning cloak.

coney, cony   an old English word for rabbit dressed to simulate more expensive peltries. see *rabbit* for the many commercial names.

coney, beaver-dyed   an old English name for rabbit, or rabbit processed to simulate beaver.

confetti dots   an allover pattern in small dots and varied colors.

confidents   curls tied with velvet bowknots. Also called heartbreakers. Also the name of a silk hood tied under the chin. French, second half seventeenth century.

Congo brown   a dark brown with an orange cast.

congress shoe   see *gaiter.*

Connolly, Sybil   see *couture, haute.*

contact lens   a tiny dome-shaped glass which adheres to the pupil of the eye, thus eliminating the need for spectacles.

continental   see *androsmane.*

continental heel   see *heel, continental, French.*

convent   a lightweight crêpe-woven cloth used for female religious habits.

conversation bonnet   see *bonnet, conversation.*

coolie coat   see *shan.*

coolie hat   see *hat, coolie.*

coonskin   see *raccoon.*

cope   a cape or cloak worn over the alb by priests and bishops. It is an exact semicircle of silk or brocade and embroidery, sometimes with hood but no sleeves. Open in front and fastened over the chest by a brooch called a morse or by a self-band. Originally an outdoor garment worn alike by laity and churchmen.

coq plumage   the lustrous black and dark green feathers of the male barnyard fowl. Used especially on European military officers' hats and the dress hats of the Italian bersaglieri.

coquard   French for "old cock," a toque or bonnet worn by Swiss and German knights in the sixteenth century. Satin and ostrich plumes attached to a linen coif or cap.

coquille   French for shell, a shell-like edging or ruching used as trimming on neckwear and baby bonnets.

coral   a branchlike formation of compound sea animals, the individual polyps of which arise by budding. Of varying shades of pink, red, oxblood and white, cut and polished and used as jewelry.

cordelière   a heavy, ropelike cotton cord with knotted ends, used as a girdle by Franciscan friars. Fashionable in women's dress in the twentieth century, made of cord and fabrics with knotted or tasseled ends.

cordonnet a fine cord of cotton, linen or silk used to edge or outline lace. Also used for fringe, tassels and embroidery.

cordovan soft, fine-grained colored leather made of goatskin at Cordova, Spain, in the Middle Ages. Now made of split horsehide, goatskin, pigskin and other skins; nonporous, durable, expensive and usually a rich, dark brown. Cordwain and cordwainer are archaic words for cordovan leather and the cordovan shoemaker of medieval times.

corduroy originally *cord du Roi* or cloth of the king; a cotton velvet with narrow or wide wale. In medieval days used for the king's livery or outdoor servants. Today it enjoys wide usage in casual clothes.

corfam a trade name for a chemically-made leather substitute by Du Pont. It is the first man-made shoe upper leather that is soft, supple and porous.

cornercap three- or four-cornered velvet cap worn in Europe with ecclesiastic or academic robes—fourteenth and fifteenth centuries.

cornet or **horned cap** of muslin or lace and of varying style, was much worn in the fourteenth and fifteenth centuries.

The starched nurse's cap of modern times is based upon that medieval headdress as is the chef's cap of stiffly starched linen which has survived to our day.

corno the ducal bonnet of the Venetian doge and dogaresse. Of brocaded satin or velvet ornamented with a band of gold galloon, pearls and jewels. Worn over a white linen coif with cap strings, late fifteenth and sixteenth centuries.

corona Latin for a crown bestowed by ancient Romans as an honor. Also, a fillet or circlet in religious vestments.

coronation braid see *braid*.

coronation cloth created in England and first seen at the coronation of Edward VII (1901–1910). A cloth used in coronation regalia, it is of wool and unfinished suitings in solid colors with gold or silver tinsel stripes about an inch apart.

coronet a lesser crown worn by nobility or persons of rank. Usually refers to the gilded circlets worn around a red velvet cap by British peers and peeresses when robed for state occasions such as coronations or the opening of Parliament. The design varies according to the rank of the wearer. The peeresses' coronets are smaller replicas of the peers' and are worn pinned to the hair, behind the tiara.

corsage a small bouquet of flowers worn on the shoulder or bosom, or carried in the hand. Also, the décolleté bodice of

corno with jeweled knob and gold circlet - Italian - 15th C

corno - crimson satin and pearls - Venetian - 16th C.

coronet of gold and pearls - Byzantine - 6th C.

cornet or Dutch coif, a starched linen cap worn by Dutch Bourgeoisie, 16th to 18th century.

cornet - Dutch - 1620

cornet - wired and embroidered cap - Dutch 1630's

cornet over wire-edged cap - German 1630

cornet of lingerie fabric with wired edge - French bourgeoisie - 1630's

cornet - sheer lawn - wired and embroidered - German - 1630's

corset of boiled leather worn under bodice - French - early 16th C.

corset or laced stomacher - 1644

corseted peasecod-bellied jacket with busk - French 16th C.

corseted "Spanish figure" - false or hanging sleeves - ruff and handkerchief - 16th C.

an evening gown. With the growth of the florist industry and refrigeration, which prolonged the life of cut flowers, the corsage became a dress accessory. Fresh Parma violets were very popular c. 1890–1910. Violets were succeeded by gardenias, orchids and camellias, formerly considered "fast." At a dance, flowers were generally worn at the waistband of a dress, the lapel of a coat, or pinned to a muff. In the 1920's, with dropped, loose waistlines, flowers were pinned on the shoulder. Corsages are occasionally worn on a wristband, or pinned to an evening bag, so as not to be crushed while dancing. see *boutonnière*.

corselet   in ancient Crete, a short jacket open in front, displayed the bare bosom, but was laced tightly together under the breasts in corset fashion. After the decline of Cretan civilization about 1400 B.C., the corset does not appear again until the late European medieval period.

corset   The history of the corset began with man's desire to shape a living torso, male or female, into the prevalent mode. Its forms have varied, rarely comfortable, yet it remains ever in demand. The Cretans of about 1500 B.C. exhibit the first idea of a corset, a wide leather belt or "cinch girdle" and the smallest waist in the history of costume for man and woman. The corset in the fourteenth and fifteenth centuries was a fitted under-bodice of heavy canvas or boiled leather, for both men and women. Wooden stays were used as busks and the garment was tightly laced together. In the sixteenth century, men, women, girls, and even small boys wore the basquine, made of boiled leather and worn over a quilted underbodice. In the Renaissance the corset was reinforced with wire and pierced steel. The tapered form was known as the Spanish body. After 1600, steel and cane were replaced by whalebone; in England the garment was called stays instead of a corset. "Peasecod-bellied" was the description given the long-pointed doublet front with busk and small waist, the Spanish gift to the European mode of the courts. Ladies and courtiers dieted to acquire the Spanish figure.

By the late seventeenth century the feminine corset became slim and deeply pointed in front and laced in back. It rose high under the armpits and over the breasts, a "pair of bodies" of heavy linen or brocade reinforced with whalebone. It had piccadills around the waist to which the underskirt was secured by lacing. During the Directoire period, 1795–1799, the mode was no longer dictated by Versailles but was launched in Paris at summer gardens and public winter balls. Following a trend of ancient Greek and Roman style, a bandeau which held the breasts firm was worn under slip or chemise and the torturous corset was replaced by a muslin corsetwaist fitted to the normal figure and only slightly boned. After the French Revolution, English tailors seized the ascendancy in taste and design, and have held it ever since. In the first half of the nineteenth century, the masculine trend was toward a fitted waist acquired by wearing a corset or basque belt of boned canvas or leather. The nineteenth century meant the tightly fitted, boned and laced bodice of the 1830's and 1840's for women and was the return to the corset of steel stays. Reaching from bosom to hips, shaped to a small waist, it hooked in front and laced in back. The corset of the 1890's was of heavy cotton coutil, boned to produce the fashionable wasp waist. An eighteen-inch waist was the desired measurement of the day, and called the hourglass silhouette. Twentieth century—Paul Poiret was responsible for the demise of the armorlike corset with the creation of his Empire style in 1912. His mannequins wore the brassière, which he designed. A similar garment had been worn as a night garment in earlier periods and as a kind of corsetwaist for young girls. In the 1920's, the body-garment emerged as a natural form-fitting piece. It was built in many styles: an all-in-one, a foundation garment, a girdle long or short, and a panty girdle, all boneless satin or elastic, both fabrics stretchable. Two-way stretch Lastex does not ride up on the body, thus bones were no longer necessary. It was comfortable and improved the figure, and for the first time in the history of costume, the form-shaping piece was worn next to the body. see *body stocking; corselet; foundation garment.*

corset busks   invented in 1829 by Jean-Julian Josselin; the first front busk closure in two pieces fastened by clamps. The corset was laced in back.

corset cover   of the nineteenth century was a low-necked, sleeveless underbodice to cover the corset to the waist. Of linen or fine muslin, it might be embroidered, lace- and ribbon-trimmed.

corset, masculine   see *basque belt.*

cosmetics   In ancient Egypt cosmetics were used by men and women. The eyes were accented with two colors, black and green, the latter powdered malachite. The cheeks were colored with red clay ointment mixed with a touch of saffron. Carmine was applied to the lips, eyelashes were tipped with black pomade and the veins of the bosom accented with blue. Women used white lead to paint the face. Creams, oils and ointments were lavishly indulged in, men employing perfumed oils for shaving. In ancient Greece, breast toiletry was an additional feature. As the tints of the complexion were enhanced by cosmetics, so the whiteness of the bosom was heightened by the use of pastes in hyacinth purple and jasper green, which came from India and was applied with a fine brush. Face-powdering came into fashion in the Renaissance and was the result of hair-powdering with the discovery of the flattering mat texture produced by a dusting of powder on the face. In rouges, there were French red, Chinese red, Spanish red, carmine, and Bavarian red wine, the latter also taken internally. Spanish papers and Spanish wool were impregnated with rouge to rub on the

Cossack officer-
cloth caftan-like
coat-woolen
muffler-cartridge
pockets-leather
belt and boots-
World War I

skin. There were many lotions and toilet waters, but plain water was carefully avoided. Venetian ladies sponged their faces with water but immediately coated them with paint. Venetian gentlemen also painted, powdered and patched.

In the sixteenth century Catherine de Medici brought the art of face-painting to the French Court. Pigments consisted of a base of white lead with vermilion paint for color. By the eighteenth century French face-painting was definitely the mark of the French upper class at court and at all fashionable assemblies. The cheeks were entirely rouged and some English ladies writing from Paris in 1733 said they were compelled to rouge because their natural color was conspicuous by contrast. Other countries did not carry the fashion to such excess, the English in fact disapproved of paint.

Cosmetics in the early days were made of crude and injurious ingredients. The bourgeoise, actresses and ladies of quality all rouged, but the coloring of the lady was a bit more subtle. When a complexion was too rosy, it was toned down with "Spanish white," or wool saturated with white lead and chalk. "Spanish papers," the first compacts, were tiny books of leaves covered with red-and-white pulverized paint. Made in the seventeenth century, they were still available in the twentieth century as a French product.

The use of cosmetics in the United States was frowned upon for centuries as only permissible as theater make-up. It took Hollywood to efface the prejudice, by the 1920's, every woman, rich or poor, could avail herself of the many beauty aids on the market. Too, they can be safely used because the contents of all preparations today are under the watchful eye of the law to insure their being harmless. In this period body paint was a passing fad for beautifying legs exposed to view by the short skirts and the sheerest of stockings. It also appeared in designs of flowers and stars painted on the face, knees and ankles. see *rachel; rice powder; rouge; fingernails; eye makeup; lipstick.*

cote-hardie-
castellated
edges-
chaperon
and liripipe-
Flemish and
German-14thC.

Cossack cap   see *calpac.*

Cossack officer   of World War I wore a dark colored cloth coat, caftanlike with flaring sleeves and skirt. Rows of cartridge pockets on either side of chest, a black satin muffler and leather belt with sword and dirk. Leather boots and astrakhan cap.

costume jewelry   designed in the 1920's for special gowns, furnishing a desired effect and color note. Jewelry with an intrinsic value so slight that silver or gold-plated metal with semi-precious or glass stones suffices. The clip, a jeweled ornament which simply clipped to a garment, was new and considered smarter than the brooch. see *temple jewelry.*

cote, cotte   old English and French for the man's and woman's outer garment. The masculine cote was a tunic varying in length halfway between waist and knee. The feminine cotte was a complete dress fitted at the waist and reaching to the floor. The word has remained in English as coat.

cote-hardie   an Italian medieval fashion worn by both sexes, full-length for women and tunic-length for men. It varied in style from the twelfth to the fourteenth centuries but generally, sleeves were long and the body closefitting.

cothurn, cothurnus, kothornos   see *buskin.*

cotta   a short white linen vestment with square yoke worn in Anglican and Roman Catholic churches from the twelfth to the fourteenth centuries, but generally, sleeves were long and the body close-fitting. Still worn by members of robed church choirs.

cottage bonnet   see *bonnet, cottage.*

cotton   the soft, fibrous substance covering the seeds of the plant; the most important of textile raw materials. Dura-

draped turban
of knitted banding—
Mme Agnès —1920's

ble, with a wide range of uses, particularly in apparel. It is inexpensive and grown around the world in suitable climate. Its substance is pure cellulose. Cotton is first mentioned in the fifth century B.C. when the Greek historian Herodotus, returning from a trip to India, told of trees from whose fleece the natives made cloth. An English explorer visiting India in 1350 described tiny lambs growing on a tree. The conquests of Arabians and the Crusaders carried cotton to Europe. When the Conquistadores arrived in the New World, they found cotton fabric being manufactured in Peru, Mexico and southeast North America. Today the bulk of the world crop is from the United States.

cotton broadcloth   a fine, durable, mercerized fabric put out in white, dyed or printed patterns. Used for men's and women's garments.

cotton crepes   crepe yarn and crepe weave used in wide range of quality, texture, and finish; white, printed and dyed. The surface comes in crinkled, plain, granite or pebble effects.

cotton, Sea Island   a cotton which has a fiber of uncommon length, silky luster, and fineness. Formerly grown on the islands off the coasts of Georgia, Florida, South Carolina and Texas. Because of the prevalence of the boll weevil in these states, it is now grown largely in the West Indies.

couching   an effective raised embroidery done with fancy braids and round cords that outline a design and then are secured to the groundwork by fine stitches over the cord.

countenances   French for the dainty small mirror, pin and needle cushion, small scissors, each one suspended by a ribbon attached to the lady's waist, sixteenth and seventeenth centuries.

Courrèges   see *couture, haute.*

Courrèges boot   see *boot, Courrèges.*

coutil drill or **ticking**   a sturdy cotton of hard-twisted yarns used for corsets and girdles before the days of lastex.

couture   from the French word for sewing; *couturier,* male dressmaker; *couturière,* feminine dressmaker: *Maison de Haute Couture,* a top dressmaking establishment. In American usage, all terms pertain to dressmaking in its highest form and creation, most fashionable and expensive.

couture, haute   some well-known names:

Adolpho   a successful native Cuban designer of millinery has established himself in New York where he is successfully creating all phases of feminine attire.

Agnès, Mme.   well-known Parisian milliner famed for her small, snugglydraped turban of tricot banding. 1920's.

Amies, Edwin Hardy   of Savile Row, London. Born of an old Kentish family in 1909. He is dressmaker to the Queen, a title he shares with Norman Hartnell. As designer of expensive readymade clothes and accessories for men and women, he opened his establishment and boutique in 1950. His has been a tremendous and international success founded upon designs that well-dressed people appreciate.

Balenciaga, Cristobal   Spanish and in the opinion of experts, the world's greatest dressmaker. Maintains couture houses in Paris, Madrid, San Sebastian and Barcelona.

Balmain, Pierre   a successful Parisian designer who first studied architecture at the École des Beaux Arts, opening his own house in Paris, 1945.

Barentzen, Patrick de   couturier of

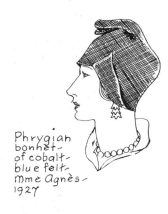

Phrygian
bonnet
of cobalt-
blue felt—
Mme Agnès—
1927

large hat
with black
wings—hat
and dress
avocado green—
black velvet coat—
black astrakhan—
Balenciaga—
1948

three-piece
ensemble-black
wool topcoat over
camel hair coat,
over sleeveless
striped sheath-
Bonnie Cashin-1950

Rome. A newcomer with many new ideas not only in feminine dress but in men's dress as well.

Beene, Geoffery   an up-and-coming American designer from Hainesville, Louisiana, who changed his mind as to his career, dropping his medical studies and taking up instead, dressmaking design.

Beer   a German by birth, he was the first couturier to open an establishment in a house on the Place Vendôme in Paris. He was famed for elegant dresses and beautiful lingerie and his success dated from around the turn of the century.

Bertin, Rose   first of the French couture and dressmaker to Queen Marie Antoinette. She was renowned for her handsome gowns and had an establishment in London for her English clientele. Ambassadors' wives from various parts of the world ordered her creations. She was loyally devoted to the queen.

Blass, Bill   a New York City Seventh Avenue designer and manufacturer who is vice-president of his successful, wholesale, ready-made business. He began his designing career in the 1940's. He served three years with the United States Army during World War II, a stint which took him to Paris. He has since become one of our top American designers.

Bohan, Marc   a gifted, artistic designer who served apprenticeship in the 1940's with Piquet, Molyneux, de Rauch and Jean Patou. He also did free-lance designing in New York City for Originala. In 1958, at the age of thirty-two, he did work for Dior for the English market. Today his title is *Marc Bohan of Christian Dior*.

Brooks, Donald   in 1962, Donald Brooks made his debut at Bendel's in New York by designing clothes for a Broadway musical, "No Strings."

Callot Soeurs   three French sisters whose house, the Maison Callot, was the leader in fashion from 1895 until just after World War I. From Maison Callot came beautiful creations in lace, chiffon, georgette and organdy. During that period, the world of fashion was in their hands.

Cardin, Pierre   made his start in the couture by first spending three years with Dior. In the 1950's he opened boutiques in London and Tokyo. In the 1960's, he added men's clothes to his list. In women's dress he added ornamental cutouts which caused some few of his creations to be labeled "kooky," but many of his designs hit the mark, causing them to be freely copied by his fellow designers.

Carven, Mme. Carmen Mollet   as a young woman studied architecture, becoming a dressmaker just before the war and the Occupation. After the liberation of Paris, Carven again opened her couture house to a successful career. Her perfume, "Ma Griffe," is a great favorite.

Cashin, Bonnie   known widely as "the great American individualist," a title bestowed upon the New York couturière when she was presented with the Coty Fashion Critics Award in 1950. In 1961, she was awarded a Coty Special Award and in 1964, received the New York Sunday Times International Fashion Special Award. She delves into every facet of costume design, at the same time giving her fashions an Oriental and Californian flare, the result of a youth spent in those parts of the world.

Cassini, Oleg Loiewski   Russian, born in Paris 1913. He was raised in Florence. He studied art and law but deciding to be a designer, opened a dress salon in Rome, 1933. He came to New York in 1937, became an American citizen and an international celebrity.

Chanel, Gabrielle   went to Paris as a young girl to be a milliner but became

"Chanel
Look"
revival-
navy blue
wool jersey
blue bow
tie-1954

known for her skillful and remarkable use of jersey fabrics in dresses and suits, and world famous for her perfume "Chanel, Number Five." see *Chanel, Gabrielle.*

Connolly, Sybil of Dublin, Ireland, famed for her beautiful tweeds and knits and hand-loomed linen dresses with handmade laces and embroideries.

Courrèges a Basque, who first opened his small white Paris salon in 1961, creating a sensation with women's short pants-suits, architectural-looking coats and white boots. This he followed with men's fashions.

Creed, Charles an English family of fine tailors who settled in Paris, having been persuaded to make the move by French refugee customers returning home after the French Revolution. The firm still carries on in London and Paris with a reputation over two hundred years old. The house was originally a man's tailor but early in this century, women's tailoring was included.

Daché, Lilly born in Beigles, near Bordeaux, France. She came to New York as a young woman, set up shop and became a most successful and fashionable milliner. To own a "Lilly Daché hat" was the desire of every smartly-dressed woman.

Dessés, Jean born in Egypt in 1904. Though of Greek ancestry, he is typically French. He studied law before he entered the field of fashion, opening his own couture house in 1937. His clientele has included many members of royalty and he has been more or less official couturier to the Greek royal family.

Dior, Christian 1905–1957. A former Parisian picture dealer who turned couturier, meeting with instant success. In 1947, he created a sensational change in women's fashions which became known as the "New Look." see *New Look.*

Doucet of Paris, came to the fore in the late 1870's but his establishment was founded by his grandparents in 1824 and as a lingerie house. Doucet became known for his tailleur or tailor-made suit. He was the first couturier to make fur coats with the fur to the inside as lining.

Erté the famous French artist and designer originally worked with Paul Poiret in Paris in 1912. When Erté came to New York in 1968 at the age of seventy-six, he was fêted by the Metropolitan Museum of Art with an exhibition of his early stage and fashion drawings. He planned to return to designing costumes for the Paris boutique of Paraphernalia.

Fath, Jacques 1912–1954. His successful designing reached its apex in 1948, a remarkable success which was cut short by his untimely death. He was also a painter and especially enjoyed creating for Americans.

Galanos, James of Greek descent with a flare for designing, got his start by selling his sketches on Seventh Avenue, New York, and in Hollywood. He finally settled in Los Angeles in 1951, founding "Galanos Originals." His sumptuous evening gowns are, as he himself says, "elegant and sophisticated," and his prices are high. He commutes to New York several times a year to display his collection.

Galitzine, Princess Irene of Rome, Russian-born. She specializes in lingerie and at-home gowns and it is claimed that her evening clothes are the most beautiful in Paris.

Gernreich, Rudi born in Vienna in a family that fled to the United States in 1938 when he was sixteen years of age. He studied art at the Los Angeles City Art College and became a designer in couture. His first efforts were concentrated upon knitted swimwear, followed by the topless swimsuit, and next, the soft, boneless brassière which really filled a need.

Creed- evening coat- brown velvet with black passementerie- 1939

greatcoat of black wool- velvet cap- Dior-1949

cream-colored faille
with frieze of
appliquéd crimson
velvet-three-cornered
shawl of crimson
velvet-
Lanvin-Castillo-
1955.

"after five" ensemble-
black broadtail
skirt-sleeveless
beige knitted
jumper-tailored
beige jacket-
Mainbocher-
1954

Givenchy, Hubert de born 1927 in Beauvais, France, of an aristocratic family. Studied at the École des Beaux Arts, Paris. At seventeen, he worked with Jacques Fath. Like other couturiers in the 1900's, he is following today's trend in having recently opened a ready-to-wear boutique where his models are to be had at a price quite a bit lower than the creations displayed in the main salon of his house.

Grès, Alix At first widely known as Alix, she became Madame Grès to the admiring world. She always worked as an artist, draping and manipulating fabrics as if she were a sculptor. An original mark of her skill was her manner of cutting into silks and cloths on the bias. Another sign of the artist was her great talent in color combinations.

Griffe, Jacques Born in the village of Carcassonnne in southern France where his mother was a successful milliner. When twenty years old, he went to Paris to work for Vionnet, sending five years there. World War II intervened and he served in the Zouave Regiment until 1942. From then on, he became a most successful couturier. He came to America in 1952, his clientele consisting of royalty and many well-known English and American ladies.

Hartnell, Norman of London. Dressmaker to the Queen and other members of the Royal Family. He had his first success with crinoline *robes de style* made for the Queen Mother. He specializes in elaborately embroidered gowns for State occasions, of which the Queen's coronation dress is the outstanding example.

Khanh, Emmanuelle a young French designer who had modeled for Balenciaga and Givenchy. She made all her own clothes in an effort to create new designs for a "New Era," and displayed her first collection in 1961 when it at once took hold.

Lanvin, Jeanne great-aunt of Bernard, the present ruler of the haute-couture House of Lanvin founded in 1890. Madame Lanvin was famous for her *robes de style* and the beautiful embroideries with which she finished the gowns. Today, the women's division is handled by the well-known Paris designer, Jules-Francois Crahay, and Mrs. Bernard Lanvin. Mr. Lanvin is in charge of a ready-to-wear boutique, which opened in Paris in 1968.

Lelong, Lucien 1889–1958. An internationally-known Paris dress designer and perfume maker. He was the first couturier to launch perfumes as part of couture.

Lucile, Lady Duff Gordon a titled English woman with establishments in London, Paris, New York and Chicago. She was a designer of great talent and famous for her elegant, beautiful gowns, suits and coats. Died 1937.

Mainbocher (Main-Rousseau-Bocher) born in Chicago. In the U.S. Army and demobilized in France 1919. He was a fashion editor to Vogue and in 1930, he opened his own house of couture in Paris. After World War I, he returned to America, and established himself in New York City.

Molyneaux, Captain Edward an Irishman who first worked in London with Lucile (Lady Duff Gordon). He opened his own house in Paris after World War I, designing clothes for stars of the French and English stage and well known society women. He was also a painter.

Norell, Norman who launched his career in 1922, was originally a designer for such stars of the silent screen as Gloria Swanson and Mae Murray. He is considered an elegant designer.

Paquin House of Paquin, founded in Paris, 1892, famed for the elegance of its clothes and for exquisite lingerie. Paquin was the very first couturier to

skirt and cummerbund-
pewter gray linen-
white embroidery-
white bodice-
Sybil Connolly-
Dublin-
Ireland

leg-of-mutton
sleeves-black
astrakhan choker,
muff and pillbox
with ribbon ties-
Jacques Fath-
1953

gown of brown
chiffon-shirred
bodice-brown
velvet ribbon-
Jacques Fath-
1953

Edwardian
princess gown
of black slipper
satin with
boned bodice-
Galanos-
1953

white taffeta with
black polka dots-
flamenco flounce
set low in front-
black faille toque-
de Givenchy-
1954

93

Dior's New Look with full bosom and small waist· 1947

make use of fur as trimming on suits and coats. The mannequins, all chosen by M. Paquin, were considered the most beautiful girls in Paris.

Pertegaz, Manuel   is considered one of the most successful of Spain's designers. He opened his salon in Barcelona in the early 1940's and has been catering to Spanish and many American women since then.

Poiret, Paul   1840–1944. He was a great artist who died poor nevertheless. As a boy, he sold his costume sketches to Paquin, Redfern, Worth and many others. He designed the gowns of many of the great actresses of the day, Réjane, Sarah Bernhardt, Mary Garden and others. His friends were all the great artists of the time. In his wonderful fashions, he created the minaret skirt and the harem skirt.

Pucci, Marchese Emilo   of Florence, known for his slinky gowns of uncrushable silk jersey signed "Emilio,"

his printed leotards and his "Capri pants" of the 1960's.

Pulitzer, Lilly   originator of the American version of the shift under which one wears nothing. A socialite of Palm Beach, Florida, she designed, with the aid of her clever dressmaker, a one-piece cotton housedress which has been popular since the 1950's, known as the "Lilly."

Quant, Mary   the English originator of "Mod Fashions" which appeared in London in the 1960's. Though they shocked the fashion world, they were adopted none-the-less by that same world. As a reward for the volume of business that grew out of the Mini-Skirt, Mary Quant was awarded the Order of the British Empire.

Reboux   Maison Reboux, the Paris milliner who in the early 1920's created a revolution in women's headgear with her chic little cloche. Of chiffon or hand-

Dior's New Look with full bosom and small waist· 1947

gown of pleated mauve-pink chiffon-jersey hem-length scarf of white tied over shoulder and breasts- Grès -1952

greatcoat of broadcloth- beaver or seal collar- leather belt- felt tricorne- Griffe - 1951

evening gown
by Poiret-
chiffon with
fur bands-
metal and
wool embroidery
on cloth-
cord girdle
with tassel-
1910

empire-styled
gown with train-
gray moiré silk-
jet flower corsage-
Molyneux-1948

"dinner
shirtwaist
dress" of two
layers of white
organdie-
black velvet
belt and poppy-
Norman Norell-
1945

chinoise coat-
dress of soft
gray wool with
black braid and
buttons-
Pauline Trigère-
1948

draped
turban in
two colors-
jersey or crepe
de chine-Reboux-
1930

kerchief felt, it was manipulated into a head-hugging hat with no trimming except perhaps a couple of tucks and as many stitches, a grosgrain ribbon band and perhaps a brooch. It suited the times after World War I and all women, and it accompanied all costumes though limited to the colors beige, brown or black.

Redfern   the English house of Redfern, was established in the Rue de Rivoli, Paris in 1881 and later, branches in London and New York City. Designed gowns for Sarah Bernhardt and Mary Garden.

Renta, Oscar de la   a Dominican who lived in Spain for fifteen years, went to Paris and then came to New York in 1965 at the age of thirty-one. He joined the house of Jane Derby as designer and part owner.

Ricci, Nina   founded her Paris house with her son in 1939. She works in fabric rather like a sculptor, finishing with fine handwork. Her models are presented in French cities, European capitals and cities in North Africa, her orders usually outnumbering those of other Paris couturiers.

Rodriguez, Pedro   a Spanish couturier with salons in Madrid, Barcelona and San Sebastian. Rodriguez opened his first house in Barcelona in 1918, the second establishment in 1939 and the Madrid house in 1941.

Saint Laurent, Yves   came to Paris, 1954, from his native Algeria to receive a prize and an apprenticeship to Dior who was one of the judges. In 1957, upon Dior's sudden death, he became chief of Dior's vast empire. The "trapeze silhouette" in 1958 established his reputation and in 1962, he opened his own couture house.

Scaasi, Arnold   a successful designer from Montreal where he studied design, worked in Paris at the House of Paquin, and in New York with Charles James, an American designer with a well-founded reputation. Scaasi went into wholesale designing and now makes beautiful and expensive clothes for his clientele.

Schiaparelli, Elsa   was born in Italy. She settled in France in the early 1920's and designed for Mme. Lanvin. Being very fond of sports clothes, she designed and made sweaters which became the "rage," as did her favorite color of vibrant pink known as "shocking pink."

Schön, Mila   a German who is one of the best known of new designers in dress and furnishings. She opened a shop in Milan and has acquired an important position in style and design, being patronized by all who appreciate her flair for the unusual but wearable.

Scott, Ken   American from Indiana. He specializes in the beautifully printed silks and among designers, holds an enviable position in the art. He settled in Milan, where in 1967, he made his mark with a display of twenty-five Milanese university male students clothed in handsome pajamas. Each man escorted a mannequin in a printed flowered silk dress. His silk scarves are veritable works of art.

Sophie   of Saks Fifth Avenue, New York, outstanding as a designer and American couturière. Her clothes are noted for the beauty of their shapes, fabrics and colors and are flattering to the wearer. She is the wife of Adam Gimbel, president of Saks.

Tiffeau, Jacques   the designing partner of Tiffeau Busch of New York. A French farmer's son, who, having learned tailoring at school in France, turned to provincial tailoring. In 1951, at the age of twenty-three, he came to America where he joined the firm of Monte Sano, a Seventh Avenue house. He also took a course at the Art Students' League to learn to sketch. His designs drew notice especially when in 1964, he raised the skirt hems above the knees. He then went on to creating simple dresses with cardigan jackets which also accompanied pants. His name has become one of the outstanding of New York's couture.

Trigère, Pauline a French couturière who held forth on Seventh Avenue, New York, for a quarter century before she became all-American. She is the creator of beautiful clothes which have earned for her a high reputation, in fact, she is considered one of the best in her art.

Ungaro, Emmanuel a tailor who had worked with Balenciaga and also with Courrèges, went out on his own in Paris in 1961 when he was thirty-eight years old. He is very popular, and in 1967 following the growth of boutique craze, he opened his own ready-to-wear shop in the front of his made-to-order salon.

Valentina an American couturière who, in the early 1940's, created a short dinner dress to be worn when one's escort was attired in business clothes. Called ballerina, it was either dress or short-jacket suit, usually black in brocade or faille silk. see *ballerina*.

Valentino couturier of Rome, a contemporary newcomer with new and original ideas in the use of fabrics and colors.

Vionnet, Madeleine born in Aubervilliers, France. As a young woman, she went first to London, then returned to Paris, working for Doucet for five years. In 1912 she opened her own establishment on the rue de Rivoli and from 1918 to 1939, the Vionnet dress was every woman's desire, including royalty. She became a great success and had a definite influence upon the foremost couturiers of her period.

Weitz, John an American designer born in Berlin, educated in British public school, has been designing fashions since 1948. He claims to build fashionable clothes for functional men. He has been most successful in the United States and his clothes are carried in London and the important cities of western Europe.

Worth, Charles Frederick born in England, 1826. As a small boy he worked in London fabric shops. He left for Paris around 1846 when about twenty years old. He married his talented model and in the 1850's, the Worths opened their couture house on the rue de la Paix, which turned out to be a most successful venture. He was the first dressmaker to open a salon in Paris and to display his new creations on live mannequins. Also, he created the princess-line dress and sheath. He died in 1895.

coverall interchangeable with overalls; protective working garments of sturdy fabric. see *overalls*.

coverchief a head covering fashioned from a kerchief.

covert cloth a diagonal, twill-woven, stout woolen coating, hard- or soft-finished.

coverts short top coats worn by the British when fox-hunting. The cloth, like a gabardine, was water-repellent and tear-proof when going through coverts and thickets. Long coats, suits and raincoats were also made of the cloth which was sold in the United States in the mid-nineteenth century and called Orleans cloth.

cowboy boot see *boot, cowboy*.

cowboy dress see illustrations; *chaps*.

cowboy hat see *hat, Stetson; Ten-Gallon*.

cowhide heavy leather from cowhides are used for boots and soles. Today, however, almost any skin with natural beauty suitable for use can be transformed into a supple, durable leather. Cowhide

cowboy in Spanish-Mexican habit California-20thC.

"cowgirl" in feminine ranch dress-cotton velvet with embroidery American western

can be dressed to resemble pony or stenciled to simulate ocelot, leopard or giraffe. Such leathers, used for sportswear and trimmings, come from Denmark, Latvia, Estonia and northwest Russia.

cowichan sweater a sweater made by Indian women on Vancouver Island who card and spin the wool but never dye it; the dark areas of the designs are knit from the wool of black sheep. Used by Canadians for sportswear, twentieth century.

cowl the hood usually attached to a monk's robe. It has been imitated in feminine fashions, sometimes draped in back but also in front or just draped in a soft fold around the neck. All such forms with or without hood, are called "cowl neck."

coxcomb a narrow strip of notched red cloth which was worn on the caps of licensed jesters. An imitation of the cock's comb.

coyote see *wolf.*

coypu see *nutria.*

crackow see *poulaine.*

crape see *crepe.*

craquelé French for crackled, an effect given to silk, lace or net.

crash from the Latin *crassus,* meaning coarse; a coarse linen or a coarse woolen suiting in homespun effect obtained by weaving thick uneven cotton, linen or rayon yarns. Used for men's sportswear.

cravat a neckcloth or tie. An important fashionable accessory in the early nineteenth century. It could be folded and tied in a number of ways, some requiring considerable skill and patience. The earliest mention of the cravat dates from 1660 when a Croatian regiment visited

Croatian-
origin of
the cravat-
17th C.

cravat-haircut-
hoop earrings of
the Incroyable-
Directoire-1795

Paris, fresh from a victory over the Turks. They wore colorful linen neckerchiefs knotted around their necks, the first neckties, called royal cravattes. The cravat became so important in the early nineteenth century that a little book was published in the 1820's describing thirty-two styles of tying the piece. By 1800 the soft, folded stock of white cambric was the popular form of men's neckwear. Europeans and Americans favored the wearing of two cravats at the same time, a white one twice around the neck and a black silk one tied over it. In the 1830's colors appeared. Collar points began to turn down and by 1850 the stiff white collar with scarf tied in varied knots began to take hold. see *focal; stock.*

cravenette from the tradename for an English rainproofing process on worsted and woolen cloths, a method discovered more than half a century ago. It is still used on covert, gabardine, elastique, tricotine, whipcord and other cloths for rainwear.

crea a linen or cotton fabric much used in Spain and Spanish America for common wear.

crease-resistant term applied to textiles of cotton, linen, or rayon chemically treated to virtually eliminate wrinkling.

Creed, Charles see *couture, haute.*

crenelated see *castellated.*

crepe the generic name for a thin, almost semi-transparent fabric with a crinkly surface produced by twisting in reverse the weft and warp of hard-twisted threads. The weaving of crepe in the Orient dates back to antiquity but was not taken up in the West until after the Crusades. The Italians were the first to make crepe, in the thirteenth century. It was produced at Lyons in France in the sixteenth century, and later in England. Dull black crepe was originally used principally for mourning dress. see *cotton crepes*.

crepe-back satin   see *satin, crepe-back*.

crepe, Canton   see *Canton crepe*.

crepe, cotton   see *cotton crepe*.

crepe de chine   a popular silk fabric of long standing. Plain or printed, it is washable and extensively used for dresses, blouses and lingerie. An imitation widely used is made with cotton warp and silk filling.

crepe georgette   named for the designer, Mme. Georgette de la Plante of Paris. A highly creped, fine, sheer fabric of all silk, silk and cotton, or silk and rayon.

crepe marocain   a silk or wool combination of yarns producing a heavy dress-weight fabric.

crepe meteor   a silk or rayon face texture, lightweight and with the effect of crepe georgette. It is soft, launders and wears well. Often called satin-backed crepe because one side is satin. Used for blouses with the satin back as trim.

crepe plissé   a lightweight cotton crepe with puckered stripes, similar to seersucker. Used for men's and children's undergarments, and for nightwear.

crepe rubber   a crimped-surface natural or synthetic rubber used for soles and heels of semisports shoes.

crepe, woolen   a mourning cloth with a crimped surface. Also, a strong, lightweight worsted material, much used in ecclesiastical attire.

crepida   an ancient Roman sandal similar to the Greek krepis. The *crepida*, which was of various styles, was consid-

ered the shoe for traveler, young man and warrior.

crepine   see *caul*.

crespinette   see *caul*.

crestine   see *caul*.

Cretan dress, ancient   see illustrations.

Crete lace   a lace made on the island of Crete, of colored flax with loose bobbin stitch in geometric figures.

cretonne   gaily printed white cloth of hemp, linen or rayon, a decorator's fabric which gets its name from Creton in Normandy, France. Usually printed in floral patterns. Occasionally used for informal summer clothes, smocks and housecoats.

crew cut   a haircut of the 1940's and '50's favored by young men. The hair was cropped very closely except on top where an inch or less stood up bristly. Though also known as the G.I. or Prussian haircut of World War II, it is really a collegiate style which originated among the varsity crews to differentiate them from other undergraduates and was called the varsity cut. When the top is slightly longer and casually tousled, it becomes a feather crew or Ivy League cut.

crew hat   see *hat, crew*.

crew neck   a flat, round neckline against the throat, from a sweater neckline worn by boat crews.

crewel   a two-ply wool yarn with a slack twist used for fancy work, embroidery, laces and fringes.

crewel or **Jacobean embroidery**   a combination of varied stitches in worsted yarn, silk and cotton. A decoration for bedspreads, draperies, wall hangings and furniture covers presently enjoying a revival in fancy work. Used occasionally as

white loincloth-
red belt-blue roll-
white apron-
Cretan-1300 B.C.

boned and laced corselet-
embroidered apron-
ruffled shirt-
Cretan-1700 B.C.

decorative motifs on women's clothes, particularly on cashmere sweaters. Popular in the seventeenth and eighteenth centuries for furnishings, clothing and accessories.

criades   French for criers, screechers or brawlers; the name given to the early panniers worn by fashionable women in the seventeenth century. Hoops were encased in a petticoat of gummed canvas which "cried" and "squealed" at every move. see *panniers*.

crinoletta   a form of bustle in the late nineteenth century, in cylindrical shape of steel or whalebone, sometimes covered with narrow ruffles.

crinoline, crin   a braid for stiffening petticoats appeared early in the 1840's, made from *crin*, or horsehair, as in French. The crinoline was a petticoat corded and lined with horsehair and finished with a straw braid at the hem. Early in the 1850's, the crinoline was a quilted cotton petticoat reinforced with whalebone and worn with several starched white muslin petticoats with flounces tucked and embroidered. Eventually the many petticoats were replaced by a cagelike frame of flexible steel hoops still called a crinoline. It was invented by an Englishman and was known as Thomson's Crown Crinoline in which the

crinoline fashion-
black velvet and
lace-1842
French

skirt was cone-shaped. An improvement was the Cage Americaine with the upper half in skeleton form and only the lower half fabric-encased to reduce the weight of the garment. Victoria Cage was the trade name of a British hoop of steel patented in the late nineteenth century, giving the wearer the round hip and bustle shape which followed the crinoline. see *hoop*.

crinoline revival   in the twentieth century, the crinoline made its reappearance in full, stiff petticoats worn under the skirts of Dior's "New Look," 1947. see *New Look*.

crochet lace   a handmade lace fashioned of a single thread manipulated by a crochet hook. Sometimes the motifs are worked separately and applied to net or fabric.

crocodile   term wrongly used for alligator leather. Not legitimate in the trade, as crocodile skin has not yet been successfully tanned.

croquis   French for a quick sketch in pencil or ink, especially a fashion drawing.

cross fox   see *fox, cross*.

cross-stitch embroidery   crossed stitches "x" executed on linen or square-meshed canvas, and used chiefly for pictorial sampler work but occasionally in decorative motifs on children's or informal wear. The basic, simplest and most popular of stitches.

crotch   in sewing, the area where the two leg sections of pants, bloomers or drawers from back to front, are joined together.

crown   of Oriental origin, coming to Europe by way of Byzantium, a royal or imperial headdress or cap of sovereignty. A coronet is a lesser crown worn by persons of rank. A tiara, in secular usage

Medieval crowns

Roman
crown
of laurel

cornet head-
dress-gold
tissue and pearls-
Flemish~15th C.

royal crown over a
wimple-precious
metal and stones-
French~14th C.

English-small crown-
pearls on wires
and in coiffure-
late 16th C.

crown of
emperor-
Byzantine
6th C.

Crown of England

Viscount coronet, silver gilt
miniver-16 silver
gilt balls-red
velvet cap

Earl coronet,
with 8 tall rays
each with a ball-
red velvet cap-

coronet, marquess-
red velvet cap-four
gold strawberry
leaves-four silver
balls-jeweled
band-miniver
edge

jeweled gold
crown over
black velvet
chaperon-pleated
white frill with jewels-
French queen-late 14th C.

queen's headdress-
white velvet brim edged
with gold-gold crown
with jewels and pearls-
gauze streamers in
back-pearl earrings-
French-late 16th C.

crown-
Anglo-Saxon-
king-6th C.

two-crowned
papal tiara-
white linen
coif-
13th C.

crown of
queen-hair
in braids-
French-
12th C.

golden crown
over a wimple-
French-13th
C.

jeweled
crown over
chaperon of black
velvet-lace-edged-
French-14th C.

jeweled
crown over
black velvet
escoffion-velvet
frontlet-Scotch princess-
15th C.

crown
worn on top of brocaded
escoffion-pearl-edged
wimple-French queen-15th C.

crown or cidaris-Turkish
sultana-velvet and
silk

barrel
cuff

signifies no rank, but because it is usually jeweled its use is restricted to ladies of wealth and fashion when wearing full evening dress. see *coronet, miter, tiara.*

crow's-foot   a three-pointed embroidered motif placed as a stay at the ends of seams or to reinforce a joining with strength and finish.

crystal   see *rock crystal.*

cuaran or **rullion**   a Scotch brogue of waxed rawhide. Perforations, pinked

edges and thong laces were long a part of the design of the highlander's shoe. A writer of the seventeenth century remarks that "new good shoes are thus cut for the water to flow out when fording streams."

Cuban heel   see *heel, Cuban.*

cucullus   a hood joined to a cloak and having long ends which were wrapped around the neck. Worn in ancient Rome.

cue   see *queue.*

cuff   a turned-up fold on trouser leg or sleeve. *Barrel cuff,* a single cuff fastened by means of a button and buttonhole. *French cuff,* a double cuff of a man's shirt turned up and fastened with cuff links through buttonholes. *Mousquetaire cuffs,* ornamental wide turned-up cuffs worn by the mousquetaires, seventeenth and eighteenth centuries. The traditional open cuff on a man's jacket or coat sleeve was originated by Beau Brummell, (1778–1840), first a slit with linen frills showing and eventually the overlapping slit with buttons. *Single cuff,* a cuff without a turn-back and fastened with a button.

cuff links   a pair of gold, silver or pearl buttons connected by several chain links or a shank or a bar which fastens the turned-up shirt cuff of a man's blouse by means of a couple of buttonholes. Stiffly starched cuffs were fastened with cuff links. Usually gold. Appeared about the 1840's. see *studs.*

cuirass   originally, a piece of body armor of buff leather used in place of the earlier metal body protection. A close-fitting body garment of metal with breast-piece and back-piece reaching from neck to waistline and finished with a short hip-piece. Troopers of the sixteenth and seventeenth centuries wore metal helmet and cuirass. Still worn by some European calvary.

cuir-bouilli   French for boiled, molded leather which was used especially

for armor and corsetry in the medieval period. see *armor, armour.*

culottes   In the sixteenth century when men's haut-de-chausses or waist-high stockings were joined, becoming real breeches, they were called culottes. To-day the word is applied mostly to feminine informal dress, the culottes being long and full enough to look like a skirt. Culottes for women were first a style of divided skirt devised in the 1930's before shorts became generally acceptable for women; designed especially for bicycling in Bermuda, where strict regulations as to dress prevailed. When the wearer is standing, such culottes look like a skirt with inverted pleats at the front and back center seams. Bell bottoms as worn in the 1960's are pantaloons or pajamas and are worn by many fashionable women as lounge or informal evening costume. Such pajamas when of rich fabric appear less formal as evening dress than the décolleté gown, upon certain occasions. They were known in Italy as palazzo or party pants, and were approved wear for discothèque dancing.

cummerbund   from the Persian Hindu word, *kamarband,* a wide, soft sash worn around the waist and originally a carryall for small possessions. In the hot summer of 1893, it was adopted by Europeans and tailored in pleated black silk for wear with black tie instead of the waistcoat for summer dinner dress. Still worn with men's dress clothes and sometimes adapted for women's outfits.

curch, curchef   English and Scotch for a woman's plain cap or kerchief of white cotton or linen, as worn in the American Colonies.

curl papers   see *papillotes.*

curls   Among the ancient Romans the women wore beautiful, elaborately dressed wigs, in which the hair was braided, frizzed, curled and waved by curling irons. The hair was threaded with ribbons and strings of beads, and false hair was added if needed. The Roman lady of the first century wore a toupee of Cypriot curls, a solid mass of ringlets built up on a wire frame, reaching from ear to ear. A yellow wig was the sign of the courtesan. Many kinds of curls were popular in the seventeenth century: lover's curl at the nape of the neck hanging over the shoulder, the English ringlets, kiss curls, heartbreakers, and many others of pretty name. Masculine curls in the seventeenth century included à la comète, a long curl over one shoulder. There was also the cadenette or lovelock, a curl to one side, lower right. Favor, a curl tied with ribbon, center top. Spit curl, a slang expression of the 1890's for a single curl plastered to the forehead. Before the permanent wave era, *wire curlers* covered with leather, soft and thick, about 5 inches long, the wet hair twisted around and left to dry. *Curl papers* or *papillotes,* the wet hair twisted around curl papers, pinned and left to dry. *Curling irons* or *tongs,* a heated pair of tongs with wooden handles used to press the hair into the required shape. Pin curl, in twentieth century hairdressing, is set by winding dampened hair into a flat curl and fastening it with hairpins or clips to dry. Wire or plastic rollers became preferable by

curl papers-natural hair-solitaire tie-1745

cummerbund, embroidered bolero-fustanella-chechia and handkerchief-Anatolia

cummerbund of black silk worn with black tie-1930's

cummerbund-with chalwar-mintan (shirt) dolman jacket-tarboosh with scarf-Armenian

curling the hair in plastic rollers- contemporary

Cypriote curls on a wire frame- from Cyprus-

Cypriote curls on a wire frame- from Cyprus-

cutaway or frock coat- earliest style-1830's

the 1960's, sometimes in combination with pin curls. see *permanent wave.*

custom-made   clothes made and fitted by a custom tailor who makes clothes to order only. In British parlance, bespoke tailoring.

cutaway or frock coat- black coat with black and gray trousers- 1940's

cutaway, morning coat   a man's single-breasted coat with skirts cut away in front and hanging to the bend of the knee in back, a waistline seam, flap pockets; made of black or oxford gray cheviot or unfinished worsted. Worn with striped or checked trousers and matching or contrasting waistcoat. Its use has declined since World War II, both in Europe and in America. see *frock coat.*

cutwork embroidery   a needle-made lace also called reticella. The cut-out designs are edged with purl stitch and joined by embroidery-stitched bars. Such handiwork was the foundation of Italian lace-making in the twelfth century. see *reticella.*

cyclas or tunic- fur-lined and embroidered- worn by knight over armor- medieval

cyclas   a short, capelike cloak or tunic worn by men and women from ancient Greek and Roman times to thirteenth-century England; made of a rich silk cloth called cyclas because it was manufactured in the Cyclades. Greeks, Romans, Franks and Goths wore the garment. At the coronation of the English Henry III in the thirteenth century, the guest "citizens of London wore the cyclas over vestments of silk." In the same period, knights wore the cyclas over their armor as a surcoat.

cyprus   a black crepe veiling made in Cyprus. Used as hatbands for mourning in the sixteenth and seventeenth centuries.

Czechoslovakian embroidery   usually on linen, most often white or natural and worked with cotton, wool or silk threads in geometric folklore designs of brilliant coloring.

D

Dacca   an untwisted skein silk used in embroidery, from Dacca, India.

Dacca muslin   a very fine, sheer, cotton cloth.

Daché, Lilly   see *couture, haute.*

dacron   a trade name for polyester filaments and staple fibers, used in all types of apparel. Soft and wool-like, it shapes well in suits, shirts, ties, sweaters, socks, slacks and dresses.

dagged, petal-scalloped   fantastic, ornamental edgings of garments from the fourteenth to the seventeenth centuries, a rage that existed in England and on the Continent. It was carried to such excess that sumptuary laws were passed to forbid it. see *castellated.*

Dalmatian sleeve   see *angel sleeve.*

dalmatic   a simple robe, long and straight with long flaring sleeves, robe or gown originally from Dalmatia. It influenced Roman costume, then Byzantine, royal and clerical dress, and over the centuries was worn for European state ceremonies. In modern times it is one of the robes worn by the English sovereign at the Coronation. The Armenian bride of today wears the traditional bridal dalmatic of beautiful fabric, and the dalmatian sleeve survives in modern Western mode. Eventually the robe was shortened and elaborated with embroidery and lace, becoming part of liturgical apparel. see *sakkos.*

damascene lace   an imitation of Honiton without needlework filling, the sprigs and braces joined by corded bars.

damask   a rich fabric, known in England in the thirteenth century and in use ever since. Woven of silk or linen and made originally in Damascus. The flat-woven pattern combines satiny and flat surfaces for light and shade effects. Sword blades and other articles of steel were "damascened" to resemble the cloth.

damask, Chinese   a reversible figured fabric of linen, silk, wool or rayon. One side of satin on a twill-woven ground and the other a twill-woven motif on a satin ground.

damask, satin   see *satin damask.*

dandy   one who gives undue attention to dress and personal grooming; a fop, a beau.

dandyess, dandizette   female dandy of the English Regency period, 1811–1820.

Danish embroidery   see *hedebo embroidery.*

darned lace   any square-meshed lace on net, the pattern filled in by needlework.

darnick   see *dornick.*

dart   a pointed tuck taken up in cloth to shape a garment to the body or to cause the garment to hang better.

debutante slouch   see *boyish form.*

décolletage   a low neckline front and back, as in formal evening dress.

décolleté   adjective meaning with the

dagged edges on houppelande and chaperon— 15th C.

dalmatic and tiara worn by Serbian monk

neckline cut low, front and back, usually with bare shoulders.

deerstalker cap   see *cap, deerstalker.*

degrained leather   see *leather, degrained.*

de Joinville   a popular scarf of the nineteenth century, a variation of the Ascot puff of the 1870's. Named for Prince de Joinville, soldier and author.

delaine   a sheer woolen and cotton dress fabric, no longer in use.

Delaine Merino   an American variety of Merino sheep.

Delft blue, delf blue   a grayish, purplish blue, the predominating color on pottery made in Delft, Holland.

Delhi embroidery   East Indian stitchery worked on satin and various fabrics in chain and satin stitches with metal and silk threads.

Della Robbia colors   colors used by the Florentine sculptor and potter, Luca Della Robbia, of the fifteenth century; noted for his plaques which were covered with a soft glaze in grayed hues. The figures were usually white, in relief against a lovely blue background and often framed with a wreath of fruits in natural colors.

demi-bosom   a short bosom for semiformal or formal day wear. The bosom may be stiff or pleated.

demi-toilet   subdued evening dress.

denier   denotes the size of a fiber filament as applied to silk, rayon, acetate and synthetic fibers; based on a French measurement of a standard strand, the higher the number, the heavier the yarn. Denier in stockings refers to the thickness of the nylon yarn, the lower the denier number, the sheerer the stocking.

denim   a firm, washable fabric of twill weave in colored warp threads and white weft which creates a powdery tinge. Formerly used only for overalls, and blue jeans, but today used also for dresses and suits. Its name is a contraction of "de Nîmes" a city in France.

Denmark satin   a strong, coarse worsted fabric woven with a twill surface, formerly used for shoe uppers.

dentelle   French for lace.

dentelle au fuseau   bobbin lace.

dentelle de fille   thread lace.

dentelle de la vierge   a wide type of Dieppe point lace.

derby hat   the American term for bowler. A derby hat of lighter weight and softer felt was introduced in 1959. see *bowler.*

derby, Chola   a hat worn by Chola Indian women of La Paz, Bolivia, who must have seen, noted and acquired a man's derby in the first decade of the twentieth century. The Indians, who had always worn hard white felt hats of their own manufacture, have since worn the factory-made model in black, brown, or beige.

dernier cri   French, meaning the very latest fashion.

deshabillé, dishabille   French for negligée or undress.

Dessés, Jean   see *couture, haute.*

Devonshire brown   a rich brown supposedly the color of the soil in Devonshire, England.

dhoti   the loincloth of white cotton which the Hindu man wraps around his loins. The ends are passed to the back between the thighs and tucked in at the

Chola derby—
the hard, black
felt bowler
worn by Chola
Indian women—
La Paz, Bolivia

dhoti—
the draped
white cotton
loincloth
of the Hindu
man

waist. The dhoti is especially favored by both men and women because it is cool and comfortable in the hot climate.

diadem   A crown, emblem of regal power and sovereignty.

diagonal weave   see *twill weave.*

diamanté   French for "ornamented with diamonds"; such items as buttons, buckles and fabrics used for formal evening wear.

diamond   a precious stone; before the Middle Ages the diamond was regarded as a monarch's jewel and was mounted in scepters, crowns and other royal pieces but seldom as an individual ornament. The idea of wearing the diamond as a personal trinket was fostered by Agnès Sorel, the mistress of Charles VII of France (1403–1461). It is the hardest substance known (pure carbon) and when not cut into gems it is used as an abrasive. Usually colorless or nearly so, some specimens being of pale colors, yellow to brown, rarely blue, green, red. When cut for jewelry a remarkable brilliance comes to life. India was the chief source of diamonds for centuries, then Brazil and, presently, South Africa. see *gem cuts.*

diaper   soft, absorbent cloth used as infants' breechcloths, now generally replaced by disposable garments.

diapered fabrics   cloth embroidered all over with small conventional and geometric designs in lozenges, crescents, stars and flowers, the unit of design being repeated and connected in a diamond framework and varied in color. Originally made of costly silk in Damascus and Baghdad, the fabric has been made in cotton and linen, especially white, since the Renaissance.

diaphragm   that section of the body from the waist to the chest, more often termed the rib-cage in modern fashion writing.

dickey, dicky   an English innovation about 1809; a stiff, standing collar, followed by a separate shirt front in the 1830's. It was tucked, pleated and embroidered and of finer linen than the body garment of which it was part. see *fill-in.*

Dieppe point lace   of the seventeenth and eighteenth centuries, made at Dieppe, France; a bobbin lace of the Valenciennes type.

dimity   a sheer fabric for summer use, generally made of combed cotton. The raised, corded or checked surfaces are obtained by weaving several threads together. It was made first in Damietta, Egypt; used from the eighteenth century to the present.

dinner jacket   The dinner coat first appeared in England in the 1880's and was called the "cowes" or dress sack coat. It was described as a dress coat without tails and was used for dinners and dances in country homes. In the United States the jacket was named the "Tuxedo," because it was first worn at Tuxedo Park. In France, it is known as "the smoking," its design having originated in the smoking or lounge suits of the 1840's. It became more popular in America than in Europe, American men liking its informality. see *black tie; tuxedo.*

dinner or **theater suit**   the feminine "covered-up" look for evening of the 1930's and '40's, consisting generally of a long black skirt, a delicate blouse, a cummerbund and short jacket, emulating the informal evening dress of a lady's escort.

Dior, Christian   see *New Look; couture, haute.*

diploidion   the extra upper length of a very long chiton folded and left to hang over a tight belt. The peplos was a separate square of fabric fastened on the shoulders and left to hang. see *peplos.*

Directoire fashion-
lingerie gown-
cashmere scarf-
velvet bonnet-
1798

Directoire   1795–1799, the period in French fashion when the designers of women's dress went back to the classic robes of ancient Greece and Rome for inspiration.

Directoire   a cotton, semitransparent chemise gown which was worn over a taffeta slip. This fashion of wearing thin cottons in winter was believed to be the cause of an epidemic (probably of influenza) in Paris, 1803, which was called muslin disease.

dirndl skirt   of Tyrolese origin; a full skirt gathered at the waist, in peasant style and coloring, worn with a shirtwaist. In fashion in the U.S.A. for several decades, 1940's, 1950's, and early 1960's. see *Tyrolean dress.*

Dirndl skirt-
American mother
and daughter
fashion-1950's

ditty bag   a sailor's small box or bag in which he carries threads, needles, tapes, and other small necessaries.

djellaba, litham   a native Moroccan caftan-like robe open at the neck, of woolen cloth with long, loose sleeves and below knee-length or longer. An age-old hooded cloak of North Africa and the Near East worn by men and women.

djellaba worn under the
caftan-all sky blue- face veil
or mandeel of embroidered white
lawn-Moroccan-contemporary

Women add a scarf, the litham, a sheer embroidered square folded diagonally to cover nose, mouth and neck. Men also use the litham when the sand is blowing, but it is a plain scarf or face cloth. see *gallibaya; haik; jelab; jellaba; litham; mandeel; yasmak.*

djubbeh   see *jubbah.*

dobby, dobbie   a small loom resembling a jacquard. The fabric is also called dobby, and includes simple woven motifs such as geometric and floral designs. The textiles, cottons, rayons and silk include shirtings, huck towels, diaper cloth and dress goods. The name of the loom comes from dobby, the boy who sat atop the loom drawing up the warp threads to form the design.

doeskin   the buffed inner side of sheep, lamb or doe which is used for gloves and leather goods. Also a high-grade woolen suiting and trouser cloth, finely twilled, closely woven and in many finishes.

doeskin   a fine quality satin weave woolen cloth with a dress finish; used for waistcoat, riding habit, broadcloth coating and trousers in men's and women's costume.

dog collar   jeweled, see *collar, dog.*

dog fur   from a species of Siberian dog similar to the Eskimo dog. Foxlike fur of poor quality, much used in the nineteenth century for caps, coats, lining and muffs.

dogaline   an important, aristocratic fashion of the fourteenth century worn in Italy by both men and women. A robe of brocade or velvet, with the knee-length, flaring outer sleeves, which were often fur-lined and fur-bordered.

dogskin   a fur also called Chinese dog imported from Manchuria and Mongolia. Its use as fur is recent. Good peltries have

dolama, dolman a luxurious outer cloak of Oriental Turkish costume; a long, full robe of velvet, brocaded silk or wool with long, full sleeves slit to the elbow. The Hungarians shortened the cloak and called it a dolman. It became the short jacket of the Hussar uniform in the eighteenth century, covered across the front with braid Brandenburgs and buttons as fastenings. Also a capelike cloak restricting the arms, in the late nineteenth century.

dolama of blue velvet over a silk djubbeh-turban with fringe-Turkish

dogaline costume with long fur-lined sleeves-Italian-14th C.

dogaline costume with long fur-lined sleeves-Italian-14th C.

dolman or dolama-worn over striped caftan or djubbeh-silk sash or abnet-bonnet-Anatolian professor

dolman jacket of the hussar's uniform-usually worn slung over one shoulder-a feature was Brandenburgs and buttons-white wig with pigtail-18th C.

dolman wrap-fur-trimmed-1912

dolman-sleeved robe-black sheepskin bonnet-Russian farmer

good fur fiber and long guard hair which is bleached, dyed and left natural length. Used for trimming on popular-priced garments and for men's utility coats.

dogskin leather imported from Mongolia and China. It is soft and durable, resembling goatskin.

domino and
half mask-
18th C.

doll hat   see *hat, doll.*

dolls, fashion   see *fashion babies.*

Dom Pedro   a heavy leather brogue with one-buckle closure introduced as a work shoe by Dom Pedro, Emperor of Brazil, 1822–1834.

domet   see *outing flannel.*

domino   the hooded woolen cloak formerly worn by the clergy in winter. The wearing of the domino with a half mask originated in the eighteenth century in Venice, where it was worn to carnivals and masked balls. For such purposes, the robe was voluminous and usually of silk.

Donegal tweed   originally made by Donegal Irish peasants on hand looms, a hand-scoured, homespun tweed. Also loosely woven tweeds of Yorkshire yarns dyed and finished in Donegal. Today they are mostly machine made with the slubs woven in. For suits, topcoats and sportswear.

Dongola kid   see *kid, Dongola.*

dopatta   a scarf worn as a shawl or veil by Hindu and Mohammedan men and women in India. Of muslin or silk woven with gold and silver threads. see *uparnā.*

dorea, doria   an East Indian muslin with stripes of varied widths and colors. Probably used for the doric, see *doric.*

doric   of Oriental origin, a rectangle of sheer or fine Indian cotton, later of silk, caught together over the arms by fibulae or buttons, forming sleeves when buttoned.

dorina   the enveloping cloak of the Bosnian woman in public, covering her from head to foot and secured by a string-tied belt around the waist. It is a length of checked cloth in light color accom-

dorina-the coverall
of a Bosnian woman
in public-thin
checked cloth and
black gauze yashmak-

panied by the sheer black yashmak curtaining the face. see *feredeza.*

doris   see *dorea.*

dormeuse   French for "sleeper"; an English sleeping bonnet of the 1770's, the cap was of sheer lawn, fine shirred lace and satin ribbon with frills, which hugged the cheeks.

dormouse   a squirrel-like rodent native to Europe, some species in Asia and Africa; very fine soft fur, tawny red above, paler underneath and a white patch at the throat. Used for trimming.

d'Orsay, Count Guillaume Gabriel   French society leader and dandy, Paris and London. Also a painter and sculptor, 1801–1852.

d'Orsay pump   see *pump, d'Orsay.*

d'Orsay roll   see *hat, top.*

dot patterns   see *confetti dots; coin dots; polka dots.*

dotted Swiss, Swiss muslin   a crisp, sheer cotton fabric ornamented with small dots of matching or contrasting color which are either clipped or swivel. The

dopatta-silk or
cotton scarf with
gold and silver thread
worn by Mohammedan
and Hindu men and
women-

original cloth is still made in Switzerland and exported.

double-breasted coat or **jacket** overlapping fronts and a double row of buttons, one for closing or fastening.

doublet   see *gambeson; jerkin.*

doublet, peasecod-bellied   see *peasecod-bellied doublet.*

Doucet   see *couture, haute.*

doupioni silk   silk fibers joined at intervals making rough yarns such as those used in good quality shantung and pongee. The filament is the result of two silkworms having spun two or more cocoons together.

dowlas   originally from Daoulas in Brittany. A coarse linen cloth for working blouses made in Scotland and England in the seventeenth and eighteenth centuries. Now replaced by a stout calico.

drabbet   a coarse, drab-colored linen made in England and used for men's working smocks.

draper, draper's shop   in the eighteenth and nineteenth centuries, a skilled tailor or dressmaker kept a shop where fabrics and trimmings could be purchased. He also made garments to order.

drawers   an undergarment for the body and legs. They were worn by the Franks and Saxons from the ninth century, but in a contemporary Latin description of Charlemagne's dress, the garment is noted as "feminalia." In the sixteenth century, drawers and breeches were often confused, although drawers, being of fine linen and white, must have signified a body garment. In the seventeenth century, English gentlemen's "longe linnen" drawers are noted to wear under breeches. A type of drawers new in the seventeenth century was especially designed for Italian and French ladies who

rode horseback. And Samuel Pepys in the seventeenth century, mentions lying in his cool "holland" drawers in hot weather. Until 1800 in feminine dress, only two or three known references to this piece of apparel exist, until the transparent Empire sheath gown made some leg covering necessary. From about 1805, French and English fashion journals occasionally referred to the new item. It was the first appearance of the garment in women's dress, and it remained uncommon in German countries and England. It was worn by little girls in the 1820's but was not adopted by women until the 1830's.

drawn-work   a type of embroidery in which some threads are drawn out of the fabric and the remaining edges embroidered to complete the design.

drawstring   a manner of securing loose fabric around neck, wrist, waist or ankle by drawing a tape or cord through a slot sewn at the edge of the garment.

Dresden à la Pompadour   a fabric on which a dainty flower design is printed on the warp before weaving.

Dresden point lace   eighteenth century, made in Dresden, Saxony; of fine linen made with a square mesh formed by drawing some threads and embroidering those left. The design was usually of small flowers on a net ground in a coarser imitation of Brussels bobbin lace.

dress form   a life-size woman's torso or trunk, of papier mâché or wire, often adjustable, for the fitting and draping of garments.

dress improver   a device of two small hoops to round out a woman's hips, which developed into the bustle of the eighteen-eighties and 'nineties.

dress patterns   see *paper patterns.*

dress shield   a crescent-shaped piece of rubberized silk or cotton, worn under the arms to protect clothing from perspiration.

dressing gown   see *negligée* or *sacque*.

dressmaker   formerly a woman skilled in cutting, fitting and dressmaking who went to her customer's home several times a year to make up clothes required for the coming season. Today, the customer buys ready-made, couturier-made, or makes her own.

dressmaker suit   a more feminine version of the tailored suit of jacket, blouse and skirt. Made of softer, dressier fabrics, it permitted a wider choice of colors, some trimming, and special dressmaker details in sewing and finish.

drill, drilling   a stout, twilled cotton or linen used for men's shirts, middy blouses, linings, summer trousers and uniforms.

drip-dry   literal description of a fabric. One can wash out a garment made of drip-dry fabric, and when dry, it may be worn with little or no pressing, the garment having returned to its original form.

drugget   a heavy woolen cloth formerly used for coats, usually gray or brown. Also a coarse cloth used to protect carpet and furniture. A rug of cotton and wool also called India carpet.

druid's cloth   similar to monk's cloth; a canvaslike fabric in a rough basket weave.

du Barry   costume of the period of Louis XV, 1715 to 1774, known as Rococo Period, elaborate ornamentation in dress and furnishings—panniers, shell motifs, flowers, feathers, and ribbon bowknots. Du Barry, the favorite of Louis XV, retired from the court upon his death in 1774.

du Barry fashion—
taffeta with
ruchings and
bowknots—
powdered
hair—1762

ducal bonnet or
cap—mortar shaped—
red felt—Italian—
15 th C.

ducal bonnet   see *corno*.

ducape   a heavy corded silk of plain color, durable and popular; mentioned in inventories of the second half of the seventeenth century, and popular in the eighteenth. Used for hoods, cloaks and dresses in the American Colonies.

duchesse lace   similar to Honiton but of fine thread and daintier. A bobbin-made lace having the effect of very fine tape with flowers and floral sprays made separately and joined by brides. A favorite for bridal gowns.

duchesse satin   see *satin, duchesse*.

duck   a fabric rather like canvas or tightly woven cotton or linen, with plain and rib weaves. Of various weights and possessing great washability, it is used for work clothes and sportswear.

duckbill cap   see *cap, duckbill*.

dude   a colloquialism in the United States of unknown origin; a name given the fastidious dresser, dandy or fop, or any Easterner by the Westerner.

duffel, duffer   see *British warm*.

dulband   see *turban*.

dummy   a common term for a model or dress form.

duffer or British Warm-water-proofed cloth-concealed hood- 1950's

dungarees   workman's overalls; formerly made of an East Indian cloth dungaree but now made of denim.

dundrearies, Dundreary whiskers   see *beards*.

dupioni silk   see *doupioni silk*.

Durable Press   trademark for a chemical treatment of fabric by baking the garment in ovens, thus making the creases permanent and eliminating the need for ironing. Sportswear, blouses and dresses, men's and children's wear are frequently durable pressed.

duster   a long cover-all light coat of linen or tussore silk that men and women wore as a very necessary protection against dust, when traveling in the open motor car around the turn of the century. Today, a woman's dress-length housecoat, also an unlined summer coat. see *automobile togs*.

dust ruffle   see *balayeuse*.

Dutch collar   see *collar, Dutch*.

Dutchman's breeches   full breeches gathered to a band above the ankles. Worn with traditional costume.

duvetyn, duvetyne, duvetine   a smooth fabric resembling velvet, used for women's wear and millinery.

Dynel   trademark for synthetic staple fiber of natural gas and salt. Soft and wool-like with good draping quality. Used for knitwear, underwear and sportswear.

Dutch frock with embroidery- short-frilled apron- cornet of lawn and lace

Dutchman's breeches- wooden sabots- bearskin cap

E

earmuffs a pair of adjustable ear pads of velvet or plush attached to a metal headband used for winter protection. Worn formerly only by men and boys, especially for skiing, but now adopted by hatless young women as well. Twentieth century.

earrings favored ornaments from time immemorial. Pendant earrings were usually a symbol of rank in ancient Babylonia, Assyria and Egypt. Men and women wore rings in pierced ears, nose and lips. The European courtiers of the mid-seventeenth century delighted in the fashion of a single pearl hanging from one ear. Earrings virtually disappeared in the late nineteenth century, to be revived in the early twentieth by the appearance of a screw or clip device which permitted wearing the trinkets without piercing the ear lobes. The fashion for pierced ears was revived by young girls in the 1950's. see *chandelier earrings.*

Easter bonnet see *bonnet, Easter.*

eau de Cologne at the beginning of the eighteenth century, an Italian perfumer living in Cologne, Germany, concocted a toilet water, which became famous and is in use today as "eau de cologne." It was prepared from vegetable extracts, oils and rectified spirits but the inventor kept the formula a trade secret. see *perfume.*

échelle French for ladder; a separate front bodice panel, a form of stomacher in the seventeenth and eighteenth centuries. It was reinforced with busk and whalebone and decorated with ribbon bowknots graduated in size from bosom to waist. A variation was the cross-lacing of narrow ribbons.

Edwardian the period of Edward VII, King of England (1901–1910), which coincides with the American Gibson girl fashions. The English period recalls the hourglass silhouette for women and the long, narrow fitted suits for men.

eggplant color a rich dark muted purple.

eggshell color a creamy white or beige-white in fabrics and leather.

egret the pure white plumage of various herons which was used as the egrets of commerce. see *aigrettes; Audubon plumage law.*

Egyptian costume, ancient see illustrations, pages 115 and 116.

Egyptian lace a handmade knotted lace beaded between the meshes and used for trimming.

eider yarn a soft knitting yarn made from fine wool.

eiderdown named after the down of an eider duck. A knitted or woven cloth with napped surface and fluffy feel to both sides. Used for negligées, bathrobes and infants' wear.

Eighteenth Century costume see pages 117–127.

"échelle" French for ladder of bowknots on stomacher with busk 1685

Egyptian schenti or loincloth - beaded collarette - schenti

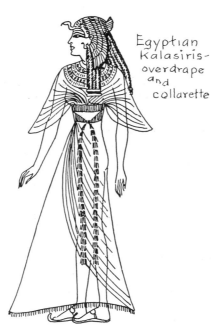

Egyptian Kalasiris - overdrape and collarette

Egyptian embroidered kalasiris with shoulder straps

Egyptian king - striped linen headdress and beard or gold postiche

bulgha - traditional Moslem slipper - yellow or red morocco

Egyptian queen - wig - gold circlet with jewels - 3rd C. - BC

Egyptian kalasiris over tunic - belt with jeweled apron

Egyptian libas - traditional pantaloons - bolero, waistcoat and fez

Egyptian

1200 B.C.
king in schenti-
kalasiris-
royal apron
and cape

king
in schenti
and
kalasiris
1420 B.C.

woman worker
wearing
the schenti
1900 B.C.

king in
pleated
schenti-
jeweled belt-
1970 B.C.

an official
in schenti
and kalasiris
1500 B.C.

a servant
wearing
the schenti-
1420 B.C.

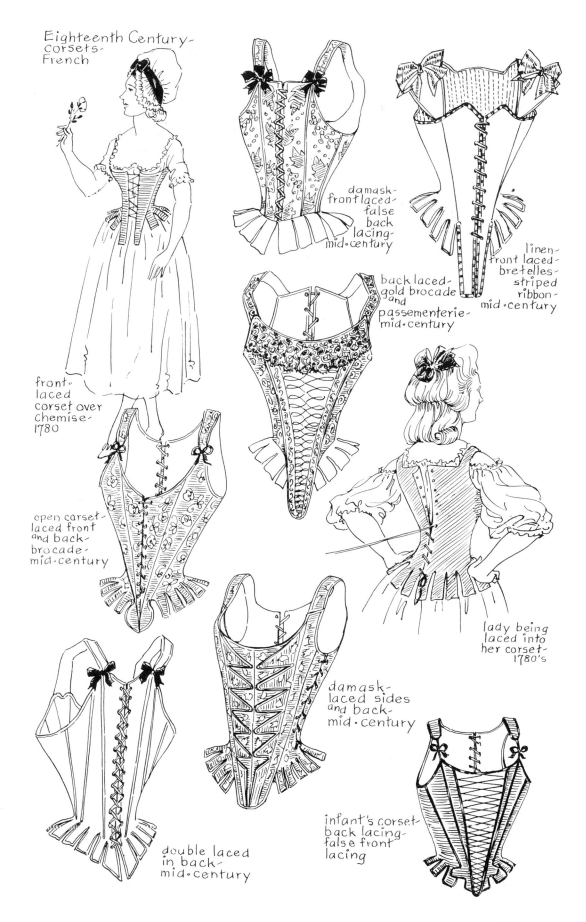

Eighteenth Century·
corsets·
French

damask·
front·laced·
false
back
lacing·
mid·century

back·laced·
gold brocade
and
passementerie·
mid·century

linen·
front·laced·
bretelles·
striped
ribbon·
mid·century

front·
laced
corset over
chemise·
1780

open corset·
laced front
and back·
brocade·
mid·century

lady being
laced into
her corset·
1780's

damask·
laced sides
and back·
mid·century

double laced
in back·
mid·century

infant's corset·
back lacing·
false front
lacing

117

Eighteenth Century -
chemise -
underpetticoat -
corset

chemise and
petticoat -
linen, lace
and bowknots -
2nd decade -
French

linen chemise
and cap -
French -
mid-century

boned chemise
with stomacher
of bowknots -
French - 1767

chemise and
corset laced
in back -
French -
1771

front-laced
corset over
chemise -
French -
1780

actress wearing
tights under
chemise -
English -
1798

cap and
chemise of the
Directoire
Period -
1798

118

Eighteenth Century-
bustle silhouette

skirt massed
high in back-
mid-century-
French-

muslin filled
with cork or
light stuffing-
tied round
waist-
1780's

polonaise over
the bustle-
pocket
openings-
French-
1778

halfskirt
of stiffened
muslin and
whalebone-
1780's

"robe à l'anglaise"
with
bustle-
1787

cushion filled
with cork or
light stuffing-
tied round
waist-
1780's

skirt massed
high in back-
English-
1780's

stuffed
bolster tied
round waist-
1780's

heavy satin
over bustle-
French-
1790's

119

Eighteenth Century-
negligée
and sports

woolen cloth
house coat
with cap
to match-
French-
1760

footed
drawers of
stockinette-
legs separate
joined at belt-
drawstring
in back-
English-
1790's

garb of a
wrestler-
breeches,
stockings
and shoes-
English-
1788

silk
house
coat with
Brandenburgs-
English-
1740

house
coat of
brocaded
silk-
fan pleats
longer than
skirt-
French-
1770

powdering
mantle of
light silk
or cotton-
French-
1780's

drawers of
linen or flannel-
late period-English

white
linen
sports
costume-
English-
mid-century

Eighteenth Century-
vest and waistcoat

embroidered
silk vest
laced in
back-
French-
1720's

vest buttoned
to left-coat
to right-
English-
1730's

elaborately
embroidered
white faille
silk-
English-1720

embroidered waistcoat-
French-
1780's

shortening
of the
vest-
French-
1770's

lace-edged
satin vest
with
stiffened
skirts-
French-
1745

striped waistcoat
of the
"incroyable"-
French-
1796

striped waistcoat
of the Directoire-
French-
1795

Eighteenth Century panniers and hoops

Watteau sack over wide panniers - 1730

wire hoops and metal bands - 1711

starched, embroidered circular petticoat - 1736

criade of gummed canvas or oilcloth and wire - 1718

silk with whalebone - pocket openings over hips - mid-century

gown over "janseniste" panniers - 1762

silk or muslin with whalebone - 1720 to 1750

wooden oval hoops - flat front and back - Venetian - 1750

pocket panniers - whalebone hoops - 1750

"janseniste" panniers with pocket openings - corset over chemise - underpetticoat - 1740 to 1770

gondola or double panniers - muslin over wooden frame - 1760

hinged metal elbow panniers - to fold under arms - 1770

122

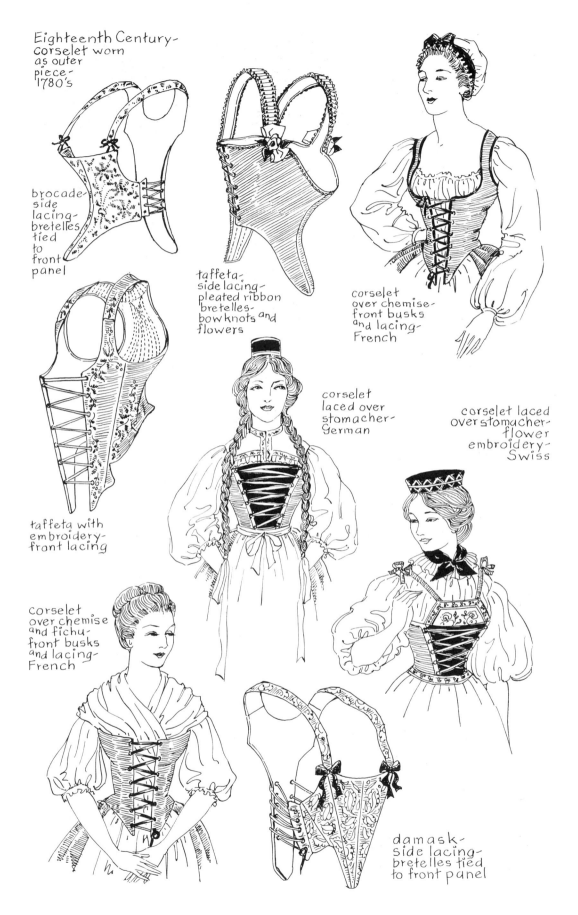

Eighteenth Century-
corselet worn
as outer
piece-
1780's

brocade-
side lacing-
bretelles
tied
to
front
panel

taffeta-
side lacing-
pleated ribbon
bretelles-
bowknots and
flowers

corselet
over chemise-
front busks
and lacing-
French

taffeta with
embroidery-
front lacing

corselet
laced over
stomacher-
German

corselet laced
over stomacher-
flower
embroidery-
Swiss

corselet
over chemise
and fichu-
front busks
and lacing-
French

damask-
side lacing-
bretelles tied
to front panel

123

Eighteenth Century
shirt and
cravat

negligée-worn
without jabot
or cravat-
English

black taffeta
solitaire-French-
1733

corset laced in
back-drawers of
linen or stockinette-
English-
1790's

gentleman's
shirt of fine
muslin-jabot
and ruffles of
point d'Alençon-
turned-down
collar-buttons
and buttonholes-
French-
mid-century

workman's
muslin shirt-
French-
first half
of period

folded cravat-
American-
early period

collar points
over black
silk cravat-
American-
1775

black
ribbon
solitaire-
lace jabot-
English-
1730's

tied cravat-
embroidered
sheer lawn-
American-
1796

linen smock
of the farmer-
English

military cravat-
black silk
over white
linen jabot-
English-
1780's

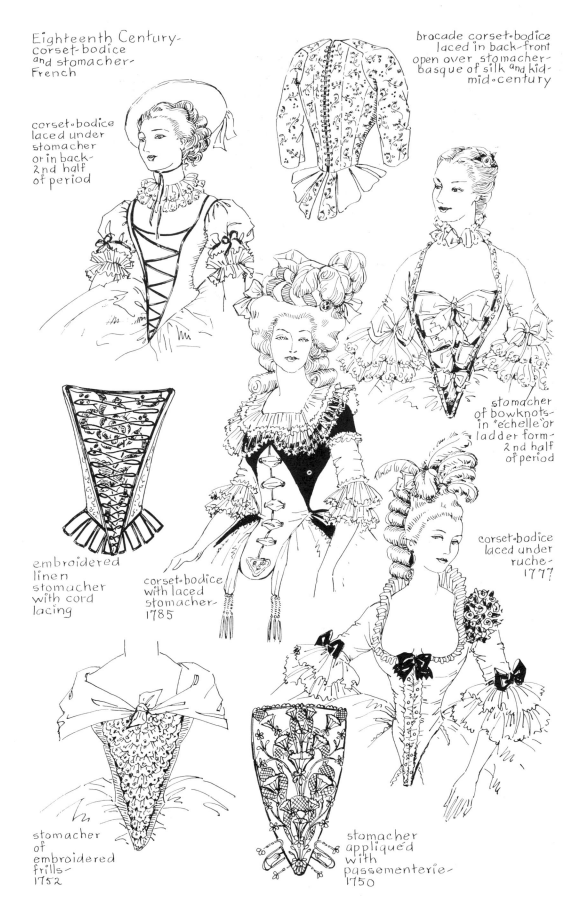

Eighteenth Century
corset-bodice
and stomacher-
French

brocade corset-bodice
laced in back-front
open over stomacher-
basque of silk and kid-
mid-century

corset-bodice
laced under
stomacher
or in back-
2nd half
of period

stomacher
of bowknots-
in "echelle" or
ladder form-
2nd half
of period

embroidered
linen
stomacher
with cord
lacing

corset-bodice
with laced
stomacher-
1785

corset-bodice
laced under
ruche-
1777

stomacher
of embroidered
frills-
1752

stomacher
appliquéd
with
passementerie-
1750

125

Eighteenth Century - negligée - the rayle - French

powdering mantle in light silk or cotton - 1725

rayle or combing jacket of fine lawn - embroidered scalloped edge - 1740's

silk or cotton rayle - corset over chemise - "modesty bit" tucked in bosom - brocaded petticoat - 1730's

negligée of white muslin - rose corset-bodice - "modesty bit" tucked in bosom - 1743

silk morning rayle worn outdoors - silk hood over white lawn hood - velvet bow - first half of period

wadded silk pelisse edged with marabou - white muslin petticoat - dormeuse bonnet of sheer white lawn - velvet ribbon - 1778

126

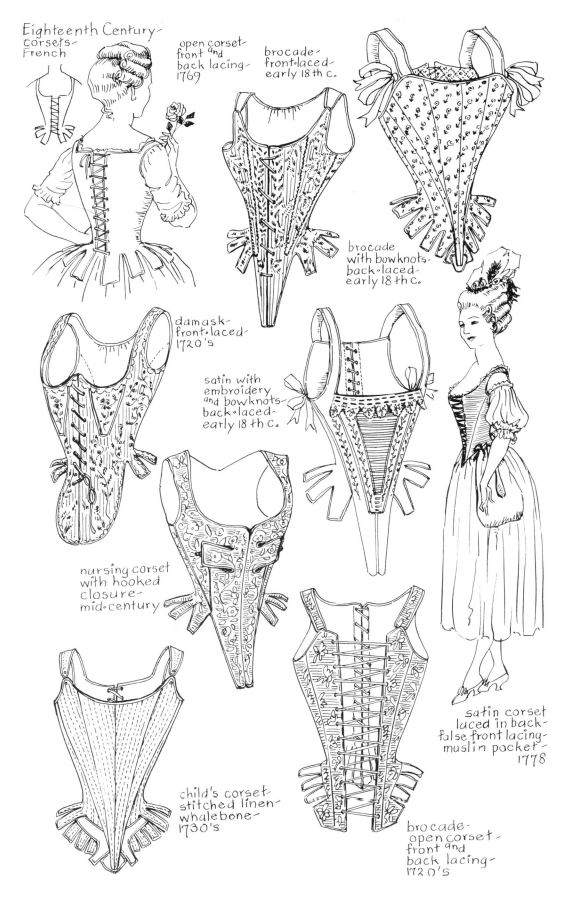

Eighteenth Century corsets—French

open corset front and back lacing—1769

brocade front-laced early 18th c.

brocade with bowknots-back-laced-early 18th c.

damask-front-laced-1720's

satin with embroidery and bowknots-back-laced-early 18th c.

nursing corset with hooked closure-mid-century

satin corset laced in back-false front lacing-muslin pocket-1778

child's corset stitched linen-whalebone-1730's

brocade-open corset-front and back lacing-1720's

127

Elizabethan-
doublet-trunk
hose-lace
whisk and
cuffs-
beaver
hat-
1597

Queen Elizabeth-
velvet and jewels-
embroidered
petticoat over
farthingale-
lace ruff and
wired gauze
conche-
late 16th C.

Eisenhower jacket   a waist-length, belted jacket in olive-drab cloth with turned collar and buttoned-cuff sleeves. Worn with a drab cloth shirt, black silk scarf and garrison cap. Named for General Dwight D. Eisenhower. see *battle jacket*.

elasticized   fabric with rubber invented by T. Hancock of Middlesex, England in 1820. It was called elastic cloth or webbing and replaced the ribbons and ribbon garters then in vogue. From 1836, when Charles Goodyear made his important discovery of a method of treating the surface of gum, the use of elastic in dress became more practical.

elastique   a steep, double twill worsted cloth similar to cavalry twill. Made elastic by being interwoven with fine threads of India rubber which renders it stretchable. Used for riding breeches, slacks and army uniforms.

elbow panniers   see *panniers, elbow*.

electric seal   see *seal, imitations*.

elephant skin   see *leather, elephant skin*.

Elizabethan costume   the mode during the reign of Queen Elizabeth I, 1558–1603. The feature of women's dress was the wheel farthingale with a long, pointed, corseted bodice and stomacher, and high heeled shoes. The queen's gorgeous ankle-length gowns permitted a glimpse of her silk stockings. Men wore the peasecod-bellied doublet and adopted the pump. The starched wired ruff appeared and lace was much used. The fabrics of this late Renaissance Period were very handsome.

elk   originally smoke-tanned hide of elk, but today of cowhide and calfskin dressed with smoke-tanned color and odor. Tanned elk is called buckskin and is a soft, pliable, oilless leather.

ell   old European measurement of cloth, different in different countries. The English ell was 45 inches but today 36 inches or more is generally accepted.

embossed   a raised pattern on velvet or plush created by shearing and pressing sections of the design flat; also a raised pattern that stands out in relief on fabrics, leather and jewelry.

embroidery   a general term for any form of ornamental needlework. Embroidery is of ancient origin, the earliest surviving examples being fifth and fourth century B.C. work from the Altai Mountains in Siberia. This is appliqué worked with horsehair, using leather, felt and woolen cloth. The earliest piece using linen is a Greek fragment, fifth century B.C. Embroidery was important in the Mediterranean area from early times; Islamic examples from Egypt, Mesopotamia, southern Italy, Sicily and Spain use a large variety of stitches, indicating an active tradition in such work and the great superiority of the Mediterranean culture and the achievement of Saracenic textile art. During the Middle Ages embroideries or hangings were used to illustrate biblical themes, episodes in the lives of the saints and even to expound religious doctrines. By the fourteenth century secular themes appeared, hunting being a particular favorite. In northern Europe English embroidery was outstanding; the oldest known piece is a chasuble of 850 A.D. The Anglo-Saxon work, which survived the Norman Conquest, was known as opus anglicanum and reached its peak in the thirteenth and fourteenth centuries. The famous Bayeux Tapestry, c. 1070, which is embroidered, not woven, is an isolated example of non-Anglo-Saxon work at this time. Opus anglicanum vestments and hangings, primarily worked in silk but using some gold, were commissioned by prelates from all over Europe. Wars and plagues brought a decline of this work, and English embroidery next attains prominence in the sixteenth and seventeenth centuries, chiefly in secular work. Besides such furnishings as hangings and cushions, much time and effort was spent on costume—everything was embroidered: jackets, caps, coifs, gloves and later aprons. The gorgeous dresses of Elizabeth I, encrusted with jewels, can be studied in many portraits.

The late eighteenth century also offered opportunities for embroidery on men's coats and waistcoats and to some extent on ladies' dresses. In Germany the prevailing style was whitework, embroidery worked in white linen thread on white linen, called opus teutonicum. Some examples of this also appeared in Italy and Switzerland. Beautiful embroideries in colored silk, mostly on vestments and ceremonial robes, were done in the Netherlands and Spain, fourteenth to sixteenth centuries.

In the Far East, especially in China and Japan, embroidery has embellished ceremonial costume for centuries. Although beautifully executed and with an exquisite use of shaded colors, the stitches employed indicate a limited repertoire of techniques. So-called peasant embroidery, worked in bright cottons or wool, has had a continuing tradition of use, especially for festival dress, in the Balkan countries, the Near East, eastern Europe and Scandinavia.

embroidery   see specific types of embroidery; Anglo-Saxon, Appenzell, appliqué, arrasene, Assisi, Ayrshire, bead, Beauvais, Berlin, Bulgarian, bullion, California, Canadian, chenille, Chinese, chromo, crewel, cross-stitch, cutwork, Czechoslovakian, Delhi, drawn-work, eyelet, flame stitch, Florentine, Genoese, Hardanger, Holbein, Jacobean, Madeira, Madras, net, opus anglicanum, Paris, Persian, Rococo, Romanian, shadow, Sicilian, Spanish blackwork, Swiss, tinsel, Turkish, Venetian, Wallachian, Yugoslavian.

emerald   a precious stone of a variety of beryl in rich green color. Oriental emerald is a rare green variety of corundum. The finest specimens, from Colombia, are usually executed in step-cut and cabochon.

emery   a sewing accessory for keeping needles polished. Usually a tiny bag of emery powder in the shape of a strawberry.

Empire fashions   the mode of the First Empire, 1804–1814. As worn by the Empress Josephine it was one of the loveliest in fashion's history. The general silhouette was that of a chemise gown, of velvet, silk or lingerie fabric worn over a sheer slip. The dress with long or short sleeves, perhaps with low décolletage, was belted under the bosom. Shawls, tiny bosom jackets and the long, enveloping redingote were in vogue. Bonnets and turbans completed the picture.

empress cloth   a cloth of the rep family much in demand in the Second French Empire, 1852–1870. It was a cloth of wool or wool and cotton, resembling merino but not twilled.

Empire fashion- formal dress- claw-hammer tails- powdered wig-1814

Empire fashion dark green velvet coat- felt bonnet with ostrich- 1814

Empress Eugénie hat, see *hat, Empress Eugénie.*

enamel opaque or semi-opaque, applied to fingernails and bare toenails.

end on end a fine check formed by a weave of alternate warp yarns of white and color. Used in cotton broadcloth, chambray and Oxford cloth for shirts, pajamas and sportswear.

engageantes French for sleeve ruffles, usually three of graduated width from elbow to wrist. Of sheer muslin, lace or embroidery and fashionable from 1660 to about 1760.

English coat see *frock coat.*

English drape a short-lived masculine fashion which appeared late in the 1920's; a one-button jacket falling loosely in front and baggy trousers with pleats at the waist. By 1938 the style had been revised to the English paddock suit with a high two-button closing.

English edging see *Angleterre.*

English foot socks see *socks, English foot.*

English gown, robe Anglaise an important fashion of the 1780's, beloved by the portrait painters of the day, especially Gainsborough, who delighted in painting their sitters in the costume. It was of unusually simple design, heavy satin with a long, full skirt and fitted bodice, gauzy sleeves and neckerchief and worn with a huge velvet hat with sweeping ostrich plumes. see *robe Anglaise; robe à la Française; Velasquez; Watteau gown.*

ensemble, feminine The three-piece costume, supplanting the severely tailored suit and coat in the 1920's. It was made in soft, colorful wools, the most popular being wool jersey and the colors beige and brown. It consisted of dress and coat, or skirt, sweater or overblouse, and coat, and eclipsed all other styles for fashionable daytime wear.

ensign blue a dark navy blue or midnight blue.

en-tout-cas a small umbrella for sun or rain, mid-nineteenth century.

entre-deux see *beading.*

envelope bag see *handbags.*

envelope chemise a lingerie piece of the twentieth century, chemise and drawers in one, 1915.

eolienne a fabric similar to poplin but lighter in weight. Usually of silk and wool or silk and cotton with crosswise corded effect in the weaving.

epaulet military and shoulder decoration suggested by the steel épaulières of armor, worn to protect the shoulders. In the seventeenth century epaulets served to hold the shoulder belt in place and thus prevent the musket from slipping. Still later, epaulets became military decoration and insignia in various armies.

"English gown" favored by portrait painters - Gainsborough hat - 1780's

They were handsome shoulder pads edged with heavy gold or silver fringe indicating the officer's rank.

epaulet sleeve   see *sleeve, epaulet; epaulettes.*

ephod   a hip-length vest of white linen with wide bretelles, worn by the Hebrew high priest. It was belted and handsomely embroidered in gold, silver, violet, purple and cerise threads. Worn in Biblical times.

ermiline   see *rabbit.*

ermine   the smallest of weasels, with cold weather coat of pure white fur, summer coat pale brown, and tip of tail always black; from Northern Asia, Europe and North America. The American species is designated weasel by the fur trade and is used for coats, jackets and trimmings. It has been used from medieval times for royal and legal robes and as heraldic insignia. It was also called miniver, which in modern British usage signifies ermine, and is geometrically spotted with black lamb pieces and worn in robes, crowns and coronets in British ceremonies. Russian ermine is the best, with Alaska weasel comparing favorably and becoming the more used in the twentieth century. The Chinese and Korean species are poor. Champagne Ermine is white ermine dyed a beige hue. see *armenian rat; weasel.*

ermine, Alaska or **Manchurian**   a larger, coarser weasel, cream to white sides with pale yellow or orange back. It resembles, but is less durable than Russian ermine.

ermine, laitice, létice   of the medieval and Renaissance periods. "A beast of whitish-gray color" resembling ermine and used for edging of neck, sleeves, tunic and ladies' trailing gowns. The width used designated the rank of the wearer.

ermine, summer stoat   the British name for the natural brown weasel which changes its protective coat to white in winter. It is light or reddish-brown above and sulphur color below the black tail. A flat, not very durable fur, small in quantity and therefore high in price, used for coats, jackets and trimming.

erminette   see *rabbit.*

escarpin   a lady's black satin slipper with ribbon ties.

esclavage   French word for slavery; a slave bracelet or slave necklace made of multi-strands of gilt chains and beads.

escoffion   an elaborate headdress of the fourteenth and fifteenth centuries which began as the golden net caul, crépine, reticulated cap of velvet or satin covered with a jeweled gilt net. It developed fantastic two-horned shapes and was finally supplanted by the tall hennin with long, flowing veil in the fifteenth century.

Eskimo dress   see illustrations, next page; *kamiks; parka; timiak; kooletah.*

espadrille   the braided cord or rope-soled canvas shoe worn by the Italians and French of the Midi, and Spaniards.

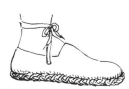

espadrille-canvas shoe with braided cord sole worn by Italians and southern French

estamene, estamin   a twilled woolen dress fabric resembling cheviot but with a rough, nappy surface.

Eton collar   see *collar, Eton.*

Eton jacket   as worn by the boys of Eton College, England. A slightly tapered coat reaching to the hips with wide lapels and open in front. It was adopted as a

ermine in winter when pure white—stoat in summer when light brown—tail always black-tipped

Eton jacket and top hat worn by boys of Eton College, England

Eskimo woman of Alaska carrying baby in parka. Tunic, shirt, breeches of sealskin, fur to the inside

Eskimo woman in modern blue parka over fur parka and fur breeches

Eskimo woman of Greenland - costume of sealskin, fur to the inside - beadwork

Eskimo of Alaska - N.W. Territory - fox or wolf with leather fringe

Eskimo of Alaska - N.W. Territory - quilted cotton parka fur-lined - dark blue fur-lined breeches - white skin boots - fur to the inside

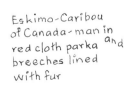

Eskimo-Caribou of Canada - man in red cloth parka and breeches lined with fur

feminine fashion in the 1860's and remains a constantly-recurring fashion with slight variation.

Etonian uniform   morning coat and silk top hat; inaugurated and worn by the boys at Eton in 1820 at the funeral of George III, who was a great benefactor of the famous public school in Buckinghamshire, England. It is still worn.

Etruscan   the costume of the farming people who lived in Etruria about 1000 B.C. reveals Greek influence, both Asiatic and European. Their few garments were covered with colorful patterns and the edges finished with characteristic decorative braids. The male tunic, a simple sheath and narrow, with the edges finished with handwork, was worn without an undergarment by the young men, but the older men wore a pleated, longer chiton underneath. The feminine short-sleeved tunic was long, snug-fitting and colorfully embroidered. The woman's cloak was a rectangle large enough to cover the whole figure. The man's cloak, called a tebenna, was a large rectangle or semicircle of woolen cloth. A favorite motif used in sculpture on tombs and smaller articles, was based upon the ancient Greek design known to us as the Greek key pattern.

étui   French name of a small box or fancy bag of pretty fabric or leather usually attached to the edge of the bodice. It was used as the container for a woman's toilet and sewing articles from the seventeenth to the nineteenth centuries.

Eugénie's wigs   the *Montero*, a huntsman's cap worn from 1600 by Spanish mountaineers, in Europe and the American colonies, and today. A round cap with a flap round back and sides which can be turned down to cover neck and cheeks in bad weather. Made of knitted yarn, woolen cloth or of fur. Named for the French Empress Eugénie who presented the fur caps to the Arctic Exploration group in 1875.

Etruscan headdress-
curls and felt cap
in tutulus shape

Etruscan headdress-
braided and curled
in tutulus shape-
jeweled tiara

"Eugénie's Wigs"-
knitted Montero
caps with fur.

evening bag   see *handbag*.

evening gown   in the time of Henry VIII, meant a night gown. see *night gown; gown*.

Evzone   a soldier of a select corps in the Greek army who wears the fustanella,

a very short flaring, pleated kilt. see *fustanella*.

eye make up   generally consists of *eye shadow*, a thin coating of cream on the lids in violet, blue or green; *eye liner*, a pencil line at the base of the lashes; *mascara*, a thin cream to darken and thicken the lashes; *eyebrow pencil*, a soft crayon pencil to outline or emphasize the brows. *False eyelashes*, which became popular in the 1960's, are made of real mink, seal, hair or plastic. The lashes are provided with a liquid or cream adhesive and applied to the base of the real lashes for each wearing.

eyeglasses or **spectacles**   Lenses for aiding impaired vision are commonly said to have been invented in the thirteenth century; by 1482, spectacle-makers had opened shops in Nuremberg. The first lenses were joined by a nosepiece which clung to the bridge of the nose. In the sixteenth century the joined lenses were attached to a vertical metal piece which could be suspended from under the front hair or hat. A great improvement in the eighteenth century were horizontal temples which hooked back of the ears. Frames were of heavy tortoise shell or horn until the nineteenth century, when lighter gold or silver frames were adopted. Notable today are improvements in plastics for frames, the harlequin shape of 1940 and the contact lenses which first appeared in the 1950's. see *contact lens; harlequin spectacles; lorgnette; pince-nez; monocle*.

eyelet embroidery   floral patterns of openwork eyelets with solid stitchery used for foliage and bowknots. see *Madeira embroidery*.

eyeleteer   a bodkin or small stiletto for punching eyelet holes for embroidery.

F

facing   a false hem sewn to the underside of edges of collar, cuffs, or edge of skirt. It usually provides a better finish than the turned-up edge of self fabric alone.

fagoting, faggoting   a kind of crisscrossed openwork stitch used in the space between two edges, as in an "open seam."

faille   a glossy fabric, soft and lustrous, woven in silk, rayon or cotton with a flat, horizontal ribbing.

Fair Isle sweater   a cardigan or pullover knit with colorful bands of geometrical designs; only the stockinette stitch is used. Supposed to have originated on Fair Isle, a small isolated island between the Orkneys and Shetlands, but actually a widespread type of knitting in the Scottish highlands and islands.

faja   the wide, crushed, brilliantly colored sash of the Spaniard's costume consisting of white shirt with bolero or manta, breeches and hose in dark blue, green or black. Still worn in most provinces.

"falbalas" and "furbelows"-
names for cut-out motifs
applied as trimming -
French -17th C.

falbala   see *furbelow*.

falderal, falderol   a piece of finery; a trifling ornament; a trinket.

faldetta   a combination cloak and hood worn by women in Malta; more commonly known as a huke, a long, black cloth wrap of Moorish origin. see *huke; haik*.

fall   a pendant ornament in costume as a cascade of lace, ruffles or ribbon. Over the top of the English hood of the sixteenth century hung a "fall" of black silk or velvet. Also a fashion new in 1966, a thick mane of hair worn pinned to the top of the head where it is usually dressed high, or cascaded into large rolls, or left

faja or wide
sash of fiesta
dress- all
dark blue and
embroidered-
white blouse-
Spanish

faldetta-a
cloak worn
by women of
Malta-of
Moorish
origin

fall- black velvet tall over white linen hood with jeweled coronet on top - Flemish - 16th C.

to hang slightly curled, or straight. Of European hair, usually in lengths of sixteen inches or more. Inexpensive falls are made of synthetic fiber.

falling band, Van Dyck   a collar of fine white lawn edged with lace, also called a rabat. A wider version which lay on the shoulders, was called a rabatine, and was also known as a Van Dyck because it is shown in many portraits painted by the Flemish artist, Sir Anthony Van Dyck (1599–1641).

false hem   see *facing.*

false sleeve   see *sleeve, false.*

falsies   see *bust forms.*

fan   used in China, Japan and India since the eleventh century B.C. The folding fan originated in Japan, it is said, about 670 A.D., reaching China in the tenth century. The Egyptian fan, a symbol of rank and power, dates back to the thirteenth century B.C. The Egyptians, Assyrians and Persians were cooled by servants or slaves carrying long-staffed fans of grasses, leaves, and feathers. From Asia Minor and Egypt, the fan reached Europe by way of Italy, where hand fans were imported from the East in the twelfth century A.D. They were made of peacock, ostrich, parrot and Indian crow feathers with jeweled ivory handles. Small, dainty, square-shaped flag fans mounted on carved ivory sticks were

carried by court ladies in the early sixteenth century. The folding fan was first used in Spain, passing to Italy and then to France, where it was introduced by Catherine de' Medici. The folded fan was made of leather, chicken skin, vellum or parchment, and decorated by the greatest artists of the day. The vogue continued into the eighteenth and nineteenth centuries, when the exquisite black lace folding fan of Spain was notable. In the early twentieth century, large ostrich feather fans were beautiful accessories with formal evening dress.

fanchon   a bonnet of the Mid-Victorian period with a bavolet or deep ruffle at the back of the head. see *capote.*

farmer's satin   an Italian imitation of real silk cloth, but the name now used for a lining fabric. see *satin, farmer's.*

"far-out" or fantastic, **"far in"** or conservative,   two popular descriptive terms for such fashions of the 1960's.

farrajiyah   a long cloak of the African desert worn by the Tuaregs. The sleeves are long and wide, resembling angel sleeves, in white or colored cotton.

farrajiyah or ksa - white cotton or wool cloak - Tuareg of middle Sahara

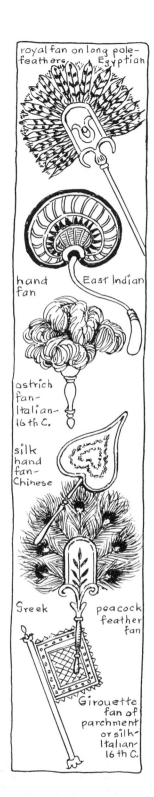

royal fan on long pole - feathers - Egyptian

hand fan   East Indian

ostrich fan - Italian - 16th C.

silk hand fan - Chinese

Greek   peacock feather fan

Girouette fan of parchment or silk - Italian - 16th C.

farthingale, verdingale, vertugadin, hoop, Catherine wheel   Of Spanish origin, worn in France during the days of Louis XIII and in England under James I and Charles I. The flat farthingale was known in England as the Saint Catherine's wheel, a mode lasting from about 1530 to 1630. An ugly fashion, gowns were sometimes made with two hoops, the hoop actually being a stuffed roll that rested upon the hips. In France, the modish woman wore the hoop under several petticoats. The skirt or outer robe was "la modeste," the next under, "la friponne" or in English, "hussy," and the under one, "le secret." The foundation petticoat was of heavy canvas or linen with wicker hoops, the stuffed bolster being placed over or under that petticoat and tied around the hips.

farthingale breeches   breeches with a small stuffed hoop resting on the hips as a protection against sword thrusts. Especially favored by the English Charles I (1625–1649).

fascia, tibiale   rolls of woven cloth and leather which were wrapped around the legs. They were worn by the Roman legionnaires and copied by the farmers and peasants in Northern Italy and Etruria.

fashion   is the current style of the moment. Fashion may be elegant, pleasing or even ugly, as long as it is the prevailing mode. *Style* is the mode of expression in any art; in costume it may be a manner of carriage, poise, line and color.

fashion babies, or fashion dolls   served as the fashion journals of past centuries. The mannequin dolls, dressed in the newest styles, were sent out from Paris as early as the fourteenth century and, according to one record, one went to the Queen of England. By the eighteenth century many were sent to European capitals from Paris where Marie Antoinette and her modiste Mlle. Bertin were the dictators of the mode. In the eighteenth century fashion babies reached New York and Philadelphia by way of London. They were eagerly awaited, as they showed the latest changes in fashion.

fastener   the mechanical slide fastener was perfected by the 1930's, manufactured in all colors and used to fasten girdles, foundation garments, dresses, coats, in fact wherever a trim, concealed closure is required; a zipper.

Fath, Jacques   see *couture, haute.*

favors   see *ribbons.*

feathers   see *aigrette; Audubon plumage law.*

fedora   a man's soft felt hat, known also as *Tyrolean hat, Alpine hat* and *Homburg,* the latter named for the place of its manufacture. The crown has a center crease from front to back. The name *Fédora* was after the heroine of Sardou's drama in Paris, 1883. A feminine fedora or alpine hat of brown felt with wings, ribbon band and spotted veil was worn for cycling in the 1890's. The masculine fedora is still the prevailing style of hat for men.

feile beag, fillebeg, filibeg, filabeg, philabeg, philibeg, kilt   the lower part of the breacan-feile laid in pleats and worn as a skirt. see *Scottish Highland dress.*

felt cloth   unwoven cloth. Wool, fur or combinations of matted fibers are felted by the use of moisture, heat, steam, pressure and hammering into a compact piece. Felt is used for hats, sportswear, house slippers, trim and many other items. Felt for hats is made of fur fibers by a process of manipulation and shrinkage that cannot be loosened without tearing. The fur of animals trapped in winter makes better felt. The principal pelts are those of beaver, muskrat, nutria, otter, and coney. Felt was used for cloaks and caps by the ancient Greeks. The matting together of wool and hair while moist was the means employed then, as today, in its manufacture.

feredeza   a baglike ankle-length cover-all of black cotton which the Balkan woman wears in public. It has long, loose sleeves and is tied with a string belt and accompanied by the yashmak. Similar in shape to the dorina, which, however, is of checked fabric and light-colored. see *dorina*.

feridgé   a luxurious cloak of woolen cloth of Turkish origin but rarely seen in Turkey today. A woman's wrap with large sleeves and cape. It reached to the floor and with it was worn the old-time head-kerchief and djellaba.

ferris-waist   trade name for a corset-waist worn by children, early 1900's. Made of strong cotton fabric reinforced with strong tape and buttoned in back, it had pendant garters for holding up stockings, and drawers were buttoned to it around the waist.

feridgé of red velvet with hanging sleeves caftan, blue satin-entari, white silk crepe chemise- red fez with blue tassels- all gilt embroidery- Turkish-Albanian

ferronière   a fine chain or narrow ribbon tied around the head with a jewel suspended in the middle of the forehead. Of Oriental origin, it was a Renaissance fashion in Europe worn with the Madonna coiffure by Italian and French ladies. In the early nineteenth century, the ferronière was worn by French and English ladies.

festoon   a garland of foliage, flowers or lace hung in scallops around a full skirt.

fez   a brimless felt or wool cap shaped in a truncated cone, dark red or black with a silk tassel in dark blue or black. Also worn swathed with linen or silk in turban fashion. The fez was made part of Turkish official dress by the ordinance of Sultan Mahmud II (1808–1839) in the early nineteenth century. All Turks, including those not Moslems, were required to wear the cap. It remained the national headdress until outlawed in 1923 when Turkey became a republic, but it is still worn by other Easterners. The fez got its name from the sacred City of Islam in French Morocco, Fez. It was supposed that the dull crimson hue from the juice of a berry which grew in the vicinity could not be had elsewhere. Following the discovery of synthetic dyes in recent times, the cap has been successfully made in France and Turkey. Jews who live in Morocco wear a black fez. see *tarboosh*.

fiber   the thread or filament used in weaving fabrics such as silk, wool, cotton, linen, asbestos and rayon. Fibers are classified as animal, vegetable, mineral and man-made.

fiber lace   a trimming for sheer fabrics, the lace made of banana and aloe fibers, frail as well as expensive.

fibula   the pin or brooch of ancient Greece and Rome, which the modern safety pin resembles. The ancient piece was simple and was basically the same

ferronière of pearls and jewels- French-1500

fez-dark blue or dark red-blue or red silk tassel

fibulae- ancient Greek safety pins

fichu—
white lawn
puffed up over
bosom—18th
and 19th C.

fitch—
furrier's name for
fur of the ferret

useful gadget, fashioned of one piece of metal wire.

fichu   a neck cloth of the eighteenth and nineteenth centuries worn with different types of gowns. Of sheer white cotton or mousseline de soie, it was draped around the throat and shoulders and usually bunched above the small tight waist, giving a pouter-pigeon look to the figure.

filament   the fiber or thread used in the weaving of a textile.

filasse   raw fiber such as jute or ramie.

filature   raw silk, the delicate untwisted silk threads reeled from the cocoons.

filet lace   a handmade lace or net having a square mesh with a pattern formed by darning stitches; known also as darned filet lace.

filibeg   see *feile beag*.

filigree   fine metal openwork of gold, silver or copper wire in delicate design used in jewelry ornamentation.

fill-in   a separate yoke with collar to be worn with dress or suit having a deep open neck. see *dicky*.

findings, notions   all work accessories of couture, such as pins, needles, threads, buttons, hooks and eyes, fasteners and braids.

fingering yarn   a finely twisted woolen yarn for knitting and crocheting.

fingernails, painted   a custom centuries old in the Orient but comparatively new in Western grooming. The ancient Egyptians used henna to color the fingernails a dark red. Modern nail lacquers appeared in 1916, and in the 1950's false, long plastic shapes to apply over one's

own by means of an adhesive. That was a short-lived fad. Toenails may be groomed as well, being manicured, creamed and painted.

finnesko   a Lapland boot made of tanned reindeer skin with the fur outside.

fisherman's sweater   traditional hand-knit sweaters of Ireland and the Hebrides, of heavy natural wool in which the lanolin has been retained to make the garment water-repellent as well as warm. A number of different stitches are used in each garment, cables, ribbing and lozenge patterns being combined in an almost infinite variety. According to legend, each sweater was different so that the families of fishermen, who frequently met death by drowning, could recognize the bodies when they were washed ashore. Also known as Aran sweaters, after the Irish islands of that name where the art of knitting has been predominant for centuries. Adopted for fashionable use as sportswear after World War II.

fisher-pekan   French name of American Indian origin. Largest of the marten species, and one of the rarest and most valuable furs. Found in the densely wooded regions of northern Canada to as far south as the Allegheny Mountains. Darkly shaded blue-brown underwool with fine, strong, dark, glossy guard hair and a rich tail, almost black. A durable fur used for scarfs and jackets.

fitch   called *polecat* or *perwitsky* in Europe. A fur from Europe and Asia, durable, creamy yellow and tawny underwool with long, shining black guard hair. The largest skins come from Denmark, Holland and Germany, smaller and silkier from Russia. Dyed, but used more often natural. When dyed sable color it is called sable-dyed fitch. Used for coats, jackets and scarfs.

flame stitch   see *Florentine embroidery*.

flammeum, ricinium the saffron-colored veil of the pagan Roman bride and the Roman lady. It was fastened to the back of the head with the long ends left to float in back. It was of Coan gauze made by the women of Coa, an island of the Dodecanese. The color was orange-yellow, which had been the festive color of the Etruscans.

flandan see *pinner.*

flannel from 1796, a demand for English flannels for scarfs and shawls developed with the wearing of muslin dresses in all seasons. A soft woolen fabric of plain and twill weave in a wide range of textures and weights in solid colors, stripes and plaids. It was used for dresses, negligées, sleepwear and quilts. During the nineteenth century red flannel was in demand all over Europe for men's winter underwear, which came to be known as "red flannels."

flannel, Canton first made in China, a heavy, warm cotton cloth widely used.

flannel, kimono see *kimono flannel.*

flannel, outing a lightweight cotton cloth popular for children's wear.

flannel, shaker see *shaker flannel.*

flannel, vegetable see *vegetable flannel.*

flapper in the early 1900's a British term for the English girl who had not yet "come out." Her hair, whether braided or hanging, "flapped in the wind." The American flapper appeared in the 1920's with short hair, short skirt and overblouse or sweater. She wore Oxfords and rolled stockings and a beret or calotte. She was named "flapper" because in winter she wore galoshes which were always unbuckled and flapping.

flash a bunch of ribbon, the remains of the ribbon-tied queue of the soldier's wig of the eighteenth century.

flat cap see *cap, flat.*

flat point lace a Venetian type of lace without any raised stitches.

flax a plant of the genus *linum* commonly cultivated for its fiber. A long, silky bast fiber used in linen. see *linen.*

flea "puce" in French; a color brought to the mode by Marie-Antoinette. There were at least a half-dozen variances of the color, such as old flea, young flea, and so on. In general, it was a reddish-brown.

fleur-de-lis "flower of Louis," the conventionalized motif based upon the iris. It was used as the royal emblem of France since Louis VII in the twelfth century and has remained a popular motif for artistic decoration.

flight boot see *boot, flight.*

floconné from the French for snow-flaked, small flakes in white on a colored ground. Machine-stitched on fabrics.

Florentine or **flame stitch embroidery** a type of canvas embroidery shaded up and down in a zigzag pattern of colors; used for draperies and covers but formerly

Fleur de lis – Louis XIV

Florodora Sextette – famous American chorus – gown of white lawn and lace – black velvet hat with ostrich – fluffy parasol – 1899

for bags, pockets and accessories. Also known as Bargello work and Hungarian point.

Florentine neckline   a broad décolletage extending from shoulder to shoulder and cut lower across the front than the back.

Florodora Sextette   a very popular number in the musical play "Florodora," 1899. The costumes were the epitome of contemporary fashion. see page 139.

flounces   strips of cloth varied in width, cut straight or bias, shirred or pleated, applied to a garment with the lower edge left free to flare. see *ruffle*.

flowers, artificial   generally of silk or velvet, used as trimming or accessories to feminine dress in the first half of the twentieth century. Some very beautiful flowers were produced, particularly in France and Italy.

fluting, goffering   usually of fine muslin for neck and sleeves. Made by an iron implement with a turn handle and ribbed with grooves which, when heated, made small pleats in ruffles or ruches. It was known as a goffering iron.

fly fringe   a silk fringe consisting of tufts or small tassels, a popular dress trimming of the nineteenth century.

fly-front   a closure to conceal buttons and buttonholes or slide fasteners. Hidden underplackets used especially on men's coats, jackets and trousers.

focal, focalia   a square of linen that the Roman legionnaire wore loosely tied around the neck and which served as handkerchief and towel. From this piece of neckwear developed the woolen cravat of the Croats, who were descendants of the peoples of a Roman-conquered province. The neckpiece eventually became the Western man's scarf. see *cravat*.

Fontanges   In 1680 the Duchesse de Fontanges, mistress of Louis XIV, her hat blown off at a royal hunting party, tied her curls in place with her garter, arranging a bowknot in front. From the happening evolved a cap of tier upon tier of upstanding, pleated, wired ruffles of lawn, lace and ribbons. The hair dressed in that style became the coiffure à la Fontanges. The cap became the bonnet à la Fontanges, and the silk-covered framework, the commode. The cap often had lappets of ribbon and lace in back and over the whole arrangement was often a black silk hood. After 1710, and much ridicule, the headdress lost its fantastic tower and ended as just a little linen or lace cap. see *commode*.

foot mantle   a woman's mantle worn in Colonial days on horseback. see *safeguard*.

footing   a narrow edging of plain lace net.

footwear   see *arctics; balmoral; batts; bicycle bal; Blücher; boots; bottine; bulgha; carbattine; culiga; chopines; chukka; cockers; escarpin; espadrille; gaiter; galoshes; geta; huaraches; jackboot; juliet; kamiks; krepis; larrigan; loafer; moccasin; mule; oxford; pattens; pedule; pegged boot; poulaines; pump; rubbers; sandals; scuffer; scuffs; shoes; slings; slippers; sneakers; solleret; tips; tsaruchia.*

forage cap   see *cap, forage.*

fore and aft cap   see *cap, fore and aft.*

forestry cloth   an olive drab cloth of twill weave made of worsted, wool, cotton and blends. Used by the United States government as uniform cloth in the Forestry Service.

Fortuny gowns   were designed by the Italian Mario Fortuny, son of the Spanish

fontange of lawn, lace and black taffeta-beauty spots—French—1680's

fontange—black velvet loops mounted on a chiffon cap—galon trimmed—18 th C.

painter. The first Fortuny gown, worn in Paris in 1910, was created for the dancer, Isadora Duncan. It was a beautiful clinging gown of permanently pleated silk, dyed in artistic color. The style became a cult, now many decades old. Though originally intended as tea gowns, they were worn by the owners as evening dress. With long sleeves or sleeveless, the gown goes over the head and is tied around the neck by a drawstring. The gowns were canceled in 1949 upon the death of the artist but occasionally a "Fortuny" is found by a collector. The term is also applied to printed velvet gowns, examples of which are in museum collections.

foulard   a twill-woven lightweight silk, plain or printed, with an allover pattern of small motifs on a solid color; also a rayon or mercerized fabric. Used especially for scarfs and dresses.

foundation garment   a gored, fitted and boned combination of corset and brassière, introduced in the late 1920's. The bosom section, also boned, furnishing the desired "uplift look."

foundation net   a stiffened, coarse net used in dressmaking and millinery.

fourchettes   small forked pieces of fabric or leather set in between glove fingers. see *trank.*

four-in-hand   a nineteenth-century scarf named after the sport of driving a four-in-hand. A long necktie, narrow around the neck with slightly widened ends; one end was placed shorter than the other and tied in front into a slip or sailor knot, then pulled tightly, straightening the knot and ends to hang vertically. It was a popular tie of the late nineteenth and early twentieth centuries.

fox   of the canine family found in Europe, North America and Asia, not south of the equator. In order of value: silver, black, cross and red, this latter most common and most important to the fur trade. see *fox, red.*

fox, blue   found in Alaska, Hudson Bay Territory, Archangel, Norway and Greenland. The finest from Archangel and Greenland; rich, smoky blue or dark brown with bluish tone. The dark color most desirable. Underwool thick and long with fine top hair. The summer coat also blue but not as rich and thick as the winter coat. Used for scarfs and jackets.

fox, common   found in North America, Europe and Asia and a few in Australia, originally carried there for hunting. Varied in size with coloring from gray through red with long, soft, glossy fur. Better quality from North America and the Arctic Circle. Dyed and used mostly for scarfs and trimming on women's cloth coats.

fox, cross   wild red fox, sometimes marked on the back with a cross of brownish black. Found in North America, Europe and Asia, the best from Hudson Bay to Labrador. Also found in ranch-bred red fox and used for scarfs.

fox, gray   found in the United States, some in Mexico and Central America. Serviceable fur of stiffer hair with close, dark underwool and coarse, regular top hair of grizzly gray. Used natural or dyed for scarfs and trimming.

fox; kit; kitt or **swift**   first two names for European species; third name American species. Small, slender fox found in the plains of the northern section of the United States and Canada, Europe, Russian steppes and Siberia. A durable fur with short, soft underfur and top hair, pale gray mixed with yellowish white. Used natural or dyed, principally for trimming.

fox, platina   Norwegian trade name for silver fox mutation. see *fox, silver or black.*

four-in-hand scarf, popular in the late 19th and early 20th centuries.

Fox - Arctic - white
from October to
spring - northernmost
America, Europe, Asia

fox, platinum   United States name of silver fox mutation. see *fox, silver or black.*

fox, pointed   the common red fox dyed black and pointed with silvery badger hairs to simulate silver fox; used for scarfs.

fox, red   found in most countries north of the equator, the strongest, most durable and finest peltries from Alaska and Kamchatka. Long, silky guard hair and underwool thick, soft and long, varying in color from pale yellow to dark red. It is dyed black to imitate natural black fox or dyed and pointed to simulate silver fox. Used for garments, scarfs, muffs, and trimming.

fox, silver or black   a mutation which appears in red fox litters. It is termed black when black the whole length of the back. The silvery quality is given by the black guard hairs which are topped with white, the underwool close and fine and the black tail tipped with white. Silver fox is the most valuable of fox furs and the most difficult to imitate. It is found in the far north, the finest coming from Labrador. Most silver fox today is scientifically ranch-bred. Used for capes, jackets and scarfs.

fox, silver pointed   thickly furred peltries lacking sufficient silver hairs, augmented by gluing in silver guard hairs taken from damaged fox pelts.

fox, South American   not a true fox, more canine than fox. Found from southern Brazil to the tip of the continent in the eastern part and in parts of Chili; the best peltries are from the southern part. Dark grayish-blue to pale, purplish blue; used natural or dyed, the guard hairs given silvery tips. Used for scarfs and trimming cloth and fur garments.

fox, white or **arctic**   found in the most northerly regions of North America,

Europe and Asia. The arctic fox becomes white from October to spring. The summer coat is a sooty-brown and yellowish white with the underwool usually gray but concealed by heavy guard hair. The imperfect peltries are dyed pale shades of gray and brown to imitate blue or black fox. Used for jackets, scarfs and trimming.

foyne   the medieval name for marten.

frangipani perfumed gloves   introduced to the European courts in the early seventeenth century by the Italian Count Frangipani. He discovered the process of making liquid perfume by treating solid scents with alcohol.

French hem   see *hem, French.*

French hood   see *hood, French.*

French seal   see *seal, French.*

frieze, frise   a stout woolen cloth with a shaggy or "friezed" pile used since the fourteenth century; first made in Wales, now in Ireland. A very warm fabric for jerkins and, "gowns," meaning overcoats.

frize, Holland   a fine bleached Holland linen of superior quality, once in great demand for men's shirts.

fringe by the yard   a narrow braid edged on one side with thread fringe, knots, or tassels as a trimming edge or decoration.

fringe, in coiffure   meaning hair cut short over the forehead and hanging either straight or curled, also called bang or bangs. see *bangs.*

frock coat, English coat, Prince Albert   single or double-breasted with skirts joined at the waistline and hanging in back to the bend of the knee. Pockets were sometimes placed in the back skirt pleats. Unlike the more formal cutaway,

frock coat -
single - breasted -
2nd half
19th C.

the skirts are not cut from the waistline center front rounding to the sides, but meet from waist to hem. Of black or Oxford gray cheviot, or unfinished worsted worn with trousers striped or checked in gray and black, and a matching or contrasting waistcoat. see *walking coat.*

frock coat, Orby   a frock coat of the first decade of the twentieth century, single-breasted with the fore and aft sections out and made without waist seams. The back had a center seam which terminated in a vent at the waist.

frogs   looped braid fastenings. see *Brandenburgs.*

frontlet   worn by ladies in the fifteenth century when foreheads were exaggeratedly bare. It was a tiny pendant loop of velvet or silk, the loop being attached to the edge of a calotte worn under the hennin or escoffion. Ladies of rank wore a loop of black velvet or gold, the loop of gold indicating that the fair wearer had an income of at least ten pounds a year.

fuchsia   a purplish red, the color of the flower.

full dress, military   the prescribed uniform worn on state occasions at home and abroad. Civilian full dress, see *tails.*

full-bottomed wig   see *wig, full-bottomed.*

fullers   workers among the Romans who washed new cloth with fuller's earth, shrank it and finally pressed it. They also cleaned soiled garments.

fuller's earth   an earthy substance of nonplastic clay resembling potter's clay, which has been used since ancient times to full cloth, i.e. remove the oil matter from cloth.

full-fashioned   a process of flat knitting in which the seam edges are shaped by reducing or adding of stitches. Used for hose, sweaters and underwear.

fur coat   the fashionable coat with "fur to the outside," was largely new in the late nineteenth century. It was originated by the Paris couturier, Doucet. Rarely until then had a fashionable coat been made with the fur to the outside.

fur, fake   synthetic fur cloths; among the imitations are Persian lamb, broadtail, beaver, sealskin and other short-haired furs. First used in the 1950's.

fur, "fun"   an expression coined in the 1960's for relatively inexpensive furs made up for young women. Moderately priced in Russian lynx, a South American skunk called zorina, and gray, cross and red foxes.

fur paws   garments and trimming made of animal paws pieced together; among those used are karakul, leopard, mink, Persian lamb and silver fox.

fur peltries   see *animal skins.*

fur, pieced   trimmings and garments are made of remnants of peltries using tails, paws and the lighter underparts. The bits of lamb, karakul, fox, squirrel, etc., are matched and joined.

fur processing   many operations including curing, tanning, dressing, dyeing, tipping, topping and feathering.

furbelows   the Anglicized word for French *falbalas*, used in the late seventeenth and eighteenth centuries to describe the decorations on court costumes, flounces, tassels, fringe, lace, braid and heavy embroidery.

furs, summer   between 1910 and 1915 fur bands ornamented gowns of chiffon and lace worn in summer, a short-lived use in trimming. By the 1940's, fur wraps

frontlet, gola chain black velvet hood-cap with frills— English-15th C.

in the form of capelets, stoles, boleros and sling jackets were in use for summer wear in the city and at resorts.

furs, tipped, topped, feathered   terms meaning that only the tips of the long guard hairs have been dyed, with a fine brush.

furs, unprime   furs taken from animals during molting season, when not in the best condition.

fused collar   see *collar, fused.*

fustanella   the short, very full and stiffly pleated kilt of the evzone, a Greek Highland soldier.

fustian   a stout cotton or flax cloth used by the Normans, especially the clergy. Originally of Oriental origin, it had been woven since the Crusades. Made in solid color, usually gray or brown, tufted or striped and sometimes rich-looking. see *beaver fustian.*

fustanella and blouse, white linen-embroidered blue cloth caftan-red cap, black tassel-Greek guard

fustanella and shirt of white cotton or linen-brown cloth bolero-slashed sleeves-Greek Highland soldier or evzone

G

Gabriel princess gown- gray silk over a crinoline- white collar- yellow gloves - 1867

gabardine   originally Spanish, *gabardina* or *paño,* meaning a woolen cloak. The woolen cloth with a raised diagonal weave which wears well. Cotton gabardine may be preshrunk and made water-repellent. In rayon, it resembles cotton gabardine. Its uses include raincoats, riding habits, uniforms, skirts, slacks and sportswear.

gabardine   name of the Jewish gown or mantle worn during the Middle Ages, usually of black cloth, silk or moiré. Ankle-length and buttoned in front to the waist.

gable headdress   the English gable- or diamond-shaped headdress; though decorative in design, it was a severe form of the hood. It was worn by older women and entirely concealed the hair. Comprising gable, wimple and gorget, the fashion lasted from 1500 to 1550.

Gabriel princess gown   a dress fitted and gored from neck and shoulder to hem, which appeared first in the 1860's and remaining popular into the first decade of the twentieth century. It was made of gray silk, fastened the length of the front with buttons or tiny bowknots and finished with a narrow white collar and a bit of black guipure braid.

gaiter or **congress shoe**   man's boot of leather with uppers of brocaded silk and side gores of elastic webbing which eliminated the opening; 1850's. see *bottine; spats.*

Gabardine-the outer cloak of Jews during the Middle Ages-hood with liripipe- 15th C.

Gable hood with wimple and gorget of white linen-long veil in back-English- 1500

gaiter trousers- or Wellington breeches with under strap- 1820's

gaiter shoe gored with elastic webbing- 1880's

gaiters or spats worn by the dude- white or tan cloth with black shoes- 1890's

145

gaiter trousers, gaiter bottoms breeches cut snugly at the ankle, extending out over the instep and held down by a strap passing under the boot. First half nineteenth century.

gaiters a cloth or leather covering for ankle or leg buttoned at the sides and a buckled-strap under foot.

Galanos, James see *couture, haute.*

galants see *ribbons.*

galatea a stout, white cotton twill, printed or striped, used in beach, sports and children's shoes.

galilla; whisk a small neat collar of sheer lawn mounted on pasteboard or held out fan-shaped by a wire edge, accredited to Philip IV of Spain, (1621–1665). Its Spanish name was galilla; to the English and American colonists, it was a whisk. It was a semi-circular and was often edged with lace.

Galitzine, Princess Irene see *couture, haute.*

gallibiya the traditional cotton robe, long-sleeved and collarless of the Arabic-speaking world.

galligaskin, gaskin wide breeches or hose of the seventeenth century worn by seamen and sportsmen. In the early nineteenth century, they were leggings buckled and strapped under the foot.

galliochios, galoshes meaning Gaulish shoes. Wooden-soled shoes with leather straps which protected fine shoes from rough stone pavements. Worn from ancient Roman times, through European periods and American colonial days.

galloon, galon a fancy finishing braid used both in costume and upholstery work. A narrow passementerie of cotton, silk, velvet, gold or silver cording.

gallowes, galluses, braces, brettelles see *suspenders.*

galoshes, modern a thick wooden clog with wide leather strap or uppers. Also of water-proofed canvas with heavy rubber sole and fastened with metal clips. Known as arctics.

galuchat French for polished sharkskin, first used by Galuchat of Paris in the eighteenth century. He introduced pebbled or grained leather. see *shagreen; sharkskin.*

galyak, galyac flat thin fur of lamb or kid born prematurely or dead, with or without moiré design. Of poor wearing quality and used for trimming.

gamashes in the seventeenth century, leggings of cotton cloth or velvet worn with shoes and riding boots to protect the fine leather. Linen leggings remained the distinguishing mark of peasant or farmer for centuries. see *spatterdashes.*

gallibiya, kibr or caftan-silk with embroidered tasseled cord-kaffiyeh and agal-Saudi Arabia

galligaskin or gaskin-leather legging with straps and buckles-1815-1850

galoshes or wooden clogs to protect shoes on the street-lady's and gentlemens'. 17th C.

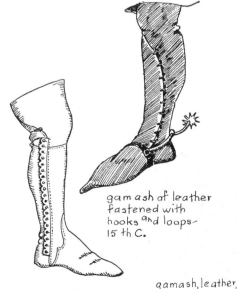

gamash of leather fastened with hooks and loops-15th C.

gamash of deerskin with buttons and separately cut vamp-English-mid 15th C.

gamash, leather, laced on inner side, 15th C. Often worn under boot during 15th and 16th C.

gambeson, pourpoint or jacket-stuffed with wool or cotton and quilted-worn by men, women and children

gambeson or **pourpoint**   a doublet, often sleeveless, of leather or cloth, stuffed and quilted. It was worn as a pad under armor in the Middle Ages and in civil dress by men, women and children.

gambeto   a thick woolen cloth short topcoat worn by the men of Catalonia in Spain instead of the mantua or plaid.

Gandhi cap   see *cap, Gandhi.*

gandoura, gandourah, gondura   a long-sleeved or sleeveless shirt or chemise of cotton or wool worn in North Africa by men and women.

gansey   see *guernsey.*

Garibaldi shirt, camicia rossa   a woman's shirtwaist popular in the

Garibaldi-famed Italian hero whose red flannel shirt became the rage in the 1860's

1860's. It was a copy of the tailored red cloth shirt worn by the Italian patriot Garibaldi and his soldiers. It had long sleeves gathered to a wristband, a small turned-down collar and a tailored bosom with four buttons.

garland   a headband or fillet, usually of wool, worn by priests in Greek and Roman antiquity.

garment, garmenture   any piece of body wearing apparel.

garnet   a popular stone in Victorian jewelry. The favored color of the garnet is deep crimson and transparent; the gem may be any color but blue—there are no blue garnets. They are found in Russia, Canada and Pennsylvania, and the Near East where they were highly prized in classical times.

garter   any band or supporting strap to hold up a sock or stocking. Until the mid-nineteenth century, before the invention of elastic cloth or webbing, garters were ties of silk, cloth or leather often embroidered and sometimes adorned with rosettes. Norwich garters, as worn by the New England colonists in the early seventeenth century, were silk bands tied in large bowknots.

gartering   of Anglo Saxon costume, little exists earlier than the tenth century. Contemporary writers mention *"brech* and *hose"* cross-gartered in cloth, woolen and leather bands. Linen bands distinguished the monks from the laity, who wore woolen gartering. Gilded straps marked the head of a clan. In the Middle Ages men's chausses (stockings) reached to the waist, where they were tied to a belt, and women's chausses reached above the knee, tied by bands or ribbons.

gaskin   see *galligaskin.*

gatyák   long, flaring white pantaloons of cloth resembling a divided riding skirt and worn as such by the Hungarian cow-

gandoura, white cotton undergarment-flowered huke-black yasmak-Arabia

Gatyak-fringed white linen pantaloons and blouse-felt hat and bolero-Hungarian cowboy-contemporary

gazelle antelope of Africa

gauntlet of the mousquetaire-embroidered and fringed-17th C.

gaucho, Argentina-chiripa worn over shoulders-white cotton shirt-long full pantaloons-contemporary

boy. The pantaloons are finished with a coarse white fringe or peasant-made crochet lace. Twentieth century.

gaucho   the cowboy of Argentina, who wears a distinctive costume: the shiripa, a skirt formed of a square woolen blanket wrapped around the hips and held by a heavy, elaborate silver belt; white cotton shirt; and pantaloons tucked into high boots. Over his arm, he carries a woolen poncho and an ornamental quirt. Twentieth century.

gauge   in stockings, the number of stitches in each $1\frac{1}{2}$ inches of the nylon fabric. The higher the gauge number, the stronger the stocking.

gauntlet   a glove with a protective forearm cuff. see *glove; mousquetaire*.

gauze   a sheer, transparent fabric first made in Gaza, Palestine. Of silk, cotton or rayon, its use depending upon the yarn of which it is made, whether veilings, dresses, curtains or surgical dressings.

gauze, silk   a curtaining of thin silk in plain weave; also of cotton or rayon in leno weave.

gazelle   hide or leather from a small member of the antelope family, the best known species from Africa, Arabia and Persia. Graceful and delicately formed, the gazelle is usually brownish with silver-tone or white stomach. The sheered pelt is used for casual coats.

gem   a precious stone cut or polished. A jewel is a precious stone set and worn as an ornament.

gem cuts   *baguette*, a flat table-cut in the form of a long, narrow rectangle. *Brilliant*, mid-seventeenth century; said to have been invented by Cardinal Mazarin to increase the diamond cutter's trade. The pyramid forms and facets are doubled, making for greater brilliancy. *Cabochon:* formerly an uncut and polished stone in convex form. Now cut in convex form or smooth-arched dome and highly polished but not faceted. *Emeraude* or *emerald*, a step cut in which the shape of the gem is square or rectangular. *Marquise*, a cut in which the gem is generally elliptical in shape but with pointed ends. *Old-Mine*, a diamond cut in a now obsolete nineteenth-century style, producing less sparkle than the modern brilliant. *Rose-Cut* or *Rosette*, developed by gem-cutters in Amsterdam, 1520. A rose-cut stone is like a squat pyramid with flat base and facets in multiples of six. Small diamonds and fine garnets are often so cut. *Step* or *Trap Cut:* oblong in form with a heavy, broad table forming a series of straight facets which give the appearance of steps as they decrease in length. *Table-Cut:* evolved from the double, pyramidal shapes placed together, the points cut away. There are many variations today which may be square or oblong with four or more facets on the underside of the stone. Emeralds and sapphires are occasionally table-cut. The girdle of a gem is the edge which is grasped by the outer rim or setting.

gem weights   the metric carat is recognized as standard weight for gems. For pearls, the weight is a grain, equal to a quarter of a carat.

genappe   a smooth worsted yarn used in braid and fringes.

genet, spotted cat   the pelt of a small European spotted cat allied to the civets, from southern France, Spain and Greece. The name also applies to the European black cat reared for its pelt, soft, well-furred and more generally used in Europe than America. Common genet is dark gray spotted with black and has been in use from the Middle Ages. Use for trimming on clothing dates back to the sixth century A.D. Very little used in America, but in demand in European markets.

Geneva gown and bands   long, loose, clergyman's gown with large sleeves. Of black silk or woolen cloth buttoned down the front, a pair of white lawn bands at the neck.

Genoa lace   Genoa, Italy, was a lace-making center in the seventeenth century. It was known for bobbin, tape, macramé, needlepoint and gold and silver laces.

Genoese embroidery   done in buttonhole stitches worked over a cord of linen and the fabric cut away between the motifs. A trimming used for dress and lingerie.

georgette   see *crepe georgette.*

Gernreich, Rudi   see *couture, haute.*

gertrude   the long tunic of earliest times, worn by both sexes from the Carolingian period to the thirteenth century, when it became a general garment for infants, a baby's flannel petticoat. It was named for Saint Gertrude, (1256–1311) who was born in Saxony. Some babies, especially in Europe, still wear flannel petticoats and the name "gertrude" is still used.

geta   a Japanese clog for all kinds of weather, worn for centuries. It varies in height from two to six inches and varies widely in design.

gew-gaw   a trinket, pretty and showy but worthless.

Gibson Girl or **Shirtwaist Girl**   the type of woman immortalized by the American artist, Charles Dana Gibson (1867–1944). She wore a simple blouse of starched white linen and Ascot scarf with a habit-back tailored skirt, hair in a pompadour and sailor hat.

gibus   see *hat, gibus.*

gilet   a type of vest. The contemporary feminine gilet is a sleeveless blouse or bodice front worn under a suit jacket or to fill in the neckline of a dress.

gillie, ghillies   a shoe of the Anglo-Saxons of rawhide without a tongue but laced through self-loops by thong or woolen gartering over linen or woolen leggings.

gilt   a wash of gold or brass color applied to metal, especially jewelry, so as to make it resemble gold. Jewelry so treated is termed gilt or gold-plated. see *pinchbeck.*

gimp   a flat, narrow, ornamental braid of silk, cotton or wool often interwoven

Japanese white percale tabi fastened in back-wooden geta

Famous Shirtwaist Girl by Charles Dana Gibson, white linen shirtwaist with linen Ascot scarf

with coarse silk or metallic wire. An upholstery finish also used for costume. see *guipure*.

gingham   a popular cotton fabric of pre-dyed yarn in a plain weave but of several colors in checks, plaids and stripes.

girandole   in jewelry, an earring with several pendants or small stones framing a larger one.

girdle   a short, light corset confining the body below the waistline. see *corset*.

Givenchy, Hubert de   see *couture, haute*.

glacé kid   glove leather, smooth, glossy, and highly polished. see *kid, glacé*.

Gladstone collar   see *collar, Gladstone*.

glass fibers   produced by forcing out molten glass into a continuous thread form. Resistant to heat, moisture and chemicals.

glass suits   worn for the first time in 1965 by most of the automobile drivers in the Indianapolis 500 race. The light-weight suits protect the wearer against heat and fire. Fiberglas, trademark for fine filament glass fiber owned by Corning Fiberglas Corp.

glasses, harlequin   see *harlequin glasses*.

glasses, opera   see *opera glasses*.

glazing   a process of applying a smooth, glossy surface to a fabric, e.g., chintz or leather coated with paraffin, then calendered by being passed between heated rollers.

glen checks   one of the Scottish Glen or District checks, each one a plaid unique to the particular district.

glen plaid   a pattern of very narrow lines crossing at right angles; generally in subdued tones of brown, gray and black or navy, on a neutral background, some-times crossed at intervals with a single thread of red or bright blue or other conspicuous color. Used for suitings.

Glen Urquhart   a Scottish plaid of dark blue, dark green and black, overlaid with a fine scarlet line crossing at right angles in boxlike formation.

Glengarry cap   see *cap, Glengarry*.

Glengarry cloth   an English home-spun tweed made of the waste stock of woolen yarns.

glove   a shaped covering for the hand enclosing each finger separately in a sheath. Archaeologists claim that hand covers or gloves of leather were worn by cavemen as long ago as other leather garments, which could be hundreds of thousands of years. Such gloves were roughly dressed and sewn with a bone needle. Knitted gloves have been found in Egyptian tombs. Although gloves were worn by workmen to protect their hands, neither Persian, Greeks nor Romans wore gloves for warmth. Warriors wore gloves, as did hunters. Falconers wore gloves made of deerskin and dogskin. Gloves appeared in Europe on the hands of kings and bishops, becoming by the ninth cen-tury a symbol of power and part of official and religious dress. The medieval knight wore his lady's glove in his helmet at tournaments and battles. Most gloves were shaped like mittens, separate fingers not appearing in Europe until the eleventh century. French glovers under Louis XIV invented glacé kid gloves.

glove fastenings   The pull-on or slip-on glove has always existed but in the late nineteenth century the wrist-length

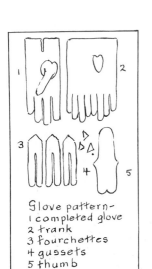

Glove pattern-
1 completed glove
2 trank
3 fourchettes
4 gussets
5 thumb

glove for ladies was closed by means of tiny pearl buttons and buttonholes. There was also a style with silk cord which laced alternating hooks from the wrist down. A recent style is the fastening on the back of the hand from the base of the fingers down, by a zipper or buttons and buttonholes.

glove, free-finger or **three dimensional**   from the trade name of a glove designed (1938) with a strip making the side walls of all five fingers in one piece.

glove lengths   wrist-length (shortie) one-button; mid-forearm, four- or five-button; elbow, eight-button; above elbow, twelve-button; shoulder, sixteen-button.

glove, shortie   a short or wrist-length glove of the Victorian Age which was revived as a slip-on, especially in chamois, in the 1920's and later in cotton, nylon, and leathers.

glove stretcher   a long, slim pair of wooden or ivory tweezers to stretch the glove fingers before putting on, often necessary in the days of tight-fitting gloves.

glover's stitch   the seams are to the outside of the glove and alternately stitched on each side, the thread drawn through on one side and then on the other.

gloves, York tan   see *York tan gloves.*

goat, angora   see *angora goat.*

goat, gray   fur of a half-grown goat which has turned gray; used for trimming.

goat, pulled or **mouflon**   Mongolian goat with guard hair plucked, leaving long, silky, furlike hair resembling the wild sheep known as mouflon in gray, white or smoky-blue.

goatee, goatbeard   a man's chin beard trimmed into a long, spiky tuft like the beard of the male goat.

goatskin   a leather prepared in all finishes and colors and dressed to imitate antelope and deerskin. Nearly all of the goatskin in American-made shoes is imported from the Far East.

gob cap   see *cap, gob.*

godet, gore, gusset   a tapering or triangular piece of cloth inserted for extra width or flare. An umbrella is made of gore-shaped pieces, and skirts are often gored. With the appearance of elastic webbing in the nineteenth century, gored shoes came into vogue for both men and women.

Godey's Lady's Book   the first American woman's magazine, a periodical dealing with women's fashions, needlework and etiquette. It was founded in Philadelphia in 1830 by Antoine Godey and published until 1898.

goffering   see *fluting.*

gold cloth or **tissue**   cloth with metal warp of gold color and silk weft. An evening fabric for wraps, gowns and trimming.

gold lace   formerly made of gold wire; later a lace of braid with silk weft threads covered with gilt or gold leaf.

golf   the feminine outfit for golfing in the 1890's called for a tailored linen shirtwaist with separate skirt, a Norfolk jacket or a short golf cape of tweed which matched the skirt, and a little felt fedora. The tailored shirtwaist or shirtwaist dress was replaced by a real sports frock in the 1920's. Worn over shorts, it buttoned down center front. It appeared in the 1930's and was suitable for both golf and tennis.

goatee beard

black silk top hat-French-1890's

gondolier net of
black silk braid
with ribbon -
French - 1870's

greatcoat,
carrick or
coachman's
coat - heavy,
warm coat -
1814

golf hose   heavy knitted woolen or worsted hose with a deep, decorative cuff which turns down below the knee. Worn with knickerbockers.

golf shoes   Oxfords made with protruding buttons or nails on the soles to prevent slipping.

gondolier net   fashion of the 1870's; a wide-meshed hairnet of narrow black braid or ribbon held by a cadogan bow in back and sometimes by one on top of the head.

gondoura   see *gandoura*.

gore   see *godet; gusset*.

gorget   originally a collarlike piece of steel armor protecting the throat. By 1600 steel armor tended to disappear, the buff-coat taking its place. Only the steel or silver gorget, a small crescent-shaped piece suspended from a fine chain around the neck, remained, engraved with the officer's grade. It was worn with full uniform by both American and British officers in the Revolutionary War. The word *gorget* was also applied to some wimples and headkerchiefs when covering the feminine head and throat.

gorro   the traditional cap of the Catalonians in Spain. A knitted yarn stocking cap and very often two, a tasseled one hanging down in back and a second on top drooping over the forehead. In red, purple and brown.

gourgandine   a corselet of silk or velvet with few stays, laced in front, of the late Louis XIV period. It was worn en negligée with a handsome petticoat until the hour of dressing and putting on a real corset.

gown   from the Saxon word *gunna*, a long, loose garment worn by all Anglo-Saxon women for centuries. It was also called a cote, surcoat or robe. From the fourteenth to the seventeenth centuries, the word gown was applied to any long, loose robe, masculine or feminine. In the sixteenth century the fashionable man wore a gown over his doublet or jerkin. It was circular in cut, open in front, short or long, and capelike. Gown, today, is also used for the robe, academic or clerical, of either sex, and for evening dresses.

gown, academic   see *academic gown*.

Goya, Francisco José de (1746–1828) Spanish court painter to Charles III and Charles IV. He followed Velásquez and like him, left many memorable portraits illustrating the court styles of his day.

grain leather   see *leather, grain*.

Granada   the Italian *granito* or grainy-surfaced cloth, a fine-finished fabric of worsted stock.

granite cloth   a lightweight, durable fiber made of twisted yarns and sometimes linen; a figured weave in a pebbly, hard-finished surface. Used for men's and women's outer-wear.

grass cloth   a fabric made in China, loosely woven of vegetable fibers. It comes in the natural brown color, bleached or dyed; used for sportswear.

gray   a combination in varying degrees of white and black. Pearl gray is one of the lightest shades, charcoal gray one of the darkest.

gray, charcoal or carbon   a very dark gray, almost black, fashionable for men's suits after World War II.

gray goods   see *grège*.

greatcoat   any heavy overcoat.

greaves   see *cnemis*.

Ancient Greek

king in
himation
and long
chiton

chlamys
and double
girded
chiton

Ionic
chiton

chlamys
and broad
brimmed
hat

Doric
woolen
chiton

long tunic
himation
and hat-
petasos

Mycenaean
1500 B.C.

Ionic
linen chiton
himation

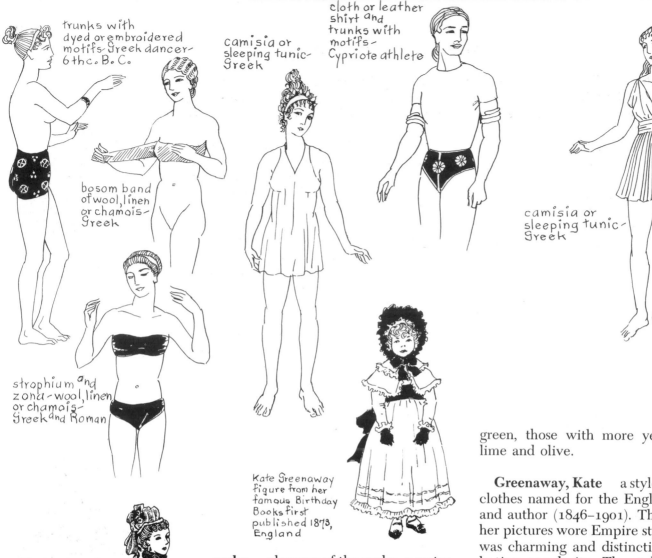

trunks with dyed or embroidered motifs-Greek dancer-6th c. B.C.

bosom band of wool, linen or chamois-Greek

camisia or sleeping tunic-Greek

cloth or leather shirt and trunks with motifs-Cypriote athlete

camisia or sleeping tunic-Greek

strophium and zona-wool, linen or chamois-Greek and Roman

Kate Greenaway figure from her famous Birthday Books first published 1873, England

"Grecian bend" due to bustle-plum-colored and lilac velvet with fur-1873

grebe plumage of the grebe, a water-bird of the loon family; silky, smooth and downlike in ivory flecked with brown. Formerly used for millinery, muffs and accessories.

Grecian bend a popular name for the fashionable lady's stance in the 1870's and 1880's when the wasp waist and bustle prevailed.

Greek costume, ancient see illustrations, page 153 and above.

Greek lace same as reticella in a heavy needlepoint lace.

green one of the three secondary colors which are green, purple and orange. Green is a combination of blue and yellow. The shades with a greater proportion of blue include jade and bottle green, those with more yellow include lime and olive.

Greenaway, Kate a style in children's clothes named for the English illustrator and author (1846–1901). The children in her pictures wore Empire style. Her work was charming and distinctive and had a lasting popularity. The style survives in the attire of child attendants in many wedding parties.

grège any fabric in untreated condition as it comes from the loom before bleaching, dyeing or finishing. Grège is also used as a fashion term for a grayish-beige color.

gremial veil an embroidered cloth or apron spread over the knees of a bishop when seated during high mass.

grenadine a silk popular in the late nineteenth century; much like marquisette and used for blouses, dresses and men's neckwear.

greys, or **petit gris** the fine white belly fur of the very small Siberian squirrel with gray black. Precious, and called "menu vair," it was used in the medieval period to line the mantles of kings, professors and court counselors.

grillage   the grill work or bars across open spaces in lacework.

grisette   a gay, free-mannered working girl in Louis XIV's day. So called because all Frenchwomen of humble condition wore dresses made of *grisette*, a coarse gray woolen fabric.

gros de londres   lightweight silk or rayon dress goods with ribs of alternating width. It is piece-dyed and made changeable or warp print in effect. A glossy finish is given the cloth that is intended for the millinery trade and dresses.

grosgrain   a stout, close-woven silk fabric or ribbon corded from selvedge to selvedge.

grosgram   a fabric popular with country women of England and the American Colonies. It has a diagonal weave of silk and wool or all wool with a rough finish. Formerly manufactured in Scotland, where heavy travel cloaks were made of it.

gros point   also known as Gros Point de Venise. A Venetian point lace with raised work and large motifs.

gros point   any embroidery worked on canvas with less than sixteen meshes per inch. There is no special gros point stitch. Aubusson stitch or Gobelin stitch are sometimes used, tent or cross stitch being more common.

guanaco, guanaquito   larger of the two wild species, guanaco and vicuña, of the South American family of which domesticated varieties are llama and alpaca. They are found high in the Peruvian Andes. Formerly, only guanacos less than twenty days old were used for fur. A soft, woolly, pale fur, reddish brown, similar to vicuña but coarser, used natural or dyed brown and dressed to simulate lynx.

guard's coat   man's traveling coat, long and loose, of tweed or homespun with inverted pleat in center back, and deep side folds held in place by a half-belt. Early twentieth century.

guepière   from the French for wasp. A small lightweight corset made to produce a tiny waist, trim above and slightly rounded below. It appeared in 1945, paving the way to the "New Look."

guernsey   a sailor's knitted woolen shirtlike garment which originated in the Channel Islands. Guernseyed means "to be wearing a guernsey."

guimpe   a short blouse of sheer white lawn or batiste with sleeves, collar and frilled neck, worn with a pinafore style of dress in the late nineteenth and early twentieth centuries. It had been a distinctive feature of the costume of the early sixteenth century, both sexes wearing the lingerie guimpe showing above the squared neckline of the period. In the twentieth century it was worn by little girls for several decades.

guipure   a heavy lace, the patterns or motifs raised into relief by twisted cords, made without a ground, the design connected by bars.

gun club checks   a pattern produced in worsted, flannel and tweed, in checks of different colors and alternating rows. Made for men's and women's wear in street dress and sportswear.

gusset   originally a piece of chain mail or plate inserted in the joints of armor for reinforcement. see *godet*.

gypsy or **Romany stripes**   of brilliant colors and varying widths, based upon designs of fabrics worn by Spanish gypsy dancers.

gypsy girl of Granada, Spain- red checked cotton dress- red satin bands-fringed, embroidered black shawl- white stockings- black slippers

H

haberdashery   a retail shop selling men's furnishings. Both the shop and the wares are called haberdashery and the dealer is a haberdasher.

habergeon, haubergeon   a high-necked, long-sleeved, hip-length tunic of chain or ring mail worn over a cloth smock by horsemen in the fifteenth century, with a leather belt to hold the sword.

habiliment   dress; attire; vestment.

habit-back skirt   a tailored sports skirt of the late Victorian period. It was usually of heavy cloth, well fitted over the hips with a reinforced, ankle-length flaring hem. An inverted pleat at center back stitched partway down accounts for the term "habit-back." see *Gibson girl*.

habutai, habutae, habutaye   a light-weight silk originally woven on hand looms, now woven on power looms in the Orient. Heavier than China silk and in natural color, it is used for dresses, blouses, jackets, office coats and pajamas.

haik   a long piece of cotton or woolen cloth, according to weather, which envelops the Algerian woman in public. It is draped over the tarboosh and the body, belted at the waist, covering the chalwar and pantaloons. Mostly of hand-woven wool, plain or striped, the haik has been and continues to be worn by both sexes of Arabs, Moors and Mohammedans for centuries. see *huke*.

hair, bobbed   see *bobbed hair*.

hair cloth   a resilient material woven of cotton or linen warp with the weft of horsehair from tail or mane. Used as a stiffening interlining in jackets or coats and in upholstery.

hair coloring   a practice many centuries old which became widespread in the mid-twentieth century with the improvement of materials and techniques. The fad for platinum blonde hair can be traced to the popularity of Jean Harlow, a cinema star of the 1930's.

hair net   an accessory centuries old, first made of silk by the Chinese. The caul or net of medieval times was made of silk or gold cord. In the 1850's the net was of braided silk, chenille or velvet ribbon fastened with small gilt buttons or buckles. Later came nets of human hair, and now they are made of nylon. see *caul*.

hair pieces   the modern commercial term for any false part of a hairdo or for a man's toupee. Women still use the word wig for a complete false hair cover. There are wiglets, switches and falls of human hair and artificial dynel. see *fall*.

hair seal   see *seal, hair*.

haircuts   see illustrations on opposite page.

hairdresser   one who designs and arranges coiffures, trims, curls or straightens, dyes, bleaches and shampoos hair.

hairlace   a net or fillet over the coiffure; a decorative fashion of the Victorian era.

Haik of white wool or cotton- worn by the Algerian woman- white lawn yashmak

Haircuts

spiral curls-wreath of olive leaves- military-Greek

frizzed hair- Persian- 9th c.B.C.

feather cut-leather fillet-charioteer- Greek

Egyptian king-wig of spiral curls- 2nd C. B.C

frame of Cypriote curls- Greek

natural hair or wig-ends rolled-Roman 4th c AD.

curls and tutulus of felt-Etruscan

bobbed hair- French-15th C.

center part moustache- mutton chops and monocle- English- 1870s

emperor's crown of laurel- ribbon- Roman- 4th C.

Norman and English- 9th c.

hair parted up and down- French Empire- c.1809

page boy- curled ends- felt béret- French-15th C.

center part- monocle- English- 1870's

football player's haircut- American-1890's

side part- 1st decade- 20th C.

cropped haircut- also called Crew, Varsity, Prussian or G.I. Bob- 1940's

157

hairline stripe   a light stripe of one-thread thickness woven into dark-colored worsted.

hairpins   from antiquity until the 1920's hairpins were fashioned of twigs, wood, bone, ivory, shell, wire and celluloid in bodkin or forked shape. But modern short hair required something different. It was solved by the bobby pin which was suggested by the wire cotter pin of modern machinery. Another twentieth century invention was the invisible hairpin of fine wire, very short and crinkled. see *bobby pin.*

half-slip   see *slip.*

haling hands   heavy work gloves worn by seamen and miners, usually of wool with leather palms. Haling derives from the word "hauling."

halter   a more or less triangular piece of sturdy material made to tie or fasten at the back of the neck and waist; for feminine wear as the only garment above the waist, leaving the arms and back bare for tanning.

halter neckline   a neckline new in the 1930's, high of neck at center front, shoulders bare and entirely bared in back. First designed for beach wear; a version for daytime and another for evening followed. The style continues to be in fashion.

hamster, golden hamster   small rodent found in parts of Europe and common in Russia and Germany. A lightweight and very flat fur, of pale yellowish brown marked with black. Used principally in Europe for men's coat linings.

handbag   a development of the twentieth century. Any small satchel or bag which holds a lady's daily traveling necessities. During periods of bouffant skirts, farthingales and hoops, there was no need of ladies' bags because large

halter neckline new in 1930's

pockets were concealed in skirt folds. As fashion changed to Directoire, a small pouch bag of handsome fabric embroidered and beaded came into vogue. This was the reticule or, humorously, "ridicule." During the style of the high-waisted, unlined Empire gowns, the soldier's leather cavalry bag or sabretache was copied in handsome fabric, embroidered, fringed and tasseled. Purses next became small and in the 1880's fabric bags had metal and jeweled mounts and steel beaded bags became favorites. In the 1890's, the new-styled pocketbook of leather was a flat, folding, book-shaped purse with compartments. In the first decade of 1900, small leather bags were popular until the saddle-bag returned. The large, flat envelope bag was of leather with many compartments and a large flap. In the 1920's and 1930's there were exquisite and costly small evening bags of fine bead embroidery and gold and silver linked mesh. The fittings of bags were now given as much thought as the exterior. Added to mirror, comb and change purse were the cigarette case and cigarette holder of beauty and value. In the present era of round-the-world travel, the large leather bag is a necessity for carrying passport, toiletries and such, as well as money. Bags for summer and sports are made in a wide variety of colorful materials and often may be simply baskets. see *shoulder bag.*

hand-blocked print   fabrics upon which the design has been printed by hand with either linoleum or wooden blocks.

hand-glasses   a nineteenth century New York name for spectacles and eyeglasses and lorgnettes.

handkerchief   a small square of linen, cotton or disposable tissue to use for wiping the nose, eyes or face. A larger square may be used as a neckerchief. Handkerchiefs may be used solely for decoration, as when tucked into the breast pocket of a man's or woman's suit. In Rome of the second century A.D. the handkerchief, a white linen square and a costly luxury, was in use on the stage in comedies and satires. Handkerchiefs were plentiful in the early Christian Era and were waved by spectators at the games. They became expensive accessories embroidered with silver and gilt and edged with fringe, forming part of church and coronation rituals. In the Medieval period, English ladies presented their men with small squares which were worn in the hatband. During the Renaissance fine sheer handkerchiefs were a fashion at the courts of France, Spain and England. Of Venetian make, they were of cambric, lawn or linen edged with beautiful lace, one corner weighted with a tassel, button or acorn. In the sixteenth century the use of all shapes and sizes of the handkerchief became general in Europe. Finally, by royal decree under Louis XIV in 1685, it became a square. Round and oval-shaped handkerchiefs had a short-lived vogue in the time of Louis XV. Early in the nineteenth century, the gentleman's handkerchief settled into an accepted size of about eighteen inches, of white linen with a hemstitched edge and an initial in one corner. The average-sized woman's handkerchief is twelve inches square. The vogue of the lace handkerchief, it is said, dates from the tearful departure of Marie-Antoinette from her beloved Austria to France. She dried her tears with a piece of lace from her gown. The ecclesiastic handkerchief, called a maniple, was carried in the hand and survives in the narrow band worn pendant from the left wrist by the celebrant at mass.

hand-pricked edge   used instead of machine-stitching on collar and lapel of a man's informal suit, a feature new in the 1930's.

hanging sleeve   see *sleeve, hanging.*

hank   a commercial length of yarn: as worsted yarn, 560 yards; silk, 120 yards; cotton, 840 yards; linen, 10 leas in England; 12 leas in Ireland and Scotland. A lea is a varying measure of yarn.

haori   a Japanese black silk coat for street wear over the kimono for men and women. The feminine, either long or knee-length, the man's knee-length and plain, while hers may be elaborately embroidered. Instead of the surplice closing of the kimono, his coat fastens in center front, tied by tiny silk cords. As on the man's kimono, the wearer's crest decorates the haori; a very small motif is embroidered or stenciled on either side of the chest, in center back and at the tops of the sleeves.

hard hat   see *boater.*

Hardanger bonnet   see *bonnet, Hardanger.*

Hardanger embroidery and **cutwork** a Norwegian embroidery worked in squares or diamond shapes on linen or canvas. All embroidery is completed before the unwanted ground is cut away. Used for edging fancy work, especially for aprons, blouses and dresses.

Hardanger skaut   traditional headgear of the Hardanger matron of Norway. A large square of stiffly starched white linen which is folded and fastened in back and worn in many different ways. The skaut is reminiscent of the headdress worn in the sixteenth century when folk dress began to take hold.

hare   fur from a rodent of the same genus as the rabbit, or jack rabbit, this latter name commonly used in the United States for both animals. The hare, larger than the rabbit, is from Central Europe and Central Siberia and used principally in the hatters' and textile trades. The colors are white, tan and bluish-gray. The very best breed in the fur industry is Belgian hare, a rather small, slender rabbit. This hare and also the chinchilla-dyed French rabbit are

skaut-Hardanger, Norway-large square of starched linen draped and pinned in place

hare "varying hare" white, tan or bluish-gray-colored in summer-white in winter. Arctic hare.

a variation of traditional Harlequin costume in black and white-red pompons

Harlequin frames-general or sports wear

alpine hat

cartwheel straw hat-black with black ribbon-French-1940's

remarkably similar to chinchilla. see *rabbit*.

hare, arctic   the long-haired hare comes from Siberia and Russia, those of arctic North America being few and not used by the fur trade. The long-haired animals are those processed to simulate white fox. White peltries are most desirable to the fur and hat trades, despite being higher priced because small in quantity.

harem skirt   see *skirt, harem*.

harem pants   see *pants, harem; culottes*.

harlequin   a character in British Pantomine derived from Arlecchino of the Italian Comedy Theatre. The traditional costume is a close-fitting one-piece garment of brightly colored diamond checks, long-sleeved and reaching to mid-calf; white stockings and black slippers; a shaven head usually simulated with a tight stocking cap; a mask with slanting eyeholes; and a lath sword. *Harlequin* used as an adjective has come to mean parti-colored.

harlequin glasses   spectacles with an upward tilt at the outer corners of the plastic frame. Introduced in the U.S. in 1944. So-called because of the resemblance to the mask traditionally worn by the Harlequin character in pantomime.

Harris Tweed   trade-mark of the Harris Tweed Association of London for a soft tweed woven on the islands of the Outer Hebrides, Harris, Lewis, etc., off the northwestern coast of Scotland. One fabric is woven from hand-spun yarn and another woven from machine-spun yarn. Used for men's and women's suits and topcoats.

Hartnell, Norman   see *couture, haute*.

Harvard shirting   a twilled cotton

cloth shirting, plain or striped, and similar to oxford cloth.

hat, Alpine or Tyrolese   a soft felt hat with a brim, generally dark green in color and banded with a dark green ribbon or a heavy cord. Usually ornamented with a feather of bristle brush.

hat, bambino   see *bambino hat*.

hat, beefeater's   see *beefeater's hat*.

hat, beaver   see *beaver hat*.

hat, bolero   a small hat with upturned boxlike brim, peaked crown, some pompons and a chin strap; worn by Spanish men when dancing the bolero.

hat, Bolivar   1783–1830, a style of felt hat worn by the great South American liberator when not in uniform.

hat, Breton sailor   see *Breton sailor*.

hat, cardinal's   see *cardinal's red hat*.

hat, cartwheel   a feminine hat with a low flat crown and a wide straight brim of even width. Usually a summer hat of straw which has appeared occasionally, in the eighteenth, nineteenth and twentieth centuries.

hat, cocked   see *Androsmane; bicorne*.

hat, continental   see *Androsmane*.

hat, coolie   a conical-shaped hat of straw, worn by men, women and children in China as protection against sun and rain.

hat, cowboy   see *hat, Stetson* or *ten gallon*.

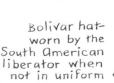

Bolivar hat- worn by the South American liberator when not in uniform

petasos-
ancient
Greek hat of
straw or felt-
from a Tanagra
statuette

the "little"
hennin-silk or
velvet-velvet frontlet-
French-15th C.

gray or
fawn-colored
cloth top hat-
English-1840's

sugar-loaf
felt bonnet-
French-15th C.

Hunting hat
over wimple-
Italian-14th C.

postilion
beaver riding hat-
powdered hair in cadogan-
1790's

black silk
hat-ribbon
band-
American 1921

leghorn
skimmer hat
over lawn cap-
English-1750's

Mexican
riding hat-gray
felt-black or
gray ribbon

black silk
topper-
French-1840's

straw sombrero-
chinstrap of colored
beads-Mexican

slouch hat
of felt-
American-
1850's

the Ten-gallon hat
of range and dude
ranch-American

bolero hat worn
over silk bandana-
black felt-
chinstrap
and pompons-
Spanish

Garibaldi's
braided pillbox cap
copied by women-1850's

doll's hat-
black ostrich-
pink cabbage
rose-velvet
ribbon-1930's

Merry
Widow straw sailor-
New York-1904

coolie hat of
straw over
headscarf-
worn by women
of Taiwan

Hats-

Albanian-
beaver
German-
1580

Spanish toqued
of velvet or
silk-jewel
band-
16th C.

Pilgrim's
hat with
buckle-
1620's

Ramillies cock-
black felt-
French-
1729

Quaker-
beaver-
silver
buckle
as worn in
Paris-1780's

bicorne of
Napoleon-black
felt-tricolor-1814

Style
Nivernois-American general-
1770's

Kevenhüller,
Androsmane
or Swiss hat-black
felt-cockade-
powdered hair-
in queue-
American general-
1780

black
bicorne-
hair tied in queue-
Spanish-circa 1800

beaver or
felt-silver
buckle-silk
band-
Puritan-1630's

black
japanned leather-
white edge-
powdered hair-
in queue-
American Marine
1775

162

Hats

mourning top hat-black silk with black faille band-worn by Abraham Lincoln

topee or topi-pith helmet-white cotton-green facing-1860's

Hungarian or pork pie hat with ribbons-1850's

Tyrolese felt hat with cord, tassel and feathers-1880's

Bersagliere-black glazed felt-coq plume-Italian-1850's

Homburg-gray felt and ribbon-worn by Prince of Wales-1890

straw boater-with silk band-monocle-English-1890's

black felt derby-1st decade-1900's

black silk topper-with d'Orsay roll-English-1880's

gray or tan felt with four dents-southern planter-American-late 19th C.

melon shape-felt or straw-worn in London, Paris and New York 1860's

163

1930 to 1940

gibus, opera or collapsible evening hat-black grosgrain or merino cloth-formal

black silk top hat-formal day or evening

polo cap-white cotton covered-reinforced

gray derby worn to the races-British

black silk hunting hat with guard

stitched tweed hat for country wear

felt riding hat-colored cord-Mexican

gray felt topper worn with cutaway coat-British

black Homburg-business or semi-formal evening

tweed grouse shooting hat

dark gray pork pie felt

Montego hat-vegetable fiber-for resort wear

black felt derby for day wear in town

snap brim-brown felt with feather

black hunting derby-reinforced

"ten-gallon hat" pale tan felt-ranch or range

tweed cap for sports

straw with dark red cotton puggree band

black velvet hunt cap-reinforced-worn with pink coat

brown leghorn-white shantung puggree band

two-tone straw-spotted silk puggree band

for duck shooting-tan gabardine-corduroy flaps

boater of sennit straw-silk club band

pith helmet for tropics-tan gabardine

panama with black grosgrain band

ski cap-dark blue gabardine-flaps inside-black ribbon

Basque béret-dark blue woolen woven in one piece

black felt Tyrolese hat-cord band-feathers

yachting cap-navy blue-gold insignia

deer shooting-bright red cloth-leather visor

164

hat, crew a sports hat of white cotton twill or natural-color linen, a four-pieced crown with button on top and ribbon band, and a stitched brim. Early 1900's. Currently a soft cotton hat with a small turned-down brim, worn to shield the eyes from glare while boating. Generally made of twill or denim and usually white; a gored crown topped with a small button, and a stitched brim.

Hat-crew hat-white cotton twill or natural color linen

hat, derby see *derby hat.*

hat, doll a small, coquettish shape with tiny ostrich plumes which was in vogue for a short period after the appearance in the 1930's of the Empress Eugénie hat. The fashion was followed by Schiaparelli's little doll hats, frivolous headpieces instead of hats, 1950's.

hat, Empress Eugénie a small, coquettish hat with tiny ostrich plumes. Its tremendous vogue in the 1930's was short.

hat, Gainsborough or **Marlborough** of black velvet or taffeta with mauve ostrich plumes and taffeta ribbons. Called Gainsborough by the British because it was often painted by Thomas Gainsborough (1727–1788). To the French, it was the Marlborough because it was worn by the Duchess of Marlborough and also because of a popular French song, "Chanson de Malbrouck." The black velvet hat was revived in the first decade of the twentieth century.

hat, gibus a collapsible opera hat of black silk faille invented and made by a Paris hatmaker named Gibus. Built over a strong spring, it closed to a flat shape for carrying under the arm. It first appeared in Paris in 1823 and was patented in 1837. Worn by gentlemen with full evening dress until the mid-twentieth century when it became smart to dispense altogether with a hat.

hat, gob's a hat of white cotton twill with four-pieced crown and stitched brim.

"Gob" is slang for the U.S. sailor. 20th century. see *cap, gob.*

hat, hard see *boater.*

hat, Hungarian or **slouch** of black felt with a rolling brim and two ribbon ends floating in back. Dates from the visit of Lajes Kossuth, the great Hungarian patriot, to England and America in 1852–1853. see *pork pie.*

hat, iron see *helmet; chapel de fer.*

hat, Korean see *Korean hat.*

hat, Marlborough see *Gainsborough hat.*

hat, mushroom see *mushroom hat.*

hat, Neapolitan a woman's summer hat with wide floppy brim and conical crown. Sheer, it was made of lacy horsehair braid or woven fiber. Usually black or straw-colored, it was originally made in Naples. Early 1900's.

hat, opera see *hat, gibus.*

hat, Panama a hat made from finely hand-plaited straw from carefully selected young leaves of the jipijapa plant. The hat is made in Ecuador, Peru and Colombia, but not Panama. It had been made for nearly three centuries when discovered by American soldiers in 1895 and so was named for Panama where it was marketed. It had been worn for a long time by the British in the tropics and in

clerical felt hat uncocked-German-18th C.

Hat-"gob's" hat of white cotton twill-four-pieced crown and stitched brim.

Gainsborough or Marlborough hat-black taffeta mauve plumes and ribbon-1870's

western scout hat of felt in light brown or gray-19th C.

"Henry Higgins's hat"
wool tweed worn by
the character in the
play "My Fair Lady" –
1950's

Pennsylvania,
Holland or
Quaker hat –
beaver, brown
or gray, 2nd half
17th century

Robin Hood

Shovel-hat worn by
Anglican and Roman
clergy

the American South where it was known as the planter's hat.

hat, picture   see *picture hat*.

hat, Pilgrims'   usually a wide-brimmed black felt hat with ribbon and a small silver buckle. Most Puritans and Pilgrims preferred very plain dress, seldom changing the style. Seventeenth century.

hat, planter's   see *hat, Panama*.

hat, pork pie   a feminine hat of the Victorian Era, small and round, known in England as the pork pie hat. Two long ribbons floating in back were named "follow me, young man." There was also a masculine pork pie hat in the same period.

hat, postilion or **postillion**   a beaver hat with high, flat-top crown and silver-buckled ribbon band. French, 1790's.

hat, Puritan   see *hat, Pilgrims'*

hat, Quaker   a "wide-awake" hat of felt or beaver with the brim rolling or cocked and commonly gray or brown. Second half of the seventeenth century.

hat, Robin Hood   a style associated with the legendary twelfth century English outlaw. A soft felt with turned-up brim, pointed crown and a long pheasant feather.

hat, sailor's   until the 1770's, a small leather tricorne which changed to a small round hard hat with a narrow brim, of varnished or japanned leather. Late in the eighteenth century the same shape appeared but of shellacked sennit, a straw. This hat was adopted by Eton College to honor Admiral Lord Nelson; it is still worn and known as a boater. see *boater; hard hat; cap, gob*.

hat, shovel   a black felt hat with low, round crown and plain flat brim turned up on both sides, protruding back and front and looking like a shovel. Worn by Anglican and Roman clerics.

hat, slouch   see *hat, Hungarian*.

hat, steeple   see *hennin*.

hat, Stetson, or **ten-gallon**   the sombrero of the American western cowboy which came to be known as the Stetson because John B. Stetson, a Philadelphia hatmaker in the 1870's, decided to produce a quality hat for cowboys.

hat, Tansui   a hat resembling the Panama, made of plant leaves grown at Tansui in Taiwan.

hat, ten-gallon   see *hat, Stetson*.

hat, top, high, silk   According to one story the high silk hat was invented in Canton about 1775 by a Chinese hatter for a Frenchman, who carried his headpiece back to Paris. Another story is that the silk hat was invented in 1760 in Florence. The hat was seen in the early 1820's but did not reach perfection until the 1830's when it was generally adopted. It was first made of polished beaver, called silk beaver, but later fashioned of plush. The d'Orsay roll was the important feature of the man's top hat in the 1830's, as it was worn by Count Gabriel d'Orsay (1801–1852). Amateur of the fine arts and a society leader in Paris and London, he was the greatest swell of his day. A few Anglo-American names for the top hat were round hat; topper or silker; John Bull, 5 and 3/4 inches high; stovepipe, 7 inches high; chimney-pot, 7 1/2 inches high; kite-high dandy, 7 3/8 inches high.

hatpin   a necessary accessory in the late Victorian and early twentieth century period. About eight inches long; often used in pairs, it secured the hat to the high-dressed coiffure. It was topped by an ornament, often gold and jeweled.

haubergeon   same as hauberk but a shorter garment.

hauberk   a hooded, long-sleeved, knee-length garment of chain or ring mail worn by nobles in the twelfth and thirteenth centuries. It was worn with a belt of leather, a steel helmet and leg and foot bands of mail.

haute couture   see *couture, haute.*

havanese or **Havana embroidery** conventional or geometric designs buttonhole-stitched in colors on heavy fabrics.

havelock—
cotton curtain
to protect neck
and cap from
the sun—Civil War

havelock   a curtain of white washable cloth which covered and protected neck and cap, copied for the soldiers in the American Civil War. Though worn by ancient Persian soldiers, it bears the name of the British General in the Sepoy mutiny, 1857, Sir Henry Havelock.

headpiece   see *fall.*

headrail   the headdress of Anglo-Saxon women from the fifth to the eleventh centuries. Of linen or cotton, it was circular, square or oblong and was wrapped around the neck like the Persian or Roman chin cloth. It was held in place by a metal fillet or crown.

heartbreakers   wired curls which trembled constantly, a fashion of the seventeenth century, worn at the nape and cheeks.

heather mixture   trade name for a combination of varicolored interwoven fibers giving the effect of heather on a moor. Used principally in tweeds and some other woolen fabrics. Used for suits and coats in men's and women's wear.

heaume   In medieval days the jousting heaume, a large helmet, was the general headdress in games and pageants, though various other styles of helmets were worn. The heaume was draped with a scarf of soft leather or silk with dagged edges and it was so attached to the heaume that it pivoted gaily in the wind. The drapery was known as the mantling or lambrequin. see *cointoise.*

hedebo embroidery   cutwork and drawnwork embroidery usually white on white and originally used by Danish peasants to ornament all garments and household linens. Used today on sheer white for collars, handkerchiefs and table linen.

hedgehog wig   see *wig, hedgehog.*

heel   The heel has been in use in the Orient for centuries. The ancient Egyptian butcher wore heels when slaughtering cattle; the Persians used heels to raise the feet off the burning sand; and the East Indians and Mongolians kept the foot in the stirrup by means of a small heel. From the flat pattens and clogs came the idea of the modern heel, which was first worn at the Italian and Spanish courts, and supposedly was the idea of Leonardo da Vinci. In the eighteenth century the gracefully curved three-inch French heel became known as the Louis XV heel returning to fashion several times since. The red heel of nobility was of Venetian origin and appeared first in the sixteenth century on the black leather shoes of royal valets and slaves.

heel, baby Louis   the low form of the Louis XV heel for women's shoes.

heel, Cuban   of medium height and

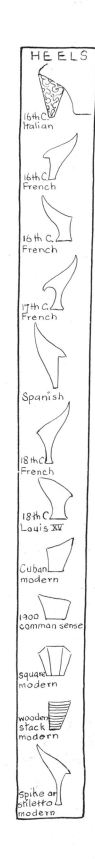

HEELS

16th C. Italian

16th C. French

16th C. French

17th C. French

Spanish

18th C. French

18th C. Louis XV

Cuban modern

1900 common sense

square modern

wooden stack modern

Spike or stiletto modern

usually built in layers or lifts of leather. Used for walking shoes.

heel, continental, French, Spanish similar in shape and very high, the difference being in the inside curve. Usually of wood covered with leather.

heel, platform   see *wedge* or *platform sole.*

heel, spike or **stiletto**   in vogue for the past several decades. Higher than the French heel, very slim and built with metal tips.

heel, sports   low, flat, and broad, and usually of layers of leather. Used for men's, women's and children's shoes.

heel, stacked   well-shaped, tapering wooden heel of varied height. Built of slim layers of wood, hence the term "stacked."

heel, wedge   see *wedge* or *platform sole.*

helmet   in general, any defensive covering for the head; specifically the headpiece in armor. The helmet of antiquity was made of boiled leather, the leather having been boiled in oil, wax or water and then steamed for hardness. The helmet of Europe following the fall of Rome was a hat fashioned of leather on a wooden frame reinforced with metal. It was a shell-like design with a serrated comb or crest of iron. About 1440 the Italians invented a small rounded shell of iron or steel with plating over the ears, neck and chin and a movable visor. Modern warfare has brought back some ancient pieces such as the padded helmet of steel or tin hat.

helmet, Bonaparte   see *Bonaparte helmet.*

helmet, pith   see *topee, topi.*

helmet, tilting   a heavy, large helmet worn in medieval jousting tournaments, a contest in which a knight would tilt another knight off his horse.

hem   the border of a garment made by folding back the edge and sewing it in place.

hem, false   see *facing.*

hem, French   a pinked edge reinforced with a line of machine stitching $\frac{1}{8}$ of an inch from the edge, turned up to the wrong side and then carefully slipstitched to the fabric with silk thread which leaves no mark after pressing.

hem, hand-rolled   for sheer fabrics and chiffon. The edge may be machine-stitched for firmness and trimmed, leaving one eighth of an inch of fabric, then folded or rolled and hand-stitched in alternating diagonal stitches, one to the fabric and one to the fold, with fine needle and thread.

hem, soft-roll   done like the French hem with a pinked edge reinforced with machine stitching. But if the garment is to be interlined, the hem may be stitched to the lining. A soft rolled hem is not pressed.

hemlines   the unstable hemline of the twentieth century began its rise in the second decade, reaching knee-length in 1925, and above, in the 1960's. Since the 1930's, there have been two distinct hemlines, full-length for formal and short for day. During the war years in the 1940's, came the short dinner dress created by Valentina, American couturière, which continues in fashion.

hemstitch embroidery   a form of punchwork executed in backstitch with a large needle called a punchwork needle. A hemstitched effect is given by drawing the thread tightly.

hemstitching   a decorative space at the top of a hem, usually on sheer fabric.

European Helmets

Gallic-Roman soldier leather and iron-painted motif-earliest centuries A.D.

spangenhelm-leather and small pieces of iron-600 A.D.

spangenhelm-worn over chain mail hood-iron and leather with noseguard-French and English-11th C.

stitched and padded leather bonnet-covered with steel casque-thin mail hood

basinet of steel over chain mail hood-13th C.

coiffette or iron skullcap

mail hood over iron skullcap-steel circlet-buckled fastening-English-13th C.

jeweled crown over mail hood-Spanish seneschal-13th C.

steel basinet with chain mail camail-jeweled circlet-shield with St. George's cross-English-14th C.

basinet with movable ventail-over mail hood-French-1386

helm or heaume of iron-1271

orle of rolled silk-two principal colors of wearer's crest-Italian-1385

chapel-de-fer or iron hat over hood of mail-French-late 13th and early 14th C.

ringed mail-no. 1-2-3 rings sewn to leather or heavy linen-no. 4 chain mail

1.   2.   3.   4.

169

European Helmets

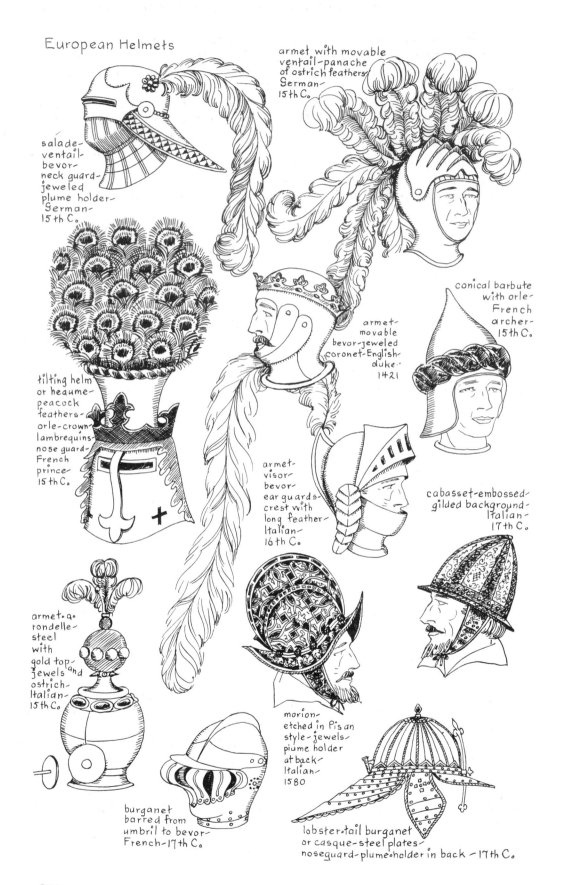

salade-ventail-bevor-neck guard-jeweled plume holder-German-15th C.

armet with movable ventail-panache of ostrich feathers-German-15th C.

tilting helm or heaume-peacock feathers-orle-crown-lambrequins-nose guard-French prince-15th C.

armet-movable bevor-jeweled coronet-English-duke-1421

conical barbute with orle-French archer-15th C.

armet-visor-bevor-ear guards-crest with long feather-Italian-16th C.

cabasset-embossed-gilded background-Italian-17th C.

armet-a-rondelle-steel with gold top-jewels and ostrich-Italian-15th C.

morion-etched in Pisan style-jewels-plume holder at back-Italian-1580

burganet barred from umbril to bevor-French-17th C.

lobster-tail burganet or casque-steel plates-noseguard-plume-holder in back -17th C.

Made by drawing out a number of horizontal threads for the space desired. Then, with threaded needle, gathering equal numbers of threads and securing the groups first at the hemline, and then, at the top of the transparent space, working from the wrong side.

henna   a tropical shrub native to Africa and Asia. A brownish, reddish-orange dye is obtained from the leaves of the plant; used for dyeing cloth and tinting the hair. A fashion of the early twentieth century.

hennin   an Oriental headdress dating back to antiquity, no two authorities agreeing to its origin. It was brought to France by Isabella of Bavaria in the latter part of the fourteenth century, its vogue lasting a hundred years. It was commonly called a steeple headdress and was usually attached to a tiny skullcap from which was suspended the black velvet frontlet on the forehead. The wearing of the frontlet was a privilege only to those having an income of ten pounds a year or more. There were many styles, each invariably draped with a veil, floating or with wired edge. The hennin became so extravagant in size that the authorities found it necessary to regulate the height according to the wearer's social position. see *escoffion*.

henrietta   a once popular cloth, little used today. A dress fabric that varied in finish, sometimes like cashmere or of the salt-and-pepper mixture type, used mostly for children's clothes. Named for Queen Henrietta Maria, wife of Charles I of England.

herringbone weave   an irregular twill weave in zigzag repetition of short diagonal lines resembling a fishbone pattern. Similar to chevron weave, a cloth for suits, topcoats and sports.

Hessian boot, Souvaroff, Hussar   see *boot, Hessian*.

hibernian embroidery   Irish hand work in satin and purl stitches done on silk, velvet or coarse net for cushions, screens and garment trimming.

hickory cloth   a coarse-twilled cotton fabric, resembling ticking but not as firm and of lighter weight, striped and checked. Used for work garments in institutions.

hides   see *animal skins*.

Highland dress   see *Scottish Highland dress*.

himation   the cloak of men and women in ancient Greece. It comprised a piece of fabric, usually white, about $1\frac{1}{2}$ by three yards in size, draped about the figure and over one shoulder. Young men and philosophers are pictured wearing it as the sole garment, in which case it appears to be securely belted at the waist. Women, too, wore it without the chiton.

hip boot   see *boot, hip*.

hipster pants   a term of the 1960's applied to snug, straight pants, replicas of the cowboy's blue jeans and cut only as high as the hipline, where they are secured by a narrow leather or self belt.

hizaam   a word of varied spellings, a wide white silk sash wrapped in cummerbund fashion over the Arabian caftan, usually holding a silver dagger.

hobble skirt   see *skirt, hobble*.

hobnails   short, sharp-pointed nails with large heads used for studding heavy shoe soles and other leather accessories.

Holbein work or **Romanian embroidery**   made in conventional and geometric patterns. Done in Holbein or double running stitch and used for samplers, fine linens and garments. Of the period of Hans Holbein, the younger (1497-1543), German court painter to Henry VIII.

cap or steeple hennin
white with ribbon
black velvet fall
French - 15th C.

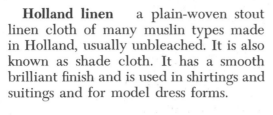

French hood-black taffeta over white satin-velvet loops-1689

Holland linen a plain-woven stout linen cloth of many muslin types made in Holland, usually unbleached. It is also known as shade cloth. It has a smooth brilliant finish and is used in shirtings and suitings and for model dress forms.

hollie point lace a needlepoint lace made in England from the mid-sixteenth century, worked in a twisted buttonhole stitch. The name is a corruption of holy point, referring to church laces. Also called hollie-work.

Homburg soft felt hat of Tyrolese origin later called Homburg because manufactured there. A tapered crown with ribbon band and curled stiff brim in black or midnight blue for semi-formal and colors for day wear.

homespun a fabric loosely woven originally by hand in a plain weave in wool, linen or cotton. Now made by machine of wool, cotton or rayon with coarse yarns in a plain tweed pattern to simulate the early homemade look.

honeycomb a weave with a small allover pattern resembling honeycomb cells; also a reversible fabric of this weave used for clothing.

Honiton lace any of the laces made in Honiton, England. Specifically, bobbin-made floral motifs, the ground later filled in with bobbin or needle-made net of varied stitches. With applied motifs, it is termed Honiton Appliqué.

hood, academic a purely ornamental hood worn with academic or ecclesiastical dress, put on over the head and hanging down in back. The length of the hood depends on the academic degree, bachelors' being the shortest and doctors' the longest, with masters' between the two. Generally of black silk on the outside but faced with the colors of the college, university or seminary, which are displayed in the turnover of the cowl. The binding, generally of velvet, indicates the subject

in which the degree has been given, such as blue for philosophy, red for divinity, purple for law, yellow for letters, green for science, white for arts.

hood, French of black velvet or silk tied under the chin; worn by English, French and American ladies for centuries with little change in style. When worn over a sheer white cap it was a flattering piece of headgear. Under Edward III (1327–1377), women of ill repute were forbidden to wear it. Madame de Maintenon, wife of Louis XIV (1643–1715), wore the hood constantly, which no doubt added to its dignity. It was worn by the Quakers and generally called the "Venerable hood." The contemporary hood follows the early model and is made of silk, wool or velvet.

hood, French of the eighteenth century worn by women of all nations including the American Colonies, was made of silk, velvet or sarsanet. It was attached to a long cape or a short shoulder cape and was then known as a capuchin after the cloak of the Capuchin monks. Quilted, fur-lined or fur-edged for winter wear, the hood of the early period was usually scarlet, cherry red or cardinal, and known as a cardinal or "red riding hood."

hood, gable, kennel, pedimental names for the English hood of the sixteenth century. A fall of black silk or black velvet hung over the top and in back. A white linen wimple and gorget were worn with it.

hood, widow's of dull black faced with white and worn over a coif and gorget, both of white linen; French, early sixteenth century.

hooded seal see *seal, hooded.*

hook and eye a device for fastening clothes; believed to have been first patented in 1808 by a Frenchman named Camus, for the production of hooks and eyes by machinery.

hood of silk over white lawn and lace cap-English-1670's

widow's hood-black cloth over gorget of white linen-French-16th C.

oop-vertugadin
f the Velasquez
ortraits-velvet
nd galon-head-
ress of curls,
eathers, ribbon
nd flowers-
panish-
58

hoop-
roundlet and
gown of crimson
brocaded damask-
slashed velvet
sleeves-feather
fan-fine
handkerchief-
Italian-16th C.

hoop-
taffeta with lace
falling band-
fine lawn fichu-
beaver hat with
plumes-English-
1630's

oop-
ale blue cloth
r silk-bodice
mbroidered-
lack velvet
rim and hat-
strich plumes-
leated rose
ilk apron-
erman-
6th C.

folding metal panniers
connected by tapes-1770's

double panniers-
Louis XV-1715-1754

hoop-robe à la
française-old blue
taffeta-stomacher
in échelle style-
pagoda lace
sleeves-ribbon
and flower trim-
French-1760's

hoop-hip-length-
whalebone and
tape

hoop-silk shirred
over whalebone

short hoop of
shirred silk over
whalebone

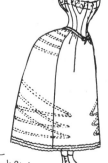

hoop-
corset and
whaleboned
petticoat in one

short
hoop-
of steel hoops
and tape-opening
in front-1857

hoop or bolster
used from
1570 to 1610

hoop-
crinoline petticoat
with steel hoops
opening in front
1857

houppelande
with long sleeves-
brocaded cloth-
sugar-loaf hat-
15th C.

hoop   a circle or circles, of a stiff material, designed to spread the skirts of a woman's dress. see *Catherine wheel; crinoline; farthingale; panniers; verdingale.*

Hoover apron   an apron with reversible front, first popular during World War I when Herbert Hoover was Food Administrator. Called a *wrap-around.*

hopsacking   a coarse, woven sacking, of hemp and jute made into bags for gathering hops. Today, made of cotton, linen and rayon and used for coats, suits and dresses.

horned cap   see *cornet.*

horsehair   mane and tail hairs of a horse used to make horsehair fiber cloth. Used for hats and stiffening.

horsehide   a tough, durable skin of lesser quality used for utility jackets, work gloves, shoe uppers, leather goods, and imitation Russian leather.

hosen   see *paltock.*

hostess gown   an at-home costume, less formal than an evening gown, with long skirt or sometimes with flaring culottes. A style that has enjoyed varying degrees of popularity since 1930.

hound's tooth check   a brilliant broken check, the design simulating canine teeth. The pattern may be woven in wool, worsted, cotton or rayon.

houppe, huppette   a pompon or bongrace of swansdown attached to a black puff protruding from under the houppelande or shawl, high on the forehead. Worn in the sixteenth century by ladies of the Low Countries. see *huke; bongrace.*

huibil grande, festival headdress
of Tehuantepec-Mexico

houppelande   a style which originated in the Low Countries, worn by both sexes from the mid-fourteenth to the early sixteenth centuries. A long, trailing and voluminous cloak with or without sleeves, wadded with cotton or fur-lined. In the fifteenth century it often had long, flaring Dalmatian sleeves and was belted.

hour-glass silhouette   see *wasp waist.*

house coat   a loose buttoned or zipped coat, long or short, for feminine at-home wear, often of a rich and elegant fabric but not necessarily so. see *hostess gown.*

housedress   see *morning dress.*

huanaco   see *guanaco.*

huaraches   Mexican peasant sling back sandals of wood with leather insole and braid edging, leather thongs laced through loops.

hug-me-tight   a facetious name for a feminine shoulderpiece, crocheted, knitted or quilted, with or without sleeves, also called a bed-jacket, late nineteenth century.

Huguenot lace   a simple lace fashioned of cutout motifs of mull applied to net.

huipil   a headdress worn with festival costume by the women of Tehuantepec, Mexico. It is all white, of cotton and lace. According to legend, the headdress was copied from some finely made baby clothes washed ashore from a Spanish shipwreck in Colonial times; the Indian women admired the garments without knowing what they were for. The word has several spelling variations.

huke, Dutch   a full-length black woolen mantle covering the figure and worn over a white linen coif with a bongrace; second half sixteenth century.

huke-
long cloak of black cloth
with covered ornament-
English-1590

huke, huque, haik   in Europe, a woman's wrap reminiscent of the period when the Saracens held sway in Spain. A square of black woolen cloth large enough to envelop the whole figure. Worn since the eleventh century, it survives in Spain and North Africa and in the Kerry cloak of Ireland. It is topped by a cloth-covered ornament. English 1590. see *houppe, huppette.*

hula skirt   skirt of rich green ti-leaves, worn by a Hawaian dancer in the classic native dance. With it is worn a bodice of embroidered silk and a flower lei.

humeral   a shoulder veil or scarf of the same color as the vestments worn by a Catholic priest giving benediction with the Blessed Sacrament.

Hungarian folk dress   see *Magyar folk dress.*

Hungarian hat   see *hat, Hungarian.*

Hungarian point   see *Florentine embroidery.*

hunt dress   in contemporary fox hunting: the Master and hunt officials wear scarlet coats, white breeches, black boots with tan tops, and black velvet visored caps; members of the hunt in formal attire wear the same as the Master and hunt officials, but with a top hat instead of a hunt cap; black or Oxford-gray coats, fawn or mustard-yellow breeches, black boots and black top hats; others in less formal garb wear approximately the same, but a hunting derby instead of top hat. Everyone wears a white shirt with a white stock. Green is worn by the Master and hunt officials in many hunts during the cubbing season and in certain hunts which have specified green instead of scarlet; green is worn generally by beaglers and harriers. (The term *pink* for scarlet is no longer used.) Collars of the hunt color and hunt buttons are worn only with the permission of the Master. Ladies have a formal coat which may be single or double-breasted and may be black, Oxford gray or dark blue; the double-breasted swallowtail coat is known as a shadbelly.

hunter's green   a rich hue of dark green, slightly yellowish, used for coats.

hunter's watch   see *watch, hunting case.*

hunting sack or **shirt**   a blouselike garment of suede, khaki or woolen, usually with turned-down collar and large patch pockets; used by trappers and huntsmen.

huppett   see *houppe.*

huque   see *huke.*

hurluberlu   a madcap wind-blown bob which appeared in 1671; a lady's hair cut short and curled into tight ringlets forming a chou-fleur (cabbage flower) on either side of the face. In vogue to the end of the century.

Hussar boot   see *Hessian boot.*

Hussar breeches   see *breeches, Hussar.*

Hussar's uniform   see *dolama, dolman.*

cloak called haik-
pleated tunic or
gandoura over
footed chalwar-
Arabian-Moor

cloak called
huke or haik-
of Moorish origin-
chopines-
Spanish-
16th C.

Incroyable cravat-
folded stock of
white cambric-1800

I

ichella the long, fringed shawl of woolen homespun cloth, woven by Auracanian Indian women of Chili. The wide border of geometric design is brilliant in color and fastened at the chest by a huge silver pin with a large disc of floral design.

idiot fringe an Americanism for the collegiate football player's haircut around the turn of the century. It was a Dutch cut with bangs.

ihenga a short full skirt, worn with the choli in northern and central India.

ihraam a form of dress expressing a religious state of self-denial, worn by the pilgrims to Mecca, the birthplace of Mohammed. Clothing consists of two lengths of white cotton without any stitching, one wrapped around the loins, the other thrown over the back, leaving shoulder and right arm free.

ikats silk fabrics of Sumatra, Java and Bali which are *chiné*, meaning that the warp threads have been printed, painted or dyed before weaving to produce a Chinese effect.

illusion a silk tulle used in veils, dresses and trimmings.

imperial a tiny beard worn by the French Emperor Napoleon III (1852–1873). It was a pointed tuft just under the lower lip.

Inca costume, traditional see illustration this page.

incroyable French for "unbelievable," of the Directoire Period, the dandy

or fop of the times. He made a cult of the extreme in dress; he peered at people through his perspective or quizzing glass,

Incan Indians of Peru-costumes of hand-woven woolen cloth-black with vivid colors-note large silver flower pin

penciled his eyebrows and used quantities of amber perfume.

indestructible voile also called indestructible flat chiffon. From the trade name for a type of sturdy all-silk voile.

Indian see *American Indian costume; bonnet, American Indian.*

Indian gown a negligée or dressing gown imported from India in the seventeenth and eighteenth centuries by the Dutch who carried on a vast trade with

imperial-a pointed tuft of hair on the chin and a moustache-Napoléon III

Incroyable-hair cut in "dog's ears"-bicorne-bulky cravat-Directoire-1795 to 1799

176

Indian gown of silk or velvet worn by both sexes-17th and 18th C.

the Orient. The robe was so important that the English king and queen had their own appointed Indian gown maker. Also called banian. see *banyan*.

Indienne   a painted or printed muslin from India which was introduced to France and England, becoming exceedingly fashionable during the seventeenth and eighteenth centuries. About the middle of the eighteenth century, shops were established in Europe for the hand-block printing of linen, cambric and cotton.

indigo   a vegetable dye obtained from a tropical plant known from earliest times; a synthetic form is now available. The color is deep, dark blue, both brilliant and permanent.

infanta style   see *robe de style*; *Velásquez*.

infula, infulae   the lappets which hang from a bishop's mitre, which originated in the pendants of a pagan priest.

inlay   a decoration or motif set into the surface of a piece of jewelry or other metals or wood.

inseam   in glove manufacture, a glove with stitched seams turned to the inside of the glove. In tailoring, the length of measure from crotch to edge of trouser leg and the forearm seam of the sleeve.

inset   an insert of fabric or lace into a garment for fit for ornamentation.

insignia   any design or characteristic mark used as a distinguishing sign or badge of honor.

insole   the inside sole of a boot or shoe whether felt or leather, attached or removable.

instep length   the length of a garment three or four inches off the floor.

insurgeant fashion   so named and worn by French women in sympathy with the American Revolutionists. It was a simplified style of the much-frilled gowns worn from 1775 to about 1782.

intaglio   a carving in a hard substance such as a gem. The design is hollowed out in reverse and below the surface.

interlace   to weave in or out, or braid together cord or ribbon, producing a symmetric design.

Inverness   a sleeveless cloak with short cape of checked woolen cloth from Inverness, Scotland. Cloth belt and leather-covered buckle. Usually worn with cap of the same cloth. 1880's.

inverted pleats   see *pleats, inverted*.

Inverness coat sleeveless and belted-woolen plaid-British. 1880's

infulae-lappets of a bishop's mitre- a pagan priest

iridescent   having a soft play of changing rainbow hues or shades in a fabric or piece of mother-of-pearl.

Irish crochet lace   copied from Spanish and Venetian needlepoint. Durable and decorative with medallions of shamrock, rose or leaf design, set in chain stitched square meshes. It is made lacy-looking by picot edge and scallops.

Irish linen   fine, plain-woven full-bleached linen cloth of Irish flax. Used for shirts, handkerchiefs, blouses, etc.

Irish poplin   originally made in France; a ribbed fabric with fine silk warp and a heavy worsted filling. Used for dresses, coats, suits, raincoats and ski suits. Carried to England and Ireland by Protestant refugees, eighteenth century.

iro, ire   a straight, uncut piece of brilliantly printed cotton worn by Nigerian women. It is draped and pinned in place forming an over tunic with kimono-like sleeves. see *agbada*.

iron, flatiron   used in pressing and smoothing cloth and garments. The pressing iron has been heated by flame, steam, gas and electricity, the electric iron being the invention of the twentieth century.

iron hat   see *helmet; chapel-de-fer*.

Isabelline   a color named after Infanta Isabella of Austria (1566–1633), daughter of Spanish Philip II. During the siege of Ostend which lasted three years,

iro–the draped overskirt of the Nigerian woman– white linen blouse– cotton underskirt and bandana– contemporary

she vowed she would not change her chemise until Ostend was taken. During that time her cream-tinted garment changed to a buff or tawny hue, a color which became fashionable and stayed in vogue for more than a century.

Isabelline   see *bear, Himalayan*.

Italian cloth   see *satin, farmers'*.

ivory   a bony substance obtained from the tusks of the walrus, narwhal, elephant, hippopotamus, also from ivory-colored bone.

ivory nut   the seed of a Venezuelan palm. When dry, it is very hard and resembles natural ivory in color. see *vegetable ivory*.

Ivy League look   a manner of masculine dressing first observed among men of Yale, Harvard and Princeton universities and some smaller colleges. A cult of the twentieth century based upon the conservative elegance made traditional by Bond Street, London, and Madison Avenue, New York. All through the straight and broad-shouldered era, the suit with the Ivy League look kept to the slender trousers, natural shoulders and narrow lapels on a straight, unshaped and above all, unpadded jacket.

Izar   the outer garment of the Moslem woman of the poorer class, a piece of white calico large enough to cover the whole person. *Izar* is the Hindu and Persian word for veil.

J

jabot ruffles which concealed the front closure of a gentleman's fine shirt. Of sheer batiste or fine lace, they were tied at the neck with a ribbon cravat string. The style originated in the Louis XIV period, surviving to the middle of the nineteenth century, reappearing from time to time in feminine dress. see *cascade*.

jabul a large cloth shawl worn as a mantle by the Moro women of the Philippine Islands.

jack a homemade coat of mail. A short jacket usually sleeveless. It was made of two layers of canvas or leather with small metal pieces in between held in place by stitching or quilting; sixteenth century.

jackboot a knee-high boot of heavy black leather with broad heel, worn by cavalrymen and fishermen. Popular in the seventeenth and eighteenth centuries.

jackets see specific types; *beer, bush, dinner, Eisenhower, Eton, lumberjack, mess, monkey, Norfolk, pea, pilot, shooting, smoking, Zouave.*

Jacobean embroidery see *crewel embroidery.*

jaconet a light, soft white cotton cloth rather like cambric but a little heavier. Used for dresses and infants' wear.

jacquard a knitting stitch in which the motif is raised in bas relief. Named for Joseph Marie Jacquard, son of a weaver who, in 1801, revolutionized the textile industry by inventing a mechanical loom to weave patterns or brocaded fabrics. The French Government bought his loom in 1806, granting him a royalty and a yearly pension. In 1837 he invented and patented another remarkable machine for making flowered net resembling handsome lace.

jade a semi-translucent gem capable of high polish, ranging in color from white to a deep green, also red, yellow and lavender. Ancient carved green is prized for its color. It has religious significance for the Chinese and is called the sacred stone of China. The choicest is semitransparent "Imperial jade." Used in carved forms and beads, also rings, pins and earrings. There are two kinds with different components: nephrite and jadeite.

jabot-origin of frills to conceal shirt closure Louis XIV period

jaguar or **American tiger** the largest member of the cat family in the Americas. It ranges from Texas and southern California over South America, except the southern end, and east of the Andes. The largest supply of peltries comes from Guiana. The fur is soft, rich, white to brownish-yellow and buff, with dark rosettes and spots larger than leopard markings. Used for coats, jackets and trimming.

jamb, jambeau a protective piece of leg armor of Medieval times.

jams flowered shorts, about knee-length, from the word pajamas, became a Nassau beach fashion when a surfer cut off the legs of his gaily-printed pajamas to make a more comfortable garment.

Japanese mink see *mink, Japanese.*

Japanese
geisha-black
satin haori
over kimona-
colorful silk obi-
white cotton tabi-
felt sandals

Japanese national costume   see *kimono.*

Japanese sable   see *sable, Japanese.*

jardinière   French for an ornamental flowerpot. A multicolored design of flowers, leaves and ribbon bowknots on a multicolored ground. Also a narrow lace of the seventeenth and eighteenth centuries which was used as an edging for linen pieces.

jargoon   see *zircon*

jaseran, jaserant   an Algerian chemise of the thirteenth century of very fine chain mail worn as body protection. Also, a jacket made of linen and sewn with overlapping metal plates. In the sixteenth century, jaserant was the name of feminine collarettes made of rows of fine gold chains.

jasey   a British colloquialism for a wig made of yarn, probably of Jersey yarn.

Java canvas   a coarse, porous canvas used for embroidery.

Japanese haori-
coat over
silk kimona

javel water   a bleaching agent and an antiseptic and disinfectant used to whiten clothes. French *eau de javel* is chlorine bleach.

jean   a stout, twilled cotton cloth which originated in Genoa, Italy, and has been used for men's, women's and children's work and play clothes since the eighteenth century. It is available in solid colors and stripes but most commonly in blue. "Blue jeans" is the common name for breeches made of the cloth in that color. see *levis.*

jelab, jellaba   a hooded woolen robe, centuries old, worn by natives of northern Africa; a three-quarter length garment for poor weather. see *djellaba, litham.*

jemima   a British term for the shoe with elastic gussets. see *bottine.*

jerkin   In the fourteenth century, the man's cote-hardie developed into a garment known as the doublet or pourpoint, both words meaning a wadded jerkin, jaque, jacket or gambeson. A similar garment for women was called jerkinet. The jerkin became a sort of waistcoat in the north of England, worn up to the early twentieth century.

jersey   an elastic cloth in tricot or stockinette stitch. The hand-knitting of wool with needles has been going on for some 2,000 years but the first knitted shirts or tunics appeared in the fifteenth century on the islands of Jersey and Guernsey in the English Channel. Guernseys, ganseys or jerseys, were knitted by women for sailors and fishermen. The knitted tunic, though it absorbed sea spray, did not feel damp. In the 1890's, when sports became fashionable, the knitted woolen garment acquired great popularity. Today knitted cloth is made of wool, cotton, silk, rayon, nylon or any possible combination of fibers. Chanel, in 1918, introduced jersey to the mode in the chemise frock and her famous suit. see *knitting; Chanel, Gabrielle.*

jersey knits, synthetic   knitted, flat or round, very popular for dress and suit fabrics in the 1960's. There are single, double and triple knits providing cloth of varied textures and weights. To be had in a variety of prints and hand-screened designs ranging from subdued to most sophisticated designs.

jester's costume   see *motley; cap and bells.*

panama
with black
grosgrain band

the Hong Kong sheath - printed copper colored silk - self-colored undershirt - large folded hat - necklace of ropes of beads - Dior

jockey cap   see *cap, jockey.*

jodhpur, chukka   an ankle-high boot with two eyelets, of suede or smooth leather and rubber or leather soles. Known by the name of East Indian origin, chukka, signifying a period of play in polo.

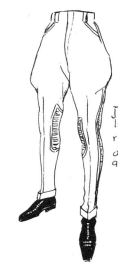

Jodhpurs - East Indian style of riding breeches adopted by men and women - 1920's

jewel neck   a high-cut, collarless neckline for day to permit the wearing of an ornamental chain, a collarette or for evening wear a necklace of beads.

jewelry, costume   see *costume jewelry.*

jewelry, paste   see *temple jewelry.*

jet, black amber   a variety of black mineral coal capable of a brilliant polish in the making of mourning jewelry, ornaments or buttons. Black jet was a vogue throughout the second half of the nineteenth century. It came from England where it was found in layers of shale and had been in use for centuries. The supply diminished and an inferior quality was supplied from Spain. White jet came from Norway and black glass imitation jet from Germany.

jinnah cap   see *cap, Jinnah.*

jipijapa   a hat made from the fibers of a palmlike plant of Central and South America. see *hat, Panama.*

Job's tears   seeds of an Asiatic grass, pearly white and capsule shape. Grown in India, strung and used as beads. Also the name of olive-green grains of chrysolite worn as gems.

jodhpurs   a style of riding breeches from India, new to the Occidental world in the second decade of the twentieth century. Full to the knees, tight from the knee to the ankle, and held down by a strap passing under the boot. The low jodhpur shoe, not the riding boot, is worn with the breeches.

Johnny collar   see *collar, mandarin.*

jonquil   the bright yellow hue of the jonquil blossom.

Joseph or **Josie**   of the eighteenth century; a lady's full-length redingote or riding coat buttoned full length down front. When unbottoned it was called a flying josie. It was made of josette, a heavy twill cotton resembling khaki.

jours   motifs in lace-making, connected by bars and brides permitting daylight to shine through. *Jours,* French for daylight.

Joseph, or "josie" when unbuttoned - riding coat or redingote - 18 th C.

jubbah or djubbeh-worn here under the dolama-Turkish

jouy prints   modern reproductions of French prints of the eighteenth century printed on white or light-toned cotton or linen, the motif in monotone. see *toile de jouy.*

jubbah   the Hindu name of a long, loose garment with long, loose sleeves worn by Parsees and Mohammedans in India and Arabia by both men and women. Made of cloth or camel's hair cloth, sometimes embroidered and sometimes fur-lined for winter wear.

jube   a padded sheepskin greatcoat with the skin to the outside, the winter coat of most Balkan peoples. Heavily embroidered in silk and wool and appliquéd with brilliantly colored woolen cloth motifs. The overlong sleeves usually have sheepskin sewn-in mittens.

Jugoslavian embroidery   stitchery worked in brightly colored yarns with various stitches, principally cross-stitch, double purl-stitch and slanting satin-stitch. Done on coarse linen.

Juliet cap   see *cap, Juliet.*

juliet shoe   a lady's house slipper of simple and graceful design with high front and quarter, and cutout U-shaped sides. Early twentieth century.

jump   British term for a contemporary short outer coat or jacket, thigh-length and buttoned down center front.

jumper   a nineteenth century playsuit for infants, top and bloomers in one piece, made of cotton cloth. see *rompers.*

sheepskin coat or jube-coat of most Balkan peoples-sewn-in sheepskin mittens-appliquéd red cloth motifs-white linen tunic and breeches-red woolen cummerbund-black sheepskin tarboosh-Bulgaria

jumper   a loose blouse or pullover for women; a one-piece, sleeveless frock worn over a guimpe or blouse; a one-piece garment with low-cut bodice, having only shoulder straps and worn over a blouse or T-shirt. see *pinafore.*

jumper frock   in the 1960's, a one-piece dress of tent or shift silhouette, sleeveless, and worn over blouse or knitted shirt with sleeves either short or long.

jumpsuit   the twentieth century work or play overalls made for men and women in cotton, denim and synthetics and usually striped, dark blue, charcoal gray or brown. The top and pantaloons are joined by a self-belt and the garment fastened in front. see *siren suit.*

jungle fighter boot   see *boot, jungle fighter.*

jusi   a delicate fabric for dresses made in the Philippine Islands. Of pure silk or silk with hemp or piña fiber. Also woven in a lacy pattern.

justaucorps   French for body coat; one of the styles of the seventeenth and eighteenth centuries, leading up to the modern man's suit jacket as a piece different from the outer cloak.

jute   a glossy fiber of two East Indian plants used chiefly for sacking, burlap, cheap twine and wrapping paper. Sometimes combined with silk or wool and made into fabric.

Juliet slipper of leather or fabric 1920's

K

kabaya   the jacket, in Western style, of the Indonesian woman's costume, most often white but also of a gay print; worn with a sarong length of contrasting printed cotton draped in skirt fashion with a deep front fold, the skirt held by a silk scarf tied around the waist.

kaffa   see *caffa*.

kaffiyeh, keffiyeh   the Arabian and Bedouin headdress of cotton, linen or silk, plain or striped, and varied in name, pattern and color. Worn for thousands of years, it remains the favorite head covering of the Arab for all occasions. He wears it even with Western dress. Folded into a triangle and placed upon the head, two points fall over the shoulders providing a tie, if wanted, and one hangs in back to protect the neck. A skullcap is often worn underneath. The scarf is held to the head by the agal which is bound around the head several times.

kaftan   see *caftan*.

kaitaka   a mat worn as a cloak by the Maoris of New Zealand. It is made of the finest flax, giving it fine texture, and is sometimes finished with a decorative border.

kalasiris   a long garment of tunic fashion worn by both men and women in ancient Egypt. It was a close-fitting sheath of woven or knitted cloth, but at the same time lightweight and transparent. It was held up by one or two shoulder straps or sometimes made with short sleeves cut in one with the body.

kalmack, kalmuk   a cloth made of

wool or shaggy cotton, resembling bearskin.

kamaka   see *camoca*.

kambal   a much-used, coarse woolen shawl or blanket in India.

kamelaukion   an ancient cap of felt or fur, tall, cone-shaped and brimless, worn by religious fanatics of various Mohammedan sects in some of their ancient rites. see *taj*.

kamiks   high boots of hairless skin into which Eskimos tuck their hairy skin trousers. Both sexes wear them, and inside the roomy boots they wear short socks of sealskin, the hair to the inside. The women of Greenland embroider their boots handsomely with intricate geometric motifs cut from dyed leather, and beaded lace patterns and feather trimming.

kamis   an Arabian undergarment in general use, of white cotton reaching to the ankles and worn over loose, wide trousers. It is embroidered around the neck and across the front with red or white silk. When worn indoors, a wide colored sash and a white cotton skullcap complete the costume.

kandys   a short skirt of goatskin or sheepskin, retaining the hair as decoration, which was the original ancient garment of the Sumerians, Babylonians, Assyrians, Persians and Hebrews. The upper part of the body was bare. see *candys, Persian*.

kangaroo, wallaby, wallaroo, wombat, koala   native Australian marsupial ani-

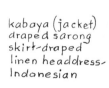

kabaya (jacket) draped sarong skirt-draped linen headdress- Indonesian

kamelaukion of felt or fur-also worn draped round with yards of cloth or silk - Persian -16th C.

"kangaroo walk-result of straight-front corset-early 1900

mals. Wallaby and wallaroo are smaller species of the kangaroo, the quantity of pelts limited, and not suitable to styling. Poor fur with no underwool, used only for sports coats and collars.

kangaroo   a soft, supple, durable shoe leather exclusively from Australia, limited because the animal is not raised commercially.

kangaroo walk   the name given by humorists to the resulting movement of a woman's figure encased in a straight-front corset at the turn of the century. see *wasp waist.*

kapa   in Yugoslavia, a small round cap in pillbox style, of black velvet with red top denoting an unmarried female; the married woman wears an all-black one. Also a national headpiece for men.

kapok   the mass of silky fibers from the seeds of the kapok or silk-cotton tree. Formerly used commercially for stuffing muffs, but now used for household needs such as pillows and mattresses.

kapta   a full-skirted tunic worn by Lapland men with rather fitted breeches. The outfit is made of reindeer skin for winter and of cloth for summer use. The skins are dehaired as well as tanned; in winter two kaptor are worn, one with fur next to the body. The colorfully embroidered costume of cap, tunic, breeches and boots, is worn by men, women and children.

karakul   a hardy breed of sheep originally from the Karakul Valley in Russia near the Caspian Sea, now native to Asia Minor.

kaross   a square rug of animal skins worn by Hottentots, a South African race allied to the Bushmen and Bantus.

kasha   a trademark for a type of soft, silky wool mixed with hair of cashmere

goat in a twill weave. Used for dresses and for men's wear.

kata   a "benediction" or ceremonial silk scarf. It is customary in Sikkim, Tibet and Bhutan, upon important occasions, to exchange scarfs between friends and guests. An ancient Tibetan rite.

Kate Greenaway frocks   see *Greenaway, Kate.*

kaunace   a skirt of dressed leather or felt, or later, woolen cloth, which was worn over a white linen tunic, high-necked and short-sleeved. It evolved from the ancient kandys worn for centuries. Both sexes wore the skirt, full-length for women and short for commoners and soldiers. The tunic of the king and high officials was fringed, tasseled and embroidered, the latter famed as "Babylonian work."

kelt   a kind of rough woolen frieze cloth usually white and rough on one side. Made in Scotland and northern England. Used for skirts, suits and coats.

Kendal green   The name of a cloth and its color. It is made by Flemish weavers working in Kendal, England. Used for skirts, suits and coats.

kepi   see *cap, forage.*

kerchief   a cloth worn as a head covering.

Kerry cloak   a full-length cloak with a hood, of black cloth, traditional in Ireland. Essentially the same garment has been worn all over Central Europe for centuries, and originated in Spain during the Saracen occupation (c. 700–1500).

kersey   a cloth which originated in Kersey, Suffolk, England. Manufactured as far back as the thirteenth century; a firm, pliable all-wool cloth, coarse and ribbed. Men's long stockings were made of it.

kapta-a full-skirted tunic of Lapland costume-of fur in winter-cloth in summer-contemporary

Kaunace embroidered - worn over linen tunic - Mesopotamian

kaunace and shawl of wool with fringe - Mesopotamian

embroidered silk or wool - over linen tunic - a felt mitre - Mesopotamian

kerseymere see *cassimere.*

kēthoneth a three-quarter-length tunic of white linen, with sleeves, worn over a full-length undergarment by the Hebrew high priest.

Kevenhüller see *Androsmane.*

khaddar a cotton homespun cloth made in India in a movement to combat the use of foreign goods.

khaki, khakee from the Hindu word meaning dusty, dust-colored. As applied to cloth, originally a durable, brownish cotton cloth used for uniforms in the Anglo-Indian army, now widely used by armed forces throughout the world.

Khanh, Emmanuelle see *couture, haute.*

khirka a shawl or mantle originally made of patches and shreds of cloth and worn by Moslem dervishes.

khurkeh, Bethlehem dress a rich, colorful costume worn by women in the Near East and still worn. A straight, narrow gown, long enough to be bloused over a wide crushed sash of figured linen or silk and still reach to the ankles. Over it is worn a short, bolero style of jacket with

kerry cloak or huke still worn in Ireland - of black cloth

Bethlehem dress - see khurkeh

kibr of white silk
worn over tobe-
gold cord neckband-
kaffeyeh and agal-
Saudi Arabia

wrist-length flaring sleeves. The dress, usually dark blue or dull red linen, is trimmed with embroidery, braids and beads in varied muted hues. see *Bethlehem headdress.*

kibr   a hooded robe with sleeves, of striped cotton or silk. An Arabian cloak which is worn over the ankle-length white cotton tobe, typical Arabian dress.

kick pleats   see *pleats, kick.*

kid   see *kidskin.*

kid, Dongola   a leather resembling French kid; made of goatskin, calfskin and sheepskin by the Dongola process of tanning and finishing.

kid, glacé   goatskin finished with a highly polished effect and smooth surface; used for gloves. *Glacé* is French for glazed.

kid, undressed   leather finished on the flesh side by the sueding process.

kid, Vici   the trade name for goatskin tanned and finished by a special method producing a bright glazed finish.

kidskin   shoe leather; a tanned leather of mature goats usually 2½ years old. It comes in all finishes and colors and is dressed to imitate antelope and deerskin. Also beautifully marked, fragile goatskins, mostly from China but also from Africa and India. In natural, gray, black and white, which may be dyed all colors, and used for shoes and bags of all styles, both masculine and feminine.

kidskin, Chinese   thousands of skins are exported from China. Gray especially in demand but dyed all colors. Those with flat or semiflat moiré pattern are used for broadtail coats and jackets.

kidskin, Mongolian   very soft under-wool, dying to any color. Often sold as

Ainu
girl in
kimono

mouflon when dressed and top hair removed. see *goat.*

Kiki skirt   a knee-high skirt made its first appearance in New York in 1923, creating a sensation when actress Leonore Ulric wore it in Picard's play, "Kiki."

kilmarnock   a broad-topped woolen cap in flat tam-o'-shanter style, of woven plaid with a pompon on top. Named for a town in Ayrshire, Scotland.

kilt   in Scottish dress, formerly the pleated section of the belted plaid which hung from waist to knees. In modern times the kilt is a separate short skirt of clan tartan, hanging in pleats from waist to knees. Worn by men in parts of Scotland and by some Scottish, Irish and Canadian regiments. Also worn by smart women for casual wear. see *breacan-feile.*

kiltie, kilty tongue   a leather tongue, usually fringed, covering the laces of a sports shoe.

kimono   a loose gown tied with a sash, part of the Japanese national dress. Worn as a dressing gown by Western women. It remains Japan's national costume, despite the fact that Western dress is now more commonly worn for travel and business. The masculine kimono is dark in color and has shorter sleeves, but otherwise is similar to the feminine robe. All garments of men and women fasten from left to right. The man's robe is ankle-length and his family crest in a tiny motif is embroidered or stenciled on each side of the chest, in center back and at the top of the sleeves. For daily wear, a wide sash called the heko-obi goes around the waist two or three times and ties in a loose bow. The kaku-obi, a sash of heavy silk, is worn on formal occasions and is tied in back in a double knot. The feminine kimono may be floor-length or shorter, the longer being held by a cord tied around the waist. Men and women of the Ainus, the original inhabitants of Japan's Hokkaido Island and a remnant race which has lived on Hokkaido for at least 7,000 years, wear a kimono somewhat different from that of the mainland over regular trousers and boots. The women's robe is ankle-length; the masculine garment reaches halfway between knee and ankle. The cloth is woven of elm-bark fiber called attush, and varies in color from a powdery blue to very dark. It is appliquéd in small geometric patterns and embroidered over in chain stitch in white geometric scrollwork. Everyday work clothes are those of the Westerner, white cotton shirt, slacks and sweater.

kimono flannel   flannelette; a soft cotton cloth printed with colorful motifs of Japanese design.

kimono sleeves   see *sleeve, kimono.*

kincob, kinkab, kinkob, kinkhob   a heavy brocaded silk with gold and silver flowers and large figures. Most often used by rich Hindus for turbans.

king klipper   a Mod note of the 1960's from London. A four-in-hand, five inches wide, of polka dot or vivid Paisley silk tied in a bulky knot and long enough to reach the belt.

kips   East Indian hides of yearling cattle, tight-grained from a breed of small oxen. Dressed to imitate box calf and cheaper leather. Kips is the commercial term for pelts fifteen to twenty-five pounds.

kirtle   the kirtle was either tunic, chemise or long petticoat, mentioned from in the fourteenth century through the reign of Queen Elizabeth I, 1558–1603, when it was made of silk, velvet, taffeta and satin, varied in colors and with elaborate trimmings. The kirtle disappeared in the seventeenth century.

kit, kitt, or **swift**   see *kit.*

kittle   a white cotton robe worn on Jewish religious occasions; a gown in which Orthodox Jews are buried.

klompen   see *shoes, wooden.*

knee breeches   breeches fitted to the knee; knickerbockers which have some fullness. "Knickers" is a more general name.

knee buckles   of plate or silver, used to fasten men's cloth knickers at the knee. Small boys' knickers were secured either by a buckled strap or an elastic band in a slot. First half twentieth century.

knickerbockers   full, baggy breeches fastened at the knee with band and buckle instead of a cuff. The name derives from Dietrich Knickerbocker, the pretended author of the *History of New York* written in 1809 by Washington Irving.

knickers   a woman's garment for winter wear worn over muslin underdrawers. Usually of wool or silk, rather full and held by knee bands.

knife pleats   see *pleats.*

knitting   a process of forming a piece of fabric by means of a single thread and

Kilmarnock, a flat-top tam-o'-shanter worn in Scotland—1820's

Knickerbockers Dutch Colonial—Ribbon ties

Knickers–19th C. buckled or buttoned bands

Plus Fours–1920's

kolah—traditional
Persian hat—black
felt or Persian lamb—
or worn draped in
turban fashion

kooletah—
coat of caribou
skin with red
leather fringe—
Canadian
Caribou Eskimo

Korean—white silk
coat and pantaloons—
horsehair hat over
black horsehair cap

a pair of needles. Knitted woolen socks found in an Egyptian Coptic tomb of a period between 400 and 500 A.D. are proof that the Egyptians knew not only how to knit, but how to shape the garment while knitting. Short socks were occasionally knitted in the ninth century and skullcaps in the thirteenth, fourteenth and fifteenth. Liturgical gloves knitted of silk were worn by churchmen. Hand-knitted silk stockings first appeared in Spain during the sixteenth century, a pair of which was presented to Henry VIII. Queen Elizabeth was the first English woman to wear silk stockings.

knob sandal   see *sandal, knob.*

knop yarn   a novelty weft yarn with variously colored knots or lumps throughout its length.

knot, Windsor   see *Windsor knot.*

knots   have served as ornaments and buttons through the ages, used especially by the Chinese and Japanese for decoration, fastening of garments, embroidery and lace-making. *Button knot*—a knot in regular size to be used as a button. *Josephine knot*—a decorative braid knot composed of two loops with the ends free for fastening. *Lover's knot*—a ribbon knot, worn as a remembrance bit. *Macramé*—a decorative knot in macramé lace. *Shoulder knot*—a shoulder ornament of braid, ribbon and lace, sometimes jeweled, worn in the seventeenth and eighteenth centuries for military and special occasions. *Tailor's knot*—a knot used at the end of the thread in sewing, a small hard knot to prevent the thread slipping through the fabric.

knots, Austrian   see *Austrian knots.*

knotted lace   a lace in which the decoration or design is executed in knots on the fabric surface, the best example of which is macramé.

koala   see *kangaroo.*

kolah   the traditional hat of the Per-

sians, a brimless hat of cloth or Persian lamb which, according to the wearer's status, may be wrapped turban-fashion with a strip of fine muslin of varied colors. Color and the winding of a ten-to-twenty yard strip indicates standing. Royalty adds a badge of aigrette plumage or a heron tuft. Worn upon special occasions today.

kolinsky mink   see *mink, kolinsky.*

koo   dark blue cotton sacks worn as everyday dress by Chinese men, women and children.

kooletah   a coat made of caribou skin worn by the Eskimos of Greenland and Labrador origin.

Korean hat   a tall-crowned, wide-brimmed hat of woven horsehair, bamboo and silk, painted black, tied under the chin with black silk ribbons. Traditionally worn by Korean men after marriage when the hair, worn in a queue by bachelors, is dressed into a tight bun on top of the head and confined by a strip of black horsehair covering the head like a skullcap. The hat is never removed, not even for sleeping. In wet weather it is covered with a conical hat of oiled paper or silk. This custom, although now passing, is still observed in some parts of Korea.

koteny   the traditional Hungarian apron worn for festivals and holidays by both young men and young women. It is decorated with embroidery and appliqué and treasured as an heirloom.

kothornus, cothurnus   see *cothurn.*

krepis   a popular Greek and Roman sandal of the fourth century. The sole was a "finger's thickness" and was held to the foot by a decorative leather strap that laced over the instep and round the ankle.

krimmer   lamb from the Crimea (Krim, the ancient Russian name). It is a curled fur of mixed, gray and black and

Korean dancing girl-yellow taffeta over red robe-trimmed with red, yellow, green and purple

korean woman's traditional white cotton dress-pink or blue

Korean bride in brilliant colored wedding dress with a tiny crown of beads

Korean wedding dress-scarlet over white-black velvet hat and boots

white hairs producing a bluish-gray color. A durable fur used for coats, jackets and trimming, especially in children's wear.

k'sa the outer cloak of the North African Moor which is skillfully draped into a wide-sleeved caped mantle. It is a straight piece of wool or cotton, indigo blue or white, about six yards long.

kulah a conical cap of felt or lambskin, the headgear of Middle Eastern monks and dervishes.

kumbi a silky fiber of the East Indian white silk cotton tree. The fiber resembles kapok, and probably, like kapok, is used for stuffing and padding.

kumya the body garment or shirt of the North African Moor. It fastens down the front with buttons and loops and is worn over full-length cotton pantaloons.

kūrtā Moslem blouse worn by men and women with trousers or pantaloons. The masculine blouse is a long white cotton shirt fastened to the left side with

button and loop. The long sleeves are buttoned to the wrists. The feminine blouse is sleeveless and reaches only to the waist.

kusak a wide silk sash worn by Turkish men, many yards long, wrapped around the waist holding the full pantaloons, long or short, in place.

kusti a sacred girdle of woolen cord worn by the Parsis in India, a religious sect which fled Persia in the seventh and eighth centuries.

K'sa-draped cloak-a straight length of cloth-indigo or white-worn by a Tuareg

kūrtā, white linen shirt-rose silk pagri (turban) brown jodphurs-moroccan shoes-worn by Sikh of Ludhiana, India

L

la modiste   in English, the "modesty bit" which was tucked into the bosom of the eighteenth century gown. It consisted of gauze or lace accented with ribbon bowknots. see *modesty bit or modesty piece.*

la robe   The surcoat disappeared in the fifteenth century and a real dress called la robe, with a fitted bodice and long, tight sleeves, joined by a belt to a full skirt, came into fashion.

Labrador scal   scc *seal, hair.*

lace   Before the creation of lace on a net ground, all laces were cords or threads of flax, cotton, mohair, aloe fiber, gold or silver. To work the braid into a pattern, the fingers were used as pegs in a sort of weaving process with braids. When looped, twisted or plaited together with a needle, it was called needlepoint. When worked with bobbins or pins on a cushion or pillow, it became pillow lace.

As a network formed of interlaced cords, lace has existed since antiquity. It had been made by slaves in Egypt, Persia, Byzance and Syria. Needle lace is mentioned by the ancient Greeks and Hebrews. It is said that Italy was the home of earliest European lace-making, but Spain claims the distinction of the art having been brought first to their country by the Saracenic invaders, the Moors. Lace is next noted in Flanders, north France and Belgium, reaching Holland, England and Ireland in the sixteenth and seventeenth centuries. The lace used for masculine linens was point de Venise, for women's lingerie point de rose, and for prelates point Colbert. During the French Revolution, because of royal patronage the lace factories in France were demolished, especially those of Chantilly. Some of the lace-makers were put to death and their patterns destroyed. "Real" lace is that made with a needle on net, bobbins on a pillow. The term can be applied to crochet or knitted lace, but never to machine-made.

See specific types of lace: *Alençon, aloe, araneus, argentan, Ave Maria, baby, Battenberg, Bavarian, Bayeux, bobbin, Bohemian, beggar's, Binche, black, blonde, Bourbon, bridal, Bruges, Brussels, Buckinghamshire, bullion, Burano, carnival, Carrickmacross, Chantilly, chenille, Crete, crochet, damascene, darned, Dieppe point, duchesse, Egyptian, fiber, filet, flat point, Genoa, gold, Greek, Irish crochet, knotted, Limerick, lisle, Maltese, margot, Mechlin, Medici, metal, mignonette, needlepoint, Northampton, Nottingham, opus araneum, orris, Paraguay, parchment, peasant, peniche, Plauen, point de gaz, point d'esprit, point de Paris, point plat, poussin, power, princess, Renaissance, reticella, Roman, rose point, Saint Gall, Saxony, Schleswig, shadow, Shetland, Spanish, Swedish, tambour, Teneriffe, thread, tondor, torchon, trolley, Turkish point, Valenciennes, Venetian, warp, yak.*

laced   an adjective meaning the tying or securing garments with lace or cord. Pertaining to men's hats, coats or uniforms, it signifies the use of braids or cords as ornamentation, now usually of gold or silver braid or cord. Gold or silver lace today is made of silk or cotton thread that is silvered or gilded.

lacis   a former name for the square net foundation or for lace marked on net.

lacquer red   a color yellowish-red in hue, similar to the finish on furniture

la robe-first appearance of the bodice-velvet hennin with veil and frontlet- French- 15th C.

obtained by using Chinese or Japanese lacquer, a spirit varnish.

laid embroidery   see *church embroidery*.

Lakoda   trade name for a skin, a natural sheared Alaska fur seal which lends itself to fine tailoring.

lamb   see *astrakan, broadtail, budge, galyak, karakul, krimmer, merino, moiré, mouflon, mouton, swakara*.

lamb, Persian   a silky, tightly curled fur, the best of the lambs from Russia, Persia, and Afghanistan. Now raised in Africa. A regular curl varying in size which opens rapidly, usually after the lamb is five days old. Silky in texture and naturally rusty, black or brown but usually dyed jet black. Persian peltries are luxurious and heavy. Those of Afghanistan have smaller, finer curl and medium weight; African, fair curl, glossy and light weight.

lamb shearlings   the sheared peltries of lambs that are about eight months old, are processed to resist curling when wet. Dyed to simulate beaver and called beaver-dyed lamb, mouton and mouton-processed lamb. From Canada, United States, Australia and Africa. The African shearlings are called capes.

lamba   a square shawl or mantle worn by Madagascan women. Woven in brilliant colors and patterned with stripes, circles, squares, discs and plaids. Part of the native costume.

lambrequin   a mantling or decorative scarf which hung from the medieval knight's helmet to protect it from heat and wet. It was also called cointoise. see *heaume; helmet; cointoise*.

lambskin   shoe lining; also the skin tanned white and dressed with wool of fine-textured sheepskin.

lamé   a silk brocaded fabric with flat threads of silver and gold. A sumptuous cloth for evening wear in gown or wrap.

laminated or **bonded fabric**   two pieces of material, one thick and one thin, or one of wool and one of silk bonded together with resin acetate. The process gives the cloth more body and the silk acts as a lining. New in the 1960's and much used.

lampas   an elaborate and decorative fabric similar to damask, woven in silk or wool and in many colors. Used in upholstery and also in simple sheath frocks.

lansdowne   a dress fabric, sheer and wiry, of silk and wool in a plain weave. Used for women's dresses.

Lanvin, Jeanne   see *couture, haute*.

Laotian costume, traditional   see illustrations on this page.

lapel   a part of the roll or "fold-back" of the front of a jacket or coat, combining collar, lapel and rever. see *collar and lapel; peaked or peak lapel*.

lapin   French for rabbit. see *rabbit*.

lapin, blocked   rabbit fur closely sheared, cut into small squares and sewn together for novelty use such as inexpensive fur coats for young people and children.

lapis lazuli   a semi-precious stone of the feldspar group sometimes noted as the sapphire of the ancients. An opaque, deep blue with a tinge of green, often marked with iron pyrites or spangled with gold.

Lapland bonnet, Laplandic, biagga gallas   a four-pointed bonnet known as the "hat of the four winds" or sorcerer's cap. Three points are stuffed with down to use as a pillow, the fourth serves as a

lamb-karakul-body about 1½ feet-tail 6 inches

Laos-chieftain's daughter-black velvet calpac and dress-red and yellow embroidery-silver hoop necklaces-contemporary

Laos-government secretary-black silk turban and coat over white shirt and trousers-ivory badge-sign of rank-contemporary

Lapland bonnet of knitted wool with tassel of reindeer strips

Lapland bonnet "the four winds"

Lavinia hat-satin with ribbon bride-French-1804

pocket and purse. Though occasionally still worn by elderly Lapp men, the peaked cap has now taken its place.

lappets   flat lace, ribbon or fabric pendants, usually a pair, attached to a cap, bonnet, crown or clerical headdress.

larrigan   knee-high, oil-tanned leather moccasins used by Canadian and United States lumbermen and trappers.

last   a mold or wooden form made on standard-size measurements over which a shoe is built. The operation is called lasting.

lastex   the rubber core around which any textile yarn may be wound. Lastex may become the warp or filling of any fabric, making that fabric stretchable in any direction. Used in all items of apparel which call for elasticity. First used successfully in the 1930's.

latchet   the fastening of a shoe or sandal, usually in the form of a narrow strap, thong or lace.

laticlave   one of two broad purple stripes down the front of the ancient Roman tunic. Two purple stripes were considered a badge of high rank.

Laton   trade name for an elastic yarn wound with cotton, very fine and very soft, for lightweight elastic garments such as underwear, swimsuits and stockings.

lava-lava   the printed calico kilt or loincloth worn by Polynesian peoples of the Pacific Islands.

lavaliere, lavalier, lavallière   a small jeweled locket worn on a chain around the neck. Named for Louise de La Vallière, mistress of Louis XIV in the 1660's. Also a man's scarf worn during the Third French Republic in 1870. It was of wide, soft silk tied in a loose knot with long ends.

lavinia hat   a large straw hat tied under the chin by a ribbon which went around brim and crown, popular early nineteenth century.

lawn   a delicate, sheer white cloth of linen or cotton in use for centuries. Made in Laon, France, in the sixteenth century and used in Elizabethan England for wimples, ruffles, ruffs, gentlemen's shirts, handkerchiefs; still used for the sleeves of Anglican bishops' robes. It has always been popular for dresses, blouses and aprons. see *bishop's or Victoria lawn.*

layette   a complete outfit for a new baby consisting of bassinet, bedding, clothing, etc.

leather   the skin or hide tanned or preserved of any beast, reptile, bird or fish. Hides are the commercial term for pelts over twenty-five pounds, also the undressed skins of full-size animals such as cows, steers, and horses. Kips are the undressed skins of smaller animals. Skins are those of calves, sheep, goat and such.

leather, boiled or **cuir bouilli**   French

for leather boiled in oil, wax or water and, while soft, molded into shape and then steamed for hardness. All parts of armor and corsets for men and women were made of it. Used from antiquity through medieval period.

leather, bull or **cow**   heavy, fibrous leather used chiefly for heels and soles, principally sole leather for heavy boots. It is also skived and dressed on the flesh side in black and colored box, grained and patent leather.

leather, chrome   tanned by the chrome method, a quick mineral process used mostly for shoes, also for glacé kid gloves.

leather, degrained   leather which has been masked, giving a smooth finished skin.

leather, elephant skin   is tanned and dressed before being shipped to the manufacturers. It requires about four years to bring it to a pliable state, and gray in color. England makes it into luggage and women's bags. Italy, Spain and Portugal make it into shoes and in the United States, it is used principally for belts and watchbands.

leather, grain   any leather dressed on the grain side of the skin; often a split from a thick tanned skin like cowhide.

leather, jack   wax leather coated with tar or pitch. Used for boots, tankards and a huge jug called a blackjack, seventeenth century.

leather, japanned or **enameled**   the dressed flesh splits of white-hair seal which are japanned. Enameling is done on the grain of the leather.

leather, man-made   see *Corfam.*

leather, patent   a japanned or lacquered leather which appeared in the first quarter of the nineteenth century and was used for harness. Seth Boyden, a harness-maker of Newark, New Jersey, made the first patent leather in the United States in 1822. It was used for the soft, little slippers then in fashion and continues to be used for slippers and for other uses such as fine handbags.

leather, roan   a low-grade sheepskin used for bookbinding, slippers, etc. It is tanned with sumac and colored to imitate ungrained morocco from which many styles of traveling cases are made.

leather, Russian   originally from Russia; a lighter leather from the hide of young cattle dressed brownish-red and black. It is tanned in willow bark, dyed with cochineal and sandalwood, which makes it insect- and moisture-resistant, and birch bark which gives it a fragrant odor.

leather, saddle   vegetable-tanned cowhide used for leather goods, including women's bags and belts and men's and women's sports shoes.

leather, Scotch grain   usually of cowhide with a pebbled grain stamped on by plates and roller. A heavy, durable leather for men's shoes.

leather stockings   Indian leggings reaching from ankle to mid-thigh, shaped to the leg and held by a thong tied to the belt. Embroidered and fringed like the moccasin. see *American Indian Costume.*

leather, synthetic   made of coated fabric, fiberboard, pasteboard, composition rubber and cellulose, the finished article resembling leather but minus its scent.

leather, vegetable   an imitation leather made of cotton waste. Put to the same uses as real leather.

leatherette, leatheroid   trade names for imitations of leather made of paper and cloth, or paper and rubber.

lederhosen   German for leather breeches or shorts held up by crossbar leather braces. Worn by men in the Tyrolean Alps, traditional Alpine dress.

leggings   leg covers of leather or cloth worn by children, reaching from foot to waist with a strap passing under the shoe. see *gaiters, gamashes, spatterdashes, spats.*

leghorn   a large picturesque hat made from finely plaited straw grown in Tuscany, Italy. It is cut green and bleached and is cultivated especially for hatmaking.

leg-o-mutton sleeve   see *sleeve, leg-o-mutton.*

lei   a flower necklace worn by Hawaiians. A thick rope of fresh, colorful, fragrant tropical flowers.

Lelong, Lucien   see *couture, haute.*

leno, leno weave   a gauze weave for men's summer shirtings. An open weave for hot weather, made in a variety of pattern effects.

leopard   a large cat, in ancient Egypt the symbol of royalty. A costly, fine fur. Due to modish demands, the fur is becoming rare, especially skins from Somaliland. The hair is short with rosettes well marked on a pale ground. The snow leopard, which is very rare, inhabits high altitudes of Tibet and Siberia. A pale yellow-gray color with long, silky hair and long fur fiber. The markings resemble spots more than rosettes. Both leopard and snow leopard coats are costly.

leotard, or **tights**   designed by a 19th century trapeze artist, Jules Leotard, the name later adopted for the garment by professional dancers. A practice costume of ballet dancers, acrobats and gymnasts. The long-sleeved garment reached from neck to crotch and was always black. In 1956 a leotard reaching from neck to toe

of stretch nylon became available in red, green and blue to be worn with Bermuda shorts, kilts, ski and skating costumes. see *body stocking.*

létice, laitice   see *ermine.*

Levantine   a firm, twilled silk cloth first made in the Levant. It was the same finish on both sides but of different colors and was used principally for robes and sashes.

leviathan canvas   a coarse, strong embroidery canvas which takes a large or double cross-stitch and a thick woolen yarn for the working of embroidery.

leviathan wool   a thick woolen embroidery yarn made of many strands and used on leviathan canvas.

levis, blue jeans   strong cotton pants of indigo blue denim reinforced with copper rivets at crucial points. The creation of Levi Strauss who went to California in 1850 seeking gold. They are worn by men, women and children for work or play.

lei-Hawaiian wreath of leaves, flowers or feathers

leotard-a garment for the practice of dancing-19th C.

levis or blue-jeans-plaid cotton shirt-black felt stetson or ten gallon hat

levis or blue-jeans-plaid cotton shirt-black felt hat-black leather boots

Levite gown - silk
and satin - straw hat
with ostrich-
powdered hair-
French - 1780's

levite gown a type of redingote with a train, inspired by the Englishman's redingote of the 1770's. There was also a redingote gown with a short, double-breasted jacket with wide lapels, which were considered very extreme.

libas the traditional Egyptian cotton pantaloons, very full and draped, reaching to knee or ankle. Worn with a white or colored shirt or a gandoura or the gallibiya or even sometimes as a waist-coat. see *gandoura.*

Liberty a trade name used by Liberty of London for fine-textured fabrics in silks, cottons and woolens.

liberty cap see *bonnet, Phrygian.*

Liberty satin see *satin, Liberty.*

Lille lace of Lille, France. A fine bobbin lace, sometimes dotted with motifs outlined with a heavy flat cordonnet.

Lillian Russell costume the fashion of the times identified with the American

actress (1861–1922). She had a handsome buxom figure and wore form-fitting gowns with a train. Her marcel-waved pompadour was topped by a large black velvet hat of Gainsborough style with ostrich plumes.

"Lilly" see *Pulitzer, Lilly* under *couture, haute.*

Lily Langtry wave a curled coiffure with crisped bangs and low chignon worn by the English actress (1852–1929), famed as the most beautiful woman in the world.

Limerick lace a pattern which originated in Limerick, Ireland, embroidered on net stretched in a tambour or embroidery frame, the stitches run through by means of a hook or a tambour needle. see *tambour lace.*

Lindbergh jacket worn by Charles A. Lindbergh, who made the first solo flight across the Atlantic from West to East, 1927; similar to the battle or Eisenhower jacket of World War II.

line a thread, string, cord or stripe; also, shape or contour.

line for line copy exact or nearly exact reproductions of Paris models made in the United States, especially on Seventh Avenue, New York.

linen the product of the flax plant, one of the five varieties of the bast family. It is thought to be older than cotton or silk of India and China, and is known to have been cultivated in Egypt for 5,000 years. A fibrous material in the stem of the flax plant produces smooth and strong fibers ranging from very coarse to very fine. Whether fine or coarse, it makes a durable fabric suitable for many items from sheerest handkerchiefs to wearing apparel of various types. In ancient Egypt linen fabrics were woven from the various bast fibers, but linen made from flax was the important and all around Egyptian

Lillian Russell-
"figure of the
day"- American
1861-1922

Lily Langtry "most beautiful
woman in the world"
wearing chinchilla

textile. During the period of the Old Kingdom, linen was treasured and stored in the royal storehouse. It varied in texture from closely woven to a very fine gauze. Pieces of five thousand years ago have been found in tombs, of a sheerness surpassing modern manufacture. So finely woven and of such transparency were some cloths that the fabric was called Egyptian lace for many centuries.

linen, book   see *book linen.*

linen, butcher's   see *butcher's linen.*

linen cambric   plain weave linen, sheer or coarse. Used for handkerchiefs and dress goods.

linen canvas   an open-mesh canvas used for embroidery.

linen, Irish   see *Irish linen.*

linen-textured rayon   a wide range of rayon fabrics with various linen textures and weights.

linene   trade name for a linen substitute, usually of cotton in a heavy, plain weave. Used for skirts, middies, aprons and such.

linge   from the French for linen. Until the twentieth century white linen was the fabric used for underclothes, often called body linen, and religious vestments.

lingerie   French for ladies' underwear, first used as an English word by *Godey's Lady's Book*, mid-nineteenth century. From about the thirteenth century until the nineteenth, underwear consisted of a shift or smock-like piece of apparel, of wool or linen and embroidered at neck and hem, called a shirte or camise. Nineteenth century underwear consisted of a chemise worn under a boned corset, a corset cover, drawers or pantalets and several petticoats, always white and made of soft cottons such as nainsook, batiste, longcloth, cambric and others, with lace

and embroidery. In the twentieth century lingerie became greatly simplified, often with garments all-in-one. Synthetic materials requiring no ironing are now widely used as is lastex for girdles and nylon for other pieces; the range of colors including prints is unlimited. Some former names for a lady's underwear were underpinnings, under-things, unmentionables, indescribables.

lingerie and corsetry   Lingerie and corsetry in the early twentieth century became practically one unit composed of bra, panties and slip. Next, an abbreviated form-fitting girdle of lastex with few or no bones was evolved which was worn with a soft, but controlling brassière. All pieces are made of sheer, yet firm, delicate synthetic silks and gauzes in pretty colors.

linsey-woolsey   a coarse, woolen linen or cotton warp cloth very popular in the American Colonies; first made at Linsey, Suffolk, England.

lipstick   a pomade for coloring the lips put up in stick form and enclosed in a tiny case, appeared in the first decade of the twentieth century. Colors ranged from white and flesh through pink to deep reds. The popular use of lipstick took hold in the 1920's, becoming scarlet-red in the 1930's. By mid-century, the blood-red mouth gave way to a pale or nude coloring which was succeeded by a more natural color. see *cosmetics.*

lipstick red   a brilliant red in costume and accessories in the 1930's and 1940's, named after the popular shade of lipstick.

liripipe, liripipium   the peak or tail of the chaperon hood. By the thirteenth century the liripipe had so lengthened that it almost touched the ground. The headpiece was worn by liveried servants in the fourteenth and fifteenth centuries. It could be folded on top of a stuffed roundlet or wrapped around the neck. It became the custom to fling the liripipe and roundlet over the left shoulder. From this custom evolved a miniature replica which is still worn on the left shoulder of the French magistrate and on the robe of the British Knights of the Garter and liveried servants. In the fifteenth century, only a noble was permitted to wear a hat with liripipe or, by its English name, tippet. see *tippet*.

lisle   a fine, hard-twisted thread of staple cotton formerly used in the manufacture of fine hosiery, underwear, gloves and many other items. It was named for the Flemish town of its origin.

lisle lace   a fine bobbin lace woven with a flowered design outlined by a cordonnet.

lisse   a fine, smooth gauze used for ruching.

litham   a sheer embroidered square folded diagonally to cover nose, mouth and neck, the ends tied, worn by Arab women. Men also use a plain litham when the sand is blowing. see *djellaba*.

little black dress   introduced by Patou of Paris in 1921. In black jersey, silk or wool, the dress became standard for day wear after five o'clock. It was decidedly chic and has remained in vogue.

Little Lord Fauntleroy   a small boy's best suit which became popular for one or two decades after the publication in 1886 of *Little Lord Fauntleroy* by the English-American novelist, Mrs. Frances Hodgson Burnett. Reginald Birch, the illustrator, chose the style of the Cavalier period for the costume of the young hero, a black velvet suit with deep lace collar, a red and black sash and a plumed hat. Sentimental mothers favored the ensemble but it was truly loathed by most of its young wearers.

liturgical headdress   The miter and tiara are both of Persian origin and were

worn by Christian and Jewish prelates alike, with no special religious significance before the eleventh century. A sign of rank was the sacred fillet of white wool with infulae or lappets. Early in the twelfth century the bishop's miter was enclosed in two pointed panels at the sides, then placed back and front where they have since remained. The white linen miter was also worn by the Levitical priest. The tall conical tiara of Asiatic origin became the papal crown, but popes wore the miter as late as the fifteenth century. The papal crown with one crown was worn by Nicholas I, (858–867 A.D.) In 1065 Alexander II added the second coronet and the third appeared with Urban V (1362–1370). In the sixteenth century a mound with a cross atop instead of a jewel completed the triple crown of the pope, and remains the symbol of his temporal power. A triple-crowned tiara was worn by the ancient Jewish high priest.

livrée, livery   In the feudal era at a stated annual date the lord of the castle made gifts of cloth or costume to the noblemen of his estate. The gift was called livrée, origin of our word "livery," the uniform of a servitor. The law governed the amount of one's possessions in wearing apparel, the size of a cloak and the width of trimming. Nobles were permitted to wear hoods with long tippets, while the commoner had to be content with just a hood.

lizard   a scaly, decorative and durable leather from Java and India, which does not crack. Used for shoes, belts, handbags, etc.

llama   a South American animal of the camel family. The coarse, woolly fleece is dyed to simulate wolf and fox. see *alpaca; guanaco; vicuña*.

llautu   a cord of fringed vicuña wool worn around the head by the ancient Peruvians as a badge of nobility.

loafer   the heeless Norwegian slipper

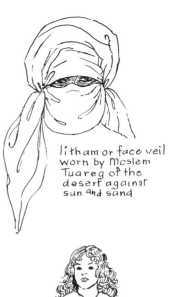

litham or face veil worn by Moslem Tuareg of the desert against sun and sand

Little Lord Fauntleroy— hero of the popular novel, whose costume set a boy's fashion— 1886

Llama- S. A. animal of the camel family

moccasin
loafer-elk tanned
leather-20th C.

first introduced in the U.S. in the 1940's; it quickly developed into a tailored style because of its comfort and slip-on qualities. Worn by men, women and children. Sometimes tasseled.

Lochlana   a trade name for a modern cloth which "feels like cashmere, wears like wool" and is made in Scotland. It is used for men's fine shirts in America.

loden   a waterproof cloth resembling Irish frieze, made by the Tyrolean peasants from the wool of their mountain sheep. It is woven and dyed in several colors but especially a bluish green known as loden green. see *toggle coat.*

loincloth, breechcloth, breechclout   a brief garment worn round the loins by primitive peoples.

long cloth   a closely woven, plain weave cotton cloth made of fine combed yarns, especially adapted to infants' wear. It was one of the first fabrics to be woven in a long piece, hence its name.

longi or sarong-type of skirt worn by men and women-Burma

longi, lungyi   a sarong-like skirt that both sexes of the Burmese wear with white cotton blouses or short jackets. The skirt is draped around the waist and hips with a deep pleat folded to the left and tucked into the belt, often giving the effect of trousers. The "acheik" longyi is a hand-loomed piece in a colorful broken pattern on silk or cotton. It is costly because it requires months to weave.

loo mask, loup   riding half masks worn by men and women in winter or strong sun. They were made of black silk or velvet, green silk or linen, and were popular in the American Colonies during the eighteenth century. see *mask.*

Loo mask of black velvet lined with white silk-French-16th C.

loom   a machine or frame of wood or metal upon which thread or yarn is woven into a textile. The threads running lengthwise form the warp, those running crosswise, the weft, woof or filling.

loongee   a large square of cotton or silk folded and carried over the shoulder. This piece, worn in Afghanistan, is used as handkerchief, muffler or sash for holding one's possessions.

Lord Chumley   a cape overcoat popular in Europe and America in the 1890's. A man's travel coat named for a play of the period.

lorgnette-
eyeglasses mounted
on a decorative
folding handle-
19th C.

lorgnette   eyeglasses mounted on a handle into which the glasses fold when not in use. In the nineteenth century they were especially fashionable as a feminine accessory. see *quizzing* or *perspective glass; opera glass.*

losh   a hide, generally elk, dressed only with oil.

lounge suit-
blue serge-
wing shirt
collar-bow
tie-English-
1880's

lounge, sack coat, sakkos   a jacket for informal wear, of British design, which appeared in the 1850's. It was a coat without a waist seam, at first considered eccentric. Single or double-breasted, it was worn generally by the 1870's and today is almost universally worn. see *sakkos*.

lounging robe   a comfortable indoor robe for lounging or extra warmth. Of flannel, velvet, silk or brocade and often lined, the length is variable. Worn by men and women.

loup   see *loo mask*.

lovat   a heather-colored fabric produced by combining blue or green with gray or beige threads.

love-lock   a single long curl over either ear, tied with a bowknot. The wearing of the love-lock prompted a celebrated French soldier, Count of Harcourt (1601–1666) to wear an earring in the exposed bare ear. This fashion was introduced into England by Charles I (1625–1649).

love-lock tied with ribbon favor-laced hat - English-17th C.

Lucile   see *couture, haute*.

lumberjack   an imitation of the coat worn by lumbermen. A straight, short jacket usually belted in back and closed in front by a slide fastener. It is made of water-repellent cotton, heavy cloth, plain or plaid, or leather and furnished with large pockets. Worn by men, women and children.

lumberjack shirt   formerly worn by Canadian lumberjacks. Always made of plaid fabric in thick wool, cotton or rayon blend and worn for work or for winter sports.

lungi or **lungee**   the long cotton cloth which the East Indian uses as turban, scarf or loincloth.

lutestring, lustring   a fine corded silk popular for ladies' dresses, seventeenth to nineteenth centuries. A narrow silk ribbon used as an eyeglass cord.

lycra spandex   trademark for a man-made fiber composed largely of "elastomer" or stretch fibers. It is used especially for feminine undergarments such as girdles, brassières, the body stocking and support stockings.

lynx, wildcat   an animal with short tail and ears tipped with tufts. Found in Norway, Sweden and North America, as far south as California. A larger animal comes from Scandinavia and Russia; the best from Hudson Bay and Sweden. Pale gray fur with fine streaks and dark spots; underhair less thick than fox. A four-inch-long silvery top hair used natural or dyed, often a lustrous black. Used for scarfs and trimming and the busby of the British hussar. A smaller form of lynx with flat, reddish or gray fur and slightly spotted fur comes from western United States and British Columbia. Used for trimming. see *caracal*.

Lyons velvet   see *velvet, Lyons*.

lumberjack-mackinaw-bush jacket or short warm-of plain or plaid wool or leather-fur collar and zipper

M

macaroni   a term in England about 1760 applied to young fops who were exquisite in dress. They wore tiny hats as did their feminine counterparts, who were also called macaronies.

macclesfield, spitalfields   fine silk scarfs manufactured and named for localities in England. Overall patterns of small design and subdued coloring. Names interchangeable. see *spitalfields*.

Macfarlane cloak   a cloth topcoat with separate sleeve capes and side slits to permit hands reaching inner pockets. British, from 1850's to end of century.

Mackinaw, Mackinac   a short, heavy, outdoor coat of woolen blanketing usually in bright plaids or wool fleece. Used by hunters and lumbermen.

Mackintosh, mac, mack   a cloak of rubber-coated fabric, therefore waterproofed; named after Charles Mackintosh (1766–1843). He designed the raincoat and patented the first waterproofing process.

macramé lace   of Arabian origin but made mostly in Genoa, Italy. A knotted lace woven in geometric patterns, often fringed with many of the ends tied together. Coarse pieces used for table covers and bedspreads; made in silk for scarfs and shawls and throws.

Madeira embroidery   white embroidery on linens and garments in conventional and floral designs in overcast eyelets, such as is made by the nuns of Madeira.

Madonna coiffure   a simple hairstyle of Renaissance Europe, the hair parted in the middle and looped in front of the ears and drawn back into a chignon. Seen in many paintings and statues of the Madonna.

madras   a muslin or cotton fabric named after the city of Madras, India, of colorful gingham in plaids, checks or stripes sometimes intermingled. There is also an East Indian madras in colorful plaid or striped silk or cotton which bleeds when laundered, creating an un usual color scheme. Used for summer apparel of both sexes. see *punjum*.

Madras embroidery   brightly printed silk and cotton handkerchiefs which are embroidered in a variety of stitches.

magenta   a color discovered in 1856 by the British chemist Sir W. H. Perkin, and the first synthetic dye. The color was later named for the Battle of Majenta, 1859. It is a bluish red in hue varying from high to a raw brilliance.

Magyar or **Hungarian dress**   notable for elaborate embroidery in brilliant colors. Applied to the feminine blouse and the man's shirt, both of white linen, an overskirt and, invariably, a long apron also for both sexes. The man's szür or greatcoat of black or white felt or leather is lavishly decorated. The costumes are often the work of a lifetime and are handed down from generation to generation.

maharmah, yashmak   a muslin cloth formerly worn over the head and lower face by Turkish and Armenian women. see *mandeel*.

mahoîtres or stuffed shoulder puffs— French. 1575

mahoîtres   high, standing, padded shoulder puffs of sleeves worn in the sixteenth century.

mail   see *chain mail.*

maillot   a knitted one-piece, tight-fitting swimsuit. Also French for swaddling clothes of a small baby. Also tights and leotard. see *bathing dress.*

Mainbocher   see *couture, haute.*

maison de couture   Parisian dressmaking establishment. see *couture.*

makeup, maquillage   the collective noun for complexion cosmetics applied to the face, comprising foundation, rouge, powder, lipstick, eye mascara, etc. *Maquillage* is the French word.

Malabar   an East Indian handkerchief of Hindu design printed in brilliant colors.

maline, malines   a silk or cotton gauze net with a plain woven hexagonal mesh. Used in veilings, ruchings and millinery work.

malo   the Hawaiian man's girdle or loincloth. Originally of tapa cloth which was made from tree bark, but now of cotton dyed in brilliant colors. Also, an ornamented royal girdle.

Maltese lace   a guipure lace in which the Maltese cross, dots and simple geometric patterns are used; formerly a bobbin lace.

mameluke sleeve   see *sleeve, mameluke.*

Manchu headdress   a cap of black satin bands shaped by a fine gold wire. Only imperial princesses were permitted to wear the headdress and, because it was so fragile, its wearing was confined to the palace. Sewn, wired and glued to it were hundreds of tiny ornaments, among them the phoenix bird, butterflies, bats, kingfisher feathers, flowers and miniature pieces made of jade, rose quartz, pearls, etc. The Manchu princess headdress of the Chi'ing dynasty was worn 1644 to 1912.

mandarin collar   see *collar, mandarin.*

mandarin robe   formerly worn by Chinese mandarins and their wives prior to the establishment of the Republic in 1912. The robe had wide long sleeves and was long, loose, and richly embroidered. The motifs were indicative of the wearer's rank as were the jeweled button atop his cap and the long string of beads of amber, coral or jade. The large squares of embroidery, one in front and one in back, told what governmental office the mandarin held. Many of the robes became fashionable as handsome evening wraps or hostess gowns for Western women in the twentieth century.

mandayas   a long outer garment resembling the cope worn during the Greek Orthodox Church services.

mandarin robe of silk with embroidery— cap with button and peacock feather

Mandeel-embroidered lawn
or linen-worn by a Moroccan
woman-other names are litham,
maharmah, yashmak and veil

mandil--Oriental
name for Persian
or Turkish turban-
16th and 17th C.

mandilion or tabard-
cloth jacket worn by
commoners and as
livery-16th and
17th C.

Mantee-a
sheer coat to display stomacher
and petticoat-Thérèse bonnet of
gauze-French-1770's

mandeel   name for the feminine Moslem veil which may be white, figured colored muslin, lacy or black and hangs over the forehead and chest.

mandil   an Oriental name for a Turkish or Persian turban.

mandilion, or tabard   a kind of dalmatic worn by common folk in inclement weather, twelfth to sixteenth centuries. A hip-length garment with hanging, open sleeves, it was put on over the head, worn by heralds, soldiers and knights. In the sixteenth and seventeenth centuries it became a piece of livery and also a short, capelike cloak worn by the Puritans. see *tabard*.

manga   a Mexican garment much like a poncho but with self-formed sleeves, formerly worn for riding.

Manila hemp   the most important cordage fiber. see *abacá*.

maniple   a narrow band worn hanging over the left forearm by the celebrant at mass; of the same material and color as the chasuble.

mannequin, manikin, mannikin   a tailor's or dressmaker's lay figure; also a living model upon which a garment is designed, fitted or displayed.

manta   from the Spanish for shawl, blanket or poncho, a large square of thick, black, coarse cotton fabric worn in the manner of the European haik. It is draped over the head, falls over the shoulder, and is pinned at the chest, and hangs to the ankles; it conceals most of the woman's form and perhaps a baby held in its folds. The short cape which a Spaniard wears over his bolero is a manta and so is the shawl, blanket, or poncho. Manta is also the name of the Spanish headdress, a square shawl, always black, of lace or silk for the aristocratic type of woman, or of thin cashmere or alpaca for the woman of lesser social standing.

man-tailored   said of a woman's suit or coat made and finished by a tailor who duplicates the fine details of well-made masculine clothes.

mantee   a feminine cloak of the eighteenth century, open in front to display stomacher and petticoat.

mantelletta   a sleeveless, short robe of silk or wool worn by high prelates of the Roman Catholic Church.

mantes   beruffled scarf-like capes of gold and silver tissue imported from Mantua in Italy in the eighteenth and nineteenth centuries. Such mantes were worn by ladies of the various European courts and society, a more conservative style being worn by commoners. There was a mante for mourning and for women of the Church, accompanied by a hood. The mante is still to be seen in various countries today.

mantilla   the lace scarf or veil, black or the white lace known as blonde, that the Spanish lady drapes over a high tortoise shell or ivory comb in her coiffure. The white shawl is worn for dress, especially to bullfights and on

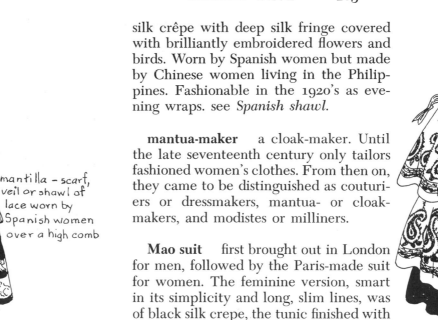

mantle of embroidered cashmere-velvet collar-felt hat-striped ribbon-French-1829

mantilla - scarf, veil or shawl of lace worn by Spanish women over a high comb

silk crêpe with deep silk fringe covered with brilliantly embroidered flowers and birds. Worn by Spanish women but made by Chinese women living in the Philippines. Fashionable in the 1920's as evening wraps. see *Spanish shawl*.

mantua-maker   a cloak-maker. Until the late seventeenth century only tailors fashioned women's clothes. From then on, they came to be distinguished as couturiers or dressmakers, mantua- or cloak-makers, and modistes or milliners.

Mao suit   first brought out in London for men, followed by the Paris-made suit for women. The feminine version, smart in its simplicity and long, slim lines, was of black silk crepe, the tunic finished with a standing collar. 1967.

maquillage   see *make-up*.

marabou   the soft fluffy feathers covering the quills of the wings and tail of the African stork. Used for trimming since 1800. Available by the yard in dyed colors and used on dresses and negligées.

marabout   a form of twisted, or thrown raw silk and the fabric made of it. Used principally for scarfs.

marcasite   a glittering mineral made especially into buckles, buttons, jewelry and other ornaments.

marcel wave   a fashion of curling the hair with irons into deep waves carefully

Easter Monday. The black Chantilly lace mantilla which later came to be associated particularly with Spanish women appeared late in the eighteenth century and was French-made.

mantilla, Watteau   see *Watteau mantilla*.

mantle   a loose garment, wrap or cape, usually without sleeves.

manton de Manilla   of the nineteenth and twentieth centuries. Shawls of heavy

Mao Suit of black silk crepe-London and Paris-1967

marcel wave invented by Marcel of Paris becoming a vogue of the 20th C.

manton de Manilla-also known as Chinese and Spanish shawls-silk crêpe with flower and bird embroidery-19th and 20th C.

Marie Antoinette costume-
"queen's gown" of gauze with
Medici collar-satin sash-
straw hat-hair cut hedgehog-
1783

arranged around the head; named for Marcel, the Parisian hairdresser who set the style. Late nineteenth century. see *permanent wave.*

margot lace   a delicate modern lace used for ruffles, flounces and trimming. It is machine-embroidered in heavy cotton thread on fragile silk net.

Marie Antoinette costume   a long-corseted bodice with low décolletage and tight sleeves with ruffles, the hooped skirt was festooned with ribbons, flowers and ruffles. The powdered coiffure was dressed with ribbons and flowers.

Marlborough hat   see *hat, Gainsborough.*

marli   a gauze much like tulle used as a ground for embroidering lace.

marlotte   a dress cloak that many modish European women wore with only slight variation in the second half of the sixteenth century. A full-length robe of simple design, in handsome brocade with a small stand-up collar and short puffed sleeves. It fastened only at the neck, flaring open over the hooped skirt of the gown.

marlotte-an overdress
with short puffed sleeves-
fastened at neck-very
fashionable-French-
16th C.

marmot   an inexpensive fur much used in Europe from a ground squirrel common in the Alps and the Pyrenees. Also, fur of the Russian and Chinese rodent dressed, dyed and striped to simulate mink, called Brazilian mink. A fur with poor durability, the best coming from Russia. It is used for coats, jackets and trimming. The American species, woodchuck or groundhog, is little used.

marquise   a woman's three-cornered riding hat; French, 1735. Occasionally worn today and still a smart hat.

marquise   a silk and lace carriage parasol of the nineteenth century; its special feature was the folding handle. see *umbrella.*

marquise   in jewelry, a finger ring set with a long, narrow cut gem, either oblong or elliptical. see *gem cuts.*

marquisette   a lightweight gauze made of cotton, rayon or silk; in white, solid colors, and novelty patterns; used for dresses.

marten   animal of the weasel and the sable species, larger than a weasel and yielding a valuable fur. Found in the northern regions of America, Europe and Asia. Russian and Siberian are most precious, American next. The underfur very fine and soft with long, rich guard hair and the animal has a handsome long tail. Most marten is blended. Used for jackets, scarfs and trimming.

marten, American; Hudson Bay sable   Found in the pine and spruce forests of North America, some in the Rocky Mountains and on the Pacific coast. A beautiful, durable fur, many of a dark color and almost as silky as Russian sable. The general color is medium- and yellowish-brown. Those of Alaska are poor. Used natural, blended or dyed if very pale and principally for scarfs and trimming.

marten, baum or **pine**   found in the

marten-fur
of the weasel
and sable species-

mountainous regions of Siberia, Norway, Germany, Switzerland, Asia Minor and the Himalayan Mountains. The best from Russia, the color ranging from pale to dark bluish-brown with fluffy underfur and silky guard hair. Used natural, blended or dyed, if pale. Used for coats, jackets, scarves and trimming.

marten, Himalayan better known as Chinese sable, yellow to yellowish-brown. Blending and tipping increases the luster. Used for jackets, scarves and trimming.

marten, Japanese the same class as the European stone marten but less costly. An inferior woolly fur with coarse top hair. Canary or dull yellowish coloring dyed various shades of brown to resemble sable. Used for scarves and trimming.

marten, stone or **beech** from Russia and Asia. Underwool grayish white and bluish with very rich, dark top hairs. The best from Russia. Used natural for jackets, scarves and trimming.

martingale the leather strap fastened to a horse's girth, intended to hold his head down and prevent his rearing. In costume, a stay, strap or partial belt to hold folds in place. On a modern coat, a belt across the back and attached at the sides to hold the fullness in place.

mascara a cosmetic cream for darkening the eyelashes.

mashru an Arabic word meaning lawful, as applied to a fabric of mixed cotton and silk. Moslems were formerly forbidden to wear pure silk at prayer.

mask an important piece in the Greek and Roman theater, the actors' faces usually masked when on the stage. The mask appeared in the European mode in the sixteenth century as a protection in bad weather. It was also worn by women who wished to appear incognito in public. By the eighteenth century, the use of the little black velvet mask or half-mask was general and worn by women and children in the American Colonies. European men and women wore the mask for the theater and the street. The small Venetian mask, called loup, or in English, loo, meaning wolf, because it frightened children, was of black velvet lined with white silk. A later mask of black and green silk covered the whole face and was held in place by a glass or silver button placed between the teeth. The earliest masks were held by a wire that curved over the forehead and on top of the head. Later, strings were attached to the sides and tied in back.

mat finish a dull, unglazed, smooth surface of silk, cloth or leather.

mat texture the flattering look of powdered skin was discovered by the fashionable use of hair powder in the seventeenth century. see *cosmetics*.

matara fur seal, of a rich, dark brown. see *seal, Alaska*.

matchcoat a British name for the garment of coarse cloth or fur worn by Indians, especially the Algonquins, along the Eastern seaboard of the American Colonies.

matelassé, matelas French for mattress, a crêpy fabric of silk, wool or other material with a net back. Machine or hand-stitched and embossed with small motifs similar to quilting or blistering. Used for dresses and wraps, early twentieth century. see *cloqué, cloguet*.

maternity wear a development of the twentieth century, when it was no longer considered proper for pregnant women to remain in seclusion as soon as their condition became evident. Dresses are made full, often hanging straight from the shoulders or a yoke; smocks or tunics are worn over a skirt which has an expandable waistline or is cut out over the abdomen.

mauve, mauveine a delicate lilac

color produced by a violet dye, obtained in 1856 by the British chemist Sir W. H. Perkin by the oxidation of aniline.

Mechlin lace   a bobbin lace made in Mechlin, Belgium; formerly any Flemish lace.

Medici collar   see *collar, Medici.*

Medici lace   French bobbin-lace similar to Cluny lace, but of finer thread. Woven closely and open in intricate pattern with one edge scalloped.

medieval, gothic, moyen-age   Historians place the Middle Ages as the period between the Fall of Rome A.D. 476 and the Fall of Constantinople in 1453. Other scholars designate the period between the tenth and fifteenth centuries as the flowering of the Gothic period. With the close of the Dark Ages, men and women were still wearing the Greco-Roman costume with its Byzantine influence but which, due to the teachings of Christianity, tended more and more to conceal the figure. In fact, religious bans governed both style and color of all laymen's dress. see illustrations.

melon sleeve   see *sleeve, melon.*

melton   a heavy, felted woolen fabric finished with a close even nap without luster. First made in England; in many grades. Used for overcoats, windbreakers, uniforms, pea jackets and regal livery.

meltonette   a lightweight women's wear cloth for suits.

Mennonite   a Protestant sect of German origin, settlers of Pennsylvania in the late seventeenth century. Their clothing was very simple, following strict rules. see *Amish.*

men's dress, modern   had its start in the 1660's when the justaucorps and the doublet changed to coat and vest. The idea came from France where Charles II of England had spent his exile. Pepys' *Diary* tells us that the change occurred in October, 1666, when Charles, giving his officials a month's notice, dressed them all in a new vest and coat after "ye Persian mode." And he adds, "it was all black and white." Today, the standard simplicity dates from the French Revolution in the 1790's. The principal change was the substitution of trousers for culottes or breeches.

mercerized, mercerizing   a permanent finish given cottons to make the yarns softer, silkier and stronger. Named for the discoverer, an English calico printer and chemist, John Mercer (1791–1866). see *schreinerize.*

merino   a breed of fine-wooled sheep originating in Spain and raised mostly for the wool. The original Spanish breed is nearly 2,000 years old. The woolly pelt is sheared and dyed to simulate more expensive furs and is also used for trimmings. The best in the world now comes from Australia. The fleeces are obtainable from Argentina, Austria, France, Germany, Ohio, U.S. and the Union of South Africa. Merino yarn is considered the best for weaving by the weaving trade, and the best for worsted and woolen knitting by the knit trade. The woven fabric resembles cashmere and is used for suits, coats and sportswear.

Merry Widow sailor   a wide-brimmed cartwheel style of feminine straw hat which appeared in 1908 during the run of the popular operetta, *The Merry Widow* by Franz Lehar.

Merveilleuse, à la La Merveilleuse   the feminine counterpart of the Incroyable during the Directoire Period in France, 1795–1799. She wore a diaphanous gown with short tight bodice and an extreme style of bonnet.

mesh bag   a lady's small handbag of flexible link mesh in gold, silver or plated

Medieval

linen loincloth
tied with tapes-
French-15th c.

linen drawers
with cloth hose
tied to tape
in slot-
13th c.

cloth hose tied
to linen shirt-
English knight-
14th c.

short
linen drawers
tied with
drawstring-
15th c.

canvas
drawers
of an
English
workman-
13th c.

cloth hose over
linen drawers-
cloth tunic-
English-
13th c.

hose into breeches-
tied to doublet-
white linen shirt-
German workman-
15th c.

shirt slit at
sides revealing
loincloth-
French farmhand-
15th c.

hose into breeches-
buttoned to doublet-
codpiece-
German-
late 15th c.

doublet with
eyelet holes for
laces-over shirt-
hose tied to doublet
over drawers-
Italian-
15th c.

cloth hose
laced to edge
of shirt or
doublet-
Italian-
15th c.

Medieval Corsets

buttoned doublet with eyelet holes for laces — undershirt — hose over drawers tied to doublet — Italian — 15 th c.

doublet over shirt — hose and boots tied to doublet — Italian — 15 th c.

parti-colored costume — cote-hardie worn over corsetto — Italian — 14 th c.

lacing the cotte worn over the chemise — French — 15 th c.

laced doublet — hose tied to doublet — French — 15 th c.

child in shirt, doublet and hose — Italian — 15 th c.

"boyish form" of the 15 th c. — reinforced canvas lining — Flemish

doublet over shirt — hose laced to doublet over drawers — French — 15 th c.

gown with bodice joined to skirt — French — 15 th c.

208

Medieval

long-sleeved shirt
worn under cuirass-
braccae
cross-gartered-
Romanesque Italian-
8th and 9th c.

tunic skirt tucked
up over linen
braies or drawers-
leather boots
cross-gartered-
French peasant-
8th to 10th c.

hair shirt worn
as a penance by
the Christian
pilgrim-
4th to 14th c.

surcoat worn
over the tunic-
French-
13th c.

brech or drawers
fastened at the knees
by drawstrings-
English-
13th c.

loose linen
brech or drawers
under woolen
tunic-English
woodsman-
13th c.

brech or drawers
ending in ties
below the knees-
drawstring belt-
English worker-
13th c.

Medieval Shapes

bliaud over
chainse-cording,
shirring and
tucks
French-
11th and 12th Cs.

cotte laced at
sides-worn over
linen chainse-
German-
12thc.

cote-hardie or
fitted gown of
brocaded silk-
Italian-
14th C.

embroidered tunic
laced in back-worn
over chainse or chemise-
German-
11th C.

fur-trimmed surcoat
over brocaded
silk cotte-
French-
14th Cs.

cote-hardie
or fitted
gown-
French-
14th C.

laced cotte
over chemise-
skirt tucked
into girdle-
French peasant-
15th C.

corselet laced at sides
over embroidered chemise-
Spanish-13th C.

210

metal. An evening bag popular in the first half of the twentieth century.

mesh fabrics   open mesh texture cloths woven of cotton, linen, wool, nylon, rayon or in combinations; used especially for men's underwear and sportswear.

Mesopotamian costume, ancient   see illustrations, pages 212, 213.

mess jacket   a short, tailless uniform jacket worn on semiformal evening occasions by officers of the Armed Services; in dark blue or white, as prescribed.

messaline   a lustrous, lightweight silk fabric of satin weave for general use in women's wear, including lingerie.

metal lace   a net foundation with motifs of gold, silver and copper threads, woven either by hand or machine.

metallic cloth   any fabric, such as lamé that has gold, silver or tinsel threaded through the design.

Mexican costume   a combination of the characteristic features of colonial Spanish style and ancient Aztec. see *huipilli; mantilla; rebozo; serape; sombrero.*

worn by midshipmen. Of heavy white twill or closely woven cotton with a dark-blue flannel sailor's collar bordered with white soutache. A black silk neckerchief, thirty-six inches square, is folded diagonally around the neck under the collar and tied in front. The blouse, a feminine fashion of the 1910's and 1920's, was popular with young girls and children, especially as a school uniform or for athletics. see *sailor suit.*

middy twill   a twill-weave cotton cloth in white and colors. see *jean.*

midnight blue   a color for men's formal or evening wear. It is claimed that midnight blue has a deep richness that looks blacker than black itself. It was introduced in the mid-1930's and is still smart.

midriff   that section of the body from the waist to the chest; the diaphragm or rib-cage.

mignonette lace   a narrow bobbin lace resembling tulle, with an open mesh.

Milan   straw manufactured in Milan, Italy, and used for women's hats.

Milanese textile   a silk or rayon warped knitted fabric which has a distinctive diagonal cross effect. Used for feminine underwear and gloves.

milaya   the long, dark mantle of cotton that the Egyptian woman wears over her cotton print dress. With men present she may draw the milaya over the lower part of her face.

military braid   see *braid.*

mess jacket-
military and
naval-worn
semi-formal
evenings. U.S.

milaya-same as haik or huke-
black cloth cover worn in street-
bur'u', a crocheted face veil-
Egyptian

middy blouse-
U.S. naval
midshipman's
blouse-
popular
feminine fashion
early 20th C.

middy blouse   a copy of the United States Navy seaman's blouse, originally

military-styled
hat-peacock
blue velvet and
ostrich-velvet
rosette-French-
1813

Mesopotamian

man and woman
wearing the kaunace-
skirt of goat or sheep
skin with long hair-
rolled fabric belt-
skin cape-
Sumerian-3000 B.C.

white linen shirt
over drawers-
rolled fabric belt-
Babylonian
workman-
2000 B.C.

shirt or tunic
of
painted leather-
Semitic-
2000 B.C.

loincloth of
painted leather-
Semitic-
1900 B.C.

soldier's white linen
shirt-copper breast
plate with leather
belt and straps-
colorful woven
hip band-
Babylonian-
1500 B.C.

shirt or tunic
of painted
leather-
Semitic-
1900 B.C.

origin of white linen
kethoneth-first of leather
with colored braid and tassels-
Semitic-1400 B.C.

212

Mesopotamian

belt and short
fringed skirt
worn over the
kandys or shirt -
Assyrian soldier
1200 B. C.

fringed skirt
worn over the
shirt-shawl
of fringe -
Assyrian king -
9th c. B. C.

kandys or shirt
with rolled fabric
belt -
Assyrian woman -
7th c. B. C.

man in
white linen
kandys or
shirt with
embroidered
corselet -
Assyrian -
9th c. B. C.

fringed white
linen shirt or
kĕthŏneth
worn under
woolen caftan -
Hebrew -
7th c. B. C.

short shirt or
kandys - rolled
fabric belt and
leather strap -
Assyro - Babylonian -
7th c. B. C.

fringed white
linen shirt or
kĕthŏneth -
Hebrew -
7th c. B. C.

handmaiden
to queen -
woolen cloth
kandys or shirt -
Assyro - Babylonian -
7th c. B. C.

213

milium   a trade name for satin lining coated on the mat side with an aluminum insulating material, or milium, with a foam back, making the garment thoroughly warm without adding weight.

mill run, or **run o' the mill**   fabric not factory-inspected and often low grade.

millinery   Fine felt, fabric and straw hats made in the Duchy of Milan in the fifteenth and sixteenth centuries were known as Millayne bonnets, hence, the English word "milainer" for the maker of feminine caps and bonnets. Felt hats were first made in England during the reign of Henry VIII.

minaret   a knee-length tunic with wired flaring edge giving the effect of a lampshade, over a slim straight skirt; created by Paul Poiret in 1912, such frivolity ending with the start of World War I, 1914.

mineral fibers   those, such as asbestos, that are procured from minerals in the earth. see *asbestos.*

minidress   a feminine frock introduced in 1966 with its hem above the knees.

miniskirt, minijupe   see *skirt.*

miniver   from the French menu-vair; a valuable fur of the Middle Ages in gray and white squirrel. Today's British usage signifies ermine or the white winter coat of the stoat or weasel, officially the fur used for state robes of British peers. see *ermine.*

mink, maük, Swedish; vision, French   the valuable fur of a semiaquatic animal of the weasel family found throughout North America, Russia, China and Japan, the very best from the Province of Quebec. Slatey or smokey dark brown, the valuable skins dark to the root. An even, close underwool, very strong, even guard

mini-dress· worn by young and mature women of 1960's

hair and a fine, bushy tail, with size and color varying according to region. Much coarse, and therefore cheap mink, comes from Louisiana, of which the smaller and finer peltries of the female and young males are the most desirable.

mink, black   see *mink, wild.*

mink, blended   natural mink of a light color, darkened by a feather dipped in dye and brushed over the longer hairs.

mink, Brazilian   see *marmot.*

mink, China   of the mink family and similar to the American and European animal. The texture, length and color of the hair varies according to district, a pale yellow necessitates dyeing.

mink, European   a natural dark, ranch mink and also, a white Aleutian mink imported from Denmark, Finland, Norway and Sweden. The skins are being fashioned into the modish coats of the day, with men favoring those of dark mink. Mink is supposedly the warmest of furs.

mink, Japanese or Jap   a smaller animal but silkier than Asiatic mink. It has shorter, darker fur and a muddy yellow color which necessitates dyeing. Used for less expensive coats and trimming.

mink-a semiquatic animal of the weasel family -

mink, kolinsky   also called red sable or tatar sable, the better quality of mink found in Siberia, China and Japan. It has short underwool, usually yellow, and long, brown, silky top hair. It is successfully dyed dark to simulate sable and is used for scarfs, coats and trimming.

mink, let-out   a manner of manufacture, the skins reshaped by being slashed into narrow diagonal strips and then resewn into long, rather than wide sections, enhancing the richness of the fur.

mink, mutation   ranch-bred or half blood, domesticated mink having nearly the same qualities as the wild animal, but the wild is stronger. Mink mutation has developed many new colors other than natural.

mink, wild   the animal living in its natural state has a finer, silky, well-furred skin with thick underfur, sturdier and more dense than the ranch-bred. Labrador wild mink is considered the finest in the world.

mino   a cape or overcoat of straw, rushes and such, worn by Japanese peasants.

mintan   the Turk's traditional fine white linen shirt which is still worn. It buttons closely down the front and has an embroidered collar.

mirrors, countenances   The making of glass mirrors on a commercial scale was first developed in Venice in the fourteenth century. From then to the middle of the seventeenth century, when large mirrors were made, fashionable men and women carried small pocket mirrors in little cases of silk or ivory. The tiny mirrors which women carried suspended on a ribbon from the waist, along with small sewing items, were called countenances.

miter or tiara   words of Greek origin, signifying a crown, the name given alike to the varied headbands worn by the Babylonians, Assyrians, Medes and Persians. The modern miter or tiara is a section of a crown worn over the forehead. Fashionable in modern times as a woman's formal evening headdress. see *liturgical headdress.*

mitten   a hand-covering usually of knitted or crocheted wool, thick cloth or leather and often lined with fur or wool. A mitten is fashioned to cover four fingers in one section with a separate stall for the thumb.

mitts   Fingerless knitted gloves were worn by the ancients as protection at work or hunting. In the medieval and Renaissance periods, such gloves were of leather and chamois. In the American Colonies of the eighteenth century, mitts of knitted or crocheted cotton or silk thread became a feminine fashion. From Paris in 1842 came mention of ladies' mitts in black lace or black velvet which were worn at tea. Mitts were still to be seen in the early twentieth century and had a short revival c. 1930.

moat collar   see *collar, moat.*

mob, mobcap   the frilled lingerie bonnet of the eighteenth century, which originated in England. It was suggested by the cap worn by the women of

Mino-cloak of straw or rushes worn over shoulders as a raincoat- Japanese

miter or tiara-papal-white with gold and jewels-head cloth-10th C.

miter or tiara-gold fillet with lappets tied in back-Jewish high priest

miter or tiara of bishop-gold embroidery on white-red lining- 12th C.

mobcap of black taffeta, black gauze and white lawn with bowknots- English-1789

mobcap of sheer white lawn over wire frame- American-late 18th C.

mobcap worn by
Charlotte Corday-
spotted white muslin-
flutted frill-taffeta
ribbon-1793

deerskin
moccasin-bead
embroidery-American
Indian

Ranelagh Market in London. Eventually any cotton bonnet was called a mobcap, or just plain mob.

moccasin   a soft leather shoe without a heel; the sole and sides are made of one piece whose edges are joined with a gathered seam to a U-shaped piece covering the instep. Moccasins worn by North American Indians were embroidered with beads and dyed porcupine quills and had a fold-over cuff tied in back. Moccasins are worn today by American woodsmen and are a favorite playshoe of American youngsters.

mocha   derived from sheepskin of hair sheep from Africa, Arabia and Persia. After the grain is removed by a severe liming process, the fibers below the grain are suèded. The color mocha is a dark, grayish brown named after an Arabian town on the Red Sea famous for its coffee.

mockado   also called mock velvet—a deep-piled velvet with better grades made in silk; cheaper, in wool. Used in the sixteenth and seventeenth centuries.

mocmain   a fiber, soft and silky, which is used for stuffing. It is from an East Indian cotton tree.

Mod   in England, a young person who affects an ultramodern version of Edwardian dress, manners and haircut, 1960's.

mode   a manner of living and dressing which depends largely upon taste and caprice of the period; fashion.

model   in costume, an original design created as a pattern from which copies will be made. Also, the mannequin or living model upon whom the creation is fitted and displayed.

modesty bit, modesty piece   a pouf of lace and ribbon worn across the top of the stays to conceal a low V or U décolletage of a gown. Eighteenth, nineteenth and early twentieth centuries.

modiste   a dressmaker or milliner who makes and sells fashionable dresses and hats for women.

mogador, mogadore   a corded tie silk with vividly colored stripes which resembles fine faille. Named for Mogadore, a seaport of Morocco.

moggan   an old Scottish term for a tight knitted sleeve or a knitted stocking without foot, formerly worn by the Highlanders.

mohair   the wiry, lustrous, strong wool of the Angora goat of Asia Minor used in mohair fabrics. see *Angora goat.*

moiré or **watered silk**   a wavy or watered pattern pressed into silk or synthetic silk by passing it between rollers engraved with the design. Used for formal gowns.

moiré   in fur, the watery design of broadtail and galyak classed as flower, lake or ribbed. Flower is like petals scattered over the ground. Lake, large, long ovals of moiré. Ribbed, when the design follows the spinal column and ribs of the animal.

mole   a very small rodent, six to seven

inches long, from North America, Europe and Asia. Skins from Scotland, northern England, Holland, Belgium, Denmark, Germany, France and Italy. Dutch, Scotch and German, preferred. Fragile, beautiful, lightweight fur of a very dark bluish-gray, with guard hair and fur fiber practically the same length. It is dyed all colors and used in coats, jackets, sweaters, linings and trimming.

moleskin cloth   a close-twilled cotton, heavy, strong and backed with a nap. Used for hunting and sports clothes.

moleskin fur   the skins of moles sewn together and used as fur; fragile.

Molyneaux, Captain Edward   see *couture, haute.*

monk bag   a small purse worn by sailors' round the neck on a cord, containing their money and valuables.

monk's hood   see *almuce.*

monk's robe   a straight, full-length garment of cloth with standing collar, buttoned from neck to hem and usually sashed with a tasseled cord. The cassock of ecclesiastics. see *cassock; soutane.*

monk's shoe   a low shoe of soft but heavy leather with heel and plain toe and a strap passing over the instep and buckled at the side.

monkey fur   from monkeys of the Colobus genus of tropical Africa. Long, silky, lustrous hair either all black or black and white with no underfur. The black is dipped in dye to darken the skin. Used for capes, muffs and trimming since the Great Exhibition in London in 1851 when a few dressed peltries were first displayed by furriers. A revival of the fur occurred in the 1920's, but it has been rarely seen in the mode since.

monkey jacket   a sailor's jacket for

rough weather. Short, heavy and snugly fitted, of dark blue cloth.

monkey suit   a colloquial term for a man's tuxedo.

Monmouth cock   see illustration.

monocle   a single unframed lens or glass of rock crystal used by men for one eye of impaired vision. It appeared in England in the 1820's and is still seen there today. The Englishman became adept in the handling of the lens which he might carry in a pocket or on a black silk cord worn round the neck.

monogram   the initials of a person's name joined into a decorative motif for engraving jewelry, embroidering pieces of apparel, or stamping leather goods.

monotone weave   a tweed of leather mixture in checks or plaids with the yarn pre-dyed in several toned-down colors.

montagnac   trade name for a woolen fabric considered one of the highest quality overcoatings available. Genuine montagnacs have varying amounts of camel and vicuña hair in them. Imported from France.

montauban   see *chapel de fer.*

montenegrin   a semifitted, caftanlike sleeveless outer garment worn by Montenegran women (Yugoslavia). It is usually embroidered in brilliant colors.

montero cap   see *cap, montero; Eugénie's wigs.*

moonstone   one of the feldspar group of gem stones, with a milky-blue sheen.

Moorish cloth   see *Turkish toweling.*

moreen   a water-embossed finished fabric of wool and cotton, coarse and stout, with ribbed effect.

the mole is trapped for its rich, soft, black fur. Found in n.a. Europe and Asia.

Monmouth Cock- beaver hat with feather fringe and white ostrich- cocked at the sides-worn by Duke of Monmouth, British-1670

monocle-fawn. colored felt hat- black ribbon band- English-1870

morion   helmet which appeared in Europe about 1550, introduced by the Spaniards, who copied it from the Moors; worn by foot soldiers in the sixteenth and seventeenth centuries. The hatlike piece had crown, brim and eartabs. see *cabasset*.

morning coat   see *frock coat*.

morning or **house dress**   simple cotton frocks that women wore for "morning chores," before the days of sports clothes and pants of the twentieth century.

Morocco   goatskin usually dyed red; originally produced by the Moors. The modern leather is of calfskin, sheepskin and other thin leathers with the pebble graining and finish imitated by printing and embossing. Used for ladies' bags, wallets, purses, men's and women's lounging slippers, etc.

morse   a clasp or brooch that fastens the liturgical cope or cloak worn by priests and bishops.

mortarboard   academic cap with flat, square top projecting beyond the round skullcap and long, silk tassel. see *catercap*.

mortier,   medieval; a deep skullcap with a flat round table-top made of pleated velvet or silk with a gold braid or ermine band around the head. Worn by certain high functionaries of the law in France.

mosaic   an inlaid design of small colored stones arranged in geometric forms; building a composition according to a prearranged pattern or picture. Used in buttons, jewelry, especially pendants and earrings.

Mother Hubbard   also known as wrapper, dressing or tea gown according to its fabric and use. Made of materials ranging from calico to fine silk and velvet,

"Mother Hubbard" or wrapper-of fabrics from cotton to silks and velvet-late 19th and 20th C.

lace and ribbon trimmed. A long, flowing gown gathered to a fitted square or round yoke and often tied with a self-belt. Worn in late nineteenth and early twentieth centuries. The American wrapper was the origin of the Hawaiian muu-muu. see *muu-muu*.

mother-of-pearl; nacre   the iridescent lining of various sea shells; used for buckles, buttons and other items requiring hard, decorative material. The first and smallest mother-of-pearl buttons, used on a man's shirt, appeared in the early nineteenth century.

motif   an ornamental design used singly or repeated, printed on fabric, embroidered, crocheted or appliquéd to a surface.

motley   dress composed of various and sundry parts and colors. The jester or fool of the Middle Ages wore a motley costume, variegated in color. see *cap and bells*.

motoring veil   see *veil*.

mouches   the French word for "flies" was used to denote beauty patches. They were made of black silk court plaster, cut in diamond shape, round, crescent and star, but always very small. see *patches*.

mouflon   a small wild sheep with an abundant mane found in regions of northern mountainous Russia and on the islands of Corsica and Sardinia. It has short, reddish-brown hair on the upper part of the body. see *goat*.

mountain sable   see *sable, mountain*.

mountmellick   embroidery used for household linens. An embroidery of coarse white cotton thread worked in large floral designs and finished with knitted fringe.

mourning band   a broad band or brassard of black cloth worn on the left coat sleeve; originally of black crepe. It was customarily worn by all men after a death in the family, when not wearing a black coat; men servants also wore it with livery. This custom is still observed in parts of Europe. In the United States the practice of wearing any kind of mourning has largely been given up since World War II, but military officers still wear a band at state funeral ceremonies.

mourning black   Among gentlefolk in the seventeenth century the wearing of mourning was carried even into negligée and nightclothes. Sheets and coverlets were black and, sometimes, the bed was painted black. Some families kept a mourning bed in reserve, to be loaned to friends when needed. There were toilet articles in black also. In the nineteenth century mourning was part of a widely accepted pattern in length of period and type of dress.

It was strictly observed by both sexes whose outer wear was black, the woman's gowns, coats and hats being trimmed with dull, heavy black crepe. One came out of mourning gradually, in purple, lavender and white for summer. With the changing way of living, mourning apparel is rarely seen in the twentieth century.

mourning colors   black was the color of mourning in Europe, as it had been in ancient Greece and the Roman Empire. The Romans of the republic wore dark blue. Purple and violet were for cardinals and kings of France. Ladies of ancient Rome and Sparta wore white, also the color of mourning in China. Until 1498, it was the color of mourning in Spain. Violet was the custom in Turkey. White silk hatbands are still customary in several English provinces. Yellow for Egypt and Burma, and in Brittany some peasant widows wear yellow caps.

mourning, white   the wearing of all white instead of all black. A royal custom probably originated by Mary, Queen of Scots, whose first husband, Francis II, King of France, left her a widow at the age of eighteen. The court was dominated by her mother-in-law, Catherine de Medici, who was already wearing mourning for the former king, IIenri II, and the difference in costume afforded the younger queen some distinction.

mousquetaires, musketeers   bodyguards of the kings of France, which originated in the sixteenth century. In the seventeenth century, under Louis XIV, there were two companies, known as the Blacks and the Grays, from the colors of their horse blankets. No uniforms were adopted until the eighteenth century which followed the mode of the cocked hat, deep cuffs, collar, vest, etc.

mousquetaire collar   see *collar, mousquetaire.*

mousquetaire glove   a heavy leather glove with a flaring wrist extension fringed and embroidered with colored silk thread; seventeenth century. The feminine mousquetaire is a long glove with forearm length, a short wrist-opening with several tiny pearl buttons, which was first worn by Sarah Bernhardt in the 1870's. Eventually for formal dress it became de rigueur made with the unopened armlength. So it has remained to date, worn crushed down casually. Made mostly in white, but black, fawn color and pale tints; in glacé kid or suède were also fashionable.

mousseline   a fabric of cotton, wool or silk, very fine and soft. Also in heavier weights for use in linings and trial patterns.

mousseline de soie   a muslin of silk or rayon rather like chiffon but crisp and firm. Used for linings in collars, yokes and cuffs.

moustache, mustache   see *beards.*

mouton   French for lamb. Sheared lamb of the Merino species dyed or bleached to imitate more expensive furs, principally beaver, nutria and seal, and called mouton pressed lamb. Used for all-purpose coats for men and women; heavy, warm and durable.

Moygashel, Inc.   the trade-mark of an imported Irish linen of excellent quality. Used for dresses, blouses and suits.

moyle   see *mule*.

Mozambique   a loosely woven dress fabric with a warp of double cotton threads and a soft cotton filling.

mozetta   a short linen shoulder cape worn over an alb. A bishop's vestment.

muffs   indispensibles, the English name, were soft bags open at each end for warming the hands. They were originated by the French in the seventeenth century. They were also used to carry the little pet dogs then so popular. For men, mostly of plush stuffed with cotton and wadding; of gold or silver tissue ornamented with ribbons and laces for the ladies. Muffs continued popular with both sexes in the eighteenth century but were used only by women in the nineteenth and early twentieth centuries. Women favored a small, fur muff in this later period.

muffetees   a pair of small muffs which many Englishmen carried in the early seventeenth century. By 1663, the large, simple muff was modish. During the 1790's, many Englishmen in deference to the public interest in Charles James Fox, the statesman and orator (1749–1806), carried very large muffs of red fox fur. Muffs were equally popular in the American Colonies and also used by men and women. The muff was a mark of dignity among older men.

muffler   an ornamental scarf or neckerchief of wool or silk, worn by men and women, especially in winter as throat protection.

mufti   a term derived from the British

muff of fox-
with ribbon
bowknot-
frockcoat
with tassels-
powdered hair-
leather jockey
boots-French-1779

mule or boudoir
slipper of velvet
or satin and lace

services in India; civilian dress worn when off-duty by naval or military officers.

mukluk   Arctic half-boot of sealskin or walrus hide with flesh side out and fur inside. Canvas top and tanned leather sole and laced with thongs. An army Arctic boot worn over a leather boot with white canvas uppers and white leather sole, 1940's.

mule or **moyle**   slippers without heels or heel counters, to the sixteenth and seventeenth centuries. They acquired heels in women's fashions in later centuries. Also called *boudoir slipper.* see *scuffs.*

mull   an old-fashioned fabric in a plain-woven, very lightweight silk or cotton. Formerly popular for women's blouses and children's frocks. Late eighteenth and early nineteenth centuries.

mummy cloth   a cloth, no doubt linen, in which Egyptian mummies were wrapped. The cloth was also used for embroidery.

mungo, mongo, mousée   reclaimed wool made from milled, felted or hard-spun woolens.

muscadine   a pastille scented with musk; the name was applied to effeminate young men of the French Revolutionary period who overdressed and used quantities of the scent.

musette bag   a soldier's leather or canvas bag on a shoulder strap for carrying provisions.

mush   a Briticism for an umbrella.

mushroom hat   of felt or straw; a simple round crown with a downward-shaped round brim, banded with ribbon.

mushru   an East Indian satin fabric, sturdy, cotton-backed and often striped or figured.

musketeers   see *mousquetaires*.

muskrat or **musquash, mushquash**   the latter name is of American Indian origin and still used in the London fur market. Muskrat is a durable fur of a prolific rodent found in the United States and Canada. The fur is dark, glossy brown or black with thick underfur and strong top hair; the three types known as northern, southern and black. The skins are worked for certain garments in let-out mink fashion and are dressed, dyed, bleached and sold under many fancy names.

muslin   a staple, plain-woven cotton first made in Mosul, Mesopotamia. It comprises weaves from sheerest batiste and soft nainsook to heavyweight bedding.

muslin model   a muslin sample of a garment design made for try-out or fitting. see *toile*.

moustache, moustachio   see *beards*.

mustard yellow   a rich brownish-yellow, the color of mustard sauce.

muted   a term applied to colors, meaning subdued values.

mutton chops   see *side whiskers*.

muu muu   The dress of the Hawaiian woman began as a cotton wrapper or robe with which the early American missionaries clothed the "pagans." The natives added charm to the garment in flower motifs and color and in the 1930's some American college girls discovered the simple style. Led to the shift as a fashionable dress. see *Mother Hubbard*.

muskrat-durable fur dressed, dyed and bleached-sold under many names

ermine cape and muff edged with tails-white silk Brandenburg-velvet gown and hat-crown of plumage

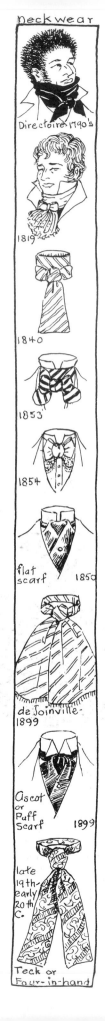

Directoire 1790's

1819

1840

1853

1854

flat scarf 1850

de Joinville 1899

Ascot or Puff Scarf 1899

late 19th-early 20th C.

Teck or Four-in-hand

N

nacre   mother-of-pearl.

nacre velvet   see *velvet, nacre.*

nail   a cloth measurement; one-sixteenth of a yard, or 2½ inches.

nail cosmetics   see *fingernails.*

nainsook   a soft, fine cotton striped, barred or plain, originally woven in India. Used for men's underwear and pajamas.

nankeen, nankin   a strong, buff-colored Chinese cotton woven of a fibrous tissue of a tree or shrub grown in the East Indies and China; named for Nanking where principally made. It was introduced into America in 1828 from Sicily and became especially popular for summer breeches and riding breeches. Also a fabric made with tussah silk or rayon in plain or twill weaves and in a natural or ecru color. Weight and texture vary with quality. see *shantung; tussah; pongee.*

nap   hairy fibers of uniform length and texture on some fabrics, lying smoothly in one direction and forming a soft surface, not a pile.

napa   a soft leather made in Napa, California, by tanning sheepskin or calfskin with a soap and oil mixture. Used the same as real leather.

Napoleon boot   see boot, Napoleon.

Napoleon collar   see *collar, Napoleon.*

napping   a finishing process to produce a soft, fuzzy surface on some cloths,

coatings and blankets. Used also on hat felts of poor quality, for the same purpose.

natural   the off-white color of undyed fabrics or yarns.

Neapolitan hat   see *hat, Neapolitan.*

near seal   see *seal, imitations.*

neck ruff   made of fur, cloth or silk held by a satin fold around the neck and finished with satin loops. 1890's. see *ruche; cartwheel.*

neckband shirt   standard contemporary masculine shirt with a neckband having buttonholes back and front for separate collar.

neckcloth   scarf, muffler, neckerchief or other neck dressing worn by men and women in the eighteenth century.

neckerchief   a kerchief for the neck.

necklace   an encircling ornament for the neck, usually in such pliable form as a string of beads or a chain of links in gold, silver, other metals or jewels. There are varied styles, see *lavalière; rivière.*

neckstock   originally a black satin or white linen cravat wrapped twice around the neck over a standing starched collar. The ends were either tied in front or buckled in back. Eighteenth and early nineteenth centuries.

neckwear, masculine   In the 1830's and 1840's the muffler tied in back, and the neckcloth in front filled in the space above the waistcoat to the chin. The

222

white evening bow tie often sported embroidered ends. It was Beau Brummell, the famous English dandy, who discovered the use of starch to stiffen his cravat to the right consistency to preserve the proper folds of the neckpiece. From then on the stiff collar or "underproper" and cuffs became important accessories in their own right. In the 1840's, collar points turned down becoming, by the 1850's, a true folded-down collar. Also in the 1850's came the small, narrow bow tie. It was stiffened by an inner lining, the bow sewn on and the scarf fastened by a strap and buckle, the first ready-made tie. see *collar; cravat; focal; four-in-hand; muffler.*

needle, steel   It is believed that the Chinese were the first to use steel needles, which were carried westward by the Moors. A needle-making industry was established in Nuremberg in 1370. The manufacture of needles was carried on in small shops during the reign of Queen Elizabeth I, eventually developing into important industries in England and Germany.

needle tapestry   embroidery worked on canvas in a variety of stitches, giving the effect of woven tapestry.

needlepoint   counted embroidery stitches worked with a needle over the threads of a canvas; the term generally refers to such work done in tent stitch.

needlepoint lace   a lace made entirely with sewing needle instead of bobbins, and worked on a paper pattern with buttonhole and blanket stitches.

needlework   see *stitch.*

negligée   an informal and usually flattering robe that a woman wears for leisure at home. Formerly it was worn during the rest period after lunch which was indulged in without the steel-boned corset.

negligée cap of red velvet-shaved head-American 1767

negligée cap   a man's cap of the wig-wearing period, worn at home and especially in the American South during hot weather. The cap, always of handsome fabric, was occasionally worn for a gentleman's portrait.

Nehru tunic   see *chogā.*

net, netting   openwork fabrics made with meshes of varied size in silk, cotton, linen, cord or twine, according to the requirements. Used for veils, dressmaking, curtains, fish nets, tennis nets, etc.

netcha   an Eskimo word for a sealskin coat.

net embroidery   various net stitches worked on a net ground, the completed piece often called lace, especially Breton.

New Look   a dramatic change in fashion which occurred in 1947. At the end of World War II a new couturier, Christian Dior of Paris (1905–1957), a former art dealer, turned his creative talent to feminine dress. Under his guidance the slim, flat, rather masculine figure acquired bosom, hips, abdomen and derrière with small waist and clothed in a bouffant fashion. Women donned the guipière or waist-cincher, and costumes were boned, lined and padded. The long full skirt, extravagantly bias-cut, was a welcome reaction to the skimpy clothes of wartime when fabric was often government rationed.

New Look created by Dior of Paris - corseted small waistline - long-waisted bodice - tiny suede tricorne - with jewel - 1954

New York surtout   a man's fashionable, short, black overcoat with skirts cut straight around. A wide collar to the waistline, finished with wide black silk braid; 1850's.

Newmarket surtout   a British overcoat named for Newmarket, England, a town famed for its race meets. The coat, a long, skirted, double-breasted cloak in redingote style, worn for riding and driving in the nineteenth century. It was always finished with a velvet collar.

New York surtout - short black overcoat with seam at waist - silk braid edged rolled collar - carrying black bowler - 1851

Newmarket surtout or overcoat in redingote style - chamois-colored cloth - always a velvet collar - black satin stock - black beaver hat - gaiter breeches - early 19th C.

nightcap   a negligée or undress cap which came into vogue in the late sixteenth century. It was much worn by gentlemen in the seventeenth century as undress, especially when without a wig. Nightcaps were often luxurious headpieces of velvet with embroidery, gilt and lace. A gentleman often had his portrait painted in a plain velvet cap. Women also wore nightcaps, but of sheer cottons with frills, lace and embroidery.

nightdress   old English; there were many names for the feminine sleeping garment which varied from century to century. Fifteenth and sixteenth centuries: nightdress, nightgown, night rail or rayle, night shift; seventeenth and eighteenth centuries: nightsmock, nightgown, nightdress; nineteenth to date: nightgown or nightdress.

nightgown, evening gown   in the period of Henry VIII, a night gown was an evening gown, there being record of one worn by Anne Boleyn (1507–1536) of black satin. A diary of 1771 notes that the writer and her mother called on a bride who was "dressed in a white satin nightgown."

nightshirt   a tailored garment reaching below the knees with side seams partway open. Worn by men and boys until the appearance of pajamas, late nineteenth century. Center front buttoned down to the waist; long sleeves and standing or turndown collar. Cuffs, collar and front were often decorated with red cross-stitch embroidery on white cotton or linen.

nightsmock   Ladies and gentlemen of the seventeenth century slept in "night smocks," common folk in their "day smocks," or regular clothes. The smocks of the upper class were made of "Holland fine" with cambric sleeves and point-lace edging. Inventories tell us that such owners owned one to two dozen fine smocks.

ninon   a stout silk voile with transparent surface. Used for dresses, neckwear and lingerie.

Nineteenth Century costume   see illustrations, pages 225–247.

Nithsdale   a hooded riding cloak of red cloth, often fur-lined, popular in the eighteenth century. Named for Lady Nithsdale, whose husband, a Jacobite rebel under sentence of death, escaped from the Tower of London wearing his wife's cloak, 1716.

Nineteenth Century-
Empire corset

elastic webbing
side inserts-
single front lace-
French-1803

damask zona
laced in back-
whaleboned-
French-1805

front bands of
elastic webbing-
French-1804

long, English
corset laced
in back-
1810

linen bandelette
after ancient
Greek design-
French-
1810

white
dimity
corset
laced in back-
French-1813

white ninon
corset-frilled
shoulder straps-
French-
1810

front-laced
colored
corselet over
embroidered
chemise-
French-1822

225

Nineteenth Century corset-
1830's

"instant" unlacing by pulling out whalebone rod-
French-1830

back-laced corset with yoke and whaleboned foundation cap sleeves-
French-c.1839

back-laced corset hooked in front-embroidery-
French-1837

gray satin corset laced in back-
French-1835

corset with dropped shoulder straps-double lacing through tiny pulleys-
French-c.1835

pregnancy and nursing corset-white with rose ribbon trimming-
French-1830

single back lacing-
French-1839

226

Nineteenth Century·
corset·
1840's

back·laced
corset with
reinforced
front·
French

lacing through
pulleys·two
single strings
laced from
top and
bottom
to waist·
French·
1840

back·laced
corset·
French·1845

lacings
through pulleys·
embroidered
edging·
French·
1846

single back
lacing·
embroidered
edging·
French·
1845

corset·cover
of fine
lingerie fabric·
lace·edged
sleeves·
English

Nineteenth Century-
first half-
bustle-lingerie
accessories

chemisette
and brassière-
ruff called
"Betsy"-
English-
1810

"Swiss
petticoat"
with
fan pleats-
1820

corset over
chemise-
bustle tied
over corset-
English-
c.1828

pleated
crinoline
"wheel"
tied over
corset-
French-
1840's

pair of
wicker or
wire mesh
cushions
over the
corset-
1840's

sleeve cushion
tied round
arm-
1830's

bustles of varied
shapes and sizes-
1830's

chemisettes and undersleeves-
lawn with embroidery,
lace and tucks-1840's

Nineteenth Century-
first half-
chemise

Empire chemise-
sheer cotton
or linen-
French-
first decade

lingerie nightcaps of
lawn, lace, tucks and
embroidery c.1830

batiste
chemise-
frills of
self fabric-
French-
1805

the "Swiss
petticoat-
cambric slip
with corded
hem and
embroidered
ruffle-
1820

chemise (shirt)
into separate
lingerie
shirtwaist-
French-
1829

linen
nightgown
with frills-
lace cap-
1825

chemise with
flap to conceal
corset top-
1840's

chemise
with simple
embroidery-
1820's

Nineteenth Century-
first half
waistcoat and
neckwear

pull-over
waistcoat-
muslin
cravat-
French-
1800

shawl-collared
waistcoat-
whaleboned
stock-
French-
1825

muslin stock-
striped
waistcoat-
French-
1809

velvet waistcoat-
muslin cravat-
Spanish-
1st decade

velvet waistcoat-
muslin stock-
French-
2nd decade

plush waistcoat-
piqué stock
and cravat-
French-
1828

cloth waistcoat-
Brandenburgs-
silk muffler-
pearl scarfpin-
French-
1829

piqué waistcoat-
black silk
cravat-
French-
c.1830

shawl-
collared
waistcoat-
black satin
muffler-
English-
1830's

turned-down
collar-black satin
muffler-cashmere
waistcoat-
English-
1842

striped cravat-
embroidered
waistcoat-
French-
1831

bow-tied
stock-
striped silk
waistcoat-
English-
1834

black velvet
waistcoat-
black satin
cravat-
French-
1840

230

Nineteenth Century-
first half-
shirt and
neckwear

frilled shirt-
collar points-
muslin cravat-
French-
1805

collar points-
silk scarf-
French-
1823

collar points-
muslin stock-
English-
1810

linen
smock-
English

2nd decade-
English

whaleboned
striped
silk stock-
French-
1827

collar points-
muslin stock-
French-
1820's

1820's
English

muslin
dress
stock-
French-
1829

turned-down
collar-silk cravat-
French-
1830's

1820's
English

black satin muffler
fastened with
solitaire gem-English-
1840's

collar points-
muslin stock-
two waistcoats,
muslin and
brocade-
French-
1834

collar points-
black silk
cravat-
English-
1840's

231

Nineteenth Century
first half-
negligée

organdy and
black lace-
French-
1830's

brocaded
velvet robe-
silk muffler-
French-
1839

taffeta with
pleated frilling-
French-
1839

cloth and
silk braid-
French-
1840's

the "amazon"
in masculine
robe and shirt-
French-1830's

robe of
brocaded silk-
French-
1840's

Nineteenth Century-
first half-
drawers-
pantalets

small girl
in pantalets-
English-
1810

corded
pantalets
and frock-
French-
1816

young lady
in embroidery.
edged
pantalets-
American-
1837

drawers-
knitted silk-
drawstrings
tied at sides
and inside
legs-
English-
2nd decade

muslin frock
and
pantalets-
French-
1836

front and back
of opera (open)
drawers-laced
in back-
English-
2nd decade

back view-
pantalets
with tucked
bottoms-
1830's

small boy
in pantalets
and frock-
American-
1820's

233

Nineteenth Century-
second half-
children's lingerie-
1880's

nightdress-
pink
batiste-
red wool
embroidery

bustle
petticoat tied in back-
white muslin-tucks
and embroidery

little girl's
initialed chemise-
batiste with
lace edge

bustle ruffles
buttoned on-white
muslin
and lace

boy's bodice
and drawers-
muslin with
lace edge

red flannel stays-
girl's 6 to 12-
laced in back-
whalebone
supports

long waisted
petticoat-
white muslin
with colored
embroidery

linen underdrawers-
boy's 10 to 12-
ties back
and legs

day shirt-
boy's 12 to 14-
white muslin
with white
embroidery

muslin
knickerbockers-
girl's 6 to 8-
buttoned at
sides-pleated
cambric frill-
bobbin lace
insertion-
extra fulness
in back

Nineteenth Century-
second half-
feminine
smallclothes

girl's
linen drawers-
buttoned at sides-
tucks-embroidery-
1863

winter garment-
corset cover
and bloomers-
knitted fabric-
1890's

crocheted wool
under petticoat-
white and scarlet-
1863

white
cotton
corset
cover-
lace
edging
and
insertion-
1890's

winter under
petticoat-
quilted
calico-
back
view-
1870's

corset over
chemise, drawers
and under petticoat-
striped stockings-
1870's

black
corset
over chemise
and drawers-
crocheted
lace-black
lisle or silk
stockings-
1890's

white cotton combination
corset cover and drawers-
lace, tucks and embroidery-
1890's

white cotton
combination corset
cover and drawers-
buttoned in front-
lace insertion-
embroidery edging-
1878

235

Nineteenth Century-
second half-
petticoats

short skirt
for walking-
hitched-up
outer skirt-
1862

belt with
cords and
clips to
hitch up
skirt-
1862

crinolette-
half back of
half hoops
tied to
petticoat-
1873

bustle
petticoat-
white muslin
and embroidery-
1870's

front
and back
separate-buttoned
together-white
muslin and lace-
1879

petticoat of
white cambric-
point d'esprit
lace-pink
satin ribbon-
1891

1880's

woolen moiré-
velvet ribbon

plush-
lace and
ribbon

white flannel
with
embroidery

236

Nineteenth Century-
second half-
crinoline

bloomer costume-
protest against
exaggerated
crinoline-
1857

muslin
interlined
with steel hoops-
front closing
panel-
1857

steel hoops-
embroidered
petticoat-
corset
cover-
1857

crinoline puff
with steel hoops-
ribbon ties-
worn over
petticoat-
1860

elliptical
steel hoops
held by tapes-
1867

scarlet flannel
crinoline -buckled
straps-steel
hoops-
1869

steel hoops held
by suspenders
front and back-1869

bustle
crinoline of
steel hoops-
1870

crinoline puff
with
steel hoops-
1863

237

Nineteenth Century-
second half-
bustle

steel hoops
with tape,
chemise,
corset and
petticoat-
c.1870

hoop skirt
with bustle-
steel hoops
and crinoline-
1873

stretchable
spiral
wire
bustle-
1880's

the polonaise-
taffeta and
fluted velvet
ribbon-
1869-

folding
bustle-
steel hoops
and muslin-
1880's

dress-
improver-
horsehair
and
embroidered
dimity-
1872

bustle over
corset-
rows
filled
with
down-
lace
edging-
1886

dress
improver-
horsehair
ruffles-
1872

bustle skirt
with steel
hoops-
1871

bustles and
breast forms
of braided
wire-
1880's

Nineteenth Century
second half-
chemise and
nightgown

nightgown of
linen or cotton-
tucks-fluted
frills-
1862

linen chemise-
fluted frills-
fine tucks-
1862

short linen
nightdress-red
cross-stitching-
1863

nightgown of
rose China silk-
eyelet embroidery-
point d'esprit lace-
rose satin ties-
1891

fine linen-white
hand-embroidery-
buttoned neck
to hem-embroidered
hem ruffle-
1880's

white cotton
nightgown with
embroidered
yoke, lace
and ribbon-
1894

chemise of
batiste or silk-
lace and
embroidery-
threaded
with baby
ribbon-
1890's

white cotton
nightgown-
tucks and
embroidery-
1894

239

Nineteenth Century-
second half-
negligée

negligée-white
jaconet-fitted
back-full front
held by belt-
scalloped
ruffles-
1852

negligée-French
blue cashmere
over white satin
petticoat-
appliquéd
Paisley
motifs-
1866

wrapper of old blue
cashmere-jabot and
frills of cream lace-
satin ribbon sash-
pleated hem ruffle-
1883

morning jacket-
pink Saxony
flannel with
pillow lace-
bowknots
on cuffs-
1886

tea gown of
cashmere-
Maline lace
and insertion-
shirred yoke
and cuffs-
balloon
sleeves-
1894

circular combing
mantle-white
cambric-frill of
embroidery-
satin tie-
1887

Nineteenth Century-
second half-
corsetry

waistband laced
in front-pleats
in back-
1862

little girl's
corset laced
front and
sides-elastic
back panel-
1862

back-
laced through
pulleys-hooked in
front-1850

front
fastening-
laced in
back-
1862

plush
edging-
laced in
back-front
closure-
1867

crossed latchet
fastening back
and front-
1868

front
closure-back
lacing-hand
embroidered-
1878

laced
sides and
lower back-front
closure-ribbon
embroidery and
shirred panels-
1879

fitted corset-
cover of longcloth-
Valenciennes lace
and embroidered
insertion-
1878

known as
pear-shaped busk-
spoon busk-
swan-bill busk-
ribbon-threaded
embroidery-
back lacing-
1878

Nineteenth Century-
second half-
corsetry

girl's
buttoned
corset waist
of twill-
1880's

reinforced
waistline-
elastic inserts-
embroidery-
1880's

dancer's corset-
low back
with
lacing-
1880's

close back
lacing-flower
motifs-
embroidered
edging-
1880's

buttoned,
whaleboned garment-
corset and corset
cover in one-
fancy
braid-
1890's

corset with
skirt
supporter-front closure-
side lacings-1880's

striped
coutil with
embroidery-
front closure-
back lacing-
1890's

buttoned
corset waist-
adjustable
shoulder
straps-long
knitted
drawers-
black cotton
stockings-
1880's

infant's
corset
waist-
buttons
to hold
stockings
and underclothes-1890's

satin corset-
back closure-
wide front busk-
eyelet embroidery-
1890's

Nineteenth Century-
second half-
the shirtwaist

linen camicia-
lace edging-
corselet with straps
to tie up sleeves-
Italian
peasant

chemisette or
habit shirt to
wear with vest-
lawn with tucks,
embroidery and
frilling-satin tie-
1852

camicia rosso
or Garibaldi red
shirt-silk with
black braid-black
velvet tie-1862

tailored shirtwaist
of striped percale-
pearl buttons-
silk tie-1896

vest of
fawn color
cashmere-
standing collar-
silk tie-
1863

shirtwaist of
lawn with
embroidered
insertion-
black baby
ribbon-black
satin stock-
1899

shirtwaist of
the Gibson girl -
heavy white
linen or piqué
with Ascot tie
1899

lingerie
neckwear-
butterfly bow-
back of neck-
embroidered jabot-front-
late 1890's

243

Nineteenth Century-
second half-
shirt and sleepwear

Garibaldi red
shirt-"camicia
rosso"-smock
design-tied
silk scarf-
c.1860

false bosom-
dickey-linen
with tucks-
1850's

linen shirt
buttoned in back-
tucked front-
Napoleon or
Windsor scarf
of black satin-
woven elastic
braces-
1850's

dress shirt buttoned
in back-crossbar
dimity bosom
with frills-
1850's

flannel undershirt-
red or white-open underarm
seams-feather
stitching-1863

dress shirt
with stiff bosom-
tab for drawers'
button-1883

nightshirt of
cotton, cotton or
woolen flannel-
1890's

dress shirt with
fluted frills-
one end tie of
pique or lawn-
1860's

nightshirt of
cotton, cotton or
woolen flannel-
1880's

pajamas
of cotton
or silk with
braid fastenings-
1890's

colored stripes on
white-white collar
and cuffs-four-in-
hand scarf-
late 1890's

Nineteenth Century-
second half-
knitwear

knit sports
shirt worn
at Oxford-
1863

knit
underdrawers-
late 1860's

knit striped
polo shirt-
1877

child's knit
bathing suit-
French-
1880's

underwaistcoat
over undershirt-
scarlet flannel-
ribbed cuffs-
lined with
chamois leather-
1880's

knit swim
suit-red and
white striped
shirt-gray
trunks-
1890's

knit "union
undergarment"-
wool, silk, cotton
or combinations-
1880's

knit swim suit-
navy blue and
red striped
shirt-blue
trunks-
1890's

cotton-Scotch
plaid-white
top-1870's

cotton-stripes
varicolored-
1860's

black silk-
flower
embroidery-
1890's

Nineteenth Century-
second half-
bathing suit

corset over
bloomers-
skirt and
tunic-blue
or black-
bag cap-
English-
1877

bustle style-
serge or flannel-
braid trim-
straw hat
over bag cap-
French-
1870's

blue flannel-
white braid-
white canvas
cape and
bag cap-
German-
1864

black or
brown
mohair-
white
braid-
French-
1880's

serge or flannel
in light color-
braid trim-
black cotton
stockings-
American-
1880's

suit and cap
turquoise blue
flannel-white
lace-ribbon
bow at neck-
English-
1880's

two-piece
knit suit-
pleated frill-
Belgian-
1890's

white flannel
metallic thread
embroidery-
flesh pink
tights with
knee-high
drawers-
French-
1890

246

Nineteenth Century-
second half-
haberdashery

dressing gown-
fawn colored
cloth-multi-
colored braid-
c.1860

waistcoat-
plain cloth
with braid-
1850's

waistcoat
over the
cambric
shirt-
1850's

lounge
jacket-red
velvet-black
satin collar
and lining-
waistcoat
figured
cloth
with
braid-
1859

double
breasted
waistcoat-
plaid cloth-
Oxford tie-
1870's

gray cloth
waistcoat
worn with
Prince Albert
wing collar-
Ascot
puff-
1890's

evening dress-
linen shirt-
stiff bosom-
poke collar-
Oxford tie of
lawn or pique-
waistcoat
of linen or
pique-
late 1890's

elastic webbing
and leather-
mid-century

embroidered
satin with
elastic and
leather-
1890

sash vest for
summer evening
dress-buckled
in back- of
ribbed or
surah silk-
1892

hooded
bathrobe of
striped cloth-
cord girdle-
1880's

elastic
garter-
1883

247

Nithsdale riding hood of red cloth often fur-lined- popular in the 18th C.

nivernois a diminutive tricorne worn by the English Macaronies with the cadogan wig in the 1770's. Named for the Duke of Nivernois, Louis-Jules Mancin Mazarani (1716–1798).

none-so-pretties fancy, decorative tapes used for trimming garments in the eighteenth century in the American Colonies.

Norell, Norman see *couture, haute.*

Norfolk jacket a sack or jacket with straight front, with or without a yoke, box pleats down front and back under which passes the self-belt. The style of yoke, pleats and pockets vary. The coat of the Duke of Norfolk's hunting suit, the first "Norfolk," appeared in the 1880's with knickerbockers, a revival of knee breeches for day wear.

Norwegian costume, traditional see illustration; *Hardanger skaut.*

nosegay a boutonnière or small bunch of fragrant flowers. see *boutonnière.*

notched lapel the V-shaped notch on the outer edge of jacket or coat where the collar is seamed to the body. A tailoring term of the early nineteenth century.

Nottingham laces many kinds of net made by machine in Nottingham, England, such as Cluny, torchon and Valenciennes, commonly called Val.

nub yarn a yarn with recurring twists or thick places used for weaving cloths such as chinchilla cloth, or ratiné lace.

nun's cotton an embroidery cotton of fine white thread.

nun's dress in 1965, after wearing the same style of habit for more than a century, the nuns of the Order of the Sisters of Mercy put on a new dress. It was designed by Sybil Connolly of Dublin who is famous for beautiful romantic ballgowns, very often made of Irish handkerchief linen and Irish crochet lace. Both the designer and nuns had hoped the habit would be changed to gray instead of black but because of teaching and nursing in many different climates, the final choice was black gabardine. In the change, some hair was permitted to show under the white cap, the dress was shorter, and pumps with Cuban heels are worn with gun-metal-colored stockings.

nun's veiling a lightweight, semitransparent woolen fabric in black, white and colors. Used in black by nuns for veiling, dresses and cloaks.

nutria; coypu, coypou an aquatic rodent half the size of the beaver, native to South America, and now found in England. The best fur is from Argentina and is called Island Nutria. Argentine fur

Setesdal dress of Norway-worn for festivals - pinafore style over blouse - "pincushion hat" with ribbons - Norway

Norfolk jacket and knickerbockers - tan and yellow plaid woolen cloth - knitted woolen hose - linen gaiters - 1880's

Northampton lace English bobbin lace of the sixteenth and seventeenth centuries imitating Flemish patterns.

is heavier and more expensive than Brazilian and Chilean, durable with soft, dense underfur after being dehaired. It is a rich bluish-brown or occasionally black. Ranch-bred, deep-piled white and champagne color are used for coats, jackets and trimming. The fur is imitated in sheared and dyed raccoon.

nylon   the strongest, finest, most elastic and all-purpose chemical fiber for clothing fabrics. As a filament, it can be blended with other man-made or natural fibers. Of weaves combined with nylon, the first and most widely used is tricot. There are silk weaves, such as taffeta, shantung, crepe, plissés, marquisettes and nets, and plain weaves in linen and cotton types. Nylon is also combined with silk and wool created by Du Pont chemists. Nylon was the first completely synthetic, commercial fiber made from air, water and coal and was created by the chemists at DuPont. see *acrilan; dacron; dynel; orlon.*

nutria or coypu-an aquatic rodent found only in S.A. Durable, soft fur, bluish brown - length to 3 feet with tail 1 foot long

O

obi   Japanese, a wide sash of brocaded silk, lined with contrasting color and inter-lined with stiffening and worn over the kimono. The obi measures fifteen inches wide and four to six yards long. The back ends are tied in a large flat bow or a large butterfly bow, the latter for brides and maidens. Inside the butterfly knot is the obiage, or small cushion for padding.

obiage   see *obi*.

ocelot; South American spotted cat a wildcat of the leopard family found from Texas to Patagonia. Abundant in Central and South America. A flat fur with short guard hair and practically no underfur. Variable markings in dots, rosettes and lines well marked. Used for coats, jackets and trimming.

off-the-rack   a Briticism for ready-made garments. see *ready-made*.

off-white   white with a faint tinge of another color; names include oyster, ivory, bone, eggshell, cream.

oil frock   a waterproof slicker coat worn by fishermen, miners and others.

oilcloth   cotton fabric which has been painted and varnished; a wide variety of uses includes cap visors, belt linings, jackets, capes and many household needs. Known in Great Britain as American cloth.

oiled silk   a silk fabric, thin and plain-woven, made waterproof by being soaked in boiled oil and dried. Used in rainwear and in items of apparel where water-proofing is required, often as a lining, although gradually being replaced by more modern water-proofing.

oilskin   a heavy cotton cloth made waterproof by being impregnated with oil and gum. Used for sailors' apparel and called oilskins or slickers. see *slicker*.

ombré   French for shaded, an adjective and weaving term for stripes of variegated colors melting into each other. Also a cloth woven, or a surface painted, in graduated hues of a special color.

omophoriom   a vestment of bishops of the Greek Church, an embroidered silk strip worn around the neck with the ends crossed on the left shoulder and falling to the knee.

onyx   a form of quartz with black and white bands. Sardonyx has red and white bands. Used in the nineteenth century for men's cufflinks, watch fobs, seals. Also in women's jewelry such as rings, earrings and brooches combined with gold.

ooze   usually calfskin with a suèded or velvety finish made by the use of a tanning liquor of oak, bark, catechu, etc.

opal   a stone composed of silica with a variable amount of water which causes an iridescent play of colors. Opals may be white or black; fire opals are reddish-orange.

opera cloak   a man's knee-length cape-like coat for evening dress wear. Of velvet or fine cloth, it had a standing collar fastened by tasseled silk cords and was worn about the 1850's. The feminine version for formal evening dress was of

opera cloak-
with velvet
collar-over
evening habit-
velvet waistcoat-
gibus, collapsible
grosgrain opera
hat-(gibus) 1834

costly brocade, velvet, silk or fine fur, the costliest being Russian sable.

opera glasses   a small binocular telescope was made for use at the opera or theater, carried by every elegant lady. Sometimes with a handle like a lorgnette, sometimes folding and carried in a leather case. It was generally mounted with mother-of-pearl, smoky or white. Still in use today.

opera hat   see *gibus*.

opera pump   see *pump, opera*.

opossum   American derivative of the American Indian name, apasum, meaning "white beast." The only pouched mammal found in North and South America. A durable long-haired fur with close, silky and whitish underfur and long guard hair in brown and silver. Used natural or dyed to simulate fitch, marten and skunk, or sheared to resemble beaver and nutria. It is popular in silvery yellow and used for coats and trimming. South American opossum of the gray, dark gray or black type is inclined to be woolly.

opossum, Australian   not a true opossum but of the phalanger family. A durable fur but unlike the American opossum, consisting of underhair and top hair; the effect is feathery, close and even. The color varies according to region from gray-blue to reddish yellow with dark and white markings, reddish most common, and gray-blue the most desirable. The fine pelts are used for coats and trimming and the lower grades for collars on sheep-lined jackets. The ringtailed opossum is found from South Queensland to South Australia. A deep bluish-gray, the underfur tinged with dull red which is used natural or dyed gray or brown. The quantity is small and used mostly for trimming.

opus anglicanum   the embroidery of Anglo-Saxon England executed in split stitch, a long outline stitch held to the ground by a tiny stitch through the center.

opus araneum lace   a handmade bobbin lace using the straight lines of the spider web (araneum) for the pattern. The term was used in the Middle Ages for embroidery in general.

orange   one of the three secondary colors with purple and green, orange being a combination of red and yellow. The shades with a greater proportion of red include vermilion and coral; those with more yellow are amber and topaz.

orange blossoms   in the nineteenth century language of flowers, orange blossoms denoted chastity. The flowers, generally artificial, were traditionally worn by brides as a chaplet holding the wedding veil in place. The custom lasted well into the twentieth century.

orby   an American-designed, man's single-breasted walking frock coat eliminating the waistline seam. A seam down center back terminated at the waist. 1907.

opossum-from Indian
name "apasam" for white
beast-durable, long-
haired fur

Orby-cutaway, frock coat or
morning coat-waistline
seam omitted-braid-bound-
American design-1907

organdie, organdy   a fine muslin in plain weave, slightly stiffened, in white and colors. Used for dresses, blouses and collars, cuffs and apron sets.

organza   a slightly stiffened sheer muslin, plain or figured, in white and colors. Used for picturesque diaphanous gowns for bride and bridesmaid apparel. Also used for *robes de style* created by Lanvin of Paris and popular in the 1920's and 1930's.

organzine   a thread used for the warp in silk weaving. Also, the name of the fabric made of the thread.

orle   a heraldic term for a wreath or torso of two colors of silk twisted together, representing the principal metal and color of the wearer's crest, worn around the knight's helmet or as a feminine head-dress. Fourteenth and fifteenth centuries.

Orleans cloth   see *covert cloth.*

orlon   trade name for a fabric made of coal, air, water, petroleum and lime-stone. It is soft, wool-like and drapes well. Used for sweaters and other sportswear.

ornament   that which is added to a costume for adornment, as a piece of jewelry.

orphreys   the tissues and bands with gold work, fringe and lace applied to chasubles, copes and vestments. They were often made separate, permitting change from one garment to another, especially on royal dress. The jeweled work of the eleventh century called anglicanum was highly valued on the

continent. The word *orphrey* originally signified both gold and Phrygia, the home of gold-embroidered tissues.

orrice   a gimp or braid trimming woven with gold or silver thread, popular in the eighteenth century.

orris   lace or braid, originally called Arras, after a town in France. Made of gold and silver thread and popular in the eighteenth century.

orris root   the aromatic rootstock of a European species of iris. It is very fragrant and when powdered, is used for perfume and sachet.

osnabruk   a coarse linen imported from Osnabruk, Prussia, used for men's jackets, shirts and breeches.

native of Africa and Arabia—now raised on ostrich farms—male, black with white plumes—female grayish

ostrich   the largest of existing birds, native to Africa but commercially raised elsewhere. The soft, curling feathers of the small useless wings and of the tail have been used in headdress since the fourteenth century. Large ostrich-feather fans, dyed all colors, were fashionable

orle of rolled silk—
two principal colors
of the wearer's
crest—Italian—1385

Orphreys—medieval motifs

Otter-Canadian or American-slender dark brown animal with valuable, durable fur— 3½ to 5 feet—tail, 1 foot

from about 1910 to 1940. The quill-holed leather is used for handbags and other leather accessories. In the late 1960's there was a revival of ostrich fringe on evening gowns and dresses.

otter, American and Canadian   found in the Northwest, the middle Atlantic region and the Pacific coast of the United States. A slender dark brown animal; the finest eastern peltry from Labrador and the finest Pacific peltry from Alaska.

otter, imitation sea   from Russia, where beaver is sheared, dyed and pointed with white hairs to simulate sea otter.

otter, river   an aquatic animal of the weasel family living on banks of rivers, streams, and along the coast of every continent but Australia. The best fur comes from the coldest regions. Varying in color according to locale, the color ranges from very dark or reddish brown to almost yellow, the most desirable being blue-black top hair with a slightly lighter-colored underfur. It is used as often un-plucked as plucked, because of lustrous silky guard hair. It is not dyed unless poor in color. It was used on men's garments for centuries; today principally for feminine coats, jackets and trimming.

otter, sea   a large, powerful species of the weasel family found in the North Pacific. A valuable fur; rich, dense, silky wool with soft, short guard hair requiring no dehairing process. It is gray-brown to rich black with occasional white or silver

hairs. It is especially valued in Russia and China and was formerly used to trim Chinese mandarin robes. Threatened with extinction, sea otters are now legally protected.

ottoman   a fabric ribbed cross-wise like faille silk but with larger, rounder ribs. The filling is of worsted, silk or cotton. Used for coats, dresses, men's waistcoats and trimmings.

outer wear   a general term for all outside apparel for men and women.

outfit   a noun comprising the complete ensemble for any specific occasion such as travel, sport, etc.

outing flannel   a cotton flannel of many uses, especially for undergarments and nightwear. Plain-woven of soft yarns and well-napped on both sides and sometimes has a wool mixture. Also called tennis flannel, domet or domett.

over-all   see *balandrana*.

overalls   loose-fitting overtrousers with a front bib held by a strap around the neck. Made for working wear of dark blue or brown denim or duck. Designed for workmen originally but used also by women and children when practical. Late nineteenth and twentieth centuries.

overblouse   any blouse that is worn outside the skirt.

overcheck   a check pattern woven over another of different color.

overcoat   a topcoat or greatcoat worn over the suit coat or jacket. see *greatcoat*.

overcoating   special fabrics woven for overcoats such as covert, melton, montagnac, cheviot.

overplaid   a finer line plaid laid over a basic ground plaid usually of neutral

dress overcoat—heavy tan broadcloth—black velvet collar—black top hat. 1890's

overcoat-black broadcloth lined with nutria-otter collar-1918

overcoat of dark blue rhinchilla cloth-chamois gloves-gray spats-1924

overcoat-Chesterfield-dark blue vicuña-black velvet collar-white silk muffler-gibus or opera hat-1941

overcoat in British Guard style-double breasted dark blue melton cloth-1942

man's Oxford-jack leather-English-17th C.

Oxford built on bootlast-tan calfskin-contemporary

tones, one check superimposed upon the other in the weaving.

oversack   a large, loosely fitting overcoat of sack or box style; also, an ulster. Worn first decade, twentieth century.

overseas cap   see *cap, overseas.*

oxford   a low shoe for men, women and children, laced or tied over the instep. The first oxford was a half-boot of heavy black jack leather, seventeenth century England. *Button oxfords* also appeared with a leather piece over the instep which buttoned to one side, on the outer side.

Oxford bags   an English fashion in which trouser bottoms flared, sometimes to a width of 24 inches; 1920's.

Oxford cloth   also called Cambridge mixture. A woolen cloth woven combining black and white or gray, producing a fabric of black or steel-colored ground lightly sprinkled with white.

oxford, gillie   a low-cut sports shoe with open lacing over the instep and the laces tied around the ankles. Late nineteenth century.

Oxford gown   see *academic gown.*

Oxford half-boot   see *boot, Oxford half-boot.*

Oxford shirting   first made in Oxford, England. A stout cotton fabric in plain or fancy basket weave or with narrow colored stripes.

oxford ties   masculine, low, soft patent leather shoes for evening dress laced and tied over the instep.

oyster white   an off-white, yellowish-gray in hue, resembling the inside of an oyster shell.

oyah   see *Turkish point lace.*

P

pac, pack a heavy felt half-boot worn in winter by loggers; also, a moccasin of oil-tanned leather.

paddock suit see *English drape.*

paenula a poncho-like garment for bad weather, worn by the Romans and earlier by the Etruscans, with or without hood, open at the neck, where a buckle or fibula fastened the wrap. It became very popular with civil, military and legal classes in ancient Rome. Though condemned and banned, the paenula eventually replaced the elegant but difficult toga even for senatorial use in the second century A.D. The paenula lengthened to the feet, a long, sleeveless cloak retaining the opening for the head. After changes of design, it became in the seventeenth century the Gothic chasuble, a church vestment. see *abolla; byrrus.*

pafti the heavy silver buckle of the Hungarian woman's belt.

page boy coiffure a medieval style adopted by young women in the 1940's. Shoulder-length hair is worn with the ends turned under.

page boy uniform of cloth with braid and buttons, a fitted short jacket with johnny collar and pillbox cap with chin strap. Worn by hotel bellboys, twentieth century.

pagoda sleeve see *sleeve, pagoda.*

pagri, puggree the turban worn by Hindu men. A large self-draped strip of cotton five to twenty-five yards long, wound round the head in varied styles, often with an end hanging in back.

paillettes, spangles, sequins tiny, round, sparkling metal discs finished in gold, silver and other colors. Pierced in the center, they are sewn to evening dress, fancy costumes and costume accessories.

paint see *cosmetics.*

paisley see *shawl.*

pajamas, pyjamas The masculine lounge and sleep costume came to the Western world from India and Persia. East Indians wore cotton pajamas in the streets and British colonials copied the custom, bringing them back to England about 1870, originally for lounge wear and finally, by the turn of the century, adopting the Eastern jacket and trousers for sleepwear instead of the nightshirt. see *nightshirt.*

pajamas, feminine cotton or silk jacket and trousers, introduced as women's sleepwear in the early 1900's

pagri of the Hindu man-large self-draped turban of printed cotton-Malayan

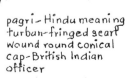

pagri-Hindu meaning turban-fringed scarf wound round conical cap-British Indian officer

palatine or pelerine-
shoulder cape of
fur carried to France
by a Palatine princess-
1671

and first worn more by little girls than by women. Beach pajamas of gaily colored cotton and lounging pajamas in rich fabrics with very wide trousers had some vogue in the 1920's and 1930's before slacks or pants were accepted for round-the-clock wear. Palazzo pajamas 1960's, so called in Italy because intended for dress evenings at-home pajamas. The wearing of pajamas by Italian women, formerly taboo, was later approved when covered with a caftan-like robe or toga. see *culottes, feminine.*

palatine, pelerine   a deep cape-like collar of lawn or lace which covered the shoulders, either cut high to the neck or in bateau line. The little cape, first made of fur and called a palatine or pelerine, was introduced into France by the Palatine Princess Charlotte Elizabeth of Bavaria, second wife of the Duc d'Orléans, brother of Louis XIV, 1671. see *pelerine.*

paletot, paddock   a single-breasted man's frock overcoat with sewn-on skirts. The names appear to be interchangeable, but some authorities claim the paddock

has a one-piece front and a skirted back, others claim the paletot is full-skirted. *Paletot* in the early seventeenth century was the French name for a silk overcoat worn over armor. It was revived in the nineteenth century for an overcoat of heavy cloth for winter use, or of light fabric for warm weather.

palisade   see *commode.*

palla   a rectangle of woolen cloth, a shawl-like wrap which was also used as bed covering. Wrapped or draped, it was worn by men, women and children in ancient Rome. see *himation; pallium.*

pallettes   in the fifteenth century armor, a pair of decorative saucer-like steel plates, one placed on each side of the chest to protect the armpits.

pallium   the Roman name for the himation, which had been the cloak of the Greeks of antiquity. Eventually it became an ecclesiastic vestment of the Roman Catholic Church. It was the characteristic

paletot or paddock-
fitted overcoat with waist
seam-pleats in back topped
by two buttons-evolution
of the redingote-1858

paletot-feminine
traveling coat-beige
and brown checked
cloth-pleats and
two buttons in back-
1886

robe of the philosopher and scholar and very often his only garment. A large piece of woolen cloth, larger than the himation. see *himation*.

Palm Beach cloth   a trademarked name for summer suiting for men and women. Originally woven of cotton and mohair, the name is now applied to other fiber-blended fabrics manufactured by the same firm.

paltock-medieval doublet worn by young men-jerkin, sleeves, parti-colored hose and codpiece secured by lacing-Italian-14th, 15th C.

paltock   a jacket worn by pages in the fourteenth and fifteenth centuries. A short, fitted doublet of cloth or silk buttoned or laced like a waistcoat to which hosen, or stockings and codpiece were fastened by lacings.

paludamentum, paludament   the official royal and military cloak worn by a Roman general. A mantle of purple woolen cloth fastened on the right shoulder.

Pamela bonnet   see *bonnet, Pamela*.

panache   a plume on a helmet, hat or cap. It is sometimes called a brush when small.

Panama hat   see *hat, Panama*.

Panamanian native dress   see *pollera*.

panel   in dressmaking, usually a featured rectangular shape and part of the design of the garment. It may be sewn close to the body or left to hang. It may also be attached to the shoulders as a train.

panes   a feature of men's and women's dress during the Renaissance. The old decoration consisted of panes or squares and slits cut onto a costume, permitting a silk lining of contrasting color to show through. It was taken up all over Europe, a fashion lasting into the 1530's. see *slashings*.

panne velvet   see *velvet, panne*.

panniers   the démodé hoop of the seventeenth century returned to fashion in a new form. It followed the hoop worn under the Watteau flying gown. Already the fashion in England, it was called hooped skirt. Adopted in France about 1730 and made of reed or whalebone shaped like a wicker birdcage, the French called it a pannier, or basket. The framework being covered with taffeta or brocade, was accordingly a taffeta or brocade hoop. At first funnel-shaped, it grew very broad at the sides and flat front and back, reaching a circumference of eight feet. Mademoiselle Margot, a couturière, invented an inexpensive pannier, making the fashion accessible to all women. see *criades*.

panniers, elbow   extremely wide panniers on which the elbows could be rested, were known as elbow panniers and the very small ones, called considérations, were for morning or negligée dress. The full skirt of the riding habit was worn over panniers. 1770's.

paludamentum-ancient military cloak of Roman general-purple woolen cloth

panes and slashes-peasecod-bellied pourpoint-trunk hose-cap with feather brush-English-16th C.

pocket panniers
accessible through side
openings - heavy silk gown-
lingerie fichu and cap-
French - 1775

pantaloons à
pont or bridge
trousers - square
front panel - worn
by French
patriot - 1793

panniers, pocket   In a popular style, pockets were formed by pulling the drapery through hip pocket holes. The dress, usually ankle length, had box pleats called Watteau pleats (1775) attached to the shoulders in back. It was a fashion that eventually spread to the bourgeoisie, becoming, finally, the habitual dress of servants. see *Watteau, Jean-Antoine.*

pant lengths, feminine   ankle length for sports and home entertaining; *Bermuda shorts* knee length, for sports; *capri pants,* same as pedal pushers but tapered; *Jamaica shorts,* ending at mid-thigh; *pedal pushers,* loose and ending mid-calf; worn for bicycling and sailing; *regulation shorts,* two inches above the knee; *short shorts,* the very shortest.

pantalettes   long ruffled drawers worn by little girls, c. 1800–1820, under the chemise.

pantalets   The classic, sheer, slim Empire gown of early 1800 made some form of garment a necessity under the dainty chemise. The result was a two-legged lingerie piece called drawers. Though frequent reference to it occurs, until 1820 it was worn only by little girls. English and French fashion journals occasionally showed evening frocks of shoe-top length with frilled satin pantalets showing below. Drawers were often false ruffles held by tapes tied at the knees. Real drawers were not adopted by women until the 1830's.

pantaloons à pont, bridge trousers   trousers which opened in front by means of a panel buttoned to the vest by three buttons, the panel operating like a draw-bridge, a style worn by sailors until the past decade. The pantaloons were also known as broadfalls or frontfalls. Worn in World War II, but changed about mid-century.

panties; step-ins   women's modern panties were a development of the twentieth century. Usually fitted over the hips, the legs flare skirtlike to a little above the knees. Originally fastened with tiny buttons on one side. An elastic waistband, eliminating a side placket, made the garment a step-in. Panties may be knee-length and close fitting, half-thigh length and flaring, called trunks, or quarter-thigh length and close-fitting, called briefs. Nylon is the preferred fabric, with a combination of nylon and wool or all wool for cold weather. Colors are generally white, pastels and black, but any color may be used in an ensemble with matching slip or petticoat. see *pantalets, pettipants, snuggies.*

pantihose or **panty stockings**   a twentieth century luxury which has never before in any age been available to women. They reach from toe to waist in a suave fit. They are to be had in all textures from sheerest to firm silk nylon or lace and in all colors.

pantoffle   the sixteenth century pantoffle was an overshoe without back quarter, leather covering only the front of the foot. It eventually became a house slipper, retaining its use and shape over the centuries to our day.

pants   a colloquialism for trousers.

pants, bearskin   see *bearskin pants.*

pants, harem   slim bloomer shape, made of supple, handsome silk. The bloomers fall into soft folds covering the knees. The body section is either a sleeveless jumper or a jacket of hip length. Designed for home wear.

pants, hipster   see *hipster pants.*

pants suit   for feminine wear, trousers and jacket of regular suitings for city, suburban and country wear; man-tailored, accompanied by simple accessories. Velvet for evening dress, permitting a soft, lingerie blouse with lace-trimmed ruffles.

pañuelo   the gauzy fichu of the traditional feminine costume of the Philippines. It is made of rengue, a starched gauze produced from native pineapple, and is beautifully embroidered in silk.

panung   the traditional feminine dress of Thailand; printed silk or cotton one yard wide and three yards long, wrapped to form a gracefully draped skirt. Worn with blouse or jacket.

panung, masculine   a straight length of cotton or silk drawn up between the legs to the back, thus forming pantaloons which reach down between knee and ankle. The traditional men's dress of Thailand.

paon   a velvet resembling panne velvet but heavier, with the nap laid in one direction.

paper clothes   introduced in the 1960's in men's undershirts and swim trunks, women's shifts and some children's clothes; inexpensive and disposable.

paper patterns   designed by Ebenezer Butterick (1826–1903), a young tailor and shirtmaker of ability. He started in the 1860's by making a pattern of the shirt worn by Italy's hero, Garibaldi, and a pattern of a suit for little boys to be made by the home dressmaker.

papier-mâché   a strong substance made of paper pulp, mixed size, and various other ingredients, especially glue, of which dress forms in particular are fashioned.

papillotes, curl papers   small folded pieces of paper around which were wound wisps of wet hair. When dry and undone, the wisps became curls. Both men and women curled their hair in this way, especially in the eighteenth century.

Paquin   see *couture, haute.*

parachute cloth   a tightly woven fabric of nylon, dacron, silk or rayon, originally perfected for parachutes, World War II. After the war, many women bought leftover parachutes and made dresses and curtains of them.

paradise feathers   elegant plumage, especially the long-tailed feathers of the adult male bird of paradise inhabiting New Guinea and adjacent islands.

paragon   a popular cloth of the seventeenth and eighteenth centuries made in Turkey. Formerly of camel's hair, resembling camlet. Used for common wear and also for upholstery.

Paraguay lace   combination hand and machine-made lace, the pattern worked in single thread spider web and wheel design. A fine weave is made for dresses and a heavier weave for other uses.

parasol   see *sunshade.*

paratrooper boot   see *boot, paratrooper.*

parchment, parchment color   beige or deep ivory, the color of the skin of goat, sheep or other animal prepared as parchment for writing on.

parchment lace   a lace formerly made of fine strips of cut-up old parchment, wound with gold, silver or silk thread and called cartisane and worked in a raised design. Mentioned in the time of Elizabeth I and similar to guipure.

pareu, pareo   a Polynesian skirt or loincloth of standard size and colors, a rectangle printed with conventional flower designs; contemporary.

Paris embroidery   a fine white cord embroidery appliquéd in satin stitch on piqué. Used in washable linens and garment accessories.

parka, anorak, amout   a hip-length hooded outer garment of sealskin, worn universally by Arctic Eskimos. It is made alike for both sexes except that the

panung-Thailand wrapped breeches worn by men and women

anorak-
Scandinavian

parka and hood of white bear-leggings of seal skin with fur side in

parka and breeches of sealskin with overdress of navy blue cotton-rick rack braid trim—modern Alaska

woman's garment has an extra hood for carrying a small child. The name *parka* comes from the Aleutian Islands; in Greenland the garment is called anorak (masculine) or amout (feminine). The modern anorak is a Scandinavian parka made of lightweight cotton or silk having wind resistance, water repellancy and allowance for ventilation, worn for sports such as skiing and sailing.

parta   the Hungarian bride's tall tiara; a glittering, bespangled headdress worn only once, built up of artificial roses of white and in delicate tints, with silk ribbons floating in back.

parta—Hungarian bride's tiara of white roses and small tinted flowers—white lawn ribbons

parti-colored clothes   worn by ladies and gentlemen of the European courts in the fourteenth and fifteenth centuries.

The whole costume was divided into variegated colors and the family coat-of-arms, emblazoned upon the dress, stamped in gold and silver leaf and colored enamels. Such costumes were passed down the family and valued as historic dress. The jester in his parti-colored costume is a survival of the period. see *motley*.

parti-colored hose, masculine   fitted and sewn tights reaching from waist to toe and being made of cloth or silk, the two legs of different colors, worn to the end of the fifteenth century.

partlet   a neckerchief, chemisette, piccadilli-band or collar which was detachable from the garment. Usually of white linen for men and embroidered or jeweled for women.

parure   a set of matching jeweled ornaments to be worn together, e.g., tiara, necklace, earrings, brooch and bracelets.

parvati   an all-cotton cloth from India, named after an ancient Indian goddess. It is handwoven, heatherlike fabric with a mixed texture and color effects, used by women for sportswear.

parti-colored surcoat over gown—French—15th C.

parti-colored hose and shoes—brocaded jerkin—Dalmatian sleeves—cap with jewel—English—13th C.

parti-colored hose—satin "gown" with velvet collar and lining—slashed sleeves—velvet cap—Italian—15th C.

pashm, pashim, pashmina Persian word for wool; the underfleece of the Tibetan goat, used for scarfs, shawls and other items.

passementerie of cotton, silk, metal and galloon and appliquéd embroidery fashioned of beads, guimpe, fringe, tassels and cording. Used for costumes of theater, church and military.

paste jewelry A lead-glass compound with considerable brilliancy used for imitation jewelry, invented by Joseph Strasser, a German jeweler, and often called Strass. The Louis XV and XVI periods are designated by connoisseurs as "the golden age of paste," the French strass being unsurpassed in design, delicacy and finish. It was worn by the aristocracy and was considered more of a substitute for, than an imitation of valuable ornaments.

pastel color a term for soft, delicate hues.

patadyong the traditional costume of Philippine women, each tribe having its own distinctive dress.

patch pocket see *pocket, patch.*

patches, mouches in ancient Rome men and women made use of the beauty spot or patch of Oriental origin. The patches were of soft leather, the Romans being skilled in the preparation of fine leather. It is recorded that the Romans, when speaking from the Tribune, wore patches. The patch was intended to simulate the mole, which was considered a beauty mark. The fashion came from Italy in the sixteenth century, called by the English "patching the face." Also worn in the seventeenth century, of black velvet, taffeta or court plaster, and carried in tiny jeweled boxes. Patches were placed near the eyes, on the cheeks the throat and breasts. Black silk patches, gummed, became fashionable in the second half of the seventeenth century,

and ladies carried them in exquisite little boxes. Mouches, as the French called them because they looked like flies, were cut in various shapes such as flowers, crescents, stars, even figures and animals. Patches were first worn in Venice in the mid-sixteenth century by the ladies of the court, hence the name "court plaster."

patchwork pieces of cloth, silk or leather of varying color and shape, sewn together to form a conventional design or, as in a quilt, a "crazy quilt" arrangement. Patchwork madras is used today in separate sports skirts and in men's sports shirts.

patent leather see *leather, patent.*

patola a wedding sari made in Gujarat, India, of a silk cloth woven in Chinese technique and known as chiné.

pattens; clogs footwear fashioned of wood, oak or poplar, raised off the ground very often by an iron ring and fastened to the foot by leather straps. They were most necessary in bad weather and when crossing the cobbled pavements. Clogs were also made of wood covered with silk to match the dainty slippers of the eighteenth century. Men, women and children wore clogs on cobbled pavements in European cities and in the American Colonies.

patadyong-Philippine traditional dress— wide-arched sleeves of rengue or pineapple cloth

pattens of oak or poplar-iron rings- English and American- 18th C.

pattern in British usage, a small sample or swatch.

patterns, dress see *paper patterns.*

pea jacket – worn by U.S. sailors – short, warm overcoat of pilot cloth – cap of same – contemporary

pattu, patteo, pattoo an East Indian shawl woven in Punjab and Kashmir. Woven also as homespun woolen cloth and tweed yardage.

pavé from the French for pavement. A jeweled setting in which the stones are set together closely to cover a metal ground.

pea or **pilot jacket** a heavy, short coat worn by sailors from 1850 on. Of closely woven cloth in dark blue. Used as a model for small boys' coats in lighter weight.

peacock feathers The peacock was introduced into England, France and Germany in the fourteenth century. The long, gorgeously colored, gold-tipped tail feathers became the favored hat ornament for prelates and nobles. The vogue lasted several centuries until the feather was finally supplanted by ostrich plumes brought from Africa.

peacockery when said of a man, meaning vanity and ostentatious display of fine clothes.

peak or **peaked lapel** a lapel which rises to a sharp point, leaving a space between the peak and collar point.

pearl the result of a dense nacre concretion formed within the shell of some mollusks. The form is variable and there are many colors, the first having a silvery or satiny luster. The best specimens are from the pearl oyster and are very costly. The pearl was a favorite jewel in the sixteenth century, worn in the coiffure, sewn to women's gowns and a single drop pearl earring worn by gentlemen. A single string around a feminine throat became classic.

pearlies the British name for costermongers, a name for apple vendors in past times. Their dress worn yearly at Epsom Downs on Derby Day is covered with white pearl buttons. Sometimes a whole

family, including children, will appear so attired. A custom still observed once a year.

pearls, baroque irregular in shape but lustrous and rich in coloring.

pearls, cultured or **Oriental** so called in the trade, first appeared about 1915. An irritant on which the pearl forms is placed in the shell and the oyster kept in a seed bed for a number of years. A process invented by the Japanese.

pearls, imitation or **simulated** a process perfected by Jaquin of Paris about 1680. Hollow blown glass is filled with essence composed of silvery particles left in the water in which whitebait has been washed.

pearls, natural the natural pearl forms when a small irritant such as a grain of sand accidently becomes lodged in an oyster's shell.

"Pearlies" – British costermongers who attend the English races in pearl-button sewn clothes

pearls, seed   very small pearls, often irregular in shape. Used in embroidery of women's costume and accessories, especially small handbags. They were popular in Victorian jewelry when the pearls were strung on horsehair and mounted in elaborate patterns to form brooches, earrings, etc., a craft requiring painstaking skill and handwork. Still in vogue today for evening bags and some bridal attire.

peasant blouse   of the Central European countries, a full blouse usually of soft white voile with a round smock-stitched neck and long full sleeves smock-stitched into wrist size with short ruffles, the smocking done in red or dark blue embroidery cotton. Popular and worn with the full dirndl skirts in the 1930's and 1940's.

peasant cloth   a gaily dyed or printed stout muslin popular for dirndl and play clothes.

peasant costume   the regional dress of people who have retained the original basic design and artistic qualities of their ancestors' clothes. Such garments reveal the influence of religion, superstition and historical events on earlier natives, and are often an inspiration to modern designers.

peasant lace   a coarse, unimpressive bobbin lace like torchon, made by European peasants.

peasant sleeve   see *sleeve, peasant.*

peasecod-bellied doublet   an extreme fashion of Spanish origin of the fifteenth and sixteenth centuries. The stuffed doublet had a wooden busk in front for shape. Worn with trunk hose.

peau d'ange   French for angel skin; a popular silk early in the twentieth century.

peau de soie   a plain-colored, firm and soft silk fabric with the same dull finish on both sides. Used for evening dresses and trimmings.

pebble grain, pebble goat   a leather, imitation leather or fabric given a grained surface by running it between rollers under pressure.

pebble weave   a rough-surfaced fabric produced by weaving together shrunken, twisted yarns.

peccary, pecari, pecary   a wild boar native to Mexico, Central and South America. The leather, limited in quantity, is fine-grained, lightweight pig leather.

pectoral   a decorative, jeweled breastplate worn by Egyptian kings and Hebrew high priests. The breastplate of the Roman military was of leather and that of the Gauls was copper. A pectoral cross is a cross worn on the breast by bishops and abbots. The ancient Hebrew pectoral was composed of two large square plaques, one hanging in front and one in back joined by gold chains over the shoulders. The front plaque was set with twelve jewels on which were engraved the names of the twelve tribes.

pedal pushers   see *pant lengths, feminine.*

pedule   a rawhide boot of northern medieval Europe. Sometimes boots and breeches were made in one.

peek-a-boo blouse   a shirtwaist of sheer lawn, voile or eyelet embroidery, a popular fashion of the 1890's and the first decade of the twentieth century. It was worn over a lacy, frilled corset cover.

peg-top skirt, tonneau or **barrel**   silhouette of 1912 with bouffant fullness around the hips sloping in to the ankles. Introduced by Paquin.

peg-top trousers   trousers which were cut wide and full around the hips, slimming down sharply to the ankles; first decade of the twentieth century. Later, a widespread fashion in the 1950's.

pekin   a handsome dress silk, originally from China, with warp-wise alternating stripes of velvet and satin in contrasting colors.

pegged boot or **shoe**   leather shoes with the sole fastened to the uppers by wooden pegs.

peignoir   a lingerie jacket or robe tied at the neck; literally a combing jacket or gown, the name founded upon the French word for comb, *peign*. Worn since the sixteenth century when it was fashioned of printed cottons, velvet or brocade. Today, the available modern synthetic fabrics present a wide choice of handsome materials for the garment.

pelerine   literally, a pilgrim's cloak; in the nineteenth century a feminine short cape with long ends in front. It was made of light or heavy silk, velvet or fur, according to season. see *palatine*.

pelisse   a cloak popular from the twelfth to the fifteenth centuries and worn by men and women. A full-length robe wadded with cotton or lined with fur, with long sleeves. Sometimes the lady's train was so long that a page was needed to carry it. In the early nineteenth century the feminine pelisse again acquired popularity, following the Empire mode, high-waisted, long-sleeved, fur-lined and fur-trimmed in all lengths and styles including the spencer, hussar and canezou jacket. Men also wore the pelisse, fur-lined and fur-trimmed.

pellon   a trade name of a fabric made by a process patented in 1951, neither woven, knitted nor felted. Of several weights and thicknesses, in black and white, it is used as interlining and shape preserver.

peltries   see *animal skins*.

penang   a heavy cotton percale from Penang, Malaysia. Originally made in Calcutta and then made in England.

pencil stripe   in weaving, stripes which are two or three warps wide, of contrasting color on a ground of solid color.

penelope   British for a sleeveless, knitted jacket.

peniche lace   a Portuguese bobbin or pillow lace made with a large mesh ground, either black or white. Can be made in two ways: executing the design first and then working the reseau around it; or working it in one piece, forming pattern and ground of the same thread.

penistone   a coarse woolen cloth made from the sixteenth to the nineteenth centuries in Penistone, Yorkshire, England. It was used for cloaks and dresses. Also known as "forest white."

penitentials   a colloquial English term for garments worn by "penitents" in black or "penitential stripes."

peplos   the bloused section worn over the chiton in ancient Greece. A rectangle of woolen fabric, unsewn and fastened on the shoulders, it hung in arranged folds weighted with lead pellets. The Greek woman's gown which had various names and was costly.

peplum   to the ancient peplos of Greece it was an outer tunic while the modern peplum is usually a short flounce or overskirt suspended from bodice or belt. A woman's garment.

péplum impératrice   of the 1860's named after the French Empress, Eugénie. It was a basque bodice with a draped-up tunic or panniers.

pepper and salt mixture   a combination of black and white yarns twisted

pelisse of gray cloth with mink collar and cuffs-fastened with brandenburgs French-1823

pelisse-brown cashmere lined with wadding and mauve silk~white fur~ gray felt bonnet with feathers-1833

together and woven into cloth, giving the effect of a dark or light ground sprinkled with dark or light specks.

percale similar to cambric; plain-woven cotton fabric with a firm, smooth finish. It is printed in shirting patterns and used for pajamas and sportswear.

perfumery The use of perfumes goes back to the ancients of Biblical times when sweet-smelling odors were concocted from the juices of herbs and flowers. They were used by men and women both for religious rites and to enhance their own persons, using a pomade which they made up. It is said that in ancient Rome the use of perfume may have surpassed that of all time. It was available in liquid, solid and powdered form and was applied not only to the body, but to all articles and possessions.

The making of perfume was revived in Renaissance Italy, founded upon the knowledge brought back from the Orient by the Crusaders. René, an Italian perfumer, opened the first perfume shop in Paris about 1500, and by the mid-sixteenth century perfume pervaded all Europe. Many scents were thought to possess miraculous powers of healing as well as beautifying. Perfumes and toilet water were used by men in the eighteenth century. Frenchmen used eau de cologne and Englishmen lavender water, but American men frowned upon the use of scents of any kind. However, such items do appear in the accounts of George Washington. A truly American after-shave lotion, "Florida Water," is still catalogued today and claims to have been a favorite since 1808.

Only the most delicate flower perfumes were used by American women until the twentieth century. In modern commercial usage cologne is a less concentrated form of perfume and toilet water is even weaker than cologne. see *toiletries*.

peridot a green gem stone of the olivine mineral family.

periwig wigs and false hair had been a periodic fashion through the centuries but the last revival and rage occurred about the middle of the seventeenth century. The French word perruque became peruke in English, then perwyke, periwig and finally just plain wig. A set of ringlets, a corner of hair, or a single curl was also a wig. It was predominantly a masculine fashion until the mid-twentieth century but the wig is still a wig in feminine parlance and the masculine item is a hairpiece. see *wig*.

permanent wave, permanent the vogue of the Marcel wave in the 1890's and the early twentieth century led to the invention of the permanent wave in 1906 by Charles Nestlé, a fashionable coiffeur in London. The permanent wave was first applied by an electric heat machine; a later method using lotions instead of heat was called a cold wave. This method has the advantage of making it possible to curl the hair right to the head, obviating the need of thick protective pads, and is much faster and safer than the machine method.

permanent press see *durable press*.

perpetuana or **petuna** a woolen cloth, glossy and durable, resembling parchment in texture. Worn by the Puritans in the American Colonies, in the seventeenth and eighteenth centuries. Made in England.

Persian a tiara or bonnet of wool or leather worn by the Persian and Arabic nobleman of ancient times, in Phrygian style, over his frizzed hair. see *tāj*.

Persian costume, ancient see illustrations on next page.

Persian embroidery Ancient garments were elaborately embroidered. Appliqué work originated with the Persians in place of all-over needlework. Their contemporary embroidery features types of drawnwork, darned work and appliqué,

péplum impératrice- gray cashmere over royal blue silk- blue velvet ribbon and buttons- French-1871

Persian

leather or felt
costume over
linen shirt
and loincloth-
Persian-
6th c. B.C.

silk kandys
over linen
shirt and
loincloth-
Median-
6th c. B.C.

silk and linen
costume worn over
white linen shirt
and loincloth-
Persian-
4th c. B.C.

embroidered or
dyed linen
loincloth-
Lycian-
1400 B.C.

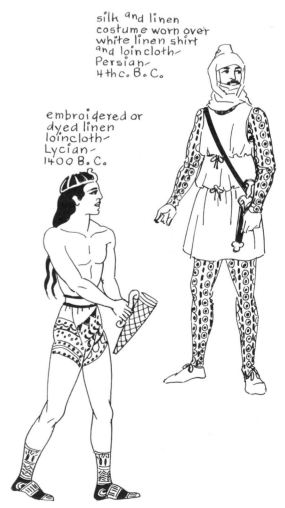

266

the designs outlined in dark color and completely filled in by various filling stitches.

Persian lamb   see *lamb, Persian.*

perspective glass   see *quizzing glass.*

peruke   the English form of *perruque* which became perwyke or periwig and finally wig. see *periwig.*

Peruvian costume, traditional   see illustrations.

perwitsky   European name for fitch or polecat. see *fitch.*

perwyke   see *periwig.*

petal-scalloped   see *dagged.*

petasos, petasus   a hat worn by the ancient Greeks, wide-brimmed and low-crowned, of felt or straw. The two-winged cap of the Greek Hermes and Roman Mercury was a petasos, as was the pointed-crowned hat of the Boeotian woman.

Peter Pan   the blouse or shirt of the costume worn by the young hero of Sir James Barrie's play, "Peter Pan." With a belted, Russian-styled tunic, he wore a round collar, bow tie and knee breeches, an ensemble which became popular for small boys. see *Peter Pan collar.*

Peter Thompson frock   a girl's private school uniform worn early in the twentieth century, designed by a navy tailor, Peter Thompson. It was a belted one-piece dress of dark blue serge or white linen with sailor collar, long sleeves and a body pleated from yoke to hem.

petersham   a heavy wool overcoating with a rough, knotty surface formerly called nigger-head. A finer, softer example is known as chinchilla.

petit gris   see *grays.*

petit point   any embroidery worked on canvas with sixteen or more mesh per inch. There is no special petit point stitch as such. see *gros point.*

petticoat   an underskirt, in modern usage. In the fourteenth century the "petticote" was an undercoat worn by both sexes, shorter than the outer coat. The feminine version was worn under an open gown and developed into a handsomely decorated skirt which was retained as an underskirt after gowns were no longer designed with an open front. see *slip, pettipants, crinoline.*

petticoat breeches   see *rhinegrave breeches, petticoat.*

pettipants, snuggies   twentieth century feminine winter underpants of nylon, knitted wool or wool jersey in colors and black, knee-length and close-fitting.

petuna   see *perpetuana.*

Philippine costume   the formal gown has a fichu and elbow-length, wide-arched butterfly sleeves of stiffly starched gauze. The skirt is floor-length with a pointed train. For tribal dress, see *patadyong; barong; tagalog; saya.*

Philippine embroidery   fine handwork in dainty floral motifs done by native women in the Philippine Islands.

phrygium   the Phrygian cap of white woolen material worn by the popes of the Middle Ages at nonliturgical ceremonies. The cap later developed into the papal tiara. see *bonnet, Phrygian.*

phulkari   Hindu word for embroidery; principally an embroidered flower pattern. Also the flower-embroidered cloth worn as shawl or mantle by the Anglo-Indian. see *chuddar.*

piccadil, pickadil, piccadilly   scalloped or castellated edgings of collars or jackets in the seventeenth century. On a

Peruvian aristocrat of pure Spanish ancestry—embroidered shawl over tortoise shell comb

Peruvian caballero habit—black and red velvet—cordovan charaparos or chaps—black leather boots

fashionable street in London lived a tailor who specialized in piccadills or edgings for ruffs. He became known as the "piccadilly tailor" and in later years the road was named for them.

picot   an edging formed of very tiny loops on cloth, ribbon, lace or braid.

picoté   adjective meaning edged or finished with picot, either by machine or hand-done.

picture hat   a wide-brimmed, richly trimmed hat, such as in Gainsborough's portraits of ladies. Banded with wide satin ribbon, weighted with gorgeous ostrich plumes and worn atop a stunning wig. see *hat, Gainsborough.*

pie-plate or **pie-tin cap**   the name given the flat-top cap worn by the sailors of the United States Navy in the nineteenth century. Of Tam'o' Shanter shape, it was held in form by a metal hoop. White cotton for summer and navy; blue woolen cloth for winter wear.

piece-dyed   fabrics, of wool, cotton or silk dyed in the piece or after weaving.

pierrette costume   the feminine counterpart of Pierrot wore a tight bodice of black or vivid-colored velvet with full white satin sleeves and skirt, muslin ruffs at neck and wrists and a peaked cap decorated with a pompon.

pierrot   a character of Italian Commedia dell'Arte, seventeenth century. He wore a voluminous smock and long, wide breeches of white satin with white pompons. The costume also included soft white slippers and a black felt calotte. The face painted white with black-arched eyebrows, red lips.

pigeon's wings   a feature of the man's powdered wig; loosely rolled puffs over the ears. First half of the eighteenth century. see *wig, bag.*

pigskin   a stout, coarse-grained leather made of hog's hide. It has a decorative surface caused by bristle holes and is long-wearing and durable. Most pigskin comes from China.

pigtail   in general, any tight braid of hair hanging down the back; specifically, the Chinese queue.

pigtail wig   see *wig, pigtail.*

piked or **peaked shoes**   see *poulaines.*

pile   a thick surface of standing threads as in velvet, produced by an extra set of warp or filling yarns which are later cut and sheared. It is to be distinguished from a cloth in which a nap lies flat.

pileus   The Greek pilos became the Etruscan and Roman pileus, a close-fitting cap with chinstrap. It was worn by soldiers and sailors and also by athletes at festivals and public games.

Pilgrims   the earliest colonists of New England. They wore the contemporary dress of seventeenth century England. see illustrations.

Philippine traditional, formal dress- wide-arched sleeves and fichu of pineapple cloth- skirt called SAYA

Pilgrim in brown cloak, hat and jerkin-sleeves red and yellow-yellow breeches with frills- white lawn collar and cuffs-spur leathers on boots

Pilgrim- underskirt and sleeve puff, violet cloth-cap, capes, sleeve and cuff of lawn-fur muff- felt hat.

pillbox   a small round hat of stiffened fabric, originally of silk or velvet sewn with pearls and worn over the chignon in eighteenth century Italy, now usually worn by women on the back of the head. see *bellboy's cap.*

pillow lace   see *bobbin lace.*

piloi   a short, felt sock of sheep or goat's hair worn by farmers in northern Greece in winter.

pilot cloth   a dark blue woolen cloth, coarse, strong and thick, twilled with a nap on one side. Used for sailors' jackets and overcoats.

pilot jacket   see *pea jacket.*

pima   a fine, strong cotton developed in Pima County, Arizona, a cross between Sea Island and Egyptian cotton. Used for tire fabrics, balloon and airplane cloths.

pin, common   originally a shank of brass wire with one end bent into a head. In the thirteenth and fourteenth centuries pins were costly, hence the expression "pin money." Englishwomen of all classes saved their money to buy pins on the first two days of January, as Parliament permitted pin merchants but two days a year on which to sell their pins. A tax was levied on the common people to pay for the English queen's pins. An act of 1483 prohibited the further import of pins so that by 1626 most ordinary pins were English. As late as 1812 the ordinary pin of brass and wire-bound head of English make was still a luxury costing as much as a dollar for a small package. In 1831, in the United States, the first successful machine for making solid-headed pins was invented by John Ireland Howe of New York.

pin, safety   developed from the ancient Greek fibula, at least 2000 years old; shaped with a loop at one end to furnish spring, with the point held by a protective hood. The modern version was invented by Walter Hunt, an American, in 1849.

piña cloth   a cloth woven from leaf fibers of the pineapple plant, chiefly in the Philippine Islands. Transparent, crisp and delicate, it is used for handkerchiefs, scarfs, dainty shawls and lace grounds.

pinafore   a sleeveless dress buttoned in back which can be worn over a blouse or chemisette, or by itself as an informal warm weather play dress; worn by women and little girls and generally made of cotton. It resembles the jumper dress but is distinguished from it by being buttoned instead of slip-on. Black sateen pinafores were once worn in school by both girls and boys to protect their other clothes, a custom which still survives in France.

pince-nez   eyeglasses which are held to the eyes by a tiny spring which clips the nose. see *eyeglasses.*

pinchbeck   an alloy of copper and zinc used for imitation jewelry. It was invented by a London watchmaker, Christopher Pinchbeck. see *gilt.*

pincheck   minute squares of color produced by interweaving colored yarns, creating a confetti look.

pine marten   see *marten, baum.*

pinking   an ornamental jagged edge given to fabric by a small machine with a ribbed roller or by the use of pinking shears, which have blades with a saw-tooth inner edge. Also used as a seam finish, to prevent raveling.

pinner   a small dainty apron of exquisite workmanship which was pinned over the front of a gown in the seventeenth and eighteenth centuries; worn by ladies-in-waiting. In the nineteenth century, pinners were often the badge of the parlor

modern pillbox pinned to chignon— Dior—1951

maid. Children's aprons were also called pinners. see *apron*.

pinner or **flandan**   of the eighteenth century; a lace-edged cap of white batiste with two floating lappets in back.

pins   see *bar pin; breastpin; brooch; clip brooch; fibula*.

pin-striped   in weaving on a solid ground, a stripe slightly thicker than a hairline stripe.

piping   a very narrow bias fold or cord, usually of contrasting color, used as an edging or seam-finish in dressmaking.

piqué   a stout, ribbed cotton fabric, sometimes of silk or rayon. Also woven in figured patterns and in a fine waffle piqué. Popular for women's dresses, blouses, separate collars and cuffs, men's shirts, waistcoats, scarfs and evening ties.

pirnie or **pirny**   a Scottish nightcap of striped woolen cloth.

pistole pocket   see *pocket, pistole*.

pith helmet   see *topee, topi*.

placket   a fold of fabric sewn to the underside of an opening in a dress to which buttons, hooks and eyes or snap fasteners were sewn. Every closure had a placket, very often secured by attached strings. The slide fastener or "zipper" eventually solved the problem with expertise.

plaid   a tartan pattern of bars of varied colors crossing each other at right angles. Also, the name used by the Scots for a traveling shawl or rug or scarf in a plaid pattern. see *Scottish Highland dress*.

plain weave   the simplest form of weave with the threads interlacing alternately at right angles. Also known as taffeta weave.

plait   a flat fold or doubling back of cloth. see *pleat*.

plaited hair   long hair braided by entwining three or more strands, one over the other, producing a ropelike contexture.

planter's hat   see *hat, Panama*.

plastic   a man-made substance capable of being molded into a form or textile.

plastron   a metal breast plate in medieval armor; a protective padded breastplate worn by the fencer; an ornamental stomacher laced to a woman's bodice as in peasant dress. see *stomacher*.

platform sole   a thick sole of cork or wood. see *wedge heel*.

platina fox   see *fox, platina*.

platinum, platina   a precious metallic element, noncorroding and grayish-white. Found as grains and nuggets in neutral gray, slightly bluish with brilliance. Made into fine jewelry and set with precious stones. Found in the Ural Mountains and Colombia.

platok   see *babushka*.

Plauen lace   of Plauen, Germany. A lace pattern embroidered on muslin, net and such and treated chemically to burn out the fabric ground.

pleated bosom   a man's white shirt for formal or semiformal day wear or semiformal evening wear. Soft or starched pleats of identical or varying widths.

pleats or **plaits**   a series of folds of cloth. In accordion pleating, the fabric is pressed so that creases of equal length alternate inward and outward; in sunburst pleating used especially in skirts, the folds gradually increase in depth. In knife pleating the folds are doubled over so that only one crease shows and these creases all point in the same direction; in box pleating the folds are in pairs, one crease pointing right and the other left.

pleats, inverted   box pleats in reverse.

pleats, kick   short, inverted pleat about four or five inches high, from the hem, placed in center back or sides of a narrow skirt for extra walking freedom.

pleats, sunburst   a type of machine-pleating used especially in skirts; the pleats radiate from waist to hem, narrowest at the top and gradually widening to the bottom.

pleats, unpressed   unstitched pleats, as in a skirt, left to flare for a soft effect.

pleats, Watteau   loose box pleats or pleats falling in center back from neck to waist, then free from waist to skirt. Eighteenth century.

plumage   since the passing of the Audubon Plumage Law only wings or plumes of goose or chicken feathers are permitted for trimming. United States. see *Audubon plumage law.*

plume   three upstanding ostrich feathers with a veil are worn with English court dress, indicating that the wearer has been "presented" to the Sovereign. They are worn slightly to the left side of the head with the tulle veil not longer than forty-five inches. This is a survival of a fashion at the court of Marie Antoinette. The three ostrich feathers which are the crest of the Prince of Wales have their origin in the arms of Anne of Bohemia, consort of Richard II (1367–1400). The custom of court presentations has been discontinued by Queen Elizabeth II.

plumpers   "beautifiers" which appeared in 1690; small, round, light balls of cork which elderly ladies carried in their cheeks to fill out the sunken spots, probably due to loss of teeth.

plus fours   knickers for sportswear, voluminous in width and length, late 1920's. The term originated in the British Army when breeches were measured as reaching to the knees, plus four inches.

plush   a fabric with pile higher than velvet. Can be made from most of the principal textile fibers; has a wide usage in imitation furs.

pocket, bellows   an outside jacket or coat pocket especially adapted to hunting and shooting. Bellowed pleats on the outside give added space and a buttoned flap keeps the pocket closed. see *saddle bag pocket.*

pocket, panniers   see *pannier pockets.*

pocket, patch   a pocket made of the garment's fabric, matching weave and design in its application; sewn to the outside of the garment.

pocket, pistole   formerly, the right hip trousers pocket, in which a gun could be carried.

pocket, saddle bag   pockets of self fabric with pleats and buttoned-down flap applied to a man's sports jacket or coat. see *pocket, bellows.*

pocket, slashed   a pocket on the inner side of the garment, reached by a finished slash on the outer side, with a flap over the opening.

pocketbook   the reticule or dressmaker type of pouch bag with drawstring top, the bag of nearly two centuries, was finally replaced by the leather pocketbook in the 1890's, a flat, folding booklet-shaped purse with compartments closed by a silver or gold ornamental latch. It was very little larger than today's wallet.

plume-court headdress- three ostrich tips and floating veil-jeweled stars- English 1890's

The sabretache of fabric or leather of the Directoire Period returned in the early twentieth century and from then on, women's leather handbags became more functional, spacious and handsome. see *handbag.*

pockets, feminine   originally made in pairs and sewn to a tape which was tied around the waist. With farthingale, over-skirt or panniers the pocket could be worn under the skirt. This fashion was prevalent c. 1650–1850, when pockets began to be inserted in skirt seams. The old pockets were often embroidered and many beautiful examples of such work have survived.

pockets, masculine   up to the Middle Ages there were no pockets in clothes. Money and necessary small articles were carried tied in a kerchief or a square of cloth. This evolved into small bags or sacs drawn closed at the top by cords, fastened to the belt and used by both sexes. Small articles like coins and keys were later carried in the codpiece, a small box or bag first designed to conceal the front opening of trunk hose of the fifteenth and sixteenth centuries. Pockets were inserted in the trunk hose of the sixteenth century. see *aumônière; codpiece.*

poet's collar   see *collar, poet's.*

point d'Alençon embroidery   see *Appenzell embroidery.*

point d'Angleterre   a bobbin lace which originated in Brussels and was smuggled into England as English lace to avoid import duty. Later, it was actually made in England.

point de gaz lace   fine needlepoint with a delicate net ground having looped meshes decorated with a realistic floral pattern. Made chiefly in Brussels, and also called Brussels rose-point lace.

point d'esprit   a fine cotton or net

with tiny dots, a Normandy lace with square or oval dots, or old guipure lace with a small figure.

point de Paris   a narrow bobbin lace with flat design on a hexagonal mesh ground. Also, a machine-made lace resembling Val lace but with a heavier outline pattern.

point plat   French for flat point lace or tulle, as opposed to raised or relief work with cordonnet.

pointed fox   see *fox, pointed.*

points   see *aglet.*

Poiret, Paul   (1880–1944) one of the greatest of French designers. He was the first to place the belt just under the bosom in true Empire style and he was responsible for the open-necked kimono bodice eliminating the set-in sleeve and high collar. He admired Oriental colors, often using brilliant hues of green, cerise, vermilion, royal blue and purple. Best known for his tunics and the hobble skirt, 1910–1914.

Poiret twill   a fine dress cloth named for the French couturier, Paul Poiret. A twill-woven fabric similar to gabardine but smoother and made also of rayon or wool blends.

poke bonnet   see *bonnet, coal scuttle.*

poke collar   see *collar, poke.*

polar seal   see *seal, imitations.*

polecat   see *fitch.*

Polish costume, traditional   see illustrations.

polished silk   called beaver, was invented in Florence, Italy, and not perfected until 1823.

Polish bridal costume of Lowicz-brilliant, deep colors-black velvet bodice, sheer white blouse-huge headdress of fresh flowers-leather boots

Polish peasant dress-red or blue jacket-white linen shirt-cap with panache of onion plant and ribbon

pollera, national Panama dress hand-embroidered in deep color-yards and yards of fine lace

polka dot   a printed pattern on silk, linen or cotton with alternating round dots, but evenly spaced. New in the first half of the nineteenth century and popular for generations. Polka dots still worn today for dresses, blouses and scarfs.

pollera   the national feminine costume of Panama, based upon the colonial dress of Spanish ladies. Of soft white voile, it has a waist-deep flaring bertha, embroidered in red and black. There are yards and yards of hand embroidery on bodice and skirt and as many yards of fine lace. The lady wears a coiffure of quivering, sparkling flowers and pearls on tiny springs.

polo cloth   a napped camel's hair and wool mixture for coating. In natural colors and dyed any color. Trademarked by the Worumbo Company.

polo coat   the twentieth century all-around coat for man or woman of natural color camel's hair; evolved from the British wait coat thrown over the shoulders between periods of play of a sport. see *camel's hair coat*.

polo shirt   a man's summer shirt, usually a pull-on of white knit cotton with round neck or Peter Pan collar.

polonaise gown   a feminine fashion from 1776 to 1787. Its special feature consisted of three panniers, one in back and two side sections which rounded away in front. The panniers of the polonaise were drawn up on cords and could also be let down to form a "flying gown." The cords were run through rings or tape loops, and were finished with tassels and rosettes, although later the panniers were sewn in position with the cords simply ornamental.

polyester   a generic name as ruled by the Federal Trade Commission for the man-made fiber composed largely of dihydric alcohol and terephthalic acid.

polo coat-natural color camel's hair-horn buttons-soft felt hat-1936

Polonaise gown with three panniers-striped and plain silk-cords, tassels and ruches-French-1776

pompadour in marcel wave created by Marcel of Paris-1903

poncho-Mexican vaquero or cowboy-white with dark blue-felt sombrero

poncho in bright colors-hand-woven and fringed-hole in center for the head-Peruvian Incan Indian

tures of the period of the Marquise de Pompadour (1721–1764), mistress of Louis XV of France. Her simple and distinctive coiffure, the hair brushed up off her face and up in back, gave its name to the pompadour style which periodically returns to favor. Worn by the Gibson girl in the 1890's and at the turn of the century. Other Pompadour items are flowered taffeta, laces, velvet ribbons, small dainty aprons, etc.

pompons ornamental colored balls of wool, feathers, silk or felt, used mostly on caps.

poncho of the South American Indian; a square of rough woolen cloth hand loomed with broad stripes of brilliant color, worn largely by Spanish-Americans. It has a hole in the center for the head, reaches below the waist and is worn by men and women. It is both cloak and blanket. Also, a waterproof garment of similar shape worn in England and America as a raincoat.

pongee a summer fabric in natural color, rough woven in tussah, a thin silk. Used in men's and women's suits and sportswear. see *tussah; shantung; nankeen.*

Used for wash-and-wear apparel when combined with cotton, rayon and other man-made filaments.

pomander sixteenth and seventeenth centuries; a small apple-shaped ball of gold or silver filigree which held a ball of musk, ambergris or other perfume. It was worn on a chain around the neck or suspended from a lady's girdle. Men, especially dandies, carried a pomander in the hand, often of hollowed-out oranges containing scent. The pomander was often carried to ward off infection. The French name is pomme d'ambre, or scented apple. Also a scented ball for wardrobes, twentieth century.

pomatum a perfumed unguent for the hair.

pomegranate an apple- or pear-shaped fruit of a thorny bush native to southwest Asia, often mentioned in early Oriental literature as symbolic of fecundity. It became the favored motif of the Indian cashmere shawls.

pompadour the name of various fea-

pony-skin   a fashion new at the beginning of the twentieth century; durable, lustrous, flat fur from the young colt or foal, at times resembling moiré karakul. From Poland, Russian Europe, Baltic states, South America and China, the Chinese fur poor. Colors beige, gray or black; dyed, bleached or used natural for coats and jackets.

poodle cloth   a fabric knitted or woven with a knotted or looped woolly surface resembling the coat of a French poodle dog.

poor boy sweater   a fashion of the 1960's, beginning in France; a knitted, vertical ribbed wool usually black, a collarless pullover sweater which clings to the figure. Worn by young women.

poplin   a lightweight ribbed fabric woven like grosgrain. Of linen or cotton warp with wool or nylon filling, usually plain-dyed; used for both masculine and feminine apparel.

poplin, Irish   see *Irish poplin.*

porosity   the porous quality of a summer fabric with meshlike spaces for coolness.

porpoise   a good-quality leather for stout shoes; really the hide of white whale, dressed for hunting and fishing boots.

Portegaz, Mañuel   see *couture, haute.*

portmonnaie   French for the pocketbook or hand purse carried by women in the late nineteenth century. see *pocketbook.*

Portuguese costume, traditional   see illustration.

possum   see *opossum*

postiche   literally, artificial. A hairpiece or wig. In ancient Egypt men wore no beard or moustache, but the pharaohs and high dignitaries wore the postiche or false beard, with which a woman, if queen, also adorned herself. The postiche was attached to a chinstrap, gold no doubt, which was part of a frame or cap worn under the bonnet or wig. Postiche today, a feminine hairpiece worn in addition to the wearer's own hair.

posy   a nosegay, small bouquet or a single flower.

pouch   a small handbag for carrying small articles.

pouf   a stuffed cushion or cushions worn under panniers. Also a small, hair-stuffed cushion worn under the high puffs of the Louis XVI coiffures.

poulaines, crackowes or **piked shoes** the style for dandies, mid-fourteenth century to about 1480. The long, pointed toes grew to such lengths that it became necessary to hold up the stuffed points by gold chains attached to the ankles or knees.

Portuguese of Aveiro in traditional dress—red sash and jacket—black trousers—black and red hat—silver buttons with braid loops

"poor boy sweater"— a phase of the "mod" trend in black—worn with straightened hair— 1960's

poulaine or piked shoe of heavy leather—French— medieval—14th C.

poulaine—blue leather laced on inner side— wooden patten— French—15th C.

Noblemen were permitted toe lengths of two feet and gentlemen, one foot; the commoner could extend only six inches beyond his toes. The shoes originated in Cracow, Poland, and became fashionable at all European courts. The French called them poulaines after Poland and the English crackowes after Cracow.

pounce   a powder in a pouncet box to rub over thin perforated paper, thus transferring a design to a fabric to be embroidered.

pourpoint   see *gambeson; jerkin; action.*

poussin lace   a type of Valenciennes bobbin lace made in Dieppe, France. Narrow and delicate, its net resembling the square of chicken wire; hence its name, French for a young chicken.

powder   see *cosmetics.*

power lace or **net**   made of thin rubber on a bobbinette machine, used mostly for girdles, corsets, brassières. The fabric stretches in all directions; new in 1966.

pre-shrunk   a manufacturer's term for fabric processed to guard against shrinking over three per cent in a standard test.

prête-à-porter   French for ready-made clothes.

pretintailles   of the late seventeenth century and Louis XIV period; cut-out motifs of lace and embroidery appliquéd or gummed to the skirts of gowns, making an elaborate ornamentation.

Prince Albert frock coat   see *frock coat.*

princess gown   a gown made of fitted sections and worn over a crinoline. Appeared first in the 1860's, a favored fashion of the first decade of the twentieth century. see *gabrielle.*

princess lace   a very fine imitation of Duchesse lace, with the motifs usually applied by hand.

princess silhouette   the lines of a dress or coat, usually gored, close-fitting to the waist and flaring to the hem. A recurring fashion in the twentieth century.

prunella, prunelle   a woolen cloth in smooth or twill weave of the eighteenth and nineteenth centuries; much used for academic and clerical robes, as well as a dress fabric.

psyche knot   a hair style with a chignon at the back of the neck, copied from representations in Greek art of the mythological princess loved by Cupid. see *chignon.*

Pucci, Emilio   see *couture, haute.*

puce or **flea color**   a deep reddish-brown color of which there are many

Prince Albert frock coat-
satin-faced lapels-
high collar-gray silk
Ascot scarf-trousers-
black with gray stripes-
silk top hat-white
spats-English-1906

princess gown-white
batiste, Valenciennes
lace, embroidery, fine
tucks-black straw
hat with aigrettes-
1909

hues. Made fashionable by Marie Antoinette.

puffed sleeve   see *sleeve, puffed.*

puffing   a form of dress trimming in bands of gathered and puffed fabric. see *panes; slashings.*

puggree, pugaree   the Hindu turban or hatband of many spellings. For the turban, a wide strip of cotton plain or striped, five to twenty-five yards long wrapped round the head in varied styles, often with a hanging end in back. Around a sun helmet or the crown of a straw hat, a wide, soft, pleated silk band, plain, figured or striped. It originated as a sun protection and is widely copied in western dress.

pull-on or **pull-over; slip-on** or **slip-over**   pertaining to any garment without front, side or back opening, put on by slipping it on over the head. A glove, sweater or girdle without opening is a pull-on or slip-on.

Pulitzer, Lilly   see *couture, haute.*

pump   a low-cut shoe without lacing or strap with thin sole and low heel. First mentioned in the sixteenth century. Pumps were worn principally by footmen which gave rise to the English practice of calling such servants "pumps."

pump, d'Orsay   1830's; the gentleman's shoe originally with cutaway sides and low broad heel; introduced by Count d'Orsay, a society dandy and leader of London and Paris. The pump remains classic today for men and women. The masculine evening shoe worn with formal evening dress is of dull black calf or patent leather with tailored black grosgrain bow. see *oxford ties.*

pump, opera, feminine   a woman's low-cut high-heeled slipper for evening wear is usually cut from a single piece of fabric of satin or velvet and untrimmed in the present mode. At times, handsome rhinestone buckles are worn and the French heel varies in height according to the mode.

punch work   open work embroidery in the round instead of the squares of drawn-thread embroidery. The round holes are made by a stiletto, and edges reinforced by embroidered stitching. Used principally for household linens, or in costume, holes required for lacing together jacket edges as a closure, etc.

punjum   madras piece goods of cotton cloth made in southern India.

pure-dye   a commercial term which, when applied to silk, means that the fabric has not been weighted more than ten per cent and therefore is washable.

Puritan hat   see *hat, Puritan.*

brown leghorn-white shantung puggree band

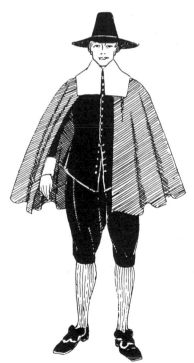

Puritan—habit black, brown or gray-white linen band and cuffs-black felt hat-gray or green stockings-spur leathers on shoes

Puritan-gown plum, gray or brown cloth-collar, cuffs and apron of white Holland linen-black felt hat

purl   a looped stitch in gold or silver thread edging on collar, cuffs and caps. Also a basic stitch in knitting.

purple   one of the three secondary colors, green, purple and orange, a combination of blue and red. The violet tones have a greater proportion of blue, the wines a greater proportion of red.

purple   The origin of the word purple is the Latin *purpura,* the name of the shellfish which yielded the famous Tyrian dye. It was not violet but a deep crimson color.

purse   see *aumônière; pocketbook; reticule.*

puttees   a narrow strip of cloth wrapped spirally around the leg from ankle to knee. Or, a fitted leather legging secured by laces, strap or catch. The first puttees appeared in the Anglo-Indian Army late in the nineteenth century. They were worn by American and British Infantry through World War I. Puttees are of East Indian origin, from *patti,* a Hindu word which signifies a strip of cloth.

pyjamas   see *pajamas.*

Q

Qiana a new man-made fiber presented in 1968 by E.I. du Pont de Nemours & Co., Inc., the producers of Nylon in the 1930's. Qiana is claimed to be the most luxurious of all silk fabrics, more silk-like than most other man-made fibers that are available on the market.

Quaker's hat see *wide-awake hat.*

Quaker fashion of many years - brown satin - white lawn kerchief fastened under belt - silk bonnet over frilled lingerie cap - 1860

Quant, Mary see *couture, haute.*

quarter the part of a shoe which forms the side, from the vamp to the heel.

quartz general term for a group of stones with a silica base, used as gems. Rose quartz is pink. Other varieties include rock crystal, amethyst, jasper, aventurine, chalcedony, bloodstone, chrysoprase, carnelian, agate and onyx.

quatre-foil spur leathers worn by the seventeenth century cavalier to conceal the fastenings of his spurs. Quatre-foil signifies a conventional, ornamental design of leaf or flower with four leaves.

Queen Elizabeth wig see *wig, Queen Elizabeth.*

queue a long braid of hair hanging in back, a Chinese fashion of centuries. In 1644, as a sign of submission, the Manchu conquerors imposed the wearing of the queue. With the establishment of the Republic in 1912, the Occidental haircut replaced it.

queue, cue wig or the tail of a wig. In the eighteenth century with the fashion of wigs on the wane, men, especially army officers, adopted a ribbon-tied queue during the hair-growing process. If extra length was desired, more hair was added and the "whip" bound with black ribbon or leather. see *wig, periwig, cue.*

quiff British slang for a man's hair oiled and dressed off the forehead, or for a forelock of hair.

quill a large stiff feather from a bird's wing or tail or a spine of the hedgehog or porcupine, sometimes used as an ornament for hats.

quilt noun or verb, a coverlet made by quilting.

quilting two pieces of cloth with a layer of cotton batting in between, the

quatre-foil spur leathers to hide spur fastenings - bucket-top boots - red soled - red heel - French - 17th C.

queue - natural hair in queue - large unlooped or uncocked hat recommended by Washington for the troops

three pieces stitched or quilted together in fancy or geometrical patterns. Quite often used for suits and skirts.

quintin   a very sheer lawn made formerly in Quintin, Brittany.

quintise   see *cointise*.

quitasol   a large fan covered with colored oil silk, which was carried for shade as well as breeze, before the invention of parasols. American, eighteenth century, but probably of Spanish origin.

quizzing or **perspective glass**   a single round lens carried on a black silk cord or ribbon, or on a chain around the neck, or mounted on a short or long handle of tortoise shell, silver or gold. Early nineteenth century. Fashionable females often had the lens set in a fan, particularly in a jeweled or painted fan.

R

rabanna   a textile imported from Madagascar. Used for hats and bags.

rabat   see *falling band*.

rabatine   see *falling band*.

rabato, rebato   a starched or wired collar band standing up at the back of the neck. Also, a support for a ruff. Early seventeenth century.

rabbi   the pair of square lawn or linen tabs attached to a starched collar band which is buttoned in back.

rabbit   a rodent of the hare family, originally from southern Europe but native today in most parts of the world. It was introduced into Australia in 1859 and the largest American imports come from Australia, Tasmania and New Zealand. Varied in color, ranging from white through gray, brown to black with white varieties coming from France, Germany, Belgium and Austria. The winter coat is whitest though not a durable fur. It is dressed and dyed to simulate better furs. Extensively used for coats, jackets and trimming and in the manufacture of felt hats. Some commercial names: angora rabbit hair; beaver-dyed coney; chinchilla coney; ermiline; erminette; French beaver; French seal; lapin; leopard-stenciled lapin; marmotine; near seal; polar seal; sealiner; squirreline. see *hare*.

raccoon   a North American mammal. A durable, long-haired fur, the best from northern United States. Also called coonskin. It is pale brown with deep underfur and long, dark and silvery-gray tophair. The poorly colored skins are dyed brown or black for the British military busby.

The fur in its natural state was popular in the first quarter of the twentieth century, used for full-length coats and as trimming on cloth coats. It is now sheared to simulate beaver and nutria; sheared, dyed and sewn like let-out mink.

raccoon coat   a craze for the huge, bulky raccoon coat in the 1920's was due to riding in open touring cars; it was particularly favored for attending football games.

rachel   a flesh color or tawny-pink color face powder, previously mostly white, which appeared in the 1880's. Named after Madame Rachel, a famous London beauty specialist.

radium   a lustrous, plain, smooth silk or rayon, which has crispness, yet supple, draping quality. Used for lingerie, linings and dresses.

wired rebato of lawn and lace-rolled gauze turban- English-1621

rabbit-rodent of the hare family-fur of many names

raccoon coat- horn buttons- black derby- 1928

raccoon- a durable, long-haired fur-N.a.mammal

281

raglan
overcoat-
tan whipcord-
similar to the
balmacaan-1939

raffia   a strong, silky smooth, straw from the leafstalk of the raffia palm of Madagascar. Used for hats, bags, baskets, and many other items.

raglan   a loose topcoat with sleeves cut to join the garment from underarm to neck. Named for Lord Raglan, who devised the design for his soldiers during the Crimean War. 1850's.

raglan sleeve   see *sleeve, raglan.*

raincoat   a garment for wear in the rain, made of synthetic fabrics, water-repellent, stain-resistant, often reversible and occasionally fur-lined. There are also some cottons, silks and woolen cloths which are oil-processed for lighter weight. Such fabrics, impregnated with oils, provide satisfactory showerproof garments and permit the use of style and material necessary in an all-purpose coat. see *cravenette; mackintosh.*

rainy daisy   see *skirt, rainy daisy.*

rajah   see *nankeen.*

ramie, rami   a perennial plant of East Asia commercially cultivated in China and Japan for its fiber. It can be spun and woven into fabrics, as is done in the United States and Europe. In Asia, it is woven into cloth and made into fishing lines, nets, laces, hats, etc. The fiber is strong and glossy.

ramillies, ramilies   a cocked hat of the eighteenth century in which the back flap turned up sharply, rising higher than the two front flaps. The two front flaps protruded outward in a spoutlike crease.

ramillies   a favorite army wig which got its name from the Battle of Ramillies in 1706, fought between the English and the French. It was an English victory under the Duke of Marlborough. The wig had a pigtail tied top and bottom with black ribbon. Sometimes the braid was looped under and tied.

raploch   a coarse, rough homespun woolen cloth made principally in Scotland.

rason   see *rhason.*

rat   a small roll or pad of false hair worn under the natural hair to shape a required silhouette, as for the pompadour. Early twentieth century. Also, fur used as costume trimming by the French couturiers during World War I. The animal was hunted and killed in the rat-infested trenches by the French soldiers, and was presumably the wood or field rat which has a clean, soft brown, black or white velvety fur.

rat, Armenian   see *ermine.*

rateen, ratinet   several coarse woolen cloths of the seventeenth and eighteenth centuries. "Ratinet" was the name of those of lighter weight of the same weave. Used for dresses, coats and capes.

ratiné, retine   cotton in a loose, plain woven cloth which can be bleached, dyed or printed and is given a high luster or other finishes. Used for dresses, suits and coats.

ratiné lace   a trimming for heavy cotton dresses. A groundwork done in heavy loops similar to Turkish toweling.

ratinet   see *rateen.*

raw silk   see *silk, raw.*

rawhide   untanned cattle hide that has undergone some preparatory processes; used for luggage, whips, laces, etc.

rayé   French for striped. An obsolete term for pin-striped fabrics whether silk, cotton or wool.

rayle, rail   a loose garment worn over the bodice, generally in cape form, for indoor or outdoor wear; another name for a combing jacket. French, eighteenth century.

rayon   a generic name for a man-made glossy fiber made of a viscous solution of modified cellulose. Also, the textile woven from such a fiber. There are many types of rayon, each with its own trade name.

rayonne   a hood much worn in the American Colonies in the second half of the seventeenth century, of black ducape, a popular heavy corded silk cloth. The hood was lined with a striped silk of contrasting color and the padded fold was turned back around the face and tied with ribbons.

razor   Latin, rasare, meaning to scrape or rase. A steel blade attached to its case or holder which also acts as a cover when not in use. Safety-razor, the twentieth century model, a smaller, more compact implement with removable blade which is easily replaced by a new one.

ready-made, ready-to-wear, off-the-rack   apparel in all sizes, of varied styles and fabrics for men, women and children, sold in shops and large stores. A twentieth century development. "Off-the-rack" is the British term.

Reboux   see *couture, haute.*

rebozo, rebosa, reboso   a piece of Mexican and South American costume centuries old. It may be either a thin, dark-colored linen scarf worn around the head and shoulders or a long, strong woolen shawl tied around the shoulders and hips as a carryall for the baby, marketing or almost anything.

red   one of the three primary colors with blue and yellow; red mixed with blue gives the secondary color purple, and, mixed with yellow, the secondary color orange. Red plus purple gives the tertiary color red-purple, red plus orange the tertiary color red-orange. The palest reds are the pink tinges, the darkest include ruby and garnet. The purple-reds include rose and crimson, the yellow reds scarlet and flame.

red feather   In medieval days, a red feather in a knight's helmet was a sign of an unusual act of chivalry performed by the wearer. According to legend, a robe of red feathers worn in the Orient meant that the wearer had donated outstanding service to the community. In Hawaii only chiefs and nobles were permitted to wear a red feather headdress.

red fox   see *fox, red.*

red riding hood   see *French hood.*

red river coat   a hooded frock coat with brass buttons, worn in Canada.

red sable   see *mink, kolinsky.*

Redfern   see *couture, haute.*

redingote   French for riding coat, originally a man's outer coat of the eighteenth century. A double-breasted coat with large collar and revers and some-

redingote—
"Levite"
Pennsylvania
or Holland hat—
velvet breeches—
lingerie cravat—
French—1780's

rebozo—a S. A. or
Mexican scarf used
as a carryall—
centuries old

redingote-
chamois color
cloth-gray
green habit-
black satin
neckcloth-
brown beaver
hat-English-
1820

redingote-black
cloth worn over
"habit" (suit)-
beaver hat-
English-1820's

redingote-mastic
color broadcloth-
toque,blue brocaded
ribbon and black
wings-1894

times a short cape; it was adopted by women late in the century. As a woman's coat it reappeared in the 1890's, still double-breasted with tailored collar and revers, a fitted body with long flaring skirt and full puffed sleeves. Made especially of mastic-colored broadcloth, it was fastened with bone buttons. see *levite gown; witzchoura.*

reefer a jacket or short overcoat, double-breasted and of very heavy cloth, worn by cattlemen, seamen and other workmen. see *pea jacket.*

reeled silk see *silk, raw.*

regalia symbols and emblems of royalty such as crown, scepter, insignia and decorations of an order. Thus, special dress and finery.

regatta a stout English twilled cotton usually in blue and white striped material, especially British.

regency the period during which a regent governs. Specifically, the French Regency (1715–1723) when the Duc

d'Orléans was regent for Louis XV, and the English (1811–1820) when George, Prince of Wales, afterward George IV, was regent for George III. These two regencies in particular, affected costume.

regimental stripes a general term for diagonal stripes on a man's necktie. In British usage, stripes in the colors of a particular regiment; such a tie may be worn with civilian dress only by officers of that regiment.

reindeer heavy, durable leather used for shoe uppers. see *caribou.*

Renaissance In Europe, the period originated in Italy, brought about by the decline of Greco-Roman influence and the undertakings of the Crusaders. It began in the thirteenth and fourteenth centuries, was fully under way at the beginning of the fifteenth, its height about the middle of the century and its climax about 1500. Costumes were ornate and made of rich materials. From the East came gems and rare stones, cloth of gold and silver tissue; from Russia and the north, came furs such as sable, vair, ermine, marten, lynx, fox (*continued on page 290*)

Renaissance
chemise tops

partlet or
guimpe of
the costume
of the
lansquenet-
German-
16th c.

laced and
sleeved doublet
over white shirt-
Italian-
16th c.

doublet
with
embroidered
partlet or
guimpe-
Italian-
1521

the frilled shirt
decolletage
worn at court-
French-
1530's

gentleman's night
shirt embroidered
and frilled-black
velvet coif-
French-1580

falling band
with
Spanish blackwork-
academic robe-
English-
1580

short doublet
with sleeves-
over white
shirt-fashion
called "braggard"-
English-16th c.

infant's
doublet with
partlet or guimpe-
French-
1st half
16th c.

shirt
embroidered
with
Spanish
blackwork-
English-
1540

Renaissance
shapes of the
early period

silhouette
of the
Italian
corsetto—
undoubtedly
of boiled
leather—
1470

high bosom and
slim body of
the "corps piqué"
(quilted linen
corset)—
French—
1520

Florentine
silhouette
of the
leather corset—
1485

chemise into
partlet or guimpe—
laced corselet—
German—
1st half
16th c.

gown
with partlet
or guimpe—
(simulated
chemise top)
Swiss—
1520

the slim
"Spanish body"
with
flat bosom—
shaped by
a leather
corset—
mid·15th c.

all·white
widow's dress—
with partlet
or guimpe—
leather
corset—
French—
mid·16th c.

gown and apron—
worn over a
linen corset—
German—
1516

laced corselet—
over a leather
or linen corset—
German—
1564

286

Renaissance
the Spanish body
and the farthingale

satin gown
over iron corset
and drum-shaped
farthingale-
French-
1581

boy's costume
over
corps piqué
and
farthingale-
Spanish-
1575

black velvet gown
with ribbon bowknots-
over iron corset-
cone-shaped
farthingale-
Spanish-
1551

brocaded and
embroidered
gown over
"busto" (iron
corset) and
"Venetians"
(bloomers)-
Venetian-
1590's

exaggerated
form of the
Spanish body-
dome-shaped
farthingale-
English-
1590

costume worn over
basquine and
French bolster
type of farthingale-
Dutch lady of the
1590's

287

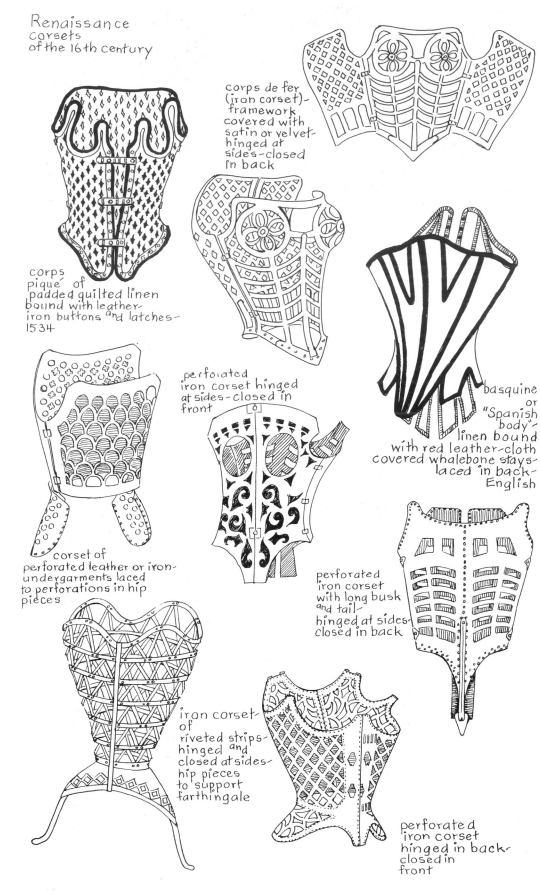

Renaissance
corsets
of the 16th century

corps de fer
(iron corset)-
framework
covered with
satin or velvet-
hinged at
sides-closed
in back

corps
piqué of
padded quilted linen
bound with leather-
iron buttons and latches-
1534

basquine
or
"Spanish
body"-
linen bound
with red leather-cloth
covered whalebone stays-
laced in back-
English

corset of
perforated leather or iron-
undergarments laced
to perforations in hip
pieces

perforated
iron corset hinged
at sides-closed in
front

perforated
iron corset
with long busk
and tail-
hinged at sides-
closed in back

iron corset-
of
riveted strips-
hinged and
closed at sides-
hip pieces
to support
farthingale

perforated
iron corset
hinged in back-
closed in
front

288

Renaissance masculine corseted shapes

brigandine-padded leather corselet with rivets-15th c.

peasecod-bellied corselet of steel with turn-buttons-French-1575

"corset"-boned and pleated jacket worn over high-collared and sleeved doublet-French-1415

soldier's quilted and fringed "jack"-(jacket)-linen or leather-Flemish-15th c.

sleeved and skirted doublet over armor-velvet and satin embroidered and jeweled-English-c.1590

brigandine-red velvet riveted with nail heads-Italian-1552

fitted doublet of small boy-English-1574

velvet jerkin worn over doublet with sleeves-Austrian-1567

peasecod-bellied doublet of slashed velvet-falling band of lace-English-1583

289

and lambskin. From Rheims came rich brocades, and from Venice, beautiful silks and velvets. The Renaissance in France reached full bloom in the reign of François I, (1515–1547). The French Court owed much of its brilliance to Italian influence. Parts of the costume were slashed and colors were lighter than those in Italy, sky-blue and white, lilac hues, rose, gold and silver being much used.

Renaissance lace   a modern lace fashioned of tape motifs joined by lace stitches. A beautiful lace when made up over pale blue or pink satin of the trailing gowns worn to semi-formal parties worn by the Gibson girl and Lillian Russell types around the turn of the nineteenth century.

reinforcing   in sewing, adding a piece of facing or binding to strengthen a spot exposed to extra wear.

remnant   the end of a bolt of cloth or a left-over piece after completion of sewing.

rengue   a Philippine fabric made from native pineapple; a delicate gauze stiffly starched. It is used for the traditional fichu and the wide-arched butterfly sleeves. see *camisa*.

Renta, Oscar de la   see *couture, haute*.

rep, repp   a cloth of silk or wool or both with a crosswise ribbed or corded surface. Also, any fabric with traverse line markings on the face. A firm material used for men's and boy's clothing and for women's suits.

repellent cloth   a fabric that repels moisture but may not be waterproof.

reprocessed wool   wool fibers woven and manufactured but never used, reduced again to fiber and spun and re-woven into fiber.

reptile   in the leather trade, the skin of an animal that crawls on its belly or short legs such as snakes, the alligator, lizard, boa, cobra and frogs, etc.

reseau   from the French for net or network of small regular meshes; the ground work or foundation of a lace pattern.

resist printing   a fabric dyed after printing the pattern in dye-resistant chemical, leaving the design white. The resist chemical is removed after dipping.

resort wear   appropriate clothes for the social life and sports activities of summer or winter resorts.

Restoration   England: the period after the commonwealth when the Stuarts returned to the throne (1660–1685). Charles II had spent his exile at the court of Louis XIV and brought the French fashions of that period back with him.

Restoration   France: 1815–1830, the return of the Bourbons after the defeat of Napoleon was marked in fashion by smaller waistlines for men and women and the return of the corset.

reticella or **Roman lace**   the first form of needlepoint lace having drawn work and cut work with geometric designs connected by picot brides. Now used principally for table linens.

reticulated headdress   the hair worn in a jewelled net. see *caul*

reticule, ridicule   a small handbag of knitted silk, beading, brocade, plush or embroidery fashionable in the eighteenth century. The slim cotton gowns permitted no pockets and as a pleasantry, the inadequate little bag was called a ridicule. It held fan, handkerchief, card money and perfume bottle. see *aumôniére; handbag*.

rever, revers   part of the turned-back or lay-over of the front of the jacket or coat, combining collar, lapels and revers.

revered   a style of drawn work or stitching ornamenting linens, handkerchiefs, sheer dresses made of cotton, lawn, percale and batiste.

reverse calf   see *calf, reverse.*

reversible coat   an outer coat that can be worn either side out, made of a single reversible fabric or of two fabrics.

rhason, rason   a cassock-like robe worn by prelates of the Greek Orthodox Church.

rhinegrave breeches   see *breeches, petticoat.*

rhinestones   small water-worn pebbles of rock crystal found mostly in the Rhine River in Germany. They are facet-cut to resemble diamonds.

ribcage   the diaphragm, or that section of the body from waist to chest.

ribbed hose   stockings knit with lengthwise deep ribs.

ribbon wire   a narrow plastic tape with wired edges for use in millinery.

ribbons, galants, favors   seventeenth century, clusters of variegated colored ribbon loops which ornamented feminine and masculine costume until the French minister Mazarin placed a ban against extravagant trimming. An elegant person often used as much as three hundred yards of ribbon on all parts of dress, including the hair.

Ricci, Nina   see *couture, haute.*

rice braid   a braid strung with cotton rice-shaped pellets.

rice net   a coarse, cotton net stiff enough for crown and brim foundation in women's hats.

rice powder   made with a base of pulverized rice. It was white and used—principally to avoid a shiny nose—until the late nineteenth century when tinted powder appeared in London.

ricinium   see *flammeum.*

rick rack   see *braid.*

ridicule   a small handbag.   see *reticule.*

riding habit   a specific costume for horseback riding, formerly jacket and skirt for riding side saddle, now jacket and breeches, wide through thighs and tight-fitting calf-length legs. see illustrations, next page; *stock.*

riding petticoat   see *safeguard.*

ring, dinner   a handsomely wrought jeweled ring for late afternoon or evening occasions.

ring, engagement   usually a gold or platinum ring set with a single gem, the solitaire diamond having become most favored. Worn on the third finger of the left hand.

ring, signet   a ring made with a flat surface upon which is engraved a monogram or crest. Originally worn by nobility to authenticate and seal letters or documents with an imprint in sealing wax.

ring, wedding   placed upon the third finger of the left hand of the bride during the ceremony. Usually a plain gold band or a jeweled circlet for the bride and, in some cases, a plain gold band for the groom. In some countries, such as Germany, worn on the third finger of the right hand.

rivière   a diamond necklace fashioned in several strands, giving the effect of a river of diamonds.

roach   see *American Indian headdress, costume.*

riding habit-
velvet brocade
and red cloth
skirt-black
hat with
red plumes-
Louis XIV-
1652

riding habit
with panniers
and waistcoat-
tricorne hat-
powdered hair-
French-18th C.

riding habit-
"London smoke"
gray cloth-velvet
collar-black
satin stock-black
silk hat-gray veil-
white muslin strap
breeches-
French-1844

riding habit-
gray cloth-
jacket braid-
edged-black
satin stock-
gray felt hat-
gray veil-
white gloves
black patent
leather boots
1885

riding habit-formal-
black melton cloth-
velvet collar-
buff cloth waistcoat-
white stock-
chamois gloves-
black silk hat-
black boots-
1925

riding-
cross-saddle habit
of whipcord-brown
coat-beige breeches-
soft, beige felt hat-
1925

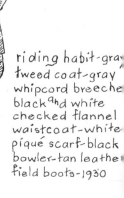

riding habit-gray
tweed coat-gray
whipcord breeches-
black and white
checked flannel
waistcoat-white
piqué scarf-black
bowler-tan leather
field boots-1930

robe à la française, Watteau gown designed by, and named after the painter, Watteau, 1730's. By 1770, it had become the formal dress for court functions. It had six box pleats stitched flat to the back and ending in a train.

robe à l'anglaise   see *English gown*

robe de style   the twentieth century infanta style, an evening fashion for which Lanvin of Paris became famous; its vogue was in the nineteen twenties and thirties. It had a tight bodice with a bouffant skirt, ankle or floor length. see *Velásquez.*

"robe de style" of heavy white satin with crystal beaded ribbons- beaded rose corsage- Lanvin 1923

robe, mandarin   see *mandarin robe.*

Robespierre collar   see *collar, Robespierre.*

Robin Hood hat   see *hat, Robin Hood.*

robings   an obsolete term for materials and trimmings for robes and gowns.

robozilla   a flattering headdress of the young women of the Balearic Isles. A headkerchief of sheer silk or gauze that covers the back of the head and ties around under the chin.

rocket or roquet- vestment of lawn and lace worn by bishops

rochette, rochet   a full-length garment of white lawn with full sleeves, worn over the cassock and under the chimere; part of an Anglican bishop's vestments.

rock crystal   a colorless form of quartz, very effective in costume jewelry when facet-cut.

rock sable   see *sable, mountain.*

rocket, roquet   a short, full, smock-like, woolen garment worn from the Middle Ages to date. In the fifteenth century, it was worn by commoners and pages with hooded shoulder cape. It was worn to the eighteenth century by men and women in Europe and the American Colonies. In the nineteenth century, worn by ecclesiastics, of white linen with the lower half from waist down, of heavy lace.

rococo   of the eighteenth century, a period of ornate extremes in Italy and Germany with the shell design predominating in jewelry, accessories, and decorative motifs.

rococo embroidery   a design style carried to extreme in asymmetrically curved forms and shell motifs. Executed in a narrow one eighth inch wide ribbon known as China ribbon.

robozilla-embroidered lawn and pleated silk gorget- Balearic Islands

rocket or roquet- medieval blouse and hood-also worn by monks

Roller Hat of felt or
straw-boys and girls-
early 20th century

roquelaure or
roquelo-cloak
of cloth, velvet
or silk-hooded,
collared or
buttoned-
early 18 th C.

white shirt
or undertunic-
Roman-
early c. A.D.

Rodriguez, Pedro   see *couture, haute.*

roll collar   see *collar, roll*

rolled hem   a very fine handkerchief hem made by rolling the edge and fastening it by minute slip stitches. Also used for scarves and sheer or chiffon dresses.

roller   a small, round hat of felt or straw with rolled brim and a ribbon band, worn by boys and girls. Early twentieth century.

romaine   a sheer fabric in a basket weave that French ladies of the sixteenth century used for head scarfs.

Roman collar   see *collar, clerical.*

Roman cut work   see *cut work embroidery.*

Roman lace   a needlepoint of geometric pattern, see reticella.

Roman stripes   cloths striped with vivid colors in different widths running in the weft direction. The name is applied to all cloths so striped, regardless of fibers. Used in dress goods, trimming and many other ways.

Romanian costume, traditional   see illustrations page 297.

Romanian embroidery   see *Holbein work.*

Romany stripes   see *gypsy stripes.*

rompers   a one-piece garment combining waist and short, full bloomers worn by young children and formerly by young girls and women for gymnasium exercises. see *jumpers.*

rondelle, rondel   a bead or gem cut into a slim disk with center hole to string between beads or gems of larger size for a necklace. Often of clear crystal to set

off colored beads. A term also used for round decorative motifs, as in embroidery.

roquelaure, roquelo   a cloak first worn in the eighteenth century by the Duke of Roquelaure, and named for him. Of heavy woolen cloth and camlet in bright colors; hooded, buttoned down the front, knee-length. It was popular in Europe and the American Colonies and worn by men and women into the early nineteenth century.

roquet, rocket   a raincape of the early eighteenth century made of heavy cloth called rocket or gray russet. Worn with or without sleeves.

rose point lace   an elaborate needlepoint lace with delicate flowers, foliage and scrolls accented with string cordonnet connected by brides and finished with buttonholed edges.

rose quartz   a milky pink to rose mineral of little value, but attractive for jewelry, especially when carved.

roseberry cloth   a lustrous cotton fabric, closely woven, mercerized, waterproofed and resembling fine reps; used for raincoats, hunting and fishing capes. A staple cheviot cloth known as Burberry cloth. see *Burberry.*

rosehube   a hat of roses worn by women of Schwyz, a canton of Switzerland. Between the wings of the lace cap the hair is held in place by a rose hat pin.

rosette   ribbon shirred or pleated into a round shape or formed of ribbon loops.

rouge   French for red; any cosmetic of that color used for lips and cheeks. see *cosmetics.*

roughers   woolen cloth as it comes from the loom before filling and perching on the horizontal bar for examination and perfecting.

Ancient Roman

Magistrate
white tunic
purple toga
gold
embroidery

Senator
white toga
purple bands
and boots

High Rank
white tunic
purple toga
gold
embroidery

Knight
white toga
and tunic
purple bands
and sandals

Young
Roman
under tunic
stola

under tunic
stola
palla

purple stola
gold
embroidery

under tunic
stola
palla

295

roundlet with draped
liripipe-silk or cloth-
French-15th C.

narrow ruche, forerunner
of the ruff - French-16th C.

ruff of starched
lawn-beaver hat
with embroidered
lady's glove and ostrich-
English-16th C.

rouleau   French for a piping or roll of ribbon; used as hat trimming or apparel.

roundlet with liripipe   a man's turban-like hat, the medieval chaperon made up over a stuffed roundlet. The noble was permitted a long tail, while that of the commoner was very short; fifteenth century. see *chaperon; liripipe.*

rubashka   the Russian smock blouse of heavy white linen with full sleeves, narrow cuffs and a narrow standing collar. Collar, cuffs and hem are embroidered, as is the left-side opening in front from collar to waist. An important garment whether worn belted with leather belt or tucked inside the trousers.

rubber   a substance obtained from the milky juice of certain tropical plants, which has been used commercially since Charles Goodyear discovered the process of vulcanization which he patented in 1844. Rubber boots and outer soles are made using this process. Rubber as a fiber for elasticized garments is composed of a core of natural or synthetic rubber around which other yarns are wrapped; this is used for garters, girdles, foundation garments, waistbands, etc.

rubber, crepe   see *crepe rubber.*

rubberized   describing waterproof fabrics such as silk impregnated with rubber or a rubber solution. The first patent for making rubberized cloth was taken out in 1801 in London by Rudolph Ackerman, but E. Mackintosh of England patented the first practical process for waterproofing in 1823. In 1820, T. Hancock of Middlesex, England, invented the first elastic fabric with rubber in it.

rubbers   low overshoes of rubber worn to protect the shoes in wet weather.

ruby   a variety of corundum crystallized and colored pale rose to deep red or "pigeon's blood." Red rubies are from

Burma, light red from Ceylon, and dark brownish red from Thailand.

ruche   a pleated or goffered strip of lace net or linen lawn, worn around the neck. Ruches appeared in Spain, in the first half of the sixteenth century, as tiny frills finishing neck and sleeves of the fine lawn masculine shirt. After the middle of the century the ruche became a fully developed ruff with lace edging. see *ruff.*

ruching   an edging for collars and cuffs of finely pleated lace or other material.

ruff   a kind of stiffly starched collar completely encircling the neck, wider than a ruche, late sixteenth and early seventeenth centuries. By the 1580's the ruff was a large cartwheel, starched and wired. The width of the fashionable ruff was about a quarter of a yard wide and the length eighteen to nineteen yards of fine linen lawn or Holland cambric. A frame of wire covered with silk thread was worn under it, the edge of the ruff also wired. Ruffs were starched in various colors, blue and green, with yellow a favorite and worn all over Europe.

ruffle   a strip of cloth fulled, pleated or gathered to a straight edge as a frill.

rullian   a Scottish brogue. see *brogue, brogan.*

rumal, remal   a silk or cotton made in Bombay, India and worn by men as headdress or turban.

rumba, rhumba   a Spanish dance costume of black satin, short black velvet jacket with cap sleeves, body bare from bolero to waistline. Long, tight black skirt with narrow, multi-colored ruffles flaring from thighs to floor.

russet   a coarse peasant cloth of yellowish-red or grayish-brown used for everyday clothes in past centuries. Russet remains the name for such garments, also for the color.

Russian-shuba of embroidered white felt with black braid edge and black Persian lamb collar-black felt hat

Russian woman in quilted cotton caftan-linen smock-white felt calpac with bride-contemporary

Romanian sheepskin bolero with black lamb and embroidery-worn over linen smock

Romanian-szür-embroidered black felt-black sleeveless jacket (sarafan)-black felt hat

Russian festival costume-sarafan, (jacket) over rubashka (smock) black lamb fur-black embroidery-soft felt hat

Russian caftan of rich brocade-velvet skirt over satin skirt-headscarf of brocade-late 19th C.

Russian blouse of white or colored linen, hip-length or a little longer with long, slightly fulled sleeves gathered into cuffs, and a standing collar opening to the left side of the neck. Collar, opening, and cuffs usually embroidered in colorful stitchery. A leather belt or tie belt is worn. see *rubashka*.

Russian costume, traditional see illustrations.

Russian embroidery done mostly on linen in brilliantly colored geometric designs. Used on collars, cuffs and wide hem borders on skirts. Also, a colorful embroidery worked in outline motifs on holland, a canvas of plain weave, sized and glazed. The canvas is cut away upon completion.

rust a reddish-yellow hue, the color of iron rust.

Russian Youth dress U.S.S.R.-dark green with red and yellow braid over red breeches-red fox cap

297

S

sable, Russian or
Siberian-15 inches
long-tail 7 inches

sack coat,
black with
black velvet
collar-beige
felt bowler-
checked breeches
chamois gloves-
English-
1850's

saad, sad colors   the grayed hues of any color, generally gray, dark brown and black. Favored by the Puritans, seventeenth century.

saba   a variety of the genus of banana grown in the Philippine Islands. A fine textured fabric produced from the fiber of the plant.

sable, Alaska or **American**   see *skunk* or *raccoon*.

sable   a marten of the weasel family from northern Europe and northern Asia. The name is from *sabelum* of Slavic origin.

sable, Chinese   also called Himalayan marten; yellow to yellowish-brown and dark golden brown. Blending and tipping is necessary to increase luster. see *marten.*

sable, Hudson Bay   see *marten, American.*

sable, Japanese   yellowish-brown peltries, coarse in texture. Lack of luster necessitates dyeing.

sable, mountain or **rock**   commercial names; the small animal is a bassarisk or ringtail and related to the raccoon. Originally from Mexico and now found in Mexico, Central America, Southwest United States from Texas to California, Oregon and Nevada. Its hair is silky like the marten pale yellow hairs. Usually dyed dark brown and illegally called mountain or rock sable. Used for scarfs and trimming.

sable, red   see *kolinsky.*

sable, Russian or **Siberian**   the most highly esteemed of all furs, known as Russian crown sable under the Romanoffs. Underhair close, fine and very soft; top hair silky, fine and flowing; durable, lightweight and very warm. Lustrous color from gray to brown, almost black. Rarely used for coats because of time and cost required to match skins. Used for scarfs and trimming on fine cloth coats or fine broadtail coats.

sable, tatar   see *mink, kolinsky.*

sabot   see *wooden shoe; klompen.*

sabotine   a shoe of rawhide with a wooden heel made as a makeshift by soldiers during World War I.

sabretache   a military leather pouch for carrying orders and dispatches by a cavalryman. It hung from the belt on the left, or sabre, side. Copied in feminine fabrics during the Directoire period and again in the early twentieth century. see *handbags.*

sabrine work   fancywork in flower appliqués applied by chain or purl stitch on jackets and borders of skirts.

sac   see *sacque.*

sachet   a small scent bag usually of silk padded with cotton, holding a powdered perfume substance called sachet powder. Used to scent garments and linens in chests and wardrobes.

sack coat   a masculine coat, plain,

Ivy League

British

ontinental
ack Coat•Masculine•Contemporary

Spanish

short and without waist seam, single or double-breasted. The Norfolk is a type of sack coat. see *lounge coat*.

sackcloth or **sacking**   coarse, heavy linen, cotton or muslin used for sports suits. Sackcloth in ancient times was worn as an act of mourning or penance because of its rough texture.

sacque, sac   a feminine short, loose jacket with sleeves usually of silk or flannel, worn with petticoat or slip as a negligée. see *Watteau sacque; bed jacket; bed sacque*.

saddle bag pocket   see *pocket, saddle bag*.

saddle oxford   a low, broad-heeled sports shoe appeared about 1915, worn by men, women and children. Of white buckskin with a saddle of black or brown leather across the vamp and a three-eyelet lacing down the instep.

safari   seal fur dyed a light brown. see *seal, Alaska*.

safeguard   a wrap-around skirt worn when riding, to protect ladies' clothes from mud and dust. Used in England and the American Colonies in the seventeenth and eighteenth centuries, and especially by farmer's wives when going to market. It was usually made of red, gray or black homespun and known by the various names of *foot mantle, fote mantle, weather skirt, riding petticoat*.

safety razor   an invention of the late nineteenth century which replaced the long blade used for centuries. A small fine precision blade of steel was protected by a guard to prevent cutting the skin, the blade easily removed for a new one, or for stropping.

saffian leather   leather made of goatskin and sheepskins, tanned with sumac and dyed bright colors. It is frequently confused with moroccan leather, because named for the Moroccan seaport called Saffi.

saffron   a species of crocus with bright yellow stamens which, when dried, are used to color and flavor food and were formerly used as a dye. The flower was known throughout the ancient Mediterranean world and the East. In medieval times it was used in Europe for dyeing linen and silk and also as a hair dye. Buddhist monks wear saffron-colored robes because the color is considered a peaceful one. The Hindu pundit wears a sacred spot of yellow on his forehead.

sagum   of Gaulish origin, worn by ancient Rome and early Germans. A folded rectangle of woolen cloth fastened by a thorn instead of a fibula. Opened out, it became the military blanket of the army. "Putting on the sagum" came to mean a declaration of war.

sailcloth   heavy duck or canvas used for sails, tents and such. It was once

Sailor Suit-white linen and navy blue cloth-collar edged white braid-rolled black silk neckerchief tied with white braid-black straw hat-black ribbon—1850

sailor suit-two-piece suit, navy, tan or white, of duck, serge, flannel or broadcloth-straw sailor hat, black and white shoes, black stockings-black braid trim—1870's

samarre-worn over vest and petticoat-velvet with padding and fur-worn in the colonies-17th and 18th C.

sampot worn by both sexes to form either pantaloons or skirt effect

popular among tailors for stiffening coat fronts. Sometimes used for casual skirts or jackets.

sailor, Breton   see *Breton sailor.*

sailor collar   see *sailor collar.*

sailor hat   see *hat, sailor's; gob's cap.*

sailor, Merry Widow   see *Merry Widow sailor.*

sailor suit   a British and American outfit worn especially by young boys. In the 1850's, a custom tailor of Bond Street, London, designed a sailor suit for Queen Victoria's children: short jacket with long trousers; headgear consisted of small round caps and flat straw hats. The fashion was seized upon by American mothers who adopted the uniform of the American Navy enlisted man though not always with regulation as to detail. The suit was usually of dark blue cloth trimmed with white braid. For small boys, the suit consisted of a loose overblouse with the sailor collar, narrow in front and broad and square in back. The sailor suit of the small boy comprised blouse and knee-pants, and the middy suit had long trousers. see *middy blouse;* illustrations on preceding page.

Saint Gall lace   a Swiss imitation of Venetian lace. A process of embroidering cotton or woolen fabric with silk or cotton thread, then dissolving the wool and retaining only the embroidery.

Saint Laurent, Yves   see *couture, haute.*

sakkos or **sacco**   from the Greek *sakkos,* meaning a bag or sac. see *lounge coat.*

sakkos; soccos   an embroidered vestment worn by bishops of the Eastern Orthodox Church, corresponding to the dalmatic of the Western Church. It is made all in one piece and symbolizes the seamless robe of Christ.

sallet or **salade**   a simple helmet with or without visor and made to extend over the back of the neck; fifteenth century.

salloo   a twilled red cotton fabric similar to calico, made in England and which became popular in East India, hence its Hindu name, *sālū.* The pretty cotton substituted occasionally for the beautiful Indian silk cholee or blouse, and the sari or luxurious scarf.

salt sacking   cotton and worsted in coarse, plain weaves and rough, homespun types in suitable summer weights which are used for sports and riding habits.

Salvation Army lassie bonnet   see *bonnet, Salvation Army lassie.*

Sam Browne belt   see *belt, Sam Browne.*

samarre; simar   a Dutch jacket of the seventeenth and eighteenth centuries worn by women over a petticoat of heavy satin, en negligée. The jacket, worn over a waistcoat, was short, loose and flaring, of velvet, plush or silk and sometimes fur-edged. Dutch masters such as Vermeer delighted in painting this costume. The samarre was popular in the American Colonies.

samite   a luxurious silk fabric of the Middle Ages interwoven with gold and silver threads was used for the robes of the nobles and ecclesiastics.

sampot   part of the typical Cambodian costume; a length of cotton or silk wrapped around the waist and drawn up in front producing the effect of full pantaloons, worn by men and women. For ceremonial occasions, Cambodian women wear the sampot draped in skirt fashion. Of beautiful, heavy silk with pleats in center front and an extra handsome scarf draped over the left shoulder, leaving the right shoulder bare.

sanbenito   a smock of sackcloth was

worn by those condemned to death by auto-da-fé during the Spanish Inquisition. The color was yellow or black, according to the degree of guilt. From 1480 through the sixteenth century.

sandals   a sole held to the foot by leather straps or cut-out uppers tied and buckled.

sandals, knob   the knob sandal or clog has been worn since ancient times in the Orient and is still worn there and by the Bedouins in the African desert. This sandal is broad and heelless with red moroccan leather straps over the instep. It is held to the foot by a large decorative knob, usually silver, between the large toe and the next.

Sanforized   a patented process of compressive shrinkage which guarantees that the cotton or linen so treated will not shrink beyond a quarter inch to the yard in either direction.

sanitize   a trade name process which renders textiles germ-proof, self-sterilizing and antiseptic, and prevents perspiration odors.

sans culottes   a name for the French Revolutionists or Jacobins, to distinguish them from the aristocrats. Literally, without breeches; the term referred to the fact that men of the people wore trousers rather than the fashionable knee breeches of the nobility. see *trousers;* illustration on next page.

Santa Claus costume   of bright red flannel or cotton velvet; coat and knickers. The coat is usually trimmed with something white and furry-looking such as plush for collar, cuffs and border. A buckled wide leather belt, boots and a fur-trimmed red cap complete the costume. The English Father Christmas wears the same costume.

sapphire   a pure variety of corundum in transparent or translucent crystals used as gems. Blue is the most valuable; sap-

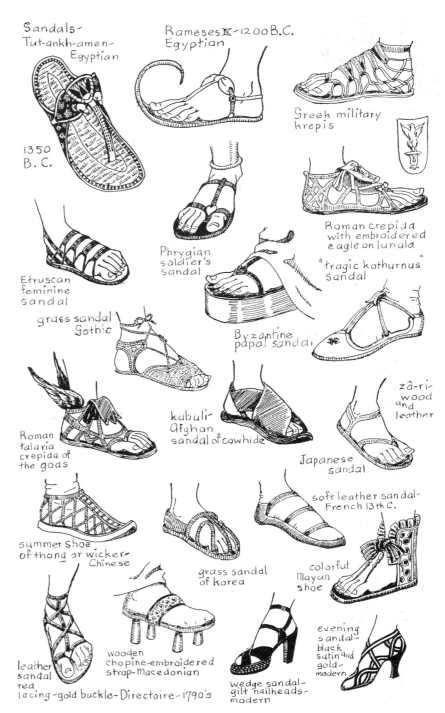

Sandals-
Tut-ankh-amen-
Egyptian
1350
B.C.

Rameses IX-1200 B.C.
Egyptian

Greek military
krepis

Etruscan
feminine
sandal

grass sandal
Gothic

Phrygian
soldier's
sandal

Roman crepida
with embroidered
eagle on lunula

Byzantine
papal sandal

"tragic kothurnus"
sandal

Roman
talaria
crepida of
the gods

kabuli-
Afghan
sandal of cowhide

zô-ri-
wood
and
leather

Japanese
sandal

summer shoe
of thong or wicker-
Chinese

grass sandal
of korea

soft leather sandal-
French 13th C.

colorful
Mayan
shoe

leather
sandal
red
lacing-gold buckle-Directoire-1790's

wooden
chopine-embroidered
strap-Macedonian

wedge sandal-
gilt nailheads-
modern

evening
sandal-
black
satin and
gold-
modern

phires occur in yellows, greens and colorless stones.

sarafan   the traditional dress of old Russia and still worn by Russian peasants. A long full skirt of brocade or wool gathered to a sleeveless bodice with either square or round neckline. It is worn over a full, soft white blouse gathered at the wrists into ruffles or cuffs. An embroidered, sleeveless jacket or bolero is also often worn. Both overdress and jacket are called sarafans.

sarape, zarape   a colorful, fringed shawl-like wrap worn by Mexicans and South American Indians. Unlike the poncho, which has a hole in the center for the head, the sarape opens down the center front. It is a larger square than the poncho and the woven motifs are more Aztec in design and color than those of the poncho. The cloak derives from the Aztecs.

Saratoga trunk   a huge and popular traveling trunk of the late nineteenth century. Used especially for summer resort vacations, it held a large wardrobe of clothes and was built with a top tray which held the fashionable large picture hats.

sari   a piece of fabric about 40 inches wide and five to seven yards long. Of cotton, silk or both, brilliantly colored or embroidered, it is worn over the choli, a short blouse of white or solid color, and a petticoat tied around the waist by a drawstring. The sari, in folds, is tucked into the drawstring and wrapped around the waist to form a skirt, the end carried up in front over the left shoulder. The end is left to hang and may be draped over the head as a hood. The sari is the most important part of the Hindu woman's dress. Girls wear it from thirteen or fourteen years of age.

sarong   a colorful piece of cotton or silk worn by both sexes of the Malay

Archipelago, Ceylon and some parts of India. Four or five yards long, it is sewn at both ends, wrapped around the hips and tucked into a sash, forming a draped skirt varying in length from knee to ankle.

sarsanet   a fine thin silk woven by the Saracens, dating from the thirteenth century, which was especially in favor from the fifteenth to the seventeenth centuries. It was used for dresses, veilings and trimmings and in more recent times, became popular in England for linings. Also spelled sarcenet, sarscenet.

sartorial   pertaining to the tailor and his work on men's clothes.

sash   a long, wide piece of fabric worn around waist, hips or over one shoulder. see *cummerbund; faja; obi.*

sash blouse   a blouse with long ends crossed in front in surplice style and tied in back.

sarong worn by a Malay woman of Singapore-plum color woven with gold motif-wrap of white damask brocaded with gold

sarong worn by Malaysian farmer—turban, shirt of printed cotton

Sassoon, Vidal   at first a London "crimper," who became in the 1960's the fashionable hairdresser of London and New York. In his hands, the permanent wave of the past half century had straightened and lengthened into a "fall" which stood high over the forehead with the long ends lying on the shoulders. Often, he curtained the forehead with a deep fringe of straight hair.

satara   a ribbed woolen cloth from Satara, India, highly dressed and lustered.

sateen   an imitation of satin made of cotton warp and cotton or wool filling, with the face of the cloth, silk or rayon. This makes for a firmer, more durable fabric. Glycerine and repeated calenderings will produce a more satiny finish. Used for linings, pajamas, and the heavier qualities of corsets, shoe linings, and such.

satin   a silk or rayon in many varieties. Of thick, close texture with smooth, glossy surface and dull back. The glossy surface is the result of finishing between hot rollers. Also made with cotton back.

satin, antique   a fabric woven to resemble an old satin, as, for instance, white turned ivory or parchment color.

satin, crepe-back   of silk, rayon or mixture; satin face and crepe back. Satin face and crepe back are often used to trim each other.

satin, damask   a satin with a rich arabesque or flower pattern, sometimes in a velvet pile. For negligée robe or evening cloak.

satin de chine   from the word *sztum*, satin being originally a Chinese creation called *zetin* and, lastly, *satin*. It was known in medieval Europe of the twelfth and thirteenth centuries and in England by the fourteenth century. Because of its exquisite texture, it became a court favorite. There are many different satin weaves in warp and filling and all costly, because silk is used to produce a lustrous and unbroken surface.

satin de lyon   satin with a ribbed back. Used for masculine evening wear trim such as top hat, waistcoat, lapel or trouser stripes.

satin, Denmark   see *Denmark satin.*

satin, duchesse   a heavy, firm, highly lustrous, soft silk material. Used for evening coats and formal gowns.

satin, farmer's   highly lustrous with cotton warp and worsted in cotton filling. Used for petticoats.

satin jean, satin turk   a twilled-back silk fabric, soft-finished and smooth-faced, used for waistcoats, linings and shoetops in the eighteenth and nineteenth centuries.

satin, Liberty   trade name for soft, closely woven fabric dyed with raw silk warp and spun silk filling. Used for turbans, blouses and linings.

satin, Skinner's   an American silk of lustrous quality and popular in the late nineteenth and twentieth centuries. Used for dresses and linings.

satin, slipper   a closely woven, semi-glossy surface with dull back used as a fabric for evening slippers and gowns.

satin stripe   a dull-surfaced fabric with a stripe of satin weave, usually used for underskirts.

saurians   any lizard-like reptile skins used for footwear. Fashionable in the 1960's.

sautoir   a long, fine gold or silver chain upon which women carried a watch, or a small gold or silver chain purse or, perhaps, a medallion, any one of which was tucked into the belt. Late nineteenth and early twentieth centuries.

Saxon embroidery   see *Anglo-Saxon embroidery.*

Saxony cloth   a suiting of Saxony wool rather like tweed or fine cheviot in solid colors and chalk stripes. Also, a long-napped, soft or velour-finished cloth like cashmere.

Saxony lace   embroidered drawn work lace of the eighteenth century; an imitation of real lace in which the ground is chemically burned out, leaving the embroidery, an imitation Brussels lace with the design worked on a tambour drum.

Saxony yarn   a fine, closely twisted knitting yarn from Saxony, Germany.

saya   the long silk sarong skirt with train which is part of Philippine and Spanish-American formal dress. Gay Philippino evening dress is worn by both sexes. In walking or dancing, the train is carried over the left forearm in graceful manner. see *Philippino traditional formal dress.*

Scaasi, Arnold   see *couture, haute.*

scabbard   a leather or metal case for dagger, sword or bayonet; the silk case for a furled umbrella.

scalloped   an edge cut into semicircular curves or projections as an ornamental design.

Scanderbeg bolero   a fur-trimmed black cloth bolero named after the Albanian chief and national hero who resisted the Turks from 1443 to 1468.

scapular   formerly a monk's working robe; now a monastic garment with front and back panels and hood but without sleeves, worn by Benedictine and Dominican friars.

scarf, artist and poet   black silk cut on the bias and hemmed all around. Worn with an easy or soft collar and tied into a loose bowknot in front. It was the favored neckwear of poets, artists and youths. Nineteenth century.

scarf, chin   see *chin scarf.*

scarf, masculine   the flat scarf of the nineteenth century appeared in the 1850's, origin of the ascot puff of the 1870's. The ascot first worn at the Ascot Heath races, was responsible for the vogue of the ready-made cravat. Variations of the style were the de Joinville, named for the Prince de Joinville and the four-in-hand, or Teck, named after the Prince of Teck. Clubs were formed of drivers of four horses harnessed to a single carriage driven by one person who was identified by his scarf, which is the origin of the name. The four-in-hand replaced the made-up scarf by the end of the century. see *ascot; four-in-hand; de Joinville scarf; Teck.*

Scanderbeg bolero–black cloth with fur–worn over white linen shirt– chalwar and cummerbund– white felt tarboosh– Albanian

scarfpin, stickpin, tiepin an ornamental pin of gold, silver or other metal about two and one half inches long, usually mounted with a jewel. The pin was placed in the cravat below the knot, thus holding the scarf in place. It was especially worn with the ascot or the four-in-hand in the late nineteenth and early twentieth centuries. The use of the scarfpin lasted past the mid-twentieth century.

scarpetti shoes with hempen soles used for rock climbing by European peasants.

schenti loincloth of the ancient Egyptians, prototype of modern shorts. The masculine garment of all classes; king and slave alike wore it with the rest of the body bare.

Schiaparelli, Elsa see *couture, haute.*

schlappe a lace cap with pleated black and white gauze fan-shaped wings, one on each side; a flattering headpiece still worn by the women of Appenzell, Switzerland.

Schleswig lace fine Danish needlepoint lace executed in religious and other motifs; seventeenth century.

Schön, Mila see *couture, haute.*

schreinerize a process to schreiner or mercerize cotton, giving it a lustrous finish by pressing it when wet between two hot, heavy steel rollers, one engraved with lines and the other smooth.

scissors a two-bladed cutting instrument, each blade three to six inches long, each with a handle joined by a pin at the center upon which they work, move and cut. see *pinking shears.*

scogger, vamp a kind of sock worn in parts of northern England. Usually of worsted, and footless; used over the arms and over shoes. Much used in Colonial America, and called *vampay.* see *vamp.*

Scotch fingering yarn a medium weight, 3-ply finely twisted woolen yarn used for crocheting and knitting.

Scotch tweed see *tweed, Scotch.*

Scott, Ken see *couture, haute.*

Scottish Highland dress in contemporary use: the kilt; a hill jacket, generally of dark green tweed with staghorn buttons, and shoulder tabs; the sporran, knee-length stockings with a skean dhu in one; and a bonaid or Glengarry cap. For dress occasions men wear a kilt in dress tartan, if entitled to one; a black velvet jacket with silver buttons; a frilled jabot and the plaid fastened on the left shoulder with a large brooch; black pumps with silver buckles; ladies wear a simple white evening dress with the clan plaid fastened on the left shoulder. see *kilt; breacan feile; sporran; skean dhu; cap, Glengarry.*

screen printing a hand process of applying color to fabric through wire or bolting cloth screens to the motif to be colored. Each design color requires a different screen. It is costlier than roller printing, but unusual color effects can be obtained by the process.

scuffer a sandal-like, lightweight play shoe with a sturdy sole used by children for play and adults for sports.

scuffs light, soft slippers without quarters in which one "scuffs" or walks barely lifting the feet. see *mule.*

scye see *armscye.*

seal a furred or haired marine, aquatic, carnivorous mammal found off the coast of Alaska, Western Canada, Uruguay, South Africa, Japan and Siberia.

seal, Alaska, matara finest of the fur seals from the herd of the Pribilof Islands, Alaska. The quantity taken is limited by the United States and Canada. A durable, handsome fur, deep-pelted and of uniformly good quality with coarse, long

schlappe–Swiss bonnet of pleated black and white gauze–Appenzell

Scottish Highland dress worn during English Prohibition Act 1746–repealed 1783

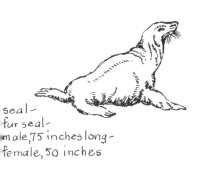

seal—
fur seal—
male, 75 inches long—
female, 50 inches

guard hairs which must be hand-plucked. A dark coat naturally lustrous, but all pelts are dyed black; matara, a dark brown; or safari, a lighter brown.

seal, baby, white coat or **wool**   the coat of month-old harp seal. A creamy white woolly coat, used natural or dyed. The older harp seal, up to five years, has mottled white patches on a bluish-black ground.

seal, cape   from the Cape of Good Hope, South Africa. It has a lighter, thinner skin and not as fine quality fur as Alaska seal.

seal, electric   see *seal, imitations.*

seal, French   see *seal, imitations.*

seal, hair   found in all parts of the world and more numerous than fur seal; taken principally for oil and leather. There are many species, but only the harp and hooded seals are common in fur markets. Formerly used for leather, but now more for sports and casual wear, especially the Labrador seal.

seal, harp   see *seal, baby.*

seal, hooded   The coat of the young seal is bluish-black with cream or white belly, used natural or dyed.

seal, imitations   electric or near seal, sheared hare; French seal, rabbit; Hudson seal, muskrat; polar seal, rabbit; seal-dyed coney, rabbit; sealing, Australian, rabbit.

seal, Labrador   see *seal, hair.*

seal, pin   fine pin-grain seal known as Levant morocco, a strong, durable leather of the white hair seal. It has an irregular grain, highly prized for bookbinding; also used for gloves and accessories.

seal, polar   see *seal, imitations.*

seam   the joining together by sewing of two pieces of fabric. The two unfinished edges are turned to the wrong side, and the smooth seam side is turned to the right side.

seam, French   the edges of two pieces of cloth stitched together on the right side, trimmed off close to the seam, then turned to the wrong side and stitched again, making a neatly finished seam without raw edges. Used in sewing fine garments.

seam, piped   a seam with a very narrow insert of fabric between the two joined pieces of fabric, either the same material or contrasting in color and texture, to show on the right side.

seam, welt   a seam first stitched on the wrong side, one edge then cut narrower to about a quarter inch. The wider edge is then folded and basted under the narrow edge and finished by stitching on the right side. This raised or swelled seam is used as decoration in tailored work.

seamstress   a woman who hand-sews and finishes as opposed to a dressmaker who cuts, fits and makes.

seed pearls   see *pearls, seed.*

seersucker   a wash-and-wear fabric of cotton, silk or rayon with or without a crinkled stripe made by varying the tensions of the warp yarns. Used for summer suits, dresses, pajamas, etc. Needs no ironing if hung very wet to dry.

selvage, selvedge   the webbed edge of a woven fabric which prevents its raveling.

sendal, cendal   a thin, silk fabric of the Middle Ages, possibly from China. It was still used in the seventeenth century. It was made both very sheer and heavy and was used for the dress of nobles and ecclesiastics. It could be painted and was used for banners.

sennit   a braided straw of fiber used by the Japanese and Chinese in making hats. The hard straw sailor is fashioned of sennit straw, coated with shellac. Sennit is a contraction of seven-knit in nautical language, after a method of braiding rope.

separates   parts of the feminine costume, coat, jacket, blouse, skirt, sweater or jumper—all of which are planned to coordinate in design and color, each part interchangeable; twentieth century.

sequins   see *paillettes.*

serge   a fabric of worsted yarn with a diagonal twill on both sides. Formerly, a popular fabric for men's and women's tailored suits and coats, especially in dark blue. Now made in wool, cotton and blends and forced to share the market with many new cloths.

serge, silk   a twilled silk fabric of a heavy grade of surah especially used for lining men's coats.

serge, wide-wale   a cloth with a definite diagonal weave, sometimes called cheviot serge.

sergedusoy, serge du soie   woolen cloth used by common folk for men's coats and waistcoats in the eighteenth century.

serul   an undergarment worn in Arabia and northern Africa; a long strip of white cotton, wrapped and tied to form short breeches and a pocket to hold the knife.

set-in sleeve   see *sleeve, set-in.*

Seventeenth Century costume   see illustrations, pages 308–315.

sewing machine   A machine for stitching or sewing, was invented, perfected and manufactured in the mid-nineteenth century, thereby creating a new world of clothes for everybody in ready-mades.

shad belly   see *hunt dress.*

shade cloth   see *Holland linen.*

shadow embroidery, shadow stitch   floral motifs worked on the wrong side of transparent fabrics.

shadow lace   a filmy, machine-made lace with shadowy flower patterns.

shadow skirt, shadow-proof panel   a panel or slim straight underskirt set into the petticoat or slip which masks the transparency of the outer skirt. A need that arose and became popular in the twentieth century when the custom of wearing several petticoats declined.

shag   a heavy woolen or silk cloth with long nap popular for men's coats and women's coats and dresses; seventeenth century.

shagreen   untanned leather prepared in Russia and the East. It is covered with seedlike granulations and dyed bright colors, chiefly green, to resemble sharkskin. Also, the name of an obsolete silk made to resemble shagreen or pebbled leather. Used for shoes, purses and bags. see *galuchat; sharkskin.*

shaker flannel   a well-napped, plain-woven, fine grade of flannel with cotton warp and wool filling. Used especially for infants' wear. Originally made by the Shakers, a religious sect.

shaker goods   a general term for plain, heavy woolen ribbed variety of socks; also fabrics and yarns manufactured by the Shaker communities in New York State and Ohio. The Shaker sect was a religious and communal group which originated in England 1747 and came to America in 1774. Their principal location was at New Lebanon, New York. Their dress was simple in design and reserved in color.

Shaker dress of alpaca with white lawn kerchief-cape of homespun-brown percale bonnet

Seventeenth Century
children in
corsets

ruff
farthingale
and corset.
French
princess-
1613

little girl in
elaborate gown
with corset
bodice-
Flemish-1st half
of century

paned and
slashed
costume over
corset-
French prince-
1613

baby-
corset doublet-
silk brocade-
linen and lace
collar and apron-
Spanish-
1602

small boy-
corset doublet-
braid-trimmed
costume-
Dutch-
1631

two-year-old
girl in farthingale
and corset-
English-
1606

corset doublet-
satin with
linen
undersleeves
and collar-
boy's dress-
Dutch-
c.1650

corset-bodice-
silk frock with
linen and lace-
French prince-
1643

Seventeenth Century
neckwear

the golilla-
starched sheer
linen lawn-
Spanish-
1620's

falling band of
fine thread lace
with strings-
English-
c.1610

falling ruff-
three layers-
linen and
point lace-
Dutch-
1624

falling band with
tassels-camisole
or brassière with
slashed sleeves-
Dutch-
1665

falling band-
Richelieu collar-
1630's

falling band
of point lace-
half shirt tied
with drawstring-
English-
1630's

cravat of
Venetian lace-
taffeta bow-
German-1687

falling band-
linen and
point lace-
French-
c.1632

"playne"
or falling band
of the judiciary-
English-
1660's

the steinkirk-
linen and lace
held in buttonhole-
French-
1693

Seventeenth Century
masculine
corset shapes

doublet with
median busk-
lace whisk-
silver gorget-
brocaded and
embroidered
silk-
English-
1616

doublet with
median busk-
slashed silk-
lawn and lace
whisk-
Dutch-
1617

young man
in satin-
median busk-
falling ruff-
Dutch-
2nd decade

slashed doublet
with corselet and
bowknots-
falling ruff-
French-
1620's

buffskin doublet
with median busk-
"playne band"-
shirt shows in
sleeve openings-
Dutch-
1620's

snug fitting vest
with sleeves-
Brandenburgs-
steinkirk cravat-
English-
1690's

elaborately
embroidered doublet-
lawn and lace whisk-
English-
1613

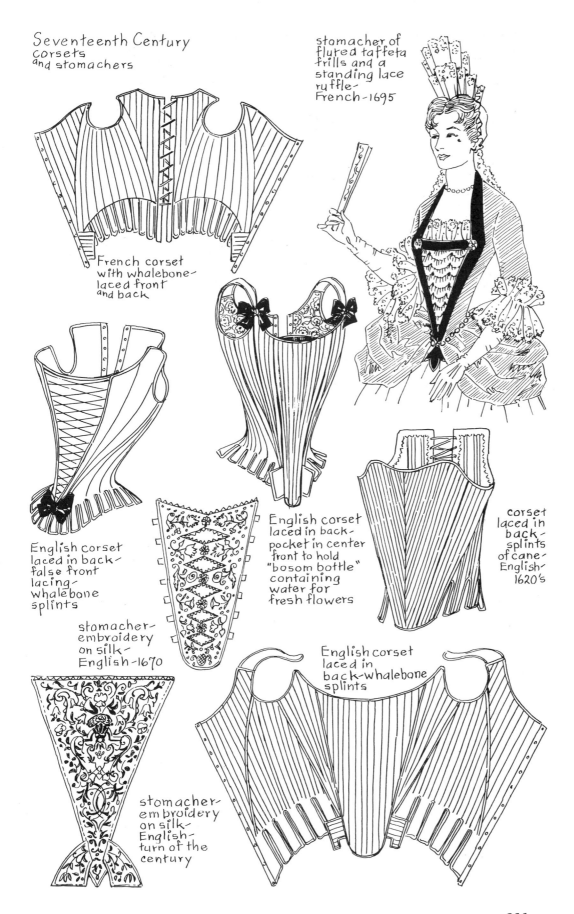

Seventeenth Century
corsets and stomachers

stomacher of fluted taffeta frills and a standing lace ruffle- French-1695

French corset with whalebone-laced front and back

English corset laced in back- false front lacing- whalebone splints

English corset laced in back- pocket in center front to hold "bosom bottle" containing water for fresh flowers

corset laced in back- splints of cane- English- 1620's

stomacher- embroidery on silk- English-1670

stomacher- embroidery on silk- English- turn of the century

English corset laced in back-whalebone splints

311

Seventeenth Century—
the boned
"corset-bodice"

false lacing
and jeweled
buttons-
French-1630

elaborately
embroidered silk
doublet-separate
lace collar, yoke
and silk oversleeves-
English-1607

the "Spanish
body"
1655

satin gown
with embroidery
and jeweled
buttons-
German-
1680

court gown
with corselet
embroidered
and jeweled-
French-
1694

boned satin
doublet with
fur collar-
Dutch-
1660

Seventeenth Century
shirts
and sundries

"half shirt"-
lace jabot-
drawstring
in edge-
English-
mid-century

brocaded silk
robe-velvet
lining-cap
to match-
French-
1690's

shirt of
fine linen
and thread
lace-rabat
and jabot
of lace
points-
English-
1632

simple linen
shirt with
"playne band"-
English-
mid-century

shirt with
lace jabot-
drawstring
puffed
sleeves-
French-
1660's

linen shirt-
ribbon loops or
galants'-petticoat
breeches-
French-
1660's

shirt with
embroidered frill-
button and bowknot-
Danish-1648

shirt with
falling band,
embroidery,
lace and
hemstitching-
English-
mid-century

linen under
drawers-
English-
1680's

Seventeenth Century
waistcoat-
gourgandine
and vest

embroidered gourgandine-
laced in front-no bones-
French-
1690's

waistcoat
embroidered-
boned in front-
laced in back-
English-
c.1670

riding
habit-skirted sleeveless
buffskin vest-linen shirt-
lace cravat-ribbon bowknots-
English-1664

negligée robe-
gourgandine
and
petticoat-
French-
1690's

quilted
waistcoat
laced in back-
hooked in front-
English-
c.1670

negligée robe-gourgandine
and petticoat-   French-1690's

embroidered
gourgandine-laced
in front-no bones-
French-1690's

Seventeenth Century
feminine lingerie

bed rayle
with
embroidered
falling band-
English-
1646

boudoir rayle-
linen with point
lace-corset over
linen chemise
with long sleeves-
French-
1628

voluminous
bed rayle for
winter use-
Dutch-
1624

embroidered
silk petticoat
over linen
chemise-
French-
1697

boudoir rayle
of silk and lace-
French-
1694

casual
morning dress-
rayle of sheer
linen and lace-
headkerchief
and long apron
to match-
French-
1683

linen drawers
with colored
embroidery-
Italian-
late 16th and early
17th c.

315

shako   a military headdress with a high stiff crown and plume. Of Hungarian origin, it was the same in European and American armies. The tall, black, polished felt with a feather pompon on the left side was prescribed by Congress in 1810. The flaring, bell-shaped polished felt shako or "tarbucket" adopted in 1913 is still worn by cadets at West Point.

shaksheer   long, full pantaloons worn by Turkish women outdoors, especially for fieldwork.

shal   see *babushka*.

shalloon   a fabric of worsted or wool, light, fine and close-woven, twilled both sides and dyed plain colors. A lining first made in Chalons, France, hence its name.

shalwar   see *chalwar*.

shamiya   the headkerchief of red, green or white silk worn by Bulgarian women. The young girl ties hers around the head, the ends floating in back; the married woman ties hers under the chin. The favored headdress when working in the fields.

shan   the dark blue cotton jacket worn by Chinese men, women and children called "everyday workaday dress." The man's jacket buttons diagonally from the neck, over the chest and under the right arm.

Shanghai dress   see *cheongsam*.

shank   the narrow part of the shoe under the arch of the foot. Also, the shaped piece of steel or leather which keeps the shoe in shape.

shank-button   a button with a metal loop or shank attached for sewing it on.

shantung   a tussah silk or rayon fabric rather like pongee with a nubby texture, used in men's and women's sportswear and summer suits. see *nankeen; pongee; tussah.*

shapka   see *calpac*.

sharkskin   leather of certain sharks and rays covered with small, hard, round granulations. Also a fabric with small pebbly or grained surface woven to resemble the leather. A summer sports fabric woven of synthetic fibers. see *galuchat, shagreen.*

shatoosh   a gossamer fabric, honey-beige in color, woven by East Indian women from hair of the beards of the Himalayan goats. The hairs are found on bramble bushes, where goats have nibbled

shako-black cloth and leather-white pompon and cords-gilt insignia-scale chinstrap-U.S. Infantry-1813

shako-black polished felt-feather pompon-ribbon band-U.S. Army-1810

shako of felt or cloth-chenille pompon-powdered hair-leather queue with bowknot-English-1807-9

leaves. The cloth is soft and costlier than vicuña. Used for hoods and scarfs.

shawl   a square or oblong covering for the neck and shoulders, often finished with fringe. Varying in size; of wool, cotton, silk, chiffon and lace, they were originally handwoven and embroidered, and later woven on power looms.

shawl collar   see *collar, shawl.*

shawls   the fashion for the cashmere shawl, a luxurious accessory, took hold in the French Empire period and lasted nearly a century. It dates from the return of Napoleon's armies from Egypt. Beautiful ones were then made in France. From Paisley in Scotland came shawls woven on power looms in intricate pomegranate or Persian cone patterns. The design required four months of work, but the actual weaving on British power looms was accomplished in a week. Ladies took lessons in the art of wearing the shawl. see *Spanish shawl.*

shearlings   see *lamb.*

sheath gown   a tubelike gown, straight, narrow and close-fitting. A recurring silhouette in the history of fashion.

sheepskin   the skin of sheep after removing the wool and finished to resemble other leathers and parchment. Sheep and lamb hair-covered peltries are important to the modern furrier due to the ever-lessening supply of wild-animal peltries. Some have wool or hair texture quite similar to that of wild animals and can be processed into imitations for coats, boots and gloves and many other fur uses.

shell   a sleeveless overblouse, which is part of an ensemble with jacket and skirt. 1950's to date.

shell edging   a scalloped edging in shell design executed in crochet work.

shepherd's check or **plaid**   a twill-woven cloth with even checks in black

and white or contrasting colors. Of wool, rayon, cotton or blends; chiefly used for sportswear.

sherryvallies   from the Spanish *zaraguellas,* loose pantaloons buttoned or laced to the belt over fine leather breeches, about two yards around the seat. Formerly for masculine riding as a protection against mud and dust.

Shetland   knitting yarn made from the wool of Shetland sheep, fine and thin with a slight twist.

Shetland cloth   a shaggy cloth made from the wool of sheep raised in the Shetland Isles off Scotland. An informal suit and overcoat cloth, lightweight and warm.

Shetland lace   an openwork needle-made lace of Shetland wool; used for infant's wear and covers, and for knitwear in lace stitches.

shields   see *dress shields.*

shift   originally, and for centuries, the chemise or shirt of white linen worn by men, women and children, basically a work or sleeping garment with long sleeves. It was smocked at the shoulders for extra fullness. In the 1950's it returned as a fashionable woman's dress worn very short. see *chemise; sheath gown.*

shingle   a feminine haircut. In the 1920's the hair was cut very short and shaped to the back of the head, just covering the ears, with a sharp point at the nape, a style revived in the 1960's.

sheath gown – blue silk and black velvet – lace and embroidery – 1910

shingle haircut – 1923

shingle coiffure with false front curls – French – 1800

shintiyan   Turkish name for wide, loose pantaloons still worn by Moslem women.

shirring   in sewing, a series of close parallel lines of running stitches drawn up to make the material set in gathers.

shirt   in general, any of certain garments for the upper part of the body; specifically, the loose garment for men and boys worn under a coat or vest, or a close-fitting undergarment. A man's business or everyday shirt is generally of fine white cotton broadcloth. Other fabrics used are airplane cloth, batiste, chambray, madras, Oxford, percale, summer piqué, poplin and a heavy voile. Also, there are figured silks or plain, plaid and striped cottons of varied colors. The shirt of deep or dark color in wine, navy, red, green or brown worn with light-toned jacket and trousers was introduced in the 1930's. The man's white shirt or nylon appeared in the late 1940's during the scarcity of white cotton and proved a sensation with its qualities of washability, quick drying and requiring very little, or no pressing. The man's dress shirt for formal evening wear with tailcoat has a starched bosom, wing collar and single or French cuffs. The man's shirt for semi-formal evening wear with dinner jacket has a plain or pleated bosom, fold collar and single or French cuffs. see specific types: *aloha; basque, boiled; chukker; Garibaldi; hunting; lumberjack; neck-band; polo.*

shirt, riding habit   worn under the waistcoat by lady and gentlemen riders of the eighteenth century. A shirt of fine cambric or lawn, usually with stiffened collar and lapels, the lapels edged with self fabric. The feminine was like the masculine, but had a tape attached at center back and tied around the waist.

shirts, shertes   The shirt or chemise with sleeves has been worn for hundreds of years by men and women. The Norman shirt of the nobleman in the fourteenth century developed neckband and cuffs. In 1442–1483, the time of Edward IV, shirts were made of wool, linen and Holland, and an occasional silk garment for royalty. In the sixteenth century, bands and cuffs were edged with embroidery. Frills next became wide and were made separate from the garment. They were fashioned of fine cambric, Holland and lawn, silk embroidered and edged with lace. An English law was passed forbidding the wearing of a pleated or embroidered shirt by a man without social rank. In the seventeenth century, there were ruffles at the neck, down the front and showing below the short doublet or jacket. The jabot and Steinkerque cravat became important in the eighteenth century. In the late eighteenth and early nineteenth centuries, the voluminous neckcloth concealed the shirtfront until Beau Brummell made a rule of displaying the ruffled shirt for day and evening wear in 1806. With that ruling, dressy gentlemen took to wearing a collar like Brummell's with points projecting upwards.

shirtwaist   the feminine adaptation of the masculine shirt at the turn of the century. Of heavy white linen or muslin, with stiff starched collar and a small bow tie or a four-in-hand. It was immortalized by the modern Charles Dana Gibson (1867–1944) in his Gibson Girl paintings.

shirtwaist dress   essentially a shirtwaist extended to dress length, with straight, gored or full skirt according to fashion. Generally buttoned to the waist, hipline, or hem, often with a fly front. Round or convertible collar; sleeves of any length or sleeveless; belted or sashed or worn loose in shift style. Any color of almost any fabric, including such formal ones as taffeta and damask. Because of its adaptability the shirtwaist dress of the 1930's has become a twentieth century classic and is considered one of America's outstanding contributions to fashion.

shocking pink   a fuchsia pink

launched by Elsa Schiaparelli, the Paris couturière, in the late 1920's.

shoddy fabric made of reclaimed wool spun from old woolen rags chopped into waste, then carded and spun into threads of varied thickness. It can be woven into cloth patterns which sell at very low price. A good-size yardage is used in less expensive men's wear. As an adjective, shoddy means cheap and of poor quality, as in fabrics, workmanship, etc.

shoe, congress see *gaiter.*

shoe, high or **high-buttoned** buttoned or laced shoes reaching well above the ankles, a fashion of the nineteenth and early twentieth centuries for winter wear.

shoe horn a shaped piece of metal or plastic used to ease the foot into a snug-fitting shoe. So named because formerly made of a polished piece of cow's horn.

shoe, juliet see *juliet shoe.*

shoe, monk a low-heeled shoe of brown calf, usually buckled at the side, a type worn by monks.

shoe, piked see *poulaines.*

shoe rose a rosette worn on the instep or vamp. Late in the sixteenth century, the new-style shoes with tongues and side pieces called for latchets or straps and colored shoestrings; the latter were tied with a lover's knot and eventually hidden by a shoe rose, a costly extravagance of the seventeenth century. Shoe roses are still part of the costume of the Warders of the Tower of London.

shoe, running an athlete's soft leather shoe with light-turned sole, with or without cleats.

shoe, saddle see *saddle Oxford.*

shoe, tennis or **sneaker** a low, laced oxford of canvas with rubber sole. Originally used largely for tennis, hence tennis shoe; *sneaker* is an Americanism.

shoe tree a form of metal or wood put inside shoes to preserve the shape when not worn.

shoe, wooden In Europe of the twentieth century, galoshes of leather with wooden soles in boot or low-shoe form continued to be the general footwear of country people, especially in winter. The work shoe or sabot of peasants in France and the Low Countries was shaped from a solid block of wood. The Dutch call theirs *klompen.* Sabots and klompen are still worn by farmers' children. Also to be seen occasionally in France worn with regional costume, are facsimiles of heeled leather slippers carved of wood, painted black and ornamented with ribbon bowknots or shoe roses.

shoemaking about 1812, the manufacture of shoe nails to replace wooden pegs; 1830, diagrams for cutting shoes; 1846, the first sewing machine patented by Howe; 1851, Singer Sewing Machine with foot treadle; 1858, the Blake machine for sewing uppers and soles together; 1860, McKay sole-sewing machine patented by Blake and McKay, making sewing possible instead of nails, then "straights" neither right nor left, finally replaced by rights and lefts, and worn by Civil War soldiers, and civilians.

shoe rose of fine lace-jewel in the center-17th C.

shoe rose of lace-white punched leather-red heel and sole-17th C.

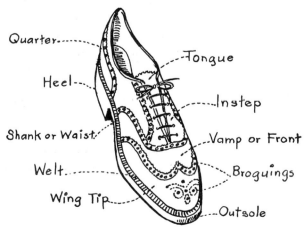

Quarter — Tongue — Heel — Instep — Shank or Waist — Vamp or Front — Welt — Broguings — Wing Tip — Outsole

shuba—
sheepskin
coat-fur to the
inside-black
woolen shirt,
"rubashka"-
black sheepskin
bonnet—Russian
farmer of Caucasia

shoepack   a heavy half-boot worn in the seventeenth century and still worn today by loggers in winter. The name is derivative of the Lenape Indian word *shipak*. It is made like the Indian moccasin without separate sole, ankle-high and of oil-tanned leather, usually white.

shooting jacket   see *bush jacket.*

shopping bag   see *tote bag.*

short warm or **car coat**   a reversible coat of two different clothes, shell and lining. Usually of Loden cloth from the Tyrol with wooden toggles and hemp loops. A continental fashion worn by men, women and children after World War II. see *British warm.*

shorts   short trousers worn by both sexes for casual or sports wear. Bermuda shorts reach the knee; Nassau shorts come to mid-thigh; Jamaica shorts are even shorter. see *pant lengths, feminine.*

shot silk   see *silk, shot.*

shoulder bag   a variation of the handbag with a long strap, to be worn either diagonally across the torso or with the bag hanging straight from one shoulder. Originating as part of the uniform of the women's services in World War II, it left the hands free and gave a trim appearance. Popular for all daytime wear during the 1940's and revived as a casual fashion in the 1960's.

shovel hat   see *hat, shovel.*

shroud   the burial garment or winding sheet used for many centuries and still in use.

shrug   a feminine jacket, waist-length or shorter.

shuba—
snow leopard-
gray or cream
color marked
with black
rosettes-red
fox cap-
Russian
Kazakh chief

shuba   a Russian sheepskin coat worn with the wool inside in winter. The skin side, which can be worn alone in milder seasons, is decorated with colorful embroidery and motifs of appliquéd dyed leather. Also worn in Rumania and Yugoslavia.

sibeline   French for sable. see *zibelline.*

Siberian chipmunk   see *chipmunk.*

Siberian dog or **fur**   see *dogskin.*

Siberian sable   see *sable, Russian.*

si-bonne   trademark of a rayon lining, soft, thin and slithery.

Sicilian, Sicilienne cloth   a kind of mohair, heavier and coarser than brilliantine. Used for men's and women's summer coats and suits.

Sicilian embroidery   see *Spanish embroidery.*

sicyonia   a shoe of reticulated design laced in front, of colored or gilt leather. Worn in ancient Rome by women and fops.

side whiskers, sideburns   long in the 1840's and even longer in the next two decades. To the English they were mutton chops or Piccadilly weepers, and to the French, cutlets or tavoris. Americans called them *dundrearies* after Lord Dundreary, a character in a popular play, *Our American Cousin,* by Tom Taylor. *Sideburns* was an American colloquialism after the general and politicians, A. E. Burnside (1824–1881). Originally, the word was burnsides. With the twentieth century, the "clean-shaven look" took over, to last until the 1960's when young men again grew sideburns.

side whiskers-
moustache and
imperial-
French-1857

silhouette   a profile or shadow outline of an object, filled in with black; also, a profile, cut with a scissors from black paper. Of ancient origin although the name dates only from mid-18th century. Etienne de Silhouette, French Minister of Finance, was notoriously unpopular for his program of taxation and economies, and his name became a term for anything of plain or simple form. In time, the word *silhouette* was applied to the outline or shape of a fashion in dress.

silk   a fiber derived from the cocoon of the silkworm and also from a species of spider. The cultivation of the mulberry tree, upon whose leaves the silkworm feeds, dates back to about 2640 B.C. in China; Chinese records of that period mention the use of silk in robes, sunshades, etc. Silk probably became known to the Mesopotamians, Egyptians and Greeks some time in the second century B.C., through Persian and Phoenician traders. Although it was worn by Cleopatra in the first century B.C. it was rarely used in Egyptian textiles until the fifth century A.D. Heliogabalus (204–222 A.D.) was the first Roman emperor to wear silk. In the Byzantine period, raw silk was imported from China and woven in the emperor's palace in Constantinople, its production being controlled by the emperor. This woven silk was valued at fabulous sums. In 360 the Persian king, victorious in a war against Constantinople, carried away the most skillful weavers. This was the foundation of the subsequent fame of Persian silks. It was in the sixth century during Justinian's reign (527–565) that Byzantine silk culture was again at its height, to last another three centuries. Under his patronage, eggs of the silkworm and seeds of the mulberry bush were brought from China by two Persian monks, concealed in their hollow bamboo staffs.

silk, artificial   see *artificial silk.*

silk cotton   a cotton-like substance enveloping the seeds of any of various trees, especially that of the balsa tree.

silk, doupioni   see *doupioni silk.*

silk, raw, reeled   silk filaments unwound from cocoons and joined onto a long thread such as is first reeled into skeins and hanks. These are the long fibers of all classes and the finest grade of silk.

silk, shot   textile term for changeable colored silk, especially taffeta, produced by the use of warp threads of one color and weft threads of another.

silk, spun   a trade term for floss, waste silk, damaged cocoons and yarns, carded and spun. Lacks some luster but makes a strong fabric.

silk, thrown   two or more twisted "singles" which are threads twisted in the direction opposite to the natural twist.

silk, weighted   silk made heavier by salts used in the dye and finish to give the cloth weight in draping, a richer look and more luster. Such treatment, however, is detrimental to the silk.

silk, wild   made from the larvae of wild silkworms and commercially valuable.

silkaline   a soft, thin cotton fabric with smooth finish resembling silk. Plain or figured and used principally for lining.

silks   see *Caledonian; China; gauze; oiled; polished; pongee; serge; shantung; Thai; tie; tied and dyed; tussah; vegetable.*

silver cloth or **tissue**   cloth made with metal warp of silver color and silk weft. Used for evening wraps, gowns and trimmings.

silver fox   see *fox, silver.*

side whiskers and moustache- French-1842

side whiskers and moustache- English-1862

side whiskers and moustache- American-1870's

silhouette- usually in profile- outline filled in with black ink

simarre-Venetian
robe worn by
magistrates
and professors-
of rich brocade-
mortarboard
cap-16th C.

sinhs, traditional
skirt of Laos-women-
wrap-around of
brocade-scarf
called uparnā-
worn by Indian
men and women

simar a lady's short "at home" jacket of brocade, velvet or plush worn over a petticoat and stomacher. The long sleeves and the edge of the jacket were banded with fur. It was a popular negligée jacket in the American Colonies. Dutch, seventeenth and eighteenth centuries.

simarre (French), **simarra** (Italian) a long, sumptuous robe of handsome brocade which originated in Venice, sixteenth century. It flared to the floor with long, wide Dalmatian sleeves. Venetian ladies wore a simarra with a long train.

sinamay a coarse, open, stiff textile woven chiefly from the Philippine abaca.

single-breasted closure of jacket and waistcoat fastened by a single row of buttons and buttonholes which appeared with the lounge jacket or sack coat in the 1850's and 1860's. see *lounge coat; sack coat.*

sinhs The traditional wrap-around skirt of Laotian women, usually of ankle-length and of beautiful brocade. It is folded into a deep front pleat. Worn with a sari-wrapped scarf of striped silk over the left shoulder, the right shoulder bare. Contemporary.

siren suit British wartime name for a "jump suit," so called because it could be quickly donned when sirens sounded for a night raid.

sisal a species of straw grown mainly in the Philippines and shipped to China; an expensive straw, finely woven with a linen finish.

sizing a finishing process in which fabrics are endowed with smoothness, stiffness and strength by the use of starch.

skaut see *Hardanger skaut.*

skean dhu a short dirk or dagger worn in the knee-length stocking of Scottish Highland dress. see *Scottish Highland dress.*

skein a quantity of yarn, silk, thread, etc. which has been taken from the reel in a loose, twisted loop.

skein-dyed applied to fabrics made of yarns, wool, cotton or silk, which have been dyed in the skein before weaving.

skeleton vest a man's backless waistcoat for summer wear, particularly with evening dress. Early 1950's.

ski a strip of wood bound one on each foot and used for gliding over snow. see *snowshoe.*

ski clothes usually stretch pants and parka for both men and women, although changing fads of fashion appear almost every season. The nature of the sport requires garments that allow freedom of action and are lightweight but warm and waterproof.

skilts knee-length Dutch breeches worn by boys and farmhands during the Revolutionary period in the American Colonies. They were very full, fit snugly at the waist, and required no suspenders.

skimmer; capeline a wide, soft-brimmed leghorn hat faced with silk, worn over a white lawn cap and tied with velvet ribbons; English, 1750's. The flat-crowned, wide-brimmed straw sailor worn by Eton students was also called a skimmer. In the late nineteenth and early twentieth centuries, the style was revived by fashionable men and women for sportswear.

skimmer
hat -leghorn
with green silk
facing-silk or
velvet ribbons-
frilled white
lawn cap-
English-
1750's

Skinner's satin   trade name for a general line of satin and lining that enjoyed a long popularity in fabrics.

skins   commercial term for pelts, weighing up to fifteen pounds of small animals such as goat, sheep, calf, etc. see *animal skins*.

skirt   that part of a costume which hangs from or below the waist. Also, an underskirt or petticoat. The skirt cut separately and sewn to a bodice first appeared in Italian court dress of the fourteenth century.

skirt, bell   a flared, gored skirt, fashionable in the 1890's, shaped by haircloth interlining from waist to hem.

skirt, circular   of the 1890's, cut circular and held in shape by haircloth interlining from waist to hem. Revived with the New Look, late 1940's.

skirt, dirndl   see *dirndl*.

skirt, habit-back   see *skirt, rainy daisy*.

skirt, harem   a divided or "trouser skirt" launched unsuccessfully in Paris about 1910. A very full skirt of soft silk, draped and gathered to the ankles to simulate Turkish pantaloons.

skirt, hobble   a very narrow, tapered ankle-length skirt. It made walking difficult, inspired ridicule, reflected in its name, the "hobble." Sometimes it was only a yard around, making a deep slit at the side a necessity for walking.

skirt, hula   the skirt of Hawaiian dancing girls, a grass skirt, knee-length or longer.

skirt, micro, miniskirt, maxiskirt   see below.

skirt, 1960's   the *micro* which just covers the hips; the *miniskirt* of a length between thigh and knee introduced by the London "Mod" designer, Mary Quant; the *maxiskirt* with hemline somewhere between knee and ankle.

skirt, peg-top   see *peg-top skirt*.

skirt, rainy daisy, or **habit back**   a sports skirt of the first decade of the twentieth century. An ankle-length, fitted cloth skirt, worn for walking, rainy days, golf and roller skating.

skirt, weather   see *safeguard*.

skirt, wrap-around   a one-piece skirt which can be made on the straight of the cloth with a few darts or tucks to shape the hips, the two straight ends overlapping in front. This has been a standard twentieth century style for some decades. Another wrap-around skirt, of the 1920's, was cut on the bias in one piece, the surplus material brought around to center front and draped into soft folds or box pleats at the waistline. In mid-century, a one-piece bias-cut skirt was introduced for casual wear, which crossed in the back and fastened with ties brought around to the front, allowing an adjustable waistline.

skiver   the grain side of split sheepskin tanned in sumac and dyed. Cheap, soft leather used for lining men's hats, pocketbooks, book binding, etc.

skivvies   U.S. Navy term for men's underwear.

skullcap   a small, round cap fitting the top of the head, without brim or peak. see *calotte* under *cap*.

skunk   from the Algonquin Indian name "Seganku." Also called black marten and Alaska sable, formerly dressed and sold as such. An American animal of the weasel family found from Hudson Bay to South America and coast to coast. Smaller numbers and poorer in quality in Mexico, Central America, Brazil and Argentina. The best skins from New York

skirt – "Hobble" with taffeta sash - lace over old blue taffeta – French – 1911

striped skunk – American animal of weasel family

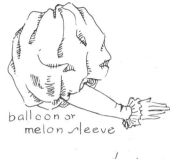

balloon or
melon sleeve

batwing
Sleeve

leg-of-mutton
sleeve, a fashion
in the 1890's

bishop
Sleeve

angel or Dalmatian
sleeves

and Ohio, very durable, silky and natural fur with flowing top hair, all black or black with a white stripe. see *civet*.

slacks   a general term for sports pants worn by either sex. Masculine sports ensembles were adopted by women in the 1920's for winter sports, and by the 1930's for other sports such as sailing. By the end of World War II slacks were accepted for feminine casual wear at any time. see *pants suit*.

slash pocket   see *pocket, slash*.

slashings   a Renaissance fashion in gentlemen's clothes. All articles of clothings were slashed, even gloves, shoes and stockings, revealing puffings of contrasting material and color. Slashings appeared in the fifteenth century and lasted to the mid-seventeenth. The decoration originated among the Swiss soldiers in 1477 when they won a battle against the Duke of Burgundy and mended their ragged uniforms with strips of tents, banners and furnishings left behind by the vanquished Burgundians. The fashion spread over Europe, reaching its height from 1520 to 1535.

slat bonnet   see *sunbonnet*.

slave bracelet   usually a link bracelet or a bracelet worn above the elbows. Also, a hoop band with loops to which the wearer adds small charms.

sleep coat   a man's coat of cotton or rayon, knee-length with half or full-length sleeves and long lapels; usually tied with self belt. Sometimes worn instead of pajamas or nightshirt, twentieth century. Also worn by women, 1960's.

sleeve, angel   the long, loose flowing sleeve of the robe or dalmatic worn in the Western church and upon English state occasions. Originally called Dalmatian sleeve.

sleeve, bag   a Flemish medieval sleeve, long and very full and soft, gathered into a plain, tight wrist cuff, fifteenth century.

sleeve, balloon or **melon**   popular in the 1890's. The forearm fitted to the elbow and a full, rounded puff from elbow to shoulder, the puff lined with muslin or buckram for stiffening. 1890's.

sleeve, batwing   a sleeve cut to fit an armhole reaching from shoulder to waist and shaped into a small cuff or fitted wristband.

sleeve, bishop's   a long, soft sleeve fitted over the upper arm and flaring at the bottom, or gathered into a band cuff. A woman's fashion of the first decade of 1900, modeled on the full linen sleeve of a prelate's rochet.

sleeve, bracelet   a three-quarter-length sleeve leaving the forearm bare halfway to the wrist to display the wearing of bracelets. Contemporary.

sleeve, cape   a sleeve cut circular and fitted to the armscye, usually elbow-length with a wide capelike flare.

sleeve, Dalmatian   see *angel sleeve*.

sleeve, dolman   attached to an armscye cut from shoulder to waistline, the sleeve itself shaping down to wrist-size.

sleeve, epaulet   a set-in sleeve with an epaulet formed of self-fabric, trimming or a roll extending around the top of the sleeve. Called "wings" in the medieval period. Late sixteenth and early seventeenth centuries.

sleeve, false or **hanging**   of Italian origin, the false or hanging sleeve was part of the outer jerkin. The sleeve which covered the arm was part of the doublet or under-jacket and often was just laced to the armscye. Medieval.

sleeve, kimono   wide at the armscye, usually cut in one with the body; characteristic of Japanese dress.

sleeve, leg-of-mutton   a fashionable sleeve of the 1890's, known as a *gigot* in French. It fitted the forearm but flared from the elbow into a balloon shape which was gathered or pleated into a fitted armscye.

sleeve, mameluke   a fashion of the French First Empire (1799–1815), named for the soldiers of a squadron of Mamelukes created by Napoleon I. A woman's sleeve, long, with a series of puffs, large at the top and diminishing in size to the wrist, finishing with frills. see *sleeve, virago.*

sleeve, melon   see *sleeve, balloon.*

sleeve, peasant   a long, full sleeve gathered or shirred into a dropped shoulder and usually shirred at the wrist.

sleeve, puffed   both masculine and feminine sleeves were elaborately puffed in varied shape and width in the sixteenth and seventeenth centuries. They were divided into sections.

sleeve, raglan   a sleeve with the seam reaching from the underarm, back and front, to the neckline. see *raglan.*

sleeve, set-in   a tailored long sleeve of dress, jacket, or coat, sewn to a fitted armscye.

sleeve, shoulder-puff   a long, fitted sleeve topped by a puff from shoulder seam to underarm depth.

sleeve, three-quarter   see *sleeve, bracelet.*

sleeve, virago   a full sleeve evenly divided into many small puffs tied by ribbon bands, the ribbon band also called viragos. Worn by men and women in the sixteenth century. see *sleeve, mameluke.*

slendang   a fine cotton scarf which the Javanese woman drapes over her shoulders.

Mameluke sleeves tied with ribbons-pleated white percale dress-French-1811

false or hanging sleeves-velvet with gold braid-gold and rose brocade gown-leather fan-ivory stick-16th C. Spanish

false sleeves-embroidered jerkin-"Venetians" with fringed silk ties-English-17th C.

remains of false sleeves-shoulder wings-leather boots-falling ruff-early 17th C.

slops-breeches
called "full slops"
laid in pleats-
brocaded silk-
English-17th C.

smock frock
of homespun,
flax or hemp-
smock
stitching-
English
farmer

slicker   A coat for rainy weather or nautical wear in waterproofed fabrics, oilskin or rubber. see *oilskin*.

slide fastener   A tape of varied length with a flexible closing device, either metal or plastic, now also in nylon, worked by a slide pull. Used first in galoshes by B. F. Goodrich Co., and named *zipper*. 1920's. see *zipper*.

slings, slingbacks   slippers with vamp or front but simply a strap in back.

slip   a feminine undergarment reaching from armpit to hemline. A full slip is a fitted slip with shaped bosom and narrow shoulder straps. Of cotton, silk or rayon, often lace-trimmed, it serves as undergarment to the dress. A half-slip is a petticoat without top, also of silk, nylon or lace-trimmed but only waist-high. Mini-slip is a very short slip. The modern slip cut on the bias became popular in the 1920's following the success of Chanel and Vionnet, about 1916, with their bias-cut gowns and dresses.

slip-on, slip-over   see *pull-on*.

slippers   for men and women, a light, low-cut shoe easily slipped on the foot for indoor use and ease, usually without the aid of fastening. Dressy, high-heeled slippers are worn by women for formal attire.

Sloppy Joe   a knitted woolen, loose-fitting pull-on worn with round or pointed white blouse collar showing at the neck and, generally, a string of pearls. Fashionable with school and college girls, 1940's.

slops   an old English term in the sixteenth and seventeenth centuries for many garments. From Spanish slops, a European fashion. see *Spanish slops*.

slotted collar   see *collar, slotted*.

slouch hat   see *hat, Hungarian; slouch; pork pie; caddie*.

slubs   slightly twisted or thick places in wool, cotton or silk woven into the cloth, as compared with skein-dyed or piece-dyed fabric woven with smooth, clean fiber.

smallclothes, smalls   eighteenth century name for close-fitting masculine breeches or underdrawers.

smock frock   a yoked shirt or loose blouse of coarse linen worn by field laborers in Europe over regular clothes, originally smocked, now often not, despite its name. Many farmers in Colonial Virginia wore smock frocks. The smock is now much worn as a coverall by professional people at work, especially artists. An obsolete English term for a woman's smock was "smicket."

smocking   stitchery which resembles a honeycomb pattern; stitches which divide and hold together tiny pleats allowing for fullness, yet at the same time giving ease to the garment.

smoked pearl   dark gray to black smoky mother-of-pearl from various sea shells; used for studs, buttons and other ornaments.

smoking jacket   a sack or lounge coat, formerly for smoking at home. Of brocade, velvet or cloth of a dark, rich color, braid bound and fastened with Brandenburgs. Worn late nineteenth and early twentieth centuries in Europe and America.

snakeskin   leather of which modern shoes, handbags, wallets and many other items are made, procured principally from farm-raised reptiles. They include the cobra, of which there are six or seven species in Asia and Africa; the boa, principally from the Amazonian region; the python of tropical Asia, Africa and Australia; the watersnake of southern United States, Malaysian Archipelago and Africa.

snap fastener, snapper   a fastener made in two metal pieces, a ball and a socket clasp, the ball fitted into the socket for closing.

sneakers   an Americanism for canvas oxfords or gymnasium shoes with rubber soles. Worn especially for tennis. see *shoe, tennis.*

snood   originally, a ribbon or fillet worn by unmarried Scottish maidens. Later, *snood* signified the coarse hairnet or fabric bag, sometimes attached to a hat, to hold a woman's hair loosely at the back of the neck, a Victorian fashion which had its origin in the medieval caul or hairnet of gold thread. The snood was a hair fashion of the 1930's, sometimes with a tiny hat attached.

snow cloth   a heavily fleeced woolen cloth such as camel's hair, blanket cloth or the like, used for winter coats.

snowshoe   an oval wooden frame with two crosspieces, strung with waterproofed thongs. It spreads the wearer's weight and allows him to walk on soft snow without sinking.

snowsuit   an outer garment for children of heavy waterproof or wadded cloth made with coat, hood and leggings in one garment. Formerly tied and buckled but now equipped with zipper fastenings.

snuffbox   a tiny box of silver, gold enamel or ivory which holds snuff, a mixture of tobacco leaf and stem, ground and perfumed. The sniffing of a pinch of snuff was a widespread habit of the eighteenth century, indulged in by men and women, especially in England. Purses to hold the snuffbox were of leather set in gold mounts or of knitted silk worked with steel beads and tasseled ends.

snuggies   see *pettipants.*

socks, bed   see *bed socks.*

socks, English foot   a separately knit sole joined at both sides to eliminate the center seam on the sole of the foot. First made for military use and then for sportswear.

socks or hose, golf   heavy knitted woolen socks worn with knickers for outdoor sports, especially golf; knee-length, often with a cuff in a decorative pattern. Shorter knitted woolen socks are worn with slacks.

solana   a crownless straw hat worn in the sixteenth century when blond hair was in fashion. Italian ladies sat in the sun with their hair spread over the wide brim of the hat to bleach the hair.

sole   the underside or bottom part of any piece of footwear.

soleae   of ancient Rome, similar in style for both sexes. They were sandals of boxwood or cowhide with leather straps for wear indoor with the tunica; those for street wear rose higher and were laced with straps. As the wearer's status rose, shoes were cut higher and enriched with gold and silver, these latter being the prerogative of magistrates.

solferino red   a bluish red named after the Battle of Solferino in Italy, 1859.

solitaire   a single gemstone, set alone. Generally designates the single diamond of the conventional engagement ring.

solitaire   a black silk ribbon which tied around a man's wig in back, and the bag which held the wig. The ribbon ends of wig and bag were brought around and tied in a bowknot in front. This was the origin of the gentleman's black silk tie, eighteenth century. see *bag wig, solitaire wig.*

solleret; bear's paw   The Italian scarpino of the sixteenth century followed the long-toed poulaine. It was called solleret because it resembled the armor foot-

solleret-escarpin or bear's paw-leather or velvet slashed over color-16th C.

snood of red chenille with velvet toque-1935

snood of red velvet with bowknot-day or evening-1939

covering of thin, articulated steel plates. The point gradually disappeared, becoming a broad, square toe. In fact, with the use of moss stuffing, it became exaggeratedly broad. In France, Germany, England and the Low Countries, the toe grew square. In the mid-sixteenth century, the English Queen Mary was forced to limit the width to six inches. The style is generally associated with Henry VIII of England and in France with François I. The bear's paw was worn by the German mercenary foot soldiers, the lansquenet, from the fifteenth to the seventeenth centuries.

sombrero   a broad-brimmed felt or straw hat, originally Spanish, worn by horsemen of Spain, Spanish America, Mexico and the United States Southwest. The Mexican brim is sometimes two feet wide and known in U.S. West as the ten-gallon hat. It is usually of tan, gray or white felt for the charro or gentleman horseman whose hat is banded and faced with silver lace, and of straw for the peon.

Sophie   see *couture, haute.*

soutache   see *braid.*

soutane   see *cassock.*

South American fox   see *fox, South American.*

southwester, sou'wester   a seaman's bad-weather hat made of rubber or tarpaulin, a canvas covered with tar, paint or other waterproofing. A wide, slanting brim, longer in back than in front.

Spandex   a man-made fiber that has the stretch properties of rubber but is lighter in weight; valuable in the world of corsetry and swimwear. Such fibers have changed these former rigid pieces of corsetry into comfortable lingerie. Trademark owned by Du Pont.

spangenhelm   followed the shell-like helmet in Europe. It was also of boiled leather with pieces of iron rising to a point and topped by a knob of wood or colored glass. The feudal lord of the ninth and tenth centuries wore such a helmet, while his followers went into battle bareheaded or wearing a felt cap.

spangles   see *paillettes.*

Spanish blackwork   of ancient Persian origin; used in the sixteenth and seventeenth centuries. An elegant and distinctive embroidery, especially on men's lingerie or fine linen shirts. It was worked in small geometric designs in black silk accented with gold or red stitches.

Spanish comb   a high comb thought to have been originally a metal head ornament to raise the kerchief or shawl off the forehead. Later made of silver and finally, in the nineteenth century, of a carved tortoise shell. When shaped like a large shell, it is called a *teja* (roof tile). Still worn today in Spain and Spanish American countries. The mantilla can be draped over it.

Spanish or **Sicilian embroidery**   a design on muslin or cambric worked like embroidery by filling in with herringbone stitches. A lacier effect can be achieved by filling in with braid and buttonhole stitches.

Spanish hair   see *wig, Spanish hair.*

Spanish heel   see *heel, Spanish; continental; French.*

Spanish lace   pure silk lace of different meshes with flat, heavy floral designs; called Spanish blonde whether white or black.

Spanish mode   of the sixteenth century, a style distinctive and elegant which had an influence upon the European mode. The Spanish gave to Europe the ruche, the ruff, the short cape, the corset,

Spanish gypsy-red velvet jacket-velvet hat, cloth sash, breeches and leggings, all black

Spanish fiesta costume, all in black and white - man of Turégano the hoop, the bombast of the padded doublet and trunk hose, followed by un-padded breeches. Knit silk stockings were a Spanish innovation and for a long time surpassed those of other countries.

Spanish papers   see *cosmetics.*

Spanish shawl   of black silk crepe edged with deep silk fringe and covered with birds and flowers in brilliant colors. Worn by Spanish women with superb grace. Nineteenth and twentieth centuries. see *manton de Manilla.*

Spanish silk kerchief   a distinct feature of Spanish dress, worn by men and women in a different manner in each province; as a head covering, over the shoulders or around the neck by women while men wear it around the brow tied like a turban.

Spanish slops or **breeches**   breeches of the sixteenth and seventeenth centuries which are noted as being "very full," as were the Dutch slops or sloppes in the same period recorded also as very wide. Slop, or sloppes, was an old English name which was applied to various other garments that were loose-fitting, such as cassocks, nightgowns or shoes.

Spanish toque   an evolution of the beret, the soft crown wired into shape, finished with a narrow brim and a jeweled necklace or "band." Fashionable in Spain, Italy, and France in the sixteenth century and worn by elegant ladies and gentlemen.

sparterie   a straw fabric for hats and shoes made of esparto grass from Algeria and Spain. Also used for footwear.

spats   a short form of cloth gaiters, after the Colonial word spatter-dashes. Spats were considered very smart in the late nineteenth and early twentieth centuries, and were worn by men and women with oxfords or pumps. Of heavy

Spanish Toque

black velvet-pink ostrich-Italian-1583

black silk and gold braid-plume-brooch-1580

black velvet toque over coif-pearls and long streamer-French-1572

black silk or velvet-jeweled band and brooch-Italian-16th C.

tiny toque over veil-pearls and feathers-German-16th C.

black silk or velvet-yellow plume, caul and cords-English-1598

black silk or velvet-pearl necklace-ostrich-aigrette-Italian-1583

black silk-jeweled band-Spanish-16th C.

silk, velvet, or felt, black-German-16th C.

iron helmet-king's archers ostrich and aigrette-French-1589

black velvet pleated crown-blue ostrich-silver band-English-1590

broadcloth in white, gray or tan and buttoned at the sides. Of linen for summer wear. see *gaiters.*

spatterdashes   high leather leggins, about 1770. The joining of legging and shoe was covered by spur leathers. see *spur leathers; gamashes.*

spectacles   see *eyeglasses*.

spectator sports clothes   any simple costume appropriate for those watching a sport but not participating in it; any casual outfit. For men, usually a sports jacket and contrasting slacks; for women a tweed or cotton suit, or a shirtwaist dress and cardigan. Topcoats and headgear depend on the weather.

spencer   a very shortwaisted jacket worn with the Empire dress of the 1790's. It was designed by Lord Spencer, who claimed fashion is so absurd that he, himself, could concoct a new style and make it a rage. And the following is his tale. He cut the tails off his own coat and went for a stroll. In two weeks all London was wearing the "spencer" and soon fashionable men and women of the Continent and the Colonies were also wearing the same little jacket. The masculine spencer has come down to the present in the mess jackets of military officers. Also worn by civilians for semiformal dinner dress in warm weather. see *Caroline spencer; canezou*.

spider web stitch   an embroidery stitch in a spider's web design, used especially at corners.

spider work   a heavy bobbin lace resembling opus araneum.

spike heel   see *heel, spike*.

spinel   a gem stone of magnesium oxide, red, brownish red, gray-blue, deep-greenish, indigo or violet. A variety from Ceylon is black. Some so-called rubies are actually spinel. The large red stone in the British Imperial State Crown known as the "Black Prince's Ruby" is a spinel and of less value than a real ruby.

spinning   the process of drawing out fine fibers into a fibrous thread or filament by twisting, either by hand or machinery. Spun silk, spun rayon, spun linen and spun glass are some of the spun textiles.

spinning jenny   an early machine for spinning wool and cotton by means of many spindles. It was invented c. 1767 by James Hargreaves, an Englishman.

spinning wheel   a machine with a single spindle formerly used for spinning yarn or thread. Driven by a wheel operated by hand or foot.

spit curl   see *beau-catcher*.

spitalfields   fine silk scarfs manufactured in a section of London called Spitalfields, the name being a mark of quality of the basket-woven silks. see *macclesfield*.

spliced heel   a trade term for hosiery made with a heel of double thickness.

sponging   a term reserved for the last operation given woolens and worsteds, meaning treating with live steam to give the final shrinkage test and finish.

sporran   a large pouch or purse worn in front of the kilt by Scottish Highlanders. It may be of leather, silver-mounted, or of animal skins with fur or hair. Evening sporrans are made of baby seal or other light-colored skins.

sports clothes   a term applied to play clothes or apparel designed so as to make the enactment of the sport easier and more successful.

sports clothes, feminine   In the late nineteenth century lawn tennis, bicycling, golf and yachting became popular, necessitating practical clothes. For golf the smart woman wore a shirtwaist and separate skirt, and a golf cape or Norfolk jacket; for bicycling, a short skirt or full bloomers with a short fitted jacket. The tailored walking skirt of shoe-top length was known as the rainy-day skirt.

sports footwear   in the Victorian period the first sports model, a laced rubber-soled shoe with fabric uppers, later

spencer jacket of velvet—white muslin gown— French Empire— 1800

Golf
1890's

Hunting 1849

Hunting
1887

Beach
dress-
1880's

Fishing-
1857

Bicycling-
1890's

Yachting-1886

Tennis-
1895

Skiing-1950's

Beach-1930's

Beach-1939

Skiing
1928

called the "sneaker," was worn for croquet, archery and lawn tennis. The ankle-high, laced leather shoe having a sole shod with protruding nails and buttons to prevent slipping, was worn for golf.

sports heel   see *heel, sports.*

sports jacket, or **coat**   a man's loosely cut jacket of tweed or cotton, worn with contrasting slacks or shorts for informal wear.

sports shirt   a man's or boy's shirt for informal wear, generally worn without a tie, open at the neck or with a harmonizing ascot tuck-in. Long or short sleeves. Made in a variety of materials, for year-round use, such as plain, checked or plaid flannel; madras and gingham; sheer nylon or mesh knit. see *aloha shirt; California sports shirt.*

spotted cat   see *genet.*

spun gold or **silver**   fiber threads which have been wound with thin metal strands.

spun rayon yarn   short lengths of filament too short to reel, twisted together and used in the same kind of weaving as cotton, linen and silk.

spun silk   see *silk, spun.*

spur   a pointed metal implement attached above the heel of a rider's boot to urge the horse by pressure.

spur leathers   large quatrefoil shapes worn especially in the seventeenth century over the instep of leather boots to conceal the fastenings of the spurs.

squirrel   a land rodent found in all parts of the world except Australia and Africa. The largest quantities of fur come from Europe and Asia, the best from Russia and Siberia, well-furred and of silky texture. Squirrel is used natural or bleached and dyed to simulate many other furs, for coats, jackets and trimming. see *miniver; vair; chinchilla.*

stacked heel   see *heel, stacked.*

stambouline   a gorgeous robe worn by Turkish Sultans. Of velvet, brocaded fabric or white satin fastened down center front with jeweled gold buttons, long, and with short sleeves. Over it was worn the doliman, a sleeveless robe with hanging sleeves. A white silk turban draped around a tarboosh completed the costume; one feather worn indoors and two feathers when in public.

stamin, stammel   a coarse woolen cloth usually dyed red; formerly used for underwear in shirt and drawers for men and as an underpetticoat for women.

stamped velvet   see *velvet, stamped.*

starch   an odorless, tasteless, powdery substance obtained from plants and diluted with water for application to garments. When dry, the starch stiffens the fabric. The starching of sheer fabrics used in caps, wimples, collars and ruffs originated in Flanders and was perfected in Holland. In 1564, a Dutch gentlewoman taught young English ladies of rank to starch. Blue, goose-green and creamy yellow were the principal colors used for ruffs and the starch employed was either English or Dutch. Starch is white today.

start-up, startop   a peasant's boot consisting of a sturdy low shoe and a separate knee-high legging of leather, wool or linen, tied top and bottom; seventeenth century.

stayhook   a small, ornamental silver hook with a pin to be fastened to the edge of the bodice for holding an étui, a fancy bag or case in which to carry toilet and sewing articles. Late nineteenth century.

stays   see *corsetry.*

steeple hat   see *hat, steeple.*

steeple headdress   see *hennin.*

steinkerk, steenkerk   a scarf of lawn,

stambouline-short-sleeves and fastened down front-over it a dolman with hanging sleeves-white silk turban-worn by sultan of Turkey

lace or black silk loosely tied, with the ends tucked into shirt or vest or drawn through a buttonhole or ring. It became a fashion in 1692 after the Battle of Steinkerk in Belgium, when the victorious French charged the opposing cavalry with their dress in disorder and cravats untied and flying. Ladies also adopted the fine white neckerchief of batiste and lace, the fashion lasting a good half century.

stencil   a cutout pattern or design to apply to another surface by painting, stippling or brushing through the openings.

step-in blouse   a blouse and drawers made in one piece, to obviate bunching at the waist; 1920's.

step-ins   see *panties*.

Stetson   see *hat, Stetson*.

sticharion   a robe or tunic of white linen, corresponding to the alb, worn by prelates of the Eastern Church.

stickpin   see *scarf pin*.

stiletto   a small instrument of bone, ivory or steel for puncturing holes to be embroidered. Used in eyelet embroidery.

stirrup-hose   overhose of the seventeenth and eighteenth centuries for horseback riding. The tops, nearly two yards wide, were edged with eyelet holes and laced to the breeches or belt.

stitch, stitchwork, needlework   employed in hand-sewing, embroidery and tapestry. Executed with an eye-needle passing through cloth, leaving a thread stitch in the fabric. All stitches, and there are more than two hundred made with needle and thread, are founded upon seven basic stitches: back stitch, blanket stitch, chain stitch, cross stitch, knot, overcast and running stitch.

stoat   see *ermine, summer*.

stock   a starched neckcloth wrapped twice around the neck and buckled in the back; successor to the cravat, eighteenth century. Still worn with riding habits by both men and women.

stockinette   an elastic or tubular textile formerly made on a knitting frame, usually cotton with a fleeced back. It was used for undergarments and stockings. Also, a close-woven, heavy elastic material, mostly white, used for livery breeches.

stockings   a close-fitting covering for the leg and foot, generally knit or woven. The word appeared first in the sixteenth century and derives from the Anglo Saxon "prican," to stick. Because hose were "stock" or "stuck" with sticking pins or needles, hose became stocken, then stocken of hose, and finally stockings. Knee-length hose were stocks. Leg coverings went through many forms before being joined together in one piece in the fourteenth century, when they reached the waist. They were secured to the short skirt of the jacket by laces with points. Women's stockings or chausses reached above the knee and were gartered. Chausses were seamed up the back and made of cloth, cotton, linen or silk. By this time in the fifteenth century, the tailor was cutting the cloth on the bias for a better fit. In the sixteenth century, chausses consisted of two sections, upper stocks and lower or netherstocks. In the mid-nineteenth century, vivid-colored silk petticoats came into fashion with stockings to match, even to horizontal stripes. Then, in the 1890's, the reaction was for black stockings worn with all shoes regardless of color. A shapely feminine leg sheathed in sheer black was considered the height of allure, the black stocking holding its own to the 1920's, with tan for sportswear. In the second decade of the twentieth century the tan silk stocking gave way to gray, taupe, beige and white for summer. Nude or blond was first worn in Paris. see *stockings, nylon; pantyhose; panty-stockings*.

steinkirk - a long, white lawn scarf looped at the neck and the ends drawn through a button-hole. full-bottomed wig - 17th C.

stockings, leather   Indian leggings of Colonial days. Reaching from ankle to mid-thigh, the side seams were fringed and embroidered and tied to the belt by thongs. Form-fitting, they were sewn to the leg and often worn to tatters.

stockings, lisle   made of a fine Egyptian cotton made silky by a mercerizing process, the result known as mercerized cotton; the wealthy woman's stockings until silk became common in the late nineteenth century.

stockings, machine-knitted   Until 1610, stockings were hand-knitted worsted, crewel, linen, jersey openwork and sewn cloth. Spanish hand-knitters excelled in their product from the sixteenth to the eighteenth centuries when France usurped the reputation. In the seventeenth century, red was for daily wear, and dress usually white.

stockings, nylon   came on the American market in 1939, followed by World War II and the curtailment of nylon until 1945. With the war's end, nylons again became available to American women. Contemporary "nylons" are available in a wide range of textures and jewel-like tones.

stockings, silk   It is noted that the first silk stockings, a Spanish invention, were worn in France by Henri II (1519–1559). Silk knits from Spain are also known to have been presented to Henry VIII. The first knit silk stockings worn by an Englishwoman were presented to Queen Elizabeth by her "silk woman," Mistress Montagne, who knitted them. The queen was so delighted with the stockings that she said that she would never wear cloth hose again. But silk stockings were not manufactured in England until the following century, though one of Elizabeth's subjects invented the first knitting and stocking frame.

stola   a full-length straight robe with short, set-in sleeves, generally of linen or

light wool, worn by women of ancient Rome.

stole or **scarf**   a long, straight, shoulder scarf of fur or velvet cloth, or knitted, often with fringed ends. Originally the stola was the ancient Roman matron's long garment. Also, an ecclesiastical vestment, a long narrow scarf with embroidery.

stomacher   a decorative and elaborate separate front panel ending in a deep point. The stomacher was essentially an evolution of the Spanish figure. Though worn over a tightly fitted bodice, it was rather like a breastplate, fashioned of steel and splints of ivory, mother-of-pearl or silver covered with satin or velvet. It was worn by men and women in the sixteenth century and by women into the seventeenth and eighteenth centuries. Laced to the figure, it was ornamented with lace, ribbons and often jewels. A favored feminine version had ribbon bowknots in graduated sizes and was called an échelle, from the French for ladder. see *échelle; plastron.*

stone marten   see *marten.*

stove-pipe   a very tall, high silk hat. see *hat, top.*

Strasbourg work   see *Roman cut work.*

strass   see *paste; jewelry.*

straw braids   about one quarter to three inches wide, used in the manufacture of hats. Made of fine straws from Italy, Switzerland, and South America, and of less expensive straws from China and Japan.

straw hats   hats made mostly of Belgian and Swiss straw in the past but now of straws grown in Japan and China.

stretch pants   women's pants for

stole and muff of ermine—white bowknot on muff—black silk gown, green velvet bonnet with green and gray ostrich—1844

sports or lounging wear made from cloth woven of stretch yarn.

stretch yarn   a fine natural or synthetic filament wrapped with silk, nylon, rayon or cotton yarn and used with such threads in weaving.

string tie   a man's very narrow necktie or scarf.

strophium   in ancient Greece, a bandelette worn outside the chiton under the bosom. It served the same purpose as the apodesme. A more elaborate piece, often ornamented with gold, pearls, and other stones. It was often worn as a filet around the head. The Roman version of the strophium was made of wool, linen or a fine, soft chamoised leather called "aluta" which was dyed purple.

studs   jeweled shirt fasteners for formal or semiformal wear in plain gold, pearls, and cabochon-cut stones. Studs fastened collar and bosom, usually gold. Tethered studs, three on a fine chain to fasten bosom front. Appeared 1840's. see *cufflinks*.

stuff   in costume, any material not made into garments.

style   in costume, the display of distinctive elegance in design and color and the fitness to the occasion. However, a costume can also be in poor taste. see *fashion*.

subarmale   a sleeveless tunic with short pleated skirt worn by ancient Roman legionnaires under the metal cuirass.

suclat   Anglo-Indian name for scarlet; also European-made woolen broadcloth for army tunics.

suede   from the French for Swedish, the velvety finish having originated in Sweden. Formerly made from kidskin only, much of the leather is now from baby lamb and calfskin.

suede, antelope-finished   a leather sueded to resemble antelope. The leathers so used are calfskin, lambskin and goatskin.

suede, camel   see *camel suede*.

suede cloth, suede finish   a knitted or woven cloth with the surface napped and shorn to simulate the leather. Suede finish is also applied to some wool and cotton fabrics.

sugar-loaf bonnet   see *bonnet, sugar-loaf*.

suit   originally a livery, uniform or habit. Now, for men, a coat or jacket with matching trousers and sometimes a matching waistcoat. For women, a coat or jacket and matching skirt, worn with a blouse or pullover.

suit, dinner   see *dinner suit*.

suit, man's   The change in western man's dress occurred first at Louis XIV's court in 1666, which Charles II of England followed in the same year by dressing his courtiers in the new vest, coat and breeches of Spanish cut. This was the habit à la française. In the first half of the eighteenth century, the long, flaring buckram-lined skirts of coat and waistcoat were modified. By the time of the French Revolution, men's costume had settled upon fitted coat and waistcoat, and longer breeches. In the late eighteenth and early nineteenth centuries, one notes the modern style of dress in London, where the English tailors had settled upon breeches below knee-length, fitted waistcoat, a long outer coat and the top hat. In the 1860's the lounge suit appeared, prototype of today's habit or suit with trousers, waistcoat and short coat or jacket, the modern man's basic dress.

suit, paddock   see *English drape*.

sultane-long skirt held up by hoops and buttons en négligé-popular in the Colonies-18th C.

sultane   a feminine robe worn in Europe and the American Colonies in early 1700's, after the Turkish emperor's robe; open down center front and caught up by buttons and loops.

summer furs   see *furs, summer*.

sun shods, Mexican   a trade name for an Indian sports sandal fashioned of two wide leather straps crossed over the instep and attached to the leather sole by nail-heads.

sun suit   a one-piece summer garment for little children.

sunbonnet, slat bonnet   of cotton fabric, plain or figured and fashioned with a brim or poke held in shape by stitched slots holding thin wooden slats. In general, the sunbonnet was a peasant type of head covering with a bavolet. It had a wide brim of straw or stiffened, starched fabric, a gathered full crown, and chin ties.

sunburst   a jeweled brooch designed with rays radiating from the center, the rays usually set with small diamonds. Late nineteenth and early twentieth centuries.

sundress   a backless dress worn for sunbathing.

sunfast   a term signifying that a dyed fabric has met a standard test for not fading by sunlight.

sunglasses   spectacles with colored lenses to protect the eyes from strong sunlight.

sunshade, parasol   from the middle of the sixteenth century both men and women used sunshades which were called "umbrellas." In the seventeenth century court sunshades were lined with gold and silver lace, becoming lighter in weight. By the eighteenth century umbrellas for rain closed but sunshades and parasols did not. Early in the nineteenth century, a tilting parasol with hinged or folding stick, named the Pompadour parasol, appeared. It was a pretty shadepiece of moiré with ruffles and fringe. see *umbrella*.

suntan era   late in the 1920's the smart world took to lounging on the beach, and immediately many kinds of oils and lotions came on the market to hasten a sun-tan or to protect a delicate skin during the process. Brownish face powders for women became the vogue and if one's skin did not take on a fashionable tan, then one painted the flesh the desired color.

supertotus   see *balandrana*.

Supp-hose   trade name for firm-holding hose and stockings for men and women. Of man-made fibers, nylon, lycra and spandex. Owned by Du Pont. see *nylon; lycra; spandex*.

supportasse   a wire frame which held up the great ruff in the sixteenth and seventeenth centuries. see *underproper*.

surah   a soft-finished silk or wool fabric, the heavier cloth called silk serge and that with high luster called satin surah. Used for dresses, men's scarfs and mufflers.

surcingle   the girdle or belt worn with a cassock.

surcoat, surcot, surcote   a fashion of the Middle Ages for men and women which derived from the armor covering worn by the Crusader to eliminate the glare of the sun upon his armor when in the East. The original covering hung straight front and back, two rectangles caught at the sides and reaching to the knees. There was a hole for the head to pass through. The lady's surcoat was short and sleeveless with wide armholes and was worn over the bliaud or gown. It was fastened by shoulder buttons.

surplice   a loose white vestment with flowing sleeves worn over a cassock by ecclesiastics during religious services in the seventeenth century, generally slipped over the head, but it sometimes was cut open in front to accommodate the wearer's wig. Still used in some denominations.

surplice bodice   any bodice or waist the closure of which overlaps in front reaching from side to side at the waist-line.

surplice collar   a collar which follows the same line of closure as the surplice bodice.

surtout, Newmarket   an overcoat made in the style of a frock coat, worn when riding or driving. It was named Newmarket after the town in England celebrated for its racing meets. Late nineteenth and early twentieth centuries. see *New York surtout; Newmarket*.

suspenders   see *braces; bretelles; gallowses; galluses*.

swag   festoons or draperies, especially as used in the late eighteenth century in interior decoration and on women's gowns.

swakara   a breed of karakul lamb from southwest Africa; lightweight, slim and supple with lustrous markings. New on the market in the 1960's.

swallowtail coat   see *tails*.

swansdown   the soft feathers of the swan used as costume trimming; also for powder puffs. Also a thick, warm cotton cloth first made in China and called Canton flannel or swansdown.

swatch   a small piece of fabric used as a sample of texture, color or design.

sweat shirt   a pullover shirt worn by athletes. Usually of thick cotton, a fine-ribbed cloth with fleecy underside. A ribbed high or round neck, wrist and hip bands. Also called T-shirt. see *turtle neck*.

sweatband   men's hats and caps are lined with a soft leather band which absorbs perspiration and prevents stain to the hat itself.

sweater   any knit or crocheted jacket or blouse; an American term formerly considered inelegant but now in general use; until the mid-twentieth century knit garments opening in front were known in England exclusively as cardigans, and those without an opening as pullovers or jumpers. The two, in a matching set, are called twin sets, a fashion more prevalent in the British Isles than America, because of climatic differences. The knitted shirt first appeared on the islands of Jersey and Guernsey. Jerseys and ganseys, as they were called, were knitted for sailors and fishermen by their wives. Because the garment made of wool and retaining its natural oil, absorbs rain and salt water without feeling damp, its fame spread over Europe, especially among working men. In the 1890's, the jersey was taken up by American sportsmen and college athletes, who called the shirt a sweater, hence its name. In the 1920's, Lanvin, Chanel and Schiaparelli took note of the sweater and, in the 1940's, Mainbocher lined sweaters with chiffon and silk and added bead embroidery. see *Aran sweater; Cowichan sweater; Fair Isle sweater; jersey; fisherman's sweater; poor boy's sweater; sloppy Joe; turtle neck sweater*.

Swedish lace   a pillow lace of the torchon type, Swedish-made.

swell, heavy swell   a Briticism for an ultra-fashionable man of the 1870's and 1880's.

swift   a box which holds a swift or reel, a turning instrument upon which is wound yarn, thread or silk.

swim suit   a one-piece knitted woolen suit for active swimming. see *maillot; Annette Kellerman*.

swirl   see *tie-about*.

swag-silk gown with panniers and swags of silk on the skirt—called Circassian gown—French—17th C.

Swiss embroidery   see *Madeira* or *eyelet embroidery*.

Swiss muslin   see *dotted Swiss*.

switch   a tress or tresses in the form of a plait or curl to add to one's own locks. Separate tresses are bound at one end. Formerly called corners of hair, in the 1960's known as falls. Though usually made of natural hair, they are now more often made of manufactured strands of acetate or nylon, which are lustrous manufactured fibers in beautiful colors and hand washable.

sword   a weapon with a long blade pointed and sharpened on both edges. Its history dates from the Bronze Age and the Iron Age. Many centuries passed before the blade became slim and lighter in weight, and further centuries before the clumsy hilt was simplified. It finally became a ceremonial ornament, a costume piece more than a weapon of defense. In modern times the sword retains its significance as a symbol of military, judicial or legal authority.

swordfisherman's cap   see *cap, swordfisherman's*.

sykchos   in ancient Greece, a soft, low leather boot of Oriental origin. Inside the boot, the Greeks wore a sock of white wool, felt or linen as protection against cold and dampness. Greek comedians wore it on the stage and from this comes the old English expression applied to actors as "gentlemen of the sock and buskin." Hence the origin of our word sock.

synthetic fabrics   artificial fabrics were introduced with the invention of rayon in 1891 when Count Hilaire de Chardonnet established the first successful rayon production. In 1886 he had experimented upon the findings of many other scientists working to produce a commercial process for manufacturing artificial silk. Its name of rayon was created by Kenneth Lord Sr. of Galey and Lord. The first finished product was shown at the Paris Exposition in 1889 and from then on, it has been produced round the globe. It is generally considered a nineteenth century European invention and a twentieth century development. In fashion, Chanel was the first couturière to use rayon, 1915. Many synthetics have been perfected and are marketed under trade names such as nylon, orlon, dacron, arnel, etc.

syrma   a long trailing robe worn by tragic actors of ancient Greece.

szür   a Hungarian cloak, decorated with embroidery or appliqué.

szür – black or white felt or leather – with fur to inside – long sleeves closed as pockets embroidered and appliquéd motifs – Hungarian

szür or cloak – white felt or leather appliquéd yellow, orange, green, purple – white woolen breeches with crochet lace – turban of green foliage – Hungarian wedding guest

T

tab   a small flap sewn to a garment to hold a section in place by a button, snap or hook.

tabard   a sleeveless or short-sleeved jacket worn by soldiers over armor and by monks and commoners. It was put on over the head and open at the sides. When worn by a knight it was embroidered with his arms and called a coat-of-arms. Heralds also wore tabards displaying the arms of the lord they served. see *mandilion*.

tabby   any of several silk fabrics of plain, watered or striped weave made in a quarter of Baghdad named Attāb.

tabi   a white cotton Japanese foot-glove with a separate stall for the large toe, and a thick sole. It fastens up the back with hooks or snaps. The only footwear for indoor use, since shoes are not worn in the house.

tabinet, tabbinet   an Irish-made poplin, often with a moiré pattern, much used in the eighteenth century.

tablion   the Roman toga gradually evolved into the full-length semicircular mantle worn by the Church and Byzantine emperors. The tablions with which it was ornamented were twelve-inch squares solidly embroidered in gold and colored silk thread and accented with varicolored jewels and pearls. The squares were placed at the front corners of the semicircular cloak and at the edge in center back.

taces   see *tass*

tack   to baste or make temporary stitches. see *tailor's tacks*.

taenia   a narrow girdle or cord worn around the hips by Greek maidens. Tied in an intricate knot, the Herculean knot was a symbol of virginity to be untied by the husband on the wedding night.

taffeta   a rich, thin silk first noted in the seventeenth century, used for doublets and pages' dress. A luxurious fabric of plain weave and several finishes in the eighteenth century; later plain-dyed, brocaded and changeable in beautiful colors.

taffeta weave   see *plain weave*.

tagal   a straw braid made from Manila hemp which comes from Tagal, a province in Java. Used for hats.

tagalog   see *barong tagalog*.

taglioni   a short braid-bound overcoat, nineteenth century. It was named after the Italian dancer, Taglioni.

tailleur   see *suit, feminine*.

tailored suit, feminine   a simple suit of cloth comprising jacket, skirt and shirtwaist. By the first decade of the twentieth century, it had become the smart street costume, in navy serge or black broadcloth. For resort wear and sportswear, it followed the English fabrics, was very often white and worn with Norfolk jacket. The style was launched by Doucet, Paris couturier in the 1880's.

tailor's chalk   talc or soapstone in small pieces for marking fabric before cutting.

Taglioni overcoat—braid trimmed and lined with plaid wool·

"tails or white tie"-formal evening dress-black or midnight blue worsted-high silk hat or collapsible opera hat-contemporary

tailor's tacks basting stitches alternating with loop stitches sewn to two pieces of material. The pieces are then cut apart, leaving marks to follow in sewing. Also called mark-stitches.

tails the colloquial name for the swallow-tailed coat. Another name is claw-hammer coat. Part of a man's formal evening dress; of black or midnight blue worsted with silk lapels and braided side seams on the trousers. "Tails" call for the stiff bosom shirt, wing collar, white tie and white waistcoat, and top hat. see *swallowtail; claw-hammer coat.*

tāj Persian or Arabic for crown; the tall, brimless cap to be seen in all Moslem countries, where it is a headdress of distinction. Its origin is the ancient tiara of the Mesopotamian valley. see *kamelaukion.*

talar Latin for ankles, hence *talaria,* winged slippers; *talaric,* ankle-length chiton or tunic. In mythology, winged shoes fastened at the ankles were worn by the Greek god Hermes and the Roman god Mercury.

talc, talcum powder an American commodity which was placed on the market about 1890. It is composed of perfumed talc and a mild antiseptic especially soothing to tender skin. Used by men, women and children, especially in hot weather.

talisman an amulet or charm, a piece of jewelry on a chain, worn around the neck to ward off evil. Nineteenth century.

tallith, taleth, tallit, tallis, talith, talit, talis the Jewish prayer shawl or tasseled white scarf bordered with blue and worn over head and shoulders.

talma a man's long cape or cloak sometimes hooded, named after the French tragedian, François Joseph Talma (1763–1826).

tam-o'-shanter a jaunty cap named after a poem by Robert Burns; of heavy brushed wool and of certain colors, the number used varying according to a man's status. Popular in the nineteenth century and still popular with women and girls in the twentieth.

tambour lace or **work** net or sheer cotton stretched on an embroidery hoop or tambour frame, formerly embroidered in the tambour stitch, now replaced by the chain stitch and worked with a crochet needle. see *Limerick lace.*

tamein the sari or sarong-like draped garment of Burmese men and women. see *lungi.*

tammy a cloth of wool or wool and cotton, often highly glazed. It has many uses and formerly was used for linings and curtains.

tanjib a fine muslin of East Indian make.

tank tops hip-length sweaters or jerseys with round neck and usually sleeveless, worn over tailored straight skirts and miniskirts. 1960's.

tanning the process of converting rawhide and skins into finished leather.

Tansui hat see *hat, Tansui.*

tapa cloth, Hawaiian a fabric made from the bark of a mulberry tree by steeping and beating. Used for many purposes including raiment on most South Pacific islands.

tapalo a coarse homespun scarf worn in Spanish-American countries.

tape firmly woven, narrow strips of cotton, linen, silk, rayon, etc., available in small rolls. Of varied widths and for varied sewing uses; such as seam tape, bias tape, mending tape, etc.

tape measure   a narrow strip of firm but flexible cloth, marked into inches and subdivisions of inches, used in sewing. Usually sixty inches long and about a half-inch in width.

tapestry   a heavy hand-woven fabric, usually figured, used as a wall hanging, furniture covering or carpet. The art of tapestry weaving originated in Flanders in the fourteenth century and spread throughout Europe. Modern tapestry can be made by machinery and is used in costume for accessories such as handbags and luggage.

tapis   a square of black silk worn on the head by Philippine peasant women.

tarboosh, tarbouch   the Arabic name of the truncated red felt cap, a cap of ancient Greek origin. Both men and women of the Mohammedan faith wear the tarboosh. The Egyptian wraps a scarf around his tarboosh and certain Indian races drape it around the kulah, a pointed skullcap. The tarboosh was introduced into India in the nineteenth century by the Indian-born educator and reformer, Sir Sayyad Ahmad. see *fez*.

tarbucket   see *shako*.

tarlatan   a thin, textured muslin with an open mesh, usually heavily sized and used as a stiffening in garments, such as the crinoline.

tarpaulin   a cloth such as canvas covered with tar or other waterproofing. Used especially for a sailor's southwester. see *southwester*.

tartan   originally the woolen cloth in plaid patterns worn in the Scottish Highlands where each clan had its distinctive tartan. Now a term for any plaid cloth resembling tartan. The patterns of a true tartan are foursquare, that is, the same color sequence is followed in each direction working out from the center square to the main cross line.

tartan velvet   a woven or printed plaid on a short-napped velvet.

tartar sable   see *mink, kolinsky*.

tartarine   an ancient and costly silk cloth supposedly woven by the people of Tartary.

tashashit   see *chechia*.

tash-tass   an East Indian cloth woven of gold and silver thread used for robes worn on ceremonial occasions.

tass or **tasses; taces**   a piece of armor which appeared in the fifteenth century. It was composed of steel bands or plates; four to eight over the hips, reaching from waist to mid-thigh, hinged on the left side and buckled on the right. It was worn until the late seventeenth century.

tassel   originally a cloak fastening; now a pendant ornament of thread or cords headed by a decorative knob top to hold the fringe intact.

tattersall   a general name for heavy woolen fancy vestings of small plaids and checks in gay colors. Named for the famous London saleroom for racing stock and thoroughbreds. Specifically, a check of narrow lines crossing at less than one-inch intervals on a neutral background.

tatting   a knotted lace edging with wide usage for lingerie and linens. Made with a small shuttle and the fingers, a single thread forming tiny loops in varied designs.

tattooing   a primitive form of body ornamentation which has been practiced since antiquity by the ancients, the North and South American Indians and still today particularly by some tribes in Africa, New Zealand and the Marquesas Islands. In more recent centuries the art rose to its highest form especially in Japan and many European aristocrats, both men and women, traveled to the Orient to have an exquisite picture tattooed on arms and chest. The old-time practice consisted of pricking the skin with sharp instruments and inserting pigments under the skin in the tiny holes. Usually powdered charcoal was used, which turned a deep blue and became indelible. Other pigments have been discovered. Slaves were often tattooed with their master's name, and sailors of all nations have delighted in being tattooed with pictures. "Body pictures" were back in fashion in the 1960's but the modern artwork was applied with ballpoint or felt-tip pens and was removable with soap and water.

taupe   the color of a mole's coat, a dark brownish-gray; from the French word for mole.

tawing   a form of mineral tanning in preparing skins with alum, salt and other agents.

tcharchaf   a name for the casual kind of dress among Moslem women of the village, which has replaced the old dress since Turkey became a republic in 1925. Under a colorful wool or silk shawl, a lace cap is worn to the eyes and the shawl held over nose and mouth. A sleeveless chemise of below-knee length covers pantaloons or chalwar, both these garments of striped cotton.

tea gown   an at-home gown of the late nineteenth and early twentieth centuries. A Victorian fashion of fitted yoke to which full sleeves and the dress body were joined. Usually of handsome fabric, lace-trimmed, and full length.

teal   a color named after the blue-winged teal, a small wild duck; a bluish green hue with low brilliance.

tebenna   the cloak of the ancient Etruscan man; a large rectangle or large semicircle of woolen cloth. see *Etruscan*.

teck band   a popular scarf of the four-in-hand style, named for the Prince of Teck. It was an imitation of the original four-in-hand necktie. Late nineteenth and early twentieth centuries. see *four-in-hand*.

teddy   also known as a combination; a feminine undergarment combining slip and panties in one piece. 1920's.

tegua   a buckskin sandal or moccasin of the Keresan Pueblo Indians of New Mexico.

teja   see *Spanish comb*.

temple jewelry   artificial jewelry of the seventeenth century made on the rue du Temple, Paris. It was an acceptable and fashionable type of what would today be called costume jewelry, set with stones of brilliant colors. Extravagant jeweled buttons were a particular fad of this time. see *costume jewelry*.

Teneriffe lace   a lace of circles and wheels similar to Paraguay lace, made chiefly in the Canary Islands.

ten-gallon hat   see *hat, Stetson*.

tennis dress   White is the conventional color for both men and women. For men, trousers or shorts and a short-sleeved shirt; for women, shorts or very short full skirt and a sleeveless blouse, or a very short one-piece dress; white ankle socks and sneakers. Like most sports attire for women, the tennis costume has become abbreviated and practical. The feminine tennis costume of the 1890's was a tailored white linen shirtwaist and separate skirt of ankle length. The skirt was of printed muslin or white linen worn with white canvas tennis shoes called balmorals or bals and black lisle stockings.

tennis flannel   see *outing flannel*.

tennis shoe   see *shoe, tennis*.

tensile strength   the strength of a fiber or piece of cloth as recorded in pounds on an instrument built for the purpose.

tent silhouette   first launched in 1951 by Balenciaga in a wonderfully simple, black woolen coat flaring widely from a low standing collar. It was followed in the 1960's by Yves Saint Laurent's A-line silhouette. And in 1967, Madame Grès used the tent silhouette in her lovely, flaring evening gowns.

terno   the traditional long evening gown of Philippine ladies, its special and unique feature being the short puffed wired sleeves called butterfly wings. Contemporary.

terry cloth   see *Turkish toweling.*

tewke   see *tuke.*

textile   woven from textile fabrics—cotton, linen, wool, silk, synthetic, etc., especially woven or knit cloth.

texture   a quality of the surface of a cloth produced by the manner of weaving and the fibers employed.

Thai silk   Oriental silk fabrics resembling nankeen, rajah, shantung and tussah made with silk or rayon in plain or twill weaves, in either natural or beautiful combinations of color. The weight and texture vary with the quality. The handwoven silks of Thailand have become widely known. In a silk-weaving village, the natives raise their own silkworms, tie the silks in tie-and-dye manner, and weave them into interesting broken patterns of fine color.

theater or **dinner suit**   see *dinner or theater suit.*

Thérèse   a huge cage of fine gauze worn over a high-dressed coiffure. It was kept in shape by very fine wire. French, 1780's. see *calash.*

thickset   a kind of cotton, fustian or velveteen used formerly for men's work clothes.

thimble   a finger guard for the sewer.

Open-ended bronze thimbles have been found among the ruins of Herculaneum, and bronze and brass thimbles have been dug up in Roman remains in the Thames. In Central Europe of the fourteenth century, leather thimbles called thummels were used. The modern thimble, a Dutch invention, reached England in the seventeenth century. First worn on the thumb, it was called a thum-bell. The tips were smooth but the sides were finely pitted.

tholia   a feminine straw hat of ancient Greece. It had a round brim and a sharply pointed crown and was worn over the head veil. This is the hat often seen in contemporary terra-cotta Tanagra figurines.

thread   a very thin filament or cord made by spinning the fibers of cotton, linen, nylon or silk, also yarns of wool hard-twisted and finished for use in sewing.

thread lace   a hand-made lace of linen thread, other than cotton or fancy thread.

three-dimensional glove   see *glove, free-finger.*

thrums   a kind of cap, knitted from the ends, usually about nine inches long, of warp threads left on the loom and which could not be woven; these are called thrums.

thummel   see *thimble.*

tiara   of Oriental origin, reaching Europe by way of Byzantium. The tiara which was worn by the ancient Persians was adopted by Christian and Jewish prelates alike. Before the eleventh century, it carried no special religious meaning. In modern times, the jeweled tiara or frontlet became a handsome evening headpiece worn by fashionable ladies with formal evening dress. Nineteenth and twentieth centuries. see *crown; coronet; miter.*

tiara, papal   jeweled triple coronets

tent coat-woolen cloth-kimona sleeve-narrow neckband-black suede pagoda cap-black fox muff-French-Balenciaga-1951

tholia-woman's hat of ancient Greece-worn over headcloth

of interwoven white folds and white lappets with gold embroidery. Worn by the Pope over a white linen coif.

Tibet cloth   a cloth woven from Tibetan goat's hair and used for dresses and wraps.

tibiale   see *fascia*.

ticking   a closely woven, heavy cotton or linen fabric of which mattress, pillow and bolster covers are made. It is usually striped but may also be printed with floral designs. Used mid-twentieth century for feminine sports clothes and summer coats.

tie   see *necktie*.

tie-about   also known as a swirl. An apron-like house dress with overlapping backs having sash ends that cross in back and tie in front.

tie clip   a piece of masculine jewelry, a clasp of gold or silver to hold the ends of a four-in-hand tie to the shirt front.

tie silks   silks such as foulard used for men's scarfs because resilient, pliable and firm in tying and knotting. Varying in weave and texture, and small-patterned.

tie tack   a small stud with a shank that pierces the necktie and shirt and screws or snaps into a little metal base.

tie wig   see *wig, tie*.

tied and dyed silks   a hand process of dyeing a silk such as surah by tying off sections to resist the dye, thereby creating interesting effects and designs. Used especially for expensive neckwear.

tied-back time   the period of the 1870's, so called by the British because all interest centered in back of feminine costume.

tiepin   see *scarfpin*.

tiffany   a gauzy silk used for head scarf or fichu in the eighteenth century; today, a muslin or transparent lawn, used for blouses or lingerie.

Tiffeau, Jacques   see *couture, haute*.

tiger   markings reproduced in tiger skin patterns printed on cloth, silk or fake fur. The fur of a real tiger is not used in costume.

tiger, American   see *jaguar*.

tights   skin-tight garments, generally covering legs and hips, worn by theatrical performers, acrobats or gymnasts, fashionable with mini-skirts and girls' fashions, 1960's.

tikka   the red spot which the Hindu woman, usually married, wears on the center of her forehead. It is a good-luck spot and may also be worn by unmarried women. It may be any color and has no caste significance.

tilter   a bustle worn under the petticoat which tilted when the wearer walked.

tilting helmet   see *helmet, tilting*.

timber wolf   Canadian-Arctic. see *wolf*.

timiak   the shirt of a Greenland Eskimo man, woman or child made of birdskins sewn together with the soft down worn next to the body. The long sleeves and neck are edged with dog fur.

tinsel cloth   cloth woven with sparkling metallic threads. Used for decorating costumes for party and holiday wear, especially Christmas fetes.

tinsel embroidery   embroidery done with tinsel threads.

tippet   originally, a liripipium, medieval, the long pendant of a hood; a pendant streamer attached to the arm; a woman's separate neckpiece of fur with long front ends of the nineteenth century. A long black scarf, similar to a stole, worn by Anglican clergy at non-sacramental services such as Matins or Evensong; the ends may be embroidered with ecclesiastical symbols. see *liripipe*.

tips   half-rubbers with a sling back, worn to protect the vamp and sole of a woman's shoe, but not the heel.

tissue   a gauze or sheer fabric of open weave, of silk, gold or silver thread.

titian   a reddish-brown color favored by the Italian painter, Tiziano Vecellio (1477–1576). A term usually descriptive of hair as Titian blond. An admired shade of hair.

tobe   Arabian undergarment, an ankle-length, loose-sleeved shirt of cotton, usually white, which slips on over the head. Worn under an outer garment, the aba, a large square which is often of brilliant colored woolen cloth.

toboggan cap   see *cap, toboggan*.

toe box   a piece of leather stiffened with gum, placed between the outer leather and lining to preserve the shape of the shoe.

toenail cosmetics   see *fingernail*.

toff   British vernacular for a dude, especially in the 1890's.

toga   During the first three centuries of our era, the Roman toga was the principal garment of both sexes but later was worn only by men. Its use was the same as the Greek himation but it was very different in shape. The Greek wrap was a rectangle and the Roman, when folded, a semi-circle. The wearing of the toga became an art with its hanging folds weighted by pellets and each fold named. The toga was the cloak of peace as the

sagum was that of war. see *himation; pallium; sagum*.

toggle   a peasant's button and loop. A small wooden block, the thickness of a finger and half as long, it is secured to the cloth by a cord around its middle. Pushed through a loop on the opposite edge for fastening.

toggle coat   an Austrian peasant-style travel coat fastened by the wooden buttons and loops called toggles. A knee-length winter coat of coarse woolen cloth with plaid lining and a removable hood. see *British warm, similar coat*.

toile   French for any cloth. A dressmaker's sample design made up in temporary fabric.

toile cirée   French for oilcloth.

toile de jouy   originally a linen or cotton printed fabric made in Jouy, France, from 1760. The design was usually a pictorial landscape or floral design and was printed in a single tone of red, blue, brown, purple or green on a natural ground. The name is now generally used for any printed fabric with similar designs. Used mainly for interior decoration but occasionally for women's summer suits or dresses.

toilet, toilette   the grooming of an individual in coiffure and costume, especially as pertaining to fashion.

toilet water   see *perfumery*.

toiletries, feminine   see *cosmetics; perfumery*.

toiletries, masculine   until the turn of the century, the use of toiletries by men was frowned upon in America but not in Europe. A change has occurred in the past half-century. To shaving cream, talcum powder and scented soap, deodorants, perfumes and toilet water have been added. There now exist many well-known toiletry

Tobe and breeches of white cotton- knitted skullcap with embroidery- Saudi Arabia merchant

tobe-worn under western jacket- over the jacket, an aba- on the head, kaffiyeh held by goat's hair agal- western cotton shirt and shoes- Arabian business man

manufacturers in Europe and America catering to the masculine market.

toilinet, toilinette   a cloth of silk or cotton warp with wool filling, closely woven in plain or loom-figured material for waistcoats.

tom-bons   full, wrapped loose pantaloons of white cotton worn by the Moslem Afghan men and women. They are full around the waist and hips, tapering down gradually to a snug fit at the ankles.

tondor lace   a Danish lace of drawnwork and embroidery, sometimes with a fine cordonet, of the seventeenth and eighteenth centuries.

tongs   an American Colonial term for work breeches or overalls made of coarse cotton or linen. Also, the first long breeches for boys of the period about 1820.

tonneau silhouette   a skirt much like the earlier peg-top model in shape and as short-lived, circa 1914.

tonsure   the shaving of the crown of the head leaving a circular fringe of hair, first practiced by monks. By the seventh century, it was a rite denoting admission to the clerical state.

tonsure wig   see *wig, tonsure.*

tontarra   see *beret.*

top boot   see *boot, top.*

top hat   see *hat, top.*

topaz   a semi-precious stone of aluminum phiosilicate, the characteristic yellow color varying from pale yellow to deep orange, occasionally blue, rarely pink, red. A yellow variety of quartz is known as Oriental topaz or yellow sapphire.

topcoat   coat worn over a suit, according to season. see *overcoat, great coat.*

topee, topi   of Hindu name and new in the 1860's, first worn by the British Army in India. Made from pith cork of the Indian spongewood tree, it is very light in weight, covered with white cotton and lined with green cloth. It is insulated against the hot sun and impervious to air and water.

tops and drops   old English for earrings with ear catches and pendants.

toque   originally a round full cap of soft material, gathered into a headband and often decorated with a small plume. In present usage, a small round brimless woman's hat, suggestive of the original shape.

toque, Spanish   see *Spanish toque.*

toquilla   the straw of a genuine Panama hat. see *jipijapa; hat, Panama.*

torchon lace   also known as Beggar's, Peasant's and Bavarian lace. A bobbin lace of heavy linen or cotton thread; the coarse pattern is used in fancy work and the fine for costume. see *Bavarian lace.*

torero   Spanish bullfighter, see illustration.

torque   a neck or arm band, usually of gold or perhaps bronze, worn by the ancient Gauls, Britons and Germans, a spirally twisted bar of gold bent into a hoop with an opening, the ends of which were fashioned into knobs or serpents' heads. Taken as spoils by the Romans, torques were awarded to the soldiers for valorous deeds.

torsade   a gold or silver fringe which edged the shoulder pads or military epaulettes designating an officer's grade. It was also used on hats.

tortoise shell   the large scales of the carapace, or shield, of a species of sea-turtle beautifully mottled and semitransparent. Used in the making of jewelry and luxury accessories such as eyeglass frames,

torero - in black velvet and gold and silver brocade - cherry-colored satin capa lined in yellow - pink stockings - torero's unique black cap - Spanish cigar and cigarette cases, Spanish combs, etc., and imitated in plastic.

tote bag   essentially a handbag based on the paper shopping bag, with deep straight sides and strong handles; open at the top. The shopping bag originated during World War II when, for lack of delivery service, shoppers carried their purchases home. Shops furnished strong paper bags with cord handles, which were universally popular. Eventually these bags were colored and decorated, serving as an advertising medium for the store.

toupee, masculine   a small patch of false hair to cover a bald spot. A small wig of the eighteenth century, with a curl or top knot at the crown of the head.

tourmaline, turmaline   a semiprecious stone, a complex silicate and magnesium with varying quantities of other minerals. Color may vary from black, brown or yellow to red, green or colorless.

tournure   French for bustle. see *bustle.*

tovaglio (Italian), **bavolet** (French) names of the European peasant bonnet with a deep ruffle at the back of the neck. It was known in the eighteenth century as a Paris fashion and called Fanchon. see *bavolet.*

tow   yarn spun from an inferior flax, used for sheetings. Tow cloth was an old-time linen homespun.

tower headdress   a tall coiffure of the seventeenth and eighteenth centuries. see *fontange.*

toyo   a cellophane-coated rice-paper straw made in Formosa, Okinawa and Japan. It is shiny and smooth and resembles panama.

tracing wheel   a small steel wheel with teeth and a handle used for marking off seams, tucks and joinings for sewing.

trademark, trade-mark name   meaning the name or symbol of a manufactured product which is legally protected by registration.

train   the trailing back section of a formal gown, attached in back to the shoulders or the waist. In the medieval period, women's skirts and, very often, men's cloaks were long, touching the floor in folds and sometimes trailing behind. In the fourteenth century the length of the train was regulated according to the wearer's rank. In Louis XIV's day, trains reached exaggerated lengths for ceremonial use. They were fastened at shoulders or waist and unhooked and put aside after the ceremony. Trains grew still longer in Louis XV's reign and were copied by Napoleon, luxuriously embroidered. The beautiful ermine-trimmed velvet robes survive in the traditional coronation attire of Great Britain. Trains continue to be worn for fashionable weddings and affairs of state but less often than in the past.

trank   the oblong leather piece marked with a glove pattern from which the glove is cut.

transfer pattern   a design for embroidery. A carbon drawing may be transferred by a hot iron, or a perforated design may be transferred by rubbing chalk through the perforations.

transformation   any small hairpiece used to change the wearer's hairstyle.

transparencies   gowns of sheer lawn or muslin painted with bouquets of colored flowers and worn over an undergown of bright colored moiré satin. Transparencies were also of gold or lace tissue worn over figured brocades. 1660's.

trapeze line   In 1958, Yves Saint Laurent, protégé of and successor to Dior,

trembling cap-gold and silver cord net with pearls-Italian-16th C.

trench coat worn by British officers, WWI- of water-proofed cotton gabardine- adopted by civilians

Trilby- a soft, felt hat, beaver-like- Tyrolese style- feather wings- 1908

was acclaimed for his Trapeze Line which evolved into the A-Line. The A-Line later became the Tent Shape in coat and dress.

trapunto   a kind of quilting worked between two pieces of fabric in which the design is stitched flat and then stuffed with cotton batting in sections, in this manner filling in each part of the design separately.

trembling cap   of gold or silver cord net banded with pearls. Italian, late sixteenth century; a conical cap with a long tail like a chaperon.

trench coat   topcoat of British officers in World War I. Of processed gabardine with an extra processed lining, it was used also by U.S. officers in World War II. The original model had reinforced shoulder flaps and gun flaps. After the war it was copied for civilian use by both sexes, soon becoming a contemporary classic.

trencher cap   same as *mortarboard*.

tressure, tressour   medieval terms for caul, reticulated or netted headdress of the fourteenth and fifteenth centuries.

trews   a Celtic garment of breeches and hose knitted in one piece. Close-fitting and worn under kilts by Highlanders and Irishmen.

tricolette   a knitted fabric made of rayon, silk or cotton and resembling jersey cloth. Used for women's clothing.

tricot   see *jersey*.

tricotine   see *cavalry twill*.

tricorne   see *cocked hat, androsmane; continental; Kevenhuller*.

Trigère, Pauline   see *couture, haute*.

trilby   a soft felt hat in Alpine shape with a plush-like texture resembling beaver. First decade of the twentieth century.

tripe   a fabric of velvet weave but not silk, now known as velveteen.

trollopée   a loose, flowing gown of the Watteau period (1715–1723), open in front and sometimes drawn up in back. It was worn as a morning dress and also called a flying gown.

trolly or **trolley lace**   as English bobbin lace; its pattern consists of flowers, sprays, dots and squares outlined with a heavy thread.

tropical worsted   summer wear woolens of lightweight mixtures in two or single-ply yarns in warp and filling. For men's and women's suitings, twentieth century.

trotcozy   a Scottish shoulder covering or small cape with cowl hood used when walking.

trotteur   French for a plain tailored woman's outfit with sturdy shoes for walking in town or country, from the French trotter, to trot. Twentieth century.

trouser skirt   see *skirt, harem*.

trousers, trowsers   of Oriental origin, worn by barbarians, as distinguished from the Greeks and Romans. The Britons then wore braccae which were made of checkered cloth. During the Roman domination, the Britons adopted Roman dress while the Scots and Irish retained their trousers, called truis. The word "trousers" appears first in the reign of Henry VIII of England. The substitution of full-length breeches for knee breeches dates from the French Revolution. Those who wore long breeches were patriots or "sans culottes," meaning without knee breeches, to distinguish them from the aristocrat. Eventually, with the addition of a jacket, the ensemble evolved into the habit or suit of the nineteenth century. Both trousers and black satin knee breeches remained the style for evening, breeches being full dress for many British and European officials. see *sans-culottes*. Trousers or long

the early nineteenth century
ay between calf and ankle
ons and loops. Made tight-
re of stockinette, buckskin
ed cotton. The most popu-
s buff or yellow nankeen
n China. Until the 1850's
very tight, with the strap
t, lasting into the 1860's.
sure gave way to a center-
nd side pockets became
ly attempt to crease
nter front of leg did not
Prince of Wales, later
upon his visit to America in
creases front, back and sides
. Creases became general by
s, having been introduced by
cers. Cuffs on trousers appeared
turn of the century, the result of
hmen turning up their trousers on
days in the muddy paddock.

trousers, bridge   see *pantalons à pont.*

trousers, peg-top   see *peg-top trousers.*

trousers, sailor   until the 1950's, made with a front fall and bell bottoms; now tailored in civilian fashion.

trousseau   the personal outfit for a bride, her clothes, jewelry, household linens, etc.

troussoire   see *chatelaine.*

truncated   the top of a cone cut off or squared, as a hat with its crown top flattened.

trunk hose   short, puffed breeches attached to the long stockings or tights which were in fashion from 1575 to 1600. Trunk hose and codpiece were secured to the doublet by points or lacings. From 1560 on, trunk hose were usually slashed or paned, revealing a full, padded lining of contrasting colored silk. see *slashing.*

trunks   a man's piece of atheletic apparel, a tight-fitting, knitted or jersey garment. It has an elastic waistband and covers the body from waist to thighs. Worn from the late nineteenth century and used for track sports and swimming.

tsaruchia   contemporary, sturdy, peaked-toed shoes worn by royal guardsmen (evzones) in Greece. Black leather with red or blue pompons.

T-shirt   a short term for tennis or sports shirt, of knitted lightweight cotton or wool with crew or V-neck and usually white. It may be sleeveless or have short or long sleeves. May also have a "mock" turtle neck.

T-strap   on a woman's shoe, a strap along the instep which joins an ankle strap at right angles, making a "T."

tubbeck or **tupak**   the tubular dress of Burmese men and women. Long, straight yardage of cotton or silk is wrapped round the body to form a straight silhouette, over which is worn a short, simple white cotton jacket.

tuck   a fold of fabric stitched in place. see *dart.*

tucker   a guimpe-like yoke of lace or embroidered fabric worn to fill in above a low-cut bodice, seventeenth and eighteenth centuries.

tuft   similar to short, upturned tassel.

tuftaffata, tuftaffaty   a heavy silk taffeta of early English and New England days. Also a "taffaty" fashionable in the Elizabethan period and the seventeenth century. It was a taffeta woven with velvet, chenille or rasied-pile stripes and was used for doublets, jerkins, gowns and petticoats.

tuke, tewke   a canvas of the fifteenth and sixteenth centuries.

trunk hose and doublet covered with cutwork, embroidery and galloon-silk hose and ribbon garters- English-1567

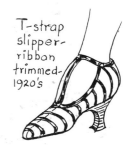

T-strap slipper- ribbon trimmed- 1920's

tulle   a very fine net or gauze of silk or cotton, first made in Nottingham, England, in 1768 on a stocking machine, wrongly supposed to have originated in France. It was made with a loosely woven tricot stitch which unraveled. Despite its poor quality, it became popular for the fashionable headdress and the huge mobcap of the period and also was inexpensive. Modern tulle is a very fine net, usually silk, and used chiefly for veiling. It was used in the 1950's for evening gowns.

tunic   a short garment worn by ancient Greeks and Romans. In modern woman's dress, a tunic is of shorter length than the basic skirt over which it is worn. A hip-length blouse; any undress jacket worn by British soldiers; the tight-fitting jacket of the British guardsman.

tunica   see *tunicle*.

tunicle   a close-fitting vestment or tunic worn by a bishop under the dalmatic.

tupu   ornamental jewelry worn by the Araucanian Indian women of Chile. A piece of silver work about ten inches long by four inches wide consisting of three heavy chains attached to a shield which fastens a cloak. From the chains hang a pendant carrying many silver coins.

tuque   a Canadian sportscap, a knitted stocking type made pointed at both ends and turned one end into the other, a doubly warm headpiece.

turban   a particular style of headdress worn by men of the Mohammedan faith, of obscure Oriental origin. A scarf of fine linen, cotton or silk folded around the head. "Dulband" was its Persian name, meaning a sash. In centuries past, it was considered an offence in Mohammedan countries for an unbeliever to wear the turban.

turban, knitted   a knitted band about

four inches wide, shaped around the head by invisible stitches. Designed by Agnés of Paris in the 1920's for the bobbed head. The turban continued to be a smart headpiece for women.

turkey red   cotton cloth and embroidery cotton dyed a brilliant, durable red, imported from Turkey. Popular in the late nineteenth century, and widely used in the peasant embroidery of the period.

turkey-back silhouette   a ladies' short coat fashionable in the 1860's. A little below hip length, it hung fairly straight in front but flared out in back from the neck over the bustle.

Turkish dress   see illustrations; *chalwar; kusak.*

Turkish embroidery   of gold, silver and silk thread, done in conventional designs and native stitches. It was worked on both sides, eliminating a "wrong side." Used for garments.

Turkish point lace, oyah   a lace made with crochet needle and colored silk in an intricate flower design in relief.

Turkish Moslem headdress banned 1928-face veil or yashmak- outer cloak or feridgé-caften over pantaloons or chalwar- baboosh on feet

Turkish tcharchaf costume-shawl embroidered- worn over lace head- piece- sleeveless chemise and chalwar of striped cotton

turkey back silhouette-silk faille-coat with hood and tassels- straw bonnet with ostrich tips- striped skirt- 1867

The turban

velvet turban-
Titus coiffure-
Directoire-
1790's

"desert turban"
with mameluke
point-hues
of red-
French-
1803

turban à la
Rachel-white
satin-gold spangles-
aigrette-French-
1833

gauze
turban
chin strap-
aigrette-
French-
1797

turban of
pleated gauze
with spangles and
band-French-1803

Turban of tulle, pearls, jewels
and aigrette-American-
1790's

turban-
pale gray
satin-Balenciaga-1944

turban-white satin with
mameluke point and pearl
fringe-French-1806

velvet turban with
aigrette and jewels-
French-1790's

The turban

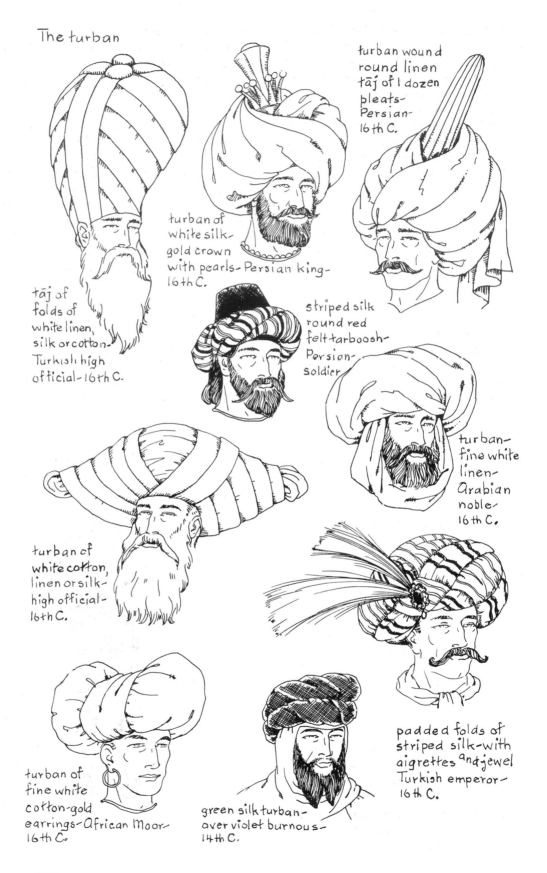

turban wound
round linen
tāj of 1 dozen
pleats-
Persian-
16th C.

turban of
white silk-
gold crown
with pearls-Persian king-
16th C.

tāj of
folds of
white linen,
silk or cotton-
Turkish high
official-16th C.

striped silk
round red
felt tarboosh-
Persian-
soldier

turban-
fine white
linen-
Arabian
noble-
16th C.

turban of
white cotton,
linen or silk-
high official-
16th C.

turban of
fine white
cotton-gold
earrings-African Moor-
16th C.

green silk turban-
over violet burnous-
14th C.

padded folds of
striped silk-with
aigrettes and jewel
Turkish emperor-
16th C.

352

Turkish toweling, terry cloth, Moorish cloth   cotton or linen woven with raised loops on both sides. Very absorbent and used chiefly for masculine and feminine bath robes, towels and wash cloths. It was first made in England in 1848, but ignored by the British. A merchant sold the goods in Turkey, where the natives used it for the draped turban. Years later, the British accepted the toweling as a British import.

turquoise   an opaque gem stone, color ranging from deep blue to pale bluish-green. The name comes from the old French name for Turkey, the best examples of the stone coming from the Near East.

turret   a crownless white linen toque worn in the twelfth century with chin-band or barbette. Worn sometimes over the wimple, flowing hair, or coiffure dressed in a chignon at the nape.

turtle   the growing scarcity and cost-liness of alligator skins for shoes and bags created a demand in the 1960's for sea turtle skins. Turtle markings are larger than alligators', the skins softer, but turtle accessories can be produced for a lower selling price. Having hard or soft shell, there are two hundred species of both the land and sea reptiles. Recently skins have come from the Caribbean Sea, the best from the coasts of Mexico and Honduras. Only the skin of the legs is usable.

turtle neck   masculine, feminine, knitted, or jersey sweater with a long, straight, tubelike collar which is rolled down to the height desired, with no front opening. A standing, knitted collar was new in the 1960's.

tuscan   a yellow straw in lacy designs from Tuscany, Italy; made from the tops of bleached wheat stalks. Used for hats.

tussah, tusseh, tussore, tusser, tussur   a type of silk which includes pongee and shantung. A very strong silk woven from the tussah silkworm of India, bred on the jujube tree. Usually in natural fawn color because it does not always dye well. Popular for dresses and men's and women's summer suits.

tutulus   Etruscan; originally the head-dress of braids worn by the flamen or pagan priest and his wife, the braids built up in conical shape. Eventually the conical shape evolved into a pointed cap with an olive twig on top tied by a fillet of wool.

tuxedo   American name for the dinner jacket, the design improvised by American millionaires living in Tuxedo Park, N.Y., who wished a less formal and more comfortable dress for small dinners. A short coat of black or midnight blue worsted with rolling silk collar, worn with a black silk waistcoat and trousers with braid side seam. In the late 1920's, a double-breasted dinner jacket made the waistcoat unnecessary. see *dinner jacket; black tie.*

tuxedo collar   see *collar, tuxedo.*

turret cap of white linen attached to coif-hair in a net-French and German-13th C.

tutulus-shaped felt hat-ringlets over forehead and curls in back-Etruscan man

tutulas headdress of braids-jeweled fillet-back hair in curls-Etruscan man

tuxedo-dinner coat or "black tie"-semi-formal evening dress-black or midnight blue cloth-contemporary

tweed, Donegal   a handscoured, homespun tweed, originally made by Donegal Irish peasants on hand looms. Also, loosely woven tweeds of Yorkshire yarns dyed and finished in Donegal. Today, mostly machine-made, with the slubs woven in. Used for suits, topcoats and sportswear.

tweed, Harris   see *Harris tweed.*

tweed, Scotch   a coarse or soft woolen fabric, usually rough-surfaced, in plain or twill weave. Made in plaids, checks or mixtures and first produced in Scotland by weavers on the Tweed River.

Twentieth Century costume   see illustrations, pages 355–379.

twill or **diagonal weave**   the strongest of all weaves, having a distinct diagonal line from selvedge to selvedge. Wool twills include serge and gabardine; cotton twills, denim and coutil or ticking.

twill, cavalry   see *cavalry twill.*

twill, middy   see *middy twill.*

twill, Poiret   see *Poiret twill.*

twist   a thread of firmly twisted silk used for making buttonholes and tailored ornaments.

twists   a trade term for woolen and worsted cloths woven of yarns of two colors twisted together, producing a mottled effect in the pattern.

Tyrian purple   a reddish-blue or bluish-red dye formerly obtained from mollusks native to the coast of Israel, where Tyre is situated. The color was famous throughout the ancient world and is often referred to in classical literature.

Tyrolean, Tyrolese   dress still worn today in the Tyrol, a province of western Austria in the Alps, bordered by Ger-(*continued on page 380*)

Tyrol-Gray cloth jacket, bright green trim, braces, jacket and belt-black leather breeches, red trim, black felt hat with feather-woolen socks-Austrian

Tyrol-black velvet over white blouse-black cotton skirt-printed cotton apron-felt hat with plumes-red socks-Austrian

Tyrol-brown suede leather breeches-jacket and vest, lacquer red-white shirt-pea green hat and braces-pheasant plume-white stockings-Italian

Tyrol-mountain maid with brandy cask-black velvet bodice and skirt-pink silk shawl fringed-pink apron-black felt hat with pink cord, tassel and flowers-Bavarian

Tyrol-white blouse-red bodice and skirt-black velvet cap of beads and flowers-jewel belt and ribbons-Italian

Tyrol guide-leather suit-jacket dull red breeches darker-waistcoat, dark green-brown cap-feather panache-gray socks-black shoes-Bavarian

Twentieth Century
bathing dress -
1900 - 1930

Annette kellerman's
swim suit - black
knitted cotton
maillot and tights -
1909

dress, bloomers,
black lisle
stockings and
corset - black or
navy mohair -
black and white
trimming -
1900

bathing corset
and brassière
of rubber
sheeting -
1915

knitted black
wool maillot
over shorts -
colored trim -
rolled black
silk stockings -
canvas shoes -
1924

black taffeta dress
and bloomers -
black and white
checked trimming -
heavy black
silk stockings -
black linen
buskins -
1915

knitted swim suit -
white wool with
navy blue polka
dots - navy trim
and shorts -
1928

355

Twentieth Century
corsetry
1900-1910

in center-
garter belt for
"straight front"
often worn over
corset-

satin
front-laced
corset-
closed back-
1904

satin brocade
with lace
and ribbon-
back-
lacing-
1901

front-laced
corset
fastened to
side of front-
1904

straighter
and longer
lines-
polka dot
fabric-
1906

whaleboned
brassière-
adjustable
shoulder straps-
1905

multi-colored
striped ribbon-
back lacing-
1905

356

Twentieth Century
lingerie
1900-1910

"French drawers"
fitted hip band
closed crotch
side-buttoned

chemise
batiste, lace
and ribbon
1902

combination
corset-cover
and petticoat
batiste, lace,
tucks, ribbon
threaded
through
entre-deux
1902

combination
corset-cover
and "umbrella
drawers"
circular
pattern
1904

nightgown
of nainsook
entre-deux with
ribbon,
embroidery,
and lace
1905

knitted
union suit
drawstring at
neck and arms
cotton, wool,
or silk

"bosom
amplifier"
cambric, lace,
beading and
ribbon
1906

gored and
tailored
taffeta
petticoat
of the period
dust ruffle
at hem

nightgown
batiste with
white
embroidery
and tucks
1909

357

Twentieth Century
negligee-
1900-1910

Japanese kimono-
interlined silk
crêpe-embroidery-
padded hem
1909

dressing
sacque-
white lawn
with lace-
box pleats-
1901

pajamas-
pongee-
embroidery
and frogs-
1902

"robe de chambre"-
violet dotted
cream flannel-
violet silk
foulard
collar and
cuffs, tucked
nainsook
1902

kimono of
striped
and plain
wash silk-
1907

matinée of
silk mull-
picot edging-
beading with
ribbon-
1904

358

Twentieth Century corsetry 1910-1920

back-lacing mercerized batiste-elastic gussets 1912

sueded tricot and lace 1912

well-boned for the heavy figure white coutil lace and ribbon 1911

brocaded satin girdle buttoned in front 1914

pink satin with elastic waistline low front lacing 1913

front lacing mercerized brocade lace edging 1918

brassière mounted on flesh colored chiffon elastic slipover snap front closure low side lacing 1913

girdle of suede cloth satin panels front and back elastic waistline 1915

brassière all-over lace lined with net ribbon band elastic straps 1913

brassière of tucked lawn and embroidery 1914

359

Twentieth Century lingerie 1910-1920

umbrella drawers nainsook with embroidery and ribbon bowknots 1912

petticoat wash silk deep lace flounce beading and ribbon 1912

combination corset cover and knickerbockers nainsook, lace edging, beading and ribbon 1913

the classic ensemble vest and knickers of glove silk pale tints 1918

combination corset cover and drawers batiste, lace, embroidery, beading and ribbon 1913

"envelope chemise" crepe de Chine with lace, beading and ribbon 1918

chemise flesh colored crepe georgette dark blue satin and embroidery 1919

princess slip white batiste lace insertion, edging, and deep flounce beading with ribbon 1913

360

Twentieth Century-
negligée and
sleepwear
1910-1920

matinée of
crepe de chine-
tucks and lace-
1912

pajamas
of cotton
wool or
wash silk-
1918

nightgown-
batiste and
cluny lace
with ribbon-
1913

negligée-satin
or velvet-crepe
georgette-
tassels-
self
ornament-
1918

pajama
lounge
suit-print
and plain
silk-coat,
trousers
and blouse-
1919

handmade
Philippine
nightgown-
white cotton
embroidery
on white
nainsook

traveling and
night robe of
striped silk-
1919

361

Twentieth Century-
corsetry-
1920-1930

evening brassière-flesh
colored satin-concealed
boning-
shirred ribbon
trim-1920

slip-on girdle
of elastic
tricot laced
at the sides-
brassière of
black Chantilly
threaded
with gold-
1925

evening
corset
hooked in
front-silk
tricotine
with lace-
back belt
of elastic-
1920

foundation
garment of
elastic tricot-
two front bones
1928

slip-on garter
belt-brocade
with elastic
back panel-
1927

maternity
girdle-satin
with front
panel of elastic
tricot-snap
closure-side
lacings-
1927

corset-girdle-
brocade and
elastic tricot-
embroidered motif-
1929

foundation
garment of
brocade, lace
and elastic
tricot-
1929

362

Twentieth Century
lingerie-
1920-1930

nightgown-
shell pink
crepe de Chine-
yoke and belt
of bias
chiffon folds-
1921

backless brassière-
pink satin-chiffon
roses-elastic
belt-1921

batiste
brassière-
lace and white
embroidery-
1921

"dance set"
brassière
and pantie-
pink glove silk-
appliqué blue
and peach-
1927

nightgown-
sheer yellow
voile and
Alençon
lace-
1929

the slip of
bias cut-
silk crepe,
chiffon or
ninon-
1925

envelope chemise
with pockets-
glove silk
and lace-
1927

for general wear-
vest and knickers
of glove silk
in pale colors

pajama of
white glove silk-
appliquéd with
black and green chiffon-
1927

Twentieth Century-
negligée-
1920-1930

negligée of two
shades of chiffon-
slashed chasuble
over slip with
pleated skirt-
1922

negligée of
satin meteor
with frills
and corsage of
crepe georgette-
1924

negligée tied to
one side-yellow
crepe de Chine-
ecru Alençon
lace-
1925

negligée of
zenana cloth
and marabou
1922

tea or dinner
pajamas of
satin with lapels
and appliqué
of lamé-
1926

364

Twentieth Century bathing dress- 1930 - 1954

knitted red woolen maillot- 1931

ballerina suit- blue and white striped rayon jersey - white trunks- 1940

halter-neck maillot of knitted black wool- 1945

knitted wool suit - purple with white and cerise stripe- 1941

the "bikini"- jacquard linen - yellow and orange- 1948

black wool jersey suit with sleeves - gilt hooks and eyes - gilt balls on cord- 1953

brown wool jersey bloomer suit with white trimming- 1953

hooded maillot of black wool jersey- 1954

Twentieth Century-
corsetry-
1930-1940

knit foundation
of Lastex and
Bemberg-
"uplift" style-
1934

step·in girdle
of Lastex, the
two·way stretch
woven fabric-
1932

all·in·one-
satin, elastic
and lace-
detachable crotch
shield·zippered
back-
1931

foundation
of satin ribbon
and net-
1933

step·in girdle of
batiste and elastic-
zipper closure-
1934

Lastex step·in
pantie girdle-
detachable
garters-
1935

step·in
corset of
pink satin-
featherboning-
zippered back-
lace brassière-
1939

strapless
brassière-
uplift bosom-
lace with
featherboning-
hooked front
closure-
1938

the French, back·laced,
side·zippered corset
which "did not take"
1939

step·in
satin corset-
side zippered
closure·front
lacing-
1939

Twentieth Century-
1930-1940
lingerie

hand-embroidered
satin slip-inserted
pleated chiffon-
1931

circular-cut
panties-silk
with lace
inserts-net
bandeau-
1931

tailored
combination-
vest, brassière
and bloomers
of glove silk-
1930

slip of
white handkerchief
linen with
eyelet embroidery-
threaded with
ribbon-
1939

nightgown-
diagonally cut-
blue and
pink crepe-
1932

nightgown-
fine white cotton-
tucks and edging-
sash ribbon in slot-
1938

367

Twentieth Century-
negligée-
1930-1940

hostess gown-
green and
silver lamé-
1936

full-length robe of
quilted calico-
lined and
piped with
contrasting
color-
1930's and '40's

pink robe-knitted
yarn or ribbon-
crepe lined-
satin trimming
and sash-
1937

hostess
pajamas-
gold brocade
coat with
black satin
trousers
and trim-
1936

gown and
coat of
sheer gray
voile-
1937

boudoir jacket-
cream satin-
ecru Alençon
lace collar-
1938

Twentieth Century-
1940-1954-
chemise slip and
petticoat

white cotton
petticoat-
white cotton
embroidery-
1947

half-slip-
black taffeta-
pleated net
with ribbon
stripes-1949

chemise slip-
black or colored-
crepe, silk or
chiffon-lace-
pleated frills-
1949

half-slip-
permanently
pleated nylon net-
1950

the
crinoline-
stiffened
net and
featherboning-
1951

full slip-
nylon
tricot and
lace- black
and pale colors-
1952

crinoline
for evening
or wedding-
plastic frame-
1952

petticoat of
tulle over taffeta-
boned Lastex
midriff-1954

petticoat of
taffeta over
organdy-ribbon
through beading-
1954

Twentieth Century
corsetry-
1940-1954

uplift and
diaphragm
control-
Lastex satin
and lace-
1944

uplift and
plunging
neckline-
plush-covered
wire-black
lace-
1945

all-in-one-
basque
silhouette-
Lastex and
satin weave-
hips of
Lastex and
net weave-
lace cups-
1940

guêpière
or waist
cincher -
boned nylon-
front lacing-
uplift, strapless
"bra"-lace
with boning-
1947

tight-waisted
corselette-
high bosom-
black satin-
1947

corselette-
flattened uplift
and long diaphragm
control of the
Renaissance-
Paris-1954

tight-waisted
girdle of
Lastex
and satin-
lace motifs-
1948

black girdle-
elasticized
nylon lace-
ruffle over
crotch shield-
1954

corselette-
half-brassière-
tight waist-
embroidered
marquisette
and satin-
long garters-
1952

Twentieth Century-
knitwear-
1940-1954

bright red
shirt and
pants-knit
rayon and
wool

summer "briefs"-
knit cotton or silk

winter panties-
knit wool,
angora or silk

vest and
panties of fine
pink knit wool

knit girdle of
Lastex and cotton
yarn-size shown
before put on

nylon stocking
embroidered
with medallion-
1954

nylon with
garter top-
elasticized
thread-
1954

bright red ski
underwear-
shirt and pants
worsted with
inner cotton
layer

nylon stockings
with lace tops-
jeweled garter buckle
1954

all-in-one-
knit wool,
rayon and cotton

371

Twentieth Century
negligée-
1940 - 1954

lounge suit-
quilted calico
jacket - black
velveteen trim
and trousers-
1947

hostess coat-
black silk jersey
combined with
aqua and coral-
1947

breakfast
cape of pink
chiffon and lace-
1948

negligée-
rose georgette
yoke outlined
with appliquéd
lace motifs-
1948

Empire negligée-
voluminous
gray taffeta-
1948

tied bed
jacket-
pink or white
nylon fleece-
net puffings-
Valenciennes
lace-
1950

peignoir of
white or pale blue
albatross-
flowered ribbon-
1952

372

Twentieth Century-
sleepwear-
1940-1954

"shortie" nightdress-
white, pink or blue
cotton-drawstring
neck-1946

pajamas of
crêpe, satin
or silk jersey-
1946

mandarin sleep
coat-white nylon
jacquard-pale
piping and frogs-
1948

nightdress-
pale blue
nylon and
lace-bloused
back-
1952

nightgown-
white georgette
and lace-
ribbon sash
in slot-
1948

pajamas-
cotton flannel-
striped and
solid color-
1953

sleep
separates-
coat and
skirt of
nylon tricot
and lace-
1953

shirtcoat-
white cotton-
embroidery
and tucks-
1954

373

Twentieth Century - bathing togs

heavy ribbed knitted wool - changeable red and black - top and trunks - 1st decade

heavy knit red wool one-piece with attached skirt - 2nd decade

two-piece - woolen jersey - navy blue and white - red striped trunks - white web belt - 1920's

elastic knit swim trunks in vivid colors - 1950's

two-piece - woolen jersey - white top - navy blue trunks - white web belt - 1930's

boxer shorts of printed linen - shirred elasticized belt - terry cloth coat 1940's and 1950's

374

Twentieth Century-
Ageless Footwear

alpargata-
hemp sandal-
black leather
ties-
Spanish
peasant

leather boot and
sandal-thong
ties-colored
stitchery and
appliqué-
Polish
woman

woman's
red babouche
or mule-
Near East

mule of the
Occidental
mode

huarache sandal-
wood with
leather
insole-
braid
edge-
metal
loops-
leather thongs-
Mexican

palm leaf
sandal-
Mexican Indian

Guatemalan
Indian sandal-
leather-
dark blue
counter

modern calfskin
version of the
Highland rawhide
cuaran
or
brogue-
origin
of
the
modern
ghillie-
Scotch

kamik-
dyed
hairless
sealskin-
blue with red
and white
skin appliqué-
colored
stitchery-
Greenland

cowboy boot-stirrup
heel-colored
inlay and
stitching-
Western U.S.

mukluk-sealskin
with fur inside-
thong or cotton
ties-
Eskimo

knob
sandal or
wooden clog-
India

laptis of birch
bark-Russian
peasant

fur anklet-
Zulu chief-
Africa

carbatine-most primitive
shoe-one
piece
rawhide-
Italian
peasant

Roman woman's
modish sandal-
white calf
skin-star
ornament

Moslem shoe of red
morocco-
peaked toe

Moslem
shoes-mules or babouches-
red morocco-turned back
counter-gold
stitchery-yellow
morocco-colored
design

18th C. pump-black
patent leather or calf-
silver buckle-dress
shoe of many
European
national
costumes

white buckskin
boot-moccasin-
Taos and
Santa Clara
Indian women
southwestern
U.S.

sabot worn by
peasants of France,
Holland and
Belgium-
all wood
or wood
and leather-
carving

zapatilla-wooden clog-
cotton upper-
bright colored-
Philippine

yellow morocco boot-
red piping and
pompon-Turkish woman's

Chinese boy's fur shoe-
felt sole-link buttons-
Central
Asia

leather-red or blue pompon-
highland troops
and shepherds-
Greek

woman's
beaded
deerskin
moccasin

n.a. Indian

tabi (sock) and
geta (clog)-
Japanese

sabot-wooden sole-
leather
uppers-
Portuguese
peasant

espadrille-
colored cloth
with braided hemp
sole-Spanish

highlow-black
kid or
suede-
bright
green
laces-
Polish
peasant
bride

Twentieth Century-
masculine
sundries

dress shirt-
stiff bosom
plain or
piqué-wing
collar-
bow tie
matching
bosom-
pearl
studs-
1910

high fold
collar-
striped silk
scarf-1910

low fold
collar-
brocaded
silk scarf-
1910

dress
waistcoat-
dull black
or white silk-
poke collar-
1912

attached collar-
buttoned down-
white oxford-
1920's

cloth day vest-
double-breasted-
1920

striped
collar-band
shirt-collar
separate-
1910

pleated
dress shirt-
pique, batiste,
voile or silk-
from 1940's

pleated
dress shirt-
batiste or silk-
matching tie and
cummerbund-
black or maroon silk-from 1930's

cotton
sports
shirt and
shorts-
1939

sports shirt
of varied
fabric and
weave-1945

short-sleeved
sports shirt-
silk or cotton
in brilliant
color-
1939

figured silk
waistcoat
for country
wear-
1953

pin collar-
small knot
in scarf-
most of
period

376

Twentieth Century-
sleepwear and
negligée

dressing gown-
cloth, silk or
velveteen-
whole
period

sleepcoat-
mercerized
cotton or
pongee-frog
fastenings-
1920's

nightshirt-
muslin
or cotton
flannel-
1st decade

sleepcoat-
cotton or
silk-1950's

"separates"-
long and short
sleeves and
breeches-
blue, gray,
maize and
wine cotton-
1953

striped
broadcloth
pajamas-
whole period

knitted pajamas for
winter wear-navy blue-
blue and white trim-
1950's

nightshirt-
cotton
broadcloth-
1950's

377

Twentieth Century-
underwear

union suit-
knitted cotton
or wool-ankle
or knee-length-
1st decade

two-piece white
cotton top and
drawers-
2nd decade

one-piece
white cotton
combination-
1920's

buttonless
combination-
white
crossbar
dimity-
1920's

two-piece
cotton mesh,
broadcloth
or pongee-
pale colors-
1930's

knitted
tee-shirt-
plaid cotton
boxer
shorts-
1950's

knitted
cotton
skeleton
shirt and
briefs-
1950's

tee-shirt and
drawers-
knitted wool-
white for general
wear-bright
red for skiing-
1950's

378

midi-length-
black and
white
striped
voile
over bras
and
shorts-
1964

nun's dress-
"mini-medieval"-
black hood
white band
and cowl-
black jumper
with shorts-
1968

maxi
length

sheer, lacy
pantyhose-1960's

bridal gown-silk
linen with Cluny
lace - wimple
headdress -
lace-edged
apron-
1964

mini-length
shirtdress
of voile with
embroidery
and buckled
belt-
1960's

Sassoon's
geometric hair-do
ending in a point
at the nape-1966

plaid jacket
over plain
mini skirt-
taffeta
turban-
1960's

mini-dress
of wool
jersey-large
felt hat-
Gernreich
1960's

beach dress-
silk brass
and bikini-
dotted voile scarf-
scarf-1960's

pantsuit
of plaid wool-large
felt hat- Tiffeau-1960's

mini-skirt suit and cap-
Tattersall cloth- Courrèges
boots-black and white
leather-1960's

plaid cloth
Scotch riding
cap-1960's

379

many, Switzerland and Italy. Costume details vary from district to district, but in general men, women and children wear the white linen blouse. Men wear a jacket and short cloth or leather breeches held up by wide embroidered cloth braces. Both sexes wear embroidered cloth waistcoats and knitted woolen hose, very often white. Colorful bands border the feminine full skirt and a large white apron usually covers it. Black leather boots are worn and black leather low shoes have heavy, flat soles, a large silver buckle frequently adorns the feminine low shoe. Hats of felt or straw are wide-brimmed and usually dressed with a barnyard feather or brush.

tyubetevka   a pillbox type of hat with flat or peaked crown ornamented with varicolored embroidery. It is known as the Uzbek cap and is popular all over Central Asia and Russia.

tzute   rectangles of hand-loomed woolen fabric, usually orange, with stripes in red and black, worn by Tzutuhil Indians of western Guatemala. The pieces are carried as handwork and are tied into turban, wide sash, rebozo, shoulder scarf, blanket, etc.

Tyrolese felt hat with cord, tassel and feathers— 1880's

tyubetevka— known as "Uzbek cap"—popular over Central Asia and Russia—of felt, ribbon and embroidery— worn by men and women

u

udones   full-length stockings of cut and sewn cloth worn by the early Christian clergy and Roman citizens. Those for the priestly class were made of white linen and later of silk. The Udo (singular) fitted over the foot to above the knee. Udones, (plural of udo) were a regular part of European dress from the fifth to the eleventh centuries. Chausse to the Normans, heuse to the Germans, and hose to the Saxons.

ulster   a heavy overcoat originally worn by men and women in Ulster, northern Ireland. A long, loose-fitting coat, usually double-breasted, with a full- or half-belt. The coat was formerly made of Ulster frieze. Worn in the U.S. in the first and second decades, twentieth century.

ultramarine   the word meaning "from beyond the sea." In medieval times, a costly pigment for painting made by pulverizing lapis lazuli; a deep blue of high saturation and low brilliance.

umbrella   from umbraculum, Latin. Babylonians, Assyrians, Greeks, Etruscans and Romans made use of the umbrella, which dates far back into antiquity. A Chinese legend notes that it was invented by the Chinese in the eleventh century B.C., and had twenty-eight ribs. It was widely used for rain in the Orient and the Near East, where it was made of leather. In the Middle Ages, it was adopted by the Catholic Church as a symbol of dignity and power. Falling into disuse, it survived in Portugal, was taken up in Italy and called an "umbrella," and then in France became a woman's fashion, with the name of "parapluie." 1787 is the first date of manufacture in England. The first umbrellas shipped to America came from India to Baltimore in 1772 and were considered feminine accessories. see *sunshades, parasols;* illustrations next page.

underdrawers   see *drawers.*

underfur   the soft, thick fur underlying the long, coarse guard hairs of a fur-bearing animal.

underpinnings   a name for feminine lingerie.

underproper   the wire frame which supported the starched ruff worn in the sixteenth and seventeenth centuries. see *supportasse.*

undershirt   the masculine body garment of knitted white lisle or wool

Ulster-heavy, long, loose, double-breasted overcoat model shown—American—1912

underwear-"underpinings" of a lady of the turn of the 20th C.—chemise of white nainsook, lace and ribbon-corset of brocaded pink coutil

Umbrella

Babylonian
and Assyrian

ancient
Greek

silk
umbrella
late 17th C.

silk tilting
parasol-about
18 inches
diameter-
1795

silk
tilting
parasol-
1796

silk with galloon
and gauze frill-
18th C

silk umbrella-
ivory and
ebony handle-
1813

parasol of
pale blue silk
with fringe-
1813

parasol of red
and blue striped
silk - red ribbon-
1880's

worn under the outer muslin, linen or silk shirt.

undervest a feminine sleeveless body garment of knitted lisle or silk worn under the corset in the nineteenth and early twentieth centuries.

underwear, feminine see *lingerie.*

underwear, masculine consists of skeleton shirt and trunks of cotton, wool or nylon.

undress, military the prescribed uniform for all ordinary occasions.

undressed kid see *kid, undressed.*

Ungaro, Emmanuel see *couture haute.*

uniform prescribed dress of certain style and color for members of a certain society, school or organization, such as a military unit.

union suit a knitted undergarment combining shirt and drawers in one piece. Of wool for winter warmth and lisle or rayon for summer. Made ankle- and wrist-lengths before the use of central heating. Today, used principally for skiing.

unpressed pleats see *pleats, unpressed.*

unprime furs see *furs, unprime.*

unwoven cloth see *felt cloth.*

uparnā a scarf worn as a shawl or veil by Hindu and Mohammedan men and women in India. Of muslin or silk woven with gold or silver threads.

uplift a brassière built to lift and hold the breasts; some are built to hold firm and flatten.

uraeus the symbol of Egyptian sovereignty, a representation of the sacred asp worn by ancient kings and queens. It was attached to the crown in the center of the forehead.

uparnā—same as dopatta—Indian scarf worn by both sexes—of silk or muslin with gold or silver threads

Uraeus—sacred asp and goddess of Lower Egypt—vulture, goddess of Upper Egypt worn by Egyptian king

uraeus—sacred asp and goddess of Lower Egypt, of silver and enamel in conventionalized style

uraeus—goddess of Lower Egypt—worn by a queen of Egypt

V

vair fur of the Russian or Siberian squirrel, a precious fur sewn in alternating gray and white pieces and worn by only kings, nobles and prelates. Medieval.

val lace see *valenciennes lace.*

valence a linen cover which the medieval knight wore on his helmet.

valencia a strong vesting material, figured or striped, of faille or cotton warp with worsted weft. Used principally for livery waistcoats.

Valenciennes or **Val lace** real lace made of linen or cotton thread. A fine bobbin lace in which the thread forms the ground and motifs, without cordonnet, on open and regular mesh. Used on handkerchiefs, baby's wear and fine lingerie. Excellent machine-made imitations are widely used. Commonly known as Val lace, and much used for dresses, blouses lingerie and hats, nineteenth and twentieth centuries.

Valentina see *couture, haute.*

Valentino see *couture, haute.*

vallancey, vallancy a large wig of the seventeenth century which shaded a gentleman's face.

vamp front of the shoe, that part of the shoe upper consisting of instep and toe.

vampy, vampay see *scogger.*

Van Dyck collar see *falling band.*

Van Dyck style the seventeenth century fashions made familiar by the portraits painted by Anthony Van Dyck, court painter to Charles I. see *cavalier.*

Van Dyck collar or falling band—white lawn embroidered— beaver hat with plume—"English ringlets"— 1630's

vanity case usually a small dressy bag or box for evening use in which the lady carries powder, lipstick and rouge, and other articles. see *compact, vanity case.*

vareuse from the French for the undervest or shirt worn by sailors for messy work; a term formerly used in the southern United States.

vasquine see *basquine.*

vat-dyed When fabric is steeped in vat dye and exposed to the air, the dye is reformed by oxidation and precipitated into the fiber, becoming fast to sun and water.

veal calf see *calf, veal.*

vegetable dye dye obtained from plants, i.e. not mineral or synthetic.

vegetable fibers those which originate from plants such as flax, cotton, jute, ramie and kapok.

vegetable flannel   a flannel made of fine wool, of German manufacture.

vegetable hair   a fibrous substance prepared from the long moss in southern United States. Used for padding, packing, etc.

vegetable horsehair   a stuffing and padding of fiber from the European dwarf fan palm.

vegetable ivory   the fruit of a tropical palm in South America. When growing, the nut is soft and creamy, but hardens and resembles animal ivory. Used almost entirely for buttons. see *ivory nut*.

vegetable silk   a fibrous material obtained from the coating of seeds of a Brazilian tree. Used for stuffing and padding.

veil   The veil has come down from the ancient cradle of civilization in the valley of Euphrates and Tigris. It is most time-honored and meaningful of costume accessories in feminine dress, and a part of as many religions as it has been of fashion. For thousands of years it has stood for bondage, humility, modesty, holiness, marriage, mourning or beauty. In Biblical times, Hebrew women wore veils of gauze as a status mark. In the Christian Church, Paul, apostle to the Gentiles, reproved women for appearing in church with uncovered heads. The feminine veil of the East was worn long before 622 A.D., the beginning of Mohammedanism and it was the adoption of the Moslem religion that carried the veil to Egypt. Though the veil continues to be worn, it is slowly disappearing in the Arab countries. A decree of Turkey in 1928 stated that the long veil worn for centuries was no longer mandatory. In the Empire and Victorian periods, veils were floating wisps of tulle or lace attached to hat or bonnet. In the last decade of the nineteenth century the taut face veil appeared, often sprinkled with chenille dots and tied over bonnet or hat. The veil more or less disappeared at the end of World War I. The short face veil in nose length survived, tied with black velvet ties to keep the hatless coiffure in order, but it has lost much of its former allure.

veil, bridal   The Greek bride wore a sheer Tyrian veil, white or colored, woven of wool or linen. It was attached to the back of her headdress or tiara, which was ornamented with pearls. A veil of yellow or saffron was worn by the Roman pagan bride, while that of the Christian bride was white or purple. In the Middle Ages, a bride's headdress was either a sheer white wimple or a tiny skullcap of pearls. The white veil is not again mentioned until the late eighteenth century when a machine for making tulle was invented in Notthingham, England in 1768. It manufactured net and lace wide enough to be used for veils and shawls. The first American bride to wear a veil is said to have been the adopted daughter of George Washington, Nellie Custis.

veil, empress demi-veil   a nose length veil worn with a tiny hat in Watteau style, early 1860's, named for the Empress Eugénie.

veil, gremial   see *gremial veil*.

veil, motoring   a long, wide chiffon veil worn at the turn of the twentieth century in the early days of automobiles. It was a necessary protection against dust, since most cars were of touring or open style and many roads unpaved. Emerald green was considered the most effective protection for the complexion.

veil, mourning   a custom of centuries that varied with different countries. The European custom called for all-black outer dress for men and women. The women, especially widows, wore a long, black, heavy crêpe veil for one year. Deep mourning was on the wane by the begin-

Lace veil-corded silk bonnet French-1806

cap of velvet or felt with frontlet and veil-French-15th C.

Bridal veil-lace net-hair dressed in Apollo's knot-shell hair pins-French-1831

capote or po bonnet-sat with straw visor and lace ve French 1801

bridal headdress-white satin band lace fans in back with jeweled brooch-1914

navy blue felt with wings and face veil-1918

fedora or Alpine hat with face veil worn bicycling-1890's

black straw with Venetian lace, ostrich and veil-French-1904

short, circular bridal veil of smoke blue tulle with a pair of birds-1937

black straw sailor-silk puggree-harem veil with chiffon hem-New York-1918

formal blac silk hunti hat-cheni veil-1930's

doll hat-pink roses and aster-pink veil-French-1940

black velvet-plumes black and royal blue-dotted veil-French-1893

navy blue sailor cap with floating veil-New York-1910

black felt bowler worn with tailored suit-coarse black mesh veil-1936

lace veil tied over a velvet toque-1920

saucer hat of white felt with black trim and dotted veil-1892

ning of the twentieth century and today has all but disappeared.

Velásquez, Diego de court painter to Philip IV of Spain. Like his contemporary, Van Dyck, he portrayed the current fashions so memorably that the style is associated with his name. He recorded the broad bell-shaped hoop flattened back and front and the slimming, long-pointed corset topped by the ruff, known today as the Infanta style, and the elegance of black for both sexes.

Velásquez Period-black velvet and galloon-sheer white embroidery-headdress of curls, bowknots, flowers and feathers-Spanish-1658

Velásquez Period-black velvet "full slops"-striped silk doublet-sheer white wisk and cuffs-cloth manta-Spanish-1620

velcro trade name of a nonmetallic, over-lapping fastener consisting of two strips of fabric faced with tiny nylon hooks which, when pressed together, hold fast. To undo, the strips are simply pulled apart. Invented by Georges de Mestral, a Swiss. First used, early 1960's on "cover-ups" in beauty salons.

veldschoen a South African Dutch shoe of untanned hide made without nails, and insole stitched to the uppers; similar to some American Indian footwear.

veldt coat a sports jacket similar to the Norfolk and worn for golf and hunting.

vellum originally a thin calf or lamb gut prepared for use as parchment. Now, fine-grained lamb, kid or calfskin prepared for the same purpose. A vegetable composition is made to resemble vellum. Used in lace-making and embroidery patterns.

vellum cloth made for the tracing of designs. A linen or cotton fabric, thin and sized on one side.

velours, beau a calfskin used for gloves which has been worked, rubbed and brushed until it resembles velvet.

veloutine a merino fabric corded and having a velvety surface.

velvet or **velours** originally made in India and imported by Genoa and Venice. It became a fabric of great luxury. In the sixteenth century, the manufacture of velvet developed in Florence, Milan and Genoa and in Lyons, France; and eventually in Germany and Holland. Velours is the French word for velvet, while the English "velours" applies to a thick-bodied, close-napped, soft type of cloth with a face finish. This latter is used for coats and felt hats, upholstery and drapery fabrics.

velvet, bagheera   a fine piece-dyed velvet, crush-resistant because of the uncut pile.

velvet, chiffon or **wedding ring**   a soft, luxurious velvet so fine that a width of it may be drawn through a wedding ring.

velvet, cut   a background of chiffon, georgette or voile with a brocaded velvet pattern. Closer-woven than transparent velvet.

velvet, Lyons   a rich stiff velvet with a back of silk, linen, cotton or rayon and a short, erect pile. Used for dresses but especially for hats.

velvet, nacré   a changeable-colored velvet made with the back of one color and the pile of another, producing an iridescent effect.

velvet, panne   woven like a plain velvet but with the pile pressed flat in one direction, giving a smooth, lustrous finish.

velvet, stamped   a velvet with an allover crushed pattern stamped on the pile by hot dies.

velvet, tartan   see *tartan velvet.*

velvet, transparent   in printed designs and solid colors and made with a rayon pile on a silk or rayon back. A soft, sheer, easily draped, lightweight velvet.

velvet, uncut   a fabric woven like velvet but with the loop warp left cut.

velveteen   a cotton velvet with short, close pile. Used for wearing apparel both feminine and masculine, especially sports clothes. see *tripe.*

velveret   a velvet with a cotton back.

venerable hood   see *French hood.*

Venetian   cotton cloth in twill or satin weave with glossy texture. Used for skirts, linings, masquerade and bathing costumes.

Venetian cloth   woolen cloth of fine texture woven either with a nap or diagonal twill. Used for dresses and skirts of medium weight.

Venetian embroidery   see *Roman cut work.*

Venetian lace   many styles of laces made in Venice such as reticella, drawn work, cut work, flat work, raised point, guipure needlepoint.

Venetians   full short breeches like knickerbockers, tied below the knees; worn in the sixteenth and seventeenth centuries.

verdigris   a color named after a greenish-blue pigment, drug or deposit that forms on copper, brass or bronze surfaces. Verdigris is sometimes called peacock or Spanish green.

verdingale   see *farthingale.*

vermilion   a brilliant red like the dye from the cochineal insect; a color varying from crimson to nearly orange.

Verona serge   a cotton and wool worsted, thin and woven with a twill.

vertugadin   see *farthingale.*

vest   see *waistcoat.*

vest, skeleton   see *skeleton vest.*

vestee   feminine, dicky which resembles a waistcoat, usually without armscyes or back. The fabric usually contrasts in color and/or texture with that of the garment.

vestings   fabrics intended for men's scarfs, vests and trimmings, such as bird's-eye linen, silk piqué, Persian patterned and corded silks.

vestments   garments and accessories of ecclesiastical attire. see *alb; chasuble; dalmatic; amice; cassock; surplice; stole; tippet; tunkle; maniple; chimere; rochet.*

Vicara   trade name of a fiber made from protein of corn. Vicara has a soft, luxurious texture like cashmere and good draping quality.

vichy   a cotton dress fabric woven of two threads of different colors.

vici kid   see *kid, vici.*

Victorian bonnets   of mid-nineteenth century, with ribbons tied under the chin, which were prim and dainty, and especially flattering to most women.

victorine   fur tippet or pelerine of the early nineteenth century.

vicuña   a wild ruminant animal of the Andes, smaller than the guanaco, living in herds from Ecuador to Bolivia. Allied to the llama and alpaca. The animal is becoming scarce· because it is much hunted for its soft wool and fur. Vicuña is the finest, softest and costliest of the wool-type fabrics. Used for overcoatings, suitings and fine sweaters.

Vietnam   a 1960's style worn by young women, a simple, straight, frock like tunic of black silk with long tight sleeves, a standing collar and a narrow belt; the skirt length between knee and ankle with fitted pantalets showing below.

Vietnamese costume   basically Chinese. see *cai-ao; caiquan; sinhs.*

vigogne yarn   a cotton yarn made up with about twenty per cent wool or wool waste.

vigoureuse, vigoureux   a worsted cloth with a mixture effect in coloring produced by printing the warp before weaving.

vinyl   a trademarked, American man-made couturière fabric introduced in 1965. Chiefly for waterproofed capes, coats and suits, and boots, belts and drapes well. It takes dye and print in brilliant colors; for skirts, hats and tote bags. Available in transparent finish and by the yard for home dressmakers. Patterns include tattersalls, stripes and dots as well as solid colors.

Vionnet, Madeleine   see *couture, haute.*

virgin wool   newly sheared wool which has not been used. Trade mark adopted, Products Labeling Act of 1929.

viscacha   a rodent allied to the Chinchilla family, a cross between chinchilla and opossum. From Argentina, it is a poor fur, commonly used in Europe for linings and trimmings, little used in the United States.

PURE VIRGIN WOOL

Trademark of quality-tested pure Virgin Wool

Vietnamese tunic or cai-co-plum-colored satin with embroidered gold Chinese motifs-trousers of white linen-black silk cap

Vietnamese woman with wicker carrying pole-white cotton jacket-black skirt called sinhs-straw hat with white cotton top

Vietnamese tunic or oudai of printed sky-blue silk -pantaloons black silk or velvet-large straw hat

viscose   wood pulp and cotton linters which, by a series of treatments in manufacture, are converted into rayon filaments and thence into a widely used fabric.

visor, vizor, vizard   in armor, the upper front piece of a helmet which was movable and could be raised to show the face. In modern usage, the projecting forepiece of a cap to protect the eyes from the sun.

viyella   the trade name for a modern twill-woven part-wool dress flannel in many weights, widths and fine colors. It is widely used for masculine, feminine and children's wear. Made in England.

voile   a fine, plain, transparent cloth of cotton, silk, rayon or wool. A crisp fabric of great strength for its weight. see *indestructible voile.*

volant   French for flounce or ruffle. see *flounce; ruffle.*

volet or **cointoise**   a scalloped pennant attached to the helmet of a chevalier in a tournament of the Middle Ages. Also, a short flowing veil attached to a woman's headdress of the same period. see *cointise; quintise.*

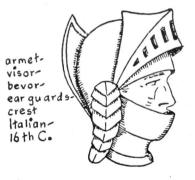

armet-
visor-
bevor-
ear guards-
crest
Italian-
16th C.

W

wadding   any mass of soft fibrous stuff used to pad, stuff or shape clothing.

wadmal, wadmol, wadmel   a woolen stuff, often coarse and hairy. Formerly used for stout warm clothes and blankets in the British Isles and Scandinavia.

waffenrock   German for a quilted tunic, doublet or tabard worn with armor. Wambais is another German name for the garment. see *mandilion; tabard*.

waffle cloth, waffle piqué, honeycomb cloth   a fabric with a honeycomb weave. Used for women's and children's apparel, dresses and coats. In white, used for men's evening ties, shirt fronts and waistcoats.

waist   a garment which clothes the body from neck to waist, a bodice or blouse.

waist cincher, waist liner, waist pincher   a foundation girdle introduced for wear with Dior's New Look of 1947. Short above and below the waistline, it was made of rayon satin, cotton lace and power net and lightly boned to produce the tiny waist. see *guepière*.

waistcoat, vest   in men's wear, a continuation of the doublet of the Middle Ages. A sleeveless but lined body jacket, waist-length, and worn between jacket and dress shirt. Made single- or double-breasted, of contrasting color or fabric or matching the suit cloth. A backless waistcoat appeared in the 1950's for summer wear. It consisted of two front pieces buttoned center front. Two narrow belt pieces, attached to the sides, buckled in back; the fronts also joined by a narrow neckband in back. see *gilet*.

wale   rib or ridges as in corduroy, piqué or any twilled fabric. "Wide wale" in corduroy is about a quarter inch wide.

walking coat   it resembled the cutaway coat in design but was a bit shorter and had pocket flaps on the hips. It varied in being quite often made of fancy suitings. see *frock coat; English coat; Prince Albert*.

walking shoe   a sturdy, comfortable, leather shoe with medium or low heel.

walking stick   see *cane*.

wallaby   any of the smaller and medium-sized kangaroos from Australia but tanned in the United States. An excellent shoe leather, close-grained and fine, yet tough. see *kangaroo*.

wallachian or **walachian embroidery**   a colorful piece of handwork executed in solid buttonhole stitch.

wallaroo   see *kangaroo*.

wallet   a flat folding purse in which is carried bills and coins, personal documents such as driving license and credit and membership cards. *A Dictionary of Men's Wear*, published 1908, W. H. Baker, says the wallet is for carrying bank notes lengthwise and billets d'amour.

wambais, wammus   a man's jacket quilted with flax or tow. More recently, chiefly in the southern United States, a heavy, loosely knitted cardigan with leather belt.

wampum   an Algonquin word for beads and strings of beads made from hard clam and whelk shells found along the coast. The original word (meaning white) was shortened by the European settlers. Beads and wampum belts became a medium of exchange between Indians and settlers.

warp   the threads that extend lengthwise in a loom and which are crossed by the weft or filling.

warp lace   a lace worked on a net in which only the warp threads are visible. Used for glass curtaining.

warp-printed   usually silks, wherein the warp threads are printed with the pattern or design before weaving, the weft threads being of neutral or plain color, producing a blurred effect.

wash and wear   a fabric treated with wrinkle-resistant properties which makes the laundered garment wearable with little or no ironing. "Wash and wear" and "drip dry" are synonymous terms for such fabrics which have been available since about 1955.

wasp waist or **hourglass silhouette**   of the 1890's and early 1900's, produced by a corset heavily boned with steel and whalebone. An eighteen-inch waist was the most desired and admired measurement.

watch   The first pocket watch was the invention of a locksmith of Nuremberg in the fifteenth century. It was egg-shaped and called a "Nuremberg live egg." A watch presented to Queen Elizabeth I is described as an armlet of gold with rubies and diamonds containing a "clock." It was really the first wrist watch but had only an hour hand; the minute hand was invented in the seventeenth century. The first thin watches appeared in 1776 and machine-made watches in 1838. A watch on a pin was worn by the Gibson Girl in 1907, and the modern wrist watch appeared in 1914. In the late nineteenth and twentieth centuries, ladies' watches were

also worn on necklace chains or on long chains with the watch tucked into a belt pocket. The wrist watch attached to a buckled leather strap was developed for the convenience of the soldier in World War I. Women also adopted the leather wrist strap, but for dress, exquisitely small watches, plain or jeweled, were worn attached to black ribbon or jeweled bands.

watch cap   see *cap, watch.*

watch, chatelaine   see *chatelaine watch.*

watch, hunting-case   a man's pocket watch with both dial and back covered; the dial covering, on a spring hinge, could be snapped shut to protect the glass from breakage. With the development of plastic unbreakable crystals, this style was given up. A smaller version was worn by ladies in the late nineteenth and early twentieth centuries, suspended from the neck on a long chain and tucked into the belt. The hunter wrist watch for ladies, mid-twentieth century, has a decorative snap lid, generally jeweled.

watch, repeater   a man's watch of the nineteenth century with a chime which struck the hours. Pressing a spring made the hour chime repeat. This obviated the necessity of lighting a candle or lamp in order to tell the time in the middle of the night.

water repellent   describes a water-resistant cloth or garment which permits a breathing through the cloth and is more comfortable to wear than a waterproofed finish. Though resistant, it is not impervious to water.

watered silk   see *moiré.*

waterfall   a headdress of the 1860's with the hair cascading from a knot on the top of the head to the nape of the neck.

wasp waist - old blue velvet and black - separate capelet - mink muff and bands - black velvet hat with blue and black ostrich - French - 1893

waterfall coiffure - tiny hat of rose taffeta with ribbon rosettes - French - 1860's

waterproof   a waterproof fabric is a cloth completely sealed against moisture.

waterproofing   various processes by which fabrics and leather are rendered impervious to water.

Watteau bonnet   a style featured in the paintings of the French painter Jean-Antoine Watteau (1684–1721). Of straw or felt with ostrich plumes and velvet ribbon. French, 1770's.

Watteau gown   the principal style of the French Regency (1715–1723) as pictured by the painter Jean-Antoine Watteau. A loose sack or dress worn over a tight bodice and very full underskirt. The gown had loose folds falling from the shoulders in back, becoming part of the skirt. The neck in front was low and the stomacher ornamented with ribbon. In the 1730's, the Watteau gown became the robe à la française with six box pleats stitched to the back and ending in a train. By 1770 this loose gown was formal dress for court functions. The robe volant or "flying gown" was a variation of the Watteau pleats, the style lasting to the 1770's.

Watteau mantilla   of flowered silk held to the figure by a cord or ribbon; A velvet hood lined with satin.

Watteau pleats   see *pleats, Watteau.*

Watteau sacque   an at-home costume of a hip-length blouse open in front over a stomacher, with pleats falling from the neck in back. Worn over several petticoats. Eighteenth century.

wearing apparel   a general term for all clothing.

weasel   any of the small slender-bodied animals of the weasel family. see *ermine; marten; mink; sable; skunk; stoat; wolverine.*

Watteau flying gown - gown and underskirt of satin - laced bodice - pagoda sleeves - velvet bowknots - lingerie cap - French - 1730

Watteau hat - straw or felt - ostrich and ribbon - powdered hair in puffs and cadogan - French - 1770's

Watteau pleats - pink taffeta gown and underskirt - edged with guimpe - lingerie cap, neck frill and sleeve ruffles - early 18th C.

Watteau or shepherdess hat of straw or silk with lace, violets and aigrettes - French - 1869

weather skirt   see *safeguard.*

weaving   in its simplest form, the art of making cloth on a frame; a process in which one makes a piece of cloth by interlacing two yarns or strands of threads at right angles. In the third century A.D. Syrian weavers in Byzantium developed the weaving of patterned fabrics by the use of shuttles.

webbing   narrow strips of elasticized woven material which are used for garters and suspenders.

wedding gown   White appears to have become customary for brides during the First Empire (1799–1815) when the tiny jackets and long coats were of rich dark colors but the dress invariably white. For well over a century white has prevailed, of heavy silk, velvet or lustrous satin with a full-length lace or tulle veil. By the mid-twentieth century, customs became less rigid and a bride might wear a gown of less conventional style and perhaps a shoulder-length headdress of tulle. see *bridal dress*.

wedding ring   see *ring, wedding*.

wedge or **platform sole**   of wood or leather for sports shoes with heel and sole in one layer and piece, flat on the ground from heel to toe. Fashionable in the 1940's. First worn in ancient Greek drama and called the "tragic kothornos."

wedgie   after Wedgies, a trademark; a wedge-heeled shoe.

weeds   garments, especially mourning attire. A black band on a man's hat or sleeve, mourning clothes or a widow's black veil. see *mourning*.

weft   the threads that cross the warp from selvedge to selvedge. see *warp*.

weighted silk   see *silk, weighted*.

weighting, loading   a process of adding body and weight to a fabric, especially silk yarn which loses weight when boiled to free it of natural gums. Sizing may also be applied to linen or cotton. see *sizing*.

Weitz, John   see *couture, haute*.

Wellington boot   see *boot, Wellington*.

Wellington half-boot   see *half-boot, Wellington*.

Welsh flannel   fine hand-woven cloth from the wool of sheep of the Welsh mountains.

welt   a cord, fold, etc., sewn to an edge or border to strengthen or trim.

West of England cloth   woolen cloths of fine reputation from the textile centers of Bradford, Huddersfield, Leeds, etc., extra fine worsteds, broadcloths, etc.

whalebone   a horny substance from the upper jaw of the baleen whale. It has served as a stiffening in costume since the Middle Ages. It was used to shape the long, peaked toes of footwear; the tall, pointed feminine hennin; the plumes of helmets and many other items. Finally, in the sixteenth century, whalebone replaced iron and steel for stays and busks of corsets and the peasecod-belly of the gentleman's doublet. Today it is obtained chiefly from the bowhead of Greenland, home of the Arctic whale, but it is scarce, as is the use of bones in today's feminine underpinings.

whang leather   a Scotch term for leather thongs, lacings and straps.

whipcord   a diagonal twill-woven fabric of hard-twisted yarns. Usually in solid colors as Oxford gray, tan and white. Used for sportswear and military uniforms.

whisk   see *gallila*.

whiskers   see *beards*.

white   the color of pure snow, reflecting all the rays of the spectrum combined.

white bob wig   see *wig, white bob.*

white coat   see *seal, baby.*

white fox   see *fox, white.*

white tie   the popular term for men's formal evening dress of black tailcoat, white waistcoat and white tie, as opposed to "black tie" which is for informal evening use.

whitney   see *witney.*

wide-awake hat   another name for the Quaker's hat, a low-crowned, broad-brimmed hat.

widow's peak   a widow's bonnet with a peak dipping over the forehead; also, a coiffure with a point of hair in the middle of the forehead. see *attifet bonnet; coiffure.*

wig   a covering of interwoven human hair or synthetic fiber shaped to the head to hide a deficiency of natural hair.

wig, Adonis   a popular hairpiece in the early eighteenth century. It was fashioned of white or gray hair.

wig, bag   a powdered wig with ends tied in a black silk bag to keep powder off the coat, the bag also worn while growing hair. Pigeon's wings often accompanied the bag over ear and cheek.

wig, barrister's wig   see *wig, full-bottomed; professional.*

wig block   a wooden block, round on top, used for making and dressing wigs.

wig, bob   a short wig of the eighteenth century worn on ordinary occasions, and for negligée by men and boys. The curled, bushy, usually white wig was a favorite with the clergy and was worn by the Quakers.

wig, campaign   worn in service and traveling. It had a curled toupee over the front of the head, pigeon's wings over the ears and the back hair in a black silk bag. Late seventeenth and early eighteenth centuries.

wig, full-bottomed   a wig with high peaks worn from 1750 through the first two decades of the nineteenth century. "Corners" of hair were inserted in concealed parts to shape its contour. The full-bottomed wig was especially favored by elderly and professional men. English and American barristers wore it to the late eighteenth century, and it has been retained to the present by the British as part of official and professional dress. A smaller wig remains part of the uniform of the coachmen of the British sovereign.

wig, hedgehog style   the natural hair was cut short on the top of the head and at the sides, the back hair tied in the black silk bag. 1785.

wig, pigeon's wings   wig with two curled puffs, one over each ear, eighteenth century.

wig powder   pure white powder, appearing in 1703, to cover the wig. Snow-white was most fashionable, gray next, and least fashionable was the brown wig dusted with brown powder. The height of the powder vogue was from 1760 to 1776. Favored colors were grayish pink, blue and violet scented with violet, chypre and pulverized starch.

wig, Spanish hair   is the most desirable hair for present-day wigs. Spanish hair is long, black, soft and shiny and easy to process. Spain is the leading exporter of hairpieces and wigs, amounting to over 25,000 pounds a year, as of the 1960's.

wig, tie or **tye**   hair simply drawn back and tied with a black silk ribbon.

wig, tonsure   the gray wig of the French abbot, made with the tonsure. Eighteenth century.

"wide-awake" Quaker hat of beaver with ribbon and buckle 1780's

Wigs

full-bottomed wig-two points- French and English-judiciary

powdered pigtail wig with pigeons' wings- 1731

full-bottomed black wig- English- 1670

full-bottomed white wig- English and American judges- 18th C.

Ramillies wig- ribbon bows and solitaire- English cavalry- 1740's

solitaire- gray powdered tie-wig with toupet- English- 1730's

powdered wig with toupet, puffs and cadogan- English- 1774

hedgehog style, wig or natural- French- 1785

powdered bag wig with pigeons' wings- silk bag and ribbon 1728

powdered bob wig- English and French-18th C

gray wig with tonsure- French abbé

white bob wig-cleric American- 18th C.

396

Wigs - Falls

wig
and
jeweled circlet-
Egyptian Queen-2033 B.C.

wig of short tube-like
curls-Egyptian-2560-
2420 B.C.

Cypriote curls-toupee
of spiral curls-Greek

Cypriote curls in
toupee form-
Roman-1st C.A.D.

coiffure à la
Zazzera-silk wig-
usually yellow-
Italian-circa 1475

natural hair
with falls-one
pendant-three
dressed in rolls

coiffure
à la Japonaise-
natural hair
with added falls
and floral piece

falls dressed
over short
hair

falls dressed
over bobbed
hair

wimple and gorget of sheer lawn-jeweled velvet band or crown-German-13 th C.

chinband, wimple and brim in white linen on a red toque-French-13 th C.

witch's costume-black cloth and white muslin-black felt hat over lingerie cap-laced bodice

wig, toupee a curled toupee over the front of the head. see *campaign wig*.

wig, white bob the white wig of elderly, clerical and professional men. American, last quarter eighteenth century.

wigan a cotton fabric, canvas-like, used to stiffen garments. from Wigan, England.

wigs, Queen Elizabeth's Queen Elizabeth I, who had as many as eighty wigs at one time, is supposed to have worn them over a shaved head. Her favorite colors were red and saffron, though she had blond hair as a young woman. By way of compliment, her ladies dyed their locks red. Her wigs were dressed with jewels, pearls and feathers. Mary, Queen of Scots, whose wigs came from France, when in prison changed her wig every other day and wore one to the executioner's block.

wild silk see *silk, wild*.

wildcat see *lynx*.

willow a straw of woven esparto grass and cotton and similar to esparterie. Used instead of buckram for higher-priced hats.

wimple a headkerchief worn in the twelfth and thirteenth centuries, square, rectangular or circular in shape, placed on top of the head and hanging to the shoulders. Known also as the headrail. It was held in place by a fillet of metal, or by a crown if worn by a lady of rank. Of fine white linen, often in colors, especially saffron yellow. After centuries of being worn by court ladies, it remained the headdress of women in general. As often as not, it was worn with a chinband.

wincey, winsey a cloth usually with cotton or linen warp and wool filling, either plain or twilled. Used especially for warm shirts, skirts and pajamas.

windblown bob the hair clipped short, simulating a windblown coif.

windbreaker a sports jacket made of leather or heavy woolen cloth with interlining or quilting, resistant to wind.

windclothes made especially for Arctic exploration and therefore of windproof materials.

Windsor cap see *cap, Windsor*.

Windsor knot see *collar, Windsor*.

wing collar see *collar, wing*.

wings puffs marking the junction of the sleeve and shoulder, a fashion of the second half of the sixteenth century.

winkle-picker in England the name for a shoe with a sharply pointed toe, fashionable the first half of the twentieth century. The term comes from a small sharp pick used when eating periwinkles, a kind of mussel.

Winterhalter another term for the crinoline period, named after the elegant portraits painted by Franz Xavier Winterhalter (1805–1873). He was a German portrait and court painter who lived in Paris from 1834 to 1870.

witch's costume a modern fancy dress imitation of the seventeenth century countrywoman's dress, featuring a steeple hat with narrow brim and a scarlet cloak. The second half of the seventeenth century was the period of most intense witch persecution in England and the American Colonies.

witch's hat as it is known today, a tall, peaked or steeple-crowned hat with a wide brim. Of black felt wool or black beaver, the hat was worn by Puritan women over a white linen or lawn cap in the seventeenth century.

witney, whitney   a sturdy woolen cloth, heavy and coarse, made in Witney, England, in the eighteenth century. It was used for coats and breeches. Also, a soft overcoat and blanket cloth resembling chinchilla, the surface tufted in transverse ridges.

witzchoura   a feminine redingote, about 1808; a long, Empire cloak, fur-lined, of Russian origin. The same style was copied in percale for summer wear, without fur.

wolf   a doglike mammal found in the forested regions of North America, Europe, Asia and Africa. The most valuable for the fur trade comes from northern sections. There are two distinct species, the large gray timber or Canadian arctic, and the small red wolf called prairie or coyote.

wolf, coyote   the Mexican name for a small species of wolf from western United States and Canada, known in the fur trade as western wolf. Cheaper than wolf and used for popular priced coats.

wolverine   a bearlike animal, largest of the weasel family. It is found in the northern regions of America, Russia, Siberia and Scandinavia. The fur is durable, warm and deep, with long top hair. It is the only fur which does not frost, and therefore was worn by the Eskimos and used as fringe and trimming by the Indians. Used as trimming in the fur trade, expensive because of limited quantity.

wombat   see *kangaroo*.

wooden shoes   see *shoes, wooden*.

wool   a natural fiber obtained from sheep which accounts for most of the wool used in clothing. Specialty fibers or wool from other animals are alpaca, camel's hair, cashmere, llama, mohair and angora goat. Not until a late period did the Egyptians wear any wool and then only for cloaks. Egyptian sheep had coarse, greasy, dark wool, the fleecy type of the Mediterranean world. The art of weaving wool was attained early in ancient times by many different peoples. When Alexander the Great, in the fourth century, invaded India, the natives were found wearing woven woolen shawls of great beauty. The Greeks learned to process and weave wool from the Egyptians, the Romans from the Greeks and by way of Rome, the knowledge passed to the Occidental world. Though the early weaving loom was a seemingly crude instrument, it is said that the fineness of texture produced using it has not been excelled to our day. In the twelfth century, the English King Henry II imported Flemish weavers into England and established weavers' guilds. He granted to the City of London the exclusive privilege of exporting woolen cloth. For many centuries the manufacture of woolen cloth was a household industry. Not until the late nineteenth century were all the processes grouped together in one building. see *shoddy; virgin wool; woolen; worsted*.

wool, Australian   see *Australian wool*.

wool batiste   an all-wool fabric, fine and lightweight, thinner than challis. Used for dresses and negligées.

wool, brushed   see *brushed wool*.

wool crepe   a lightweight woolen fabric with crepy texture of various weights and surface effects. Used for suits, dresses, blouses, etc.

woolens   woolen fabrics are made of shorter fibers than worsteds. The yarns are soft, loosely twisted and usually have a slightly fuzzy texture as in tweeds, coatings, and meltons.

worsted   a woolen fabric made of yarn which is smooth and compact and has been evenly combed, producing a long-wearing cloth such as serge or gabardine. Its name is derived from Worstead, a

witzchoura, a pelisse or fur-lined coat – velvet with astrakan lining and chinchilla trim – 1818

timber wolf – length 48 inches – tail 16 inches

wolverine – 3 to 3½ feet long – tail 6 inches

village in England, once the center of the woolen industry.

worsted yarn   a smooth-surfaced yarn spun from long-stapled pure wool fibers combed so that the fibers lay parallel to each other in weaving. The yarns are loosely twisted for knitting.

Worth, Charles Frederick   An Englishman who came to Paris before he was twenty years of age. He became a famous couturier, and in 1858 founded the House of Worth. He was the first to exhibit his creations on living mannequins. The Empress Eugénie and most European royalty were his patrons. For thirty years he was the arbiter of Paris fashions.

wraparound   see *skirt, wraparound.*

wrapper   a loose dressing robe.

wrapper   an informal house gown of the late nineteenth and early twentieth centuries, usually with ruffled neck, sleeves and hem. Fastened in front and held to the figure with a tie belt or left to hang loose. Made of a great variety of fabrics, either plain or trimmed with lace or other decoration.

wraprascal   a long, loose greatcoat of the eighteenth century used for riding by both sexes. Buttoned with large metal buttons and sometimes caped. see *Joseph* or *Josie.*

wreath   masculine, a crown or chaplet of intertwined leaves, especially laurel leaves, worn in antiquity as a sign of honor. Feminine, a garland of intertwined flowers for the Queen of May or for a bride.

wristlet   a bracelet, an ornamental ribbon; a strap to hold a watch; knitted worsted bands as protection against cold, all worn on the wrist. see *muffetees.*

wylie coat   Scotch name for a nightdress consisting of undervest and petticoat. Worn by women and children.

bathing suit and wrap·around skirt of print cotton–brown on black– Greta Plattry– 1956

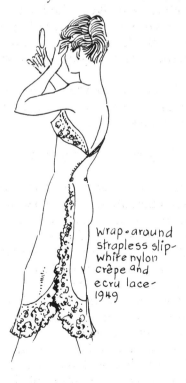

wrap·around strapless slip– white nylon crêpe and ecru lace– 1949

Y

yachting A lady's yachting costume in the late nineteenth and early twentieth centuries usually consisted of white flannel or heavy linen skirt worn with shirtwaist with stiff collar and bow tie. The jacket had full-puffed sleeves above the tight forearms. A mannish peaked cap completed the outfit. see *boating wear.*

yak lace a coarse English bobbin lace made in Northampton from Yak wool.

yard measure the English and American linear measure established in the reign of Henry II (1154–1189) by the length of the king's arm. Formerly equal to the Scotch ell. Now, the standard thirty-six inch yard.

yarmulke, yarmelke the Jewish skull-cap to be worn at all times with general dress by Orthodox Jews. Also a cap worn in reverence when reading the Torah.

yarn fibers or **filaments** used for knitting or weaving after being twisted or laid in a continuous thread.

yarn, fingering see *fingering yarn.*

yashmak, yashmac a long, narrow face screen that all Mohammedan women once wore. It has slits for the eyes, covered with strips of lace. A narrow piece of ivory, silver or gold supports the veil over the nose. It is tied by strings in back of the head. Another form of yashmak was a little black "awning" that shielded the face. Sloping down from the forehead, it was a square of black horse-hair. The wearing of the yashmak, along with the enveloping haik, is a custom centuries old among peoples of the East and Europeans living under Moorish dom-

yarmulke-
skullcap supposed to be
worn at all times by
Orthodox Jewry

yashmak of black
horsehair with silk
shawl draped over
a tarboosh -Turkish

ination. In the twentieth century cloak and veil are slowly being discarded. see *jellaba; haik; litham; maharmah.*

yellow one of the three primary colors with blue and red; yellow mixed with blue gives the secondary color green and mixed with red the secondary color orange. Yellow plus green gives the tertiary color yellow-green, yellow plus orange the tertiary color yellow-orange. Light yellows are lemon, straw and prim-rose; dark yellows are cadmium and gold.

Yugoslavian embroidery stitchery worked in brightly colored yarns with various stitches, principally cross-stitch, double purl-stitch and slanting satin stitch. Done on coarse linen.

Z

zamarra-zamarro-
the Spanish shepherd's
goatskin coat-cloth sleeves

zamarra, zamarro   a sheepskin coat worn chiefly by Spanish shepherds.

zarape   see *serape.*

zenana   the name for the harem or seraglio, formerly the women's quarters in an East Indian or Persian house from where women are, or were, secluded. Also the name of a lightweight striped fabric, the stripes simulating quilting. Of silk or flannel and used for lingerie or negligée garments.

zephyr   a sweater or loose-knit construction made of a silky, tight-twist yarn.

zephyr gingham   a plain-woven gingham with a fine, soft finish done in a variety of colors and patterns such as plaids, stripes and checks.

zephyr yarn   an embroidery and knitting yarn of a fine, soft woolen or worsted.

zibelline   a thick, lustrous woolen cloth with a long, silky nap brushed in one direction. Used for women's cloaks and capes.

zibet, zibetha   a relative of the civet cat of Africa which inhabits India, China and the Malay Peninsular. Its stripes are more numerous and regular, and it yields a scent similar to that of the civet. see *civet, civetta.*

zigzag   a line composed of even, short, sharp turns or angles. Also, an overall pattern of such lines in a cloth or braid.

zipper   the mechanical slide fastener first manufactured in the 1920's and perfected in the 1930's. Used to fasten dresses, foundation garments, or wherever a trim, concealed closure is needed.

zircon, jargoon   a mineral whose transparent varieties are used as gems; red, brownish yellow, blue, various greens and colorless. From Ceylon come smoky, pale yellow varieties, "jargon" or jargoon. Called the "poor man's diamonds."

zona   wide bands of cloth or soft leather worn by ancient Greek and Roman women over the breasts and around the hips; a wide leather belt that the Greek centurion wore under his cuirass; a hip girdle or a stomach band of wool, or heavy linen or chamoised leather.

zona belt   an outer belt or girdle that Jews and Christians in the Levant were formerly obliged to wear to distinguish them from the Moslems.

zori   the national Japanese shoe fashioned in many styles of straw, felt and wood. Sometimes the masculine sandal is slightly elevated by a low, broad heel, but the feminine shoe is always flat.

Zouave jacket   a bolero style of jacket with rounded corners, of deep, blue Arabian cloth, no collar, no buttons, but gold braid ornamentation and worn with full red cloth pantaloons. Uniform of the Zouave regiment originally formed of Kabyles of Algiers. Many Frenchmen joined the body of infantrymen and in 1838, it became a French unit and fought in the Franco-Prussian War, 1870-1871.

The uniform was copied by some independent companies of the U.S. Army in the Civil War and was also copied in feminine fashions of the 1870's.

zucchetto   a skullcap. see *cap, calotte.*

zukin   a Japanese scarf or challis to protect the coiffure, should a headcovering be needed, as in winter; the traditional protection against the sun is the parasol.

zucchetto-
skullcap worn by
Roman Catholic
ecclesiastics

Zouave jacket of
Arab blue cloth with
red braid-red cloth
pantaloons-red cap
with blue tassel-
1838

BIBLIOGRAPHY

ACCESSORIES OF DRESS—Lester and Oerke—Manuel Arts Press, Peoria, Illinois—1940

ALBUM OF AMERICAN HISTORY—James Truslow Adams—4 vols. Charles Scribner's Sons, New York, 1944-1948

AMERICAN INDIAN—Oliver La Farge—Crown Publishers, New York, 1936.

APPAREL ARTS—Anniversary Issue, 1936—Esquire, Inc., New York

BOBBINS OF BELGIUM—Charlotte Kellog—Funk and Wagnalls Co., New York, 1920

BOOK OF COSTUME—by a Lady of Rank (Mary Margaret Stanley Edgerton, Countess of Wilton) Henry Colburn, London, 1847

BRITISH COSTUME DURING XIX CENTURIES—MRS. CHARLES H. ASHDOWN—Thomas Nelson and Sons, Ltd., 1910

CLANS and TARTANS of SCOTLAND—Robert Bain—Collins, London and Glasgow

CLOTHES—James Laver—Horizon Press, Inc., New York, 1953

COSMETICS AND ADORNMENT—Max Wykes-Joyce, Philosophical Library, New York, 1961

COSTUMES ANCIENS et MODERNES—Cesare Vecellio—Firmin Didot Frères et Fils, Paris, 1859

COSTUME IN ENGLAND—F. W. Fairholt, F.S.A.—2 vols. C. Bell and Sons Ltd., London, 1846—1910-1916

COSTUME THROUGHOUT THE AGES—Mary Evans, A.M.—J. B. Lippincott and Co., Philadelphia, 1930

COSTUMES AND FASHIONS IN OLD NEW ENGLAND—Alice Morse Earle—Charles Scribner's Sons, New York, 1893

DICTIONARY OF THE AMERICAN INDIAN—John L. Stoutenburgh Jr.—Philosophical Library, New York, 1960

DICTIONARY OF MEN'S WEAR—William Henry Baker—Britton Printing Co., Cleveland, Ohio, 1908

DICTIONARY OF TEXTILE TERMS—Dan River Mills Inc.—Danville, Virginia, 1960

DICTIONNAIRE DU COSTUME—Maurice Leloir—Librairie Gründ, Paris, 1951

DIE MODE—Mittel Alter, XVI, XVII, XVIII jahrhundert—Max von Boehn—Munich, 1919, 1925, 1925, 1928—4 vols.

DRESSMAKERS OF FRANCE—Picken and Miller—Harper and Brothers, New York, 1956

EARLY AMERICAN COSTUME—Warwick and Pitz—Century Co., New York, 1929

ENCYCLOPAEDIA BRITANNICA—11th Edition, New York, 1911

ENCYCLOPEDIA OF COSTUME—James Robinson Planché—London, 1876

ENCYCLOPEDIA—NEW STANDARD—Funk and Wagnalls—New York and London, 1937

ENCYCLOPEDIA OF EGYPTIAN CIVILIZATION—translated from the French—Georges Posener-Tudor Publishing Co., New York

ENGLISH COSTUME—Dion Clayton Calthrop—Adam and Charles Black, London, 1907

EVERYDAY LIFE IN ROMAN BRITAIN—Marjorie and C. H. B. Quennell—B. T. Batsford Ltd., London, 1924

EVERYDAY LIFE IN ANGLO-SAXON, VIKING AND NORMAN TIMES—Marjorie and C. H. B. Quennell—B. T. Batsford Ltd., London, 1926

FABRIC FACTS—Fairchild Publications, Inc., New York, 1965

FIELDBOOK OF NATURAL HISTORY—E. Lawrence Palmer—McGraw Hill Book Co. Inc., New York, Toronto, 1949

FASHIONS FOR MEN—Editors of Esquire Magazine—Harper and Row, New York, 1966

FUR—A PRACTICAL TREATISE—Max Bachrach—Prentice-Hall Inc., New York, 1936-1937-1946-1947

HERITAGE OF COTTON—M. D. C. Crawford—Fairchild Publications Inc., New York, 1948

HISTORY OF AMERICAN COSTUME—1607-1870—Elizabeth McClellan—Tudor Publishing Co., New York, 1942

HISTORIC COSTUME FOR THE STAGE—Lucy Barton—Walter H. Baker Co., Boston, 1938

HISTOIRE DE LA DENTELLE—Madame Bury Palliser—Librairie de Firmin, Didot et Cie, Paris, 1892

HISTOIRE DU COSTUME EN FRANCE—J. Quicherat—Librairie Hachette et Cie, Paris, 1875

HISTORY OF CORSETS—M. D. C. Crawford and E. Guernsey—Fairchild Publications Inc., New York, 1951

HISTORY OF COSTUME—Carl Kohler—George G. Harrap and Co. Ltd., London, 1928

HISTORY OF HOSIERY—Milton N. Grass—Fairchild Publications Co. Inc., New York, 1955

HISTORY OF LINGERIE—M. D. C. and E. G. Crawford—Fairchild Publications Inc., 1952

HISTORY OF UNDERCLOTHES—G. Willet and Phillie Cunnington—Michael Joseph, Ltd., London, 1951

INDIANS—Editors of American Heritage—American Heritage Publishing Co. 1961

INDIANS OF THE AMERICAS—National Geographic Society—Washington, D.C., 1955

INDIANS OF AMERICA—Lillian Davids Fazzani—Whitman Publishing Co., Racine, Wisc., 1935

INDIAN COSTUMES OF THE UNITED STATES—Clark Wissler—American Museum of Natural History—Doubleday, Doran and Co. Inc., New York, 1940

INDIANS, NORTH AMERICAN—George Catlin—2 vols.—George Grant, Edinburgh, 1926

LANGUAGE OF FASHION—Mary Brooks Picken—J. J. Little and Ives Co. New York, 1932

LAROUSSE UNIVERSAL—2 vols.—Librairie Larousse, Paris, 1922

LE CORSET DANS L'ART ET LES MOEURS DU XIII AU XX SIÈCLES—F. Libron et H. Clouzot, Paris, 1933

LA COSTUME CHEZ LES PEUPLES ANCIENS ET MODERNES—Fr. Hottenroth

LE COSTUME HISTORIQUE—M. A. Racinet—Firmin Didot et Cie., Paris, 1888—6 vols.

LOVE OF A GLOVE—C. Coddy Collins—Fairchild Publications Inc., New York, 1945

MALE AND FEMALE COSTUME; From the Notebooks of BEAU BRUMMEL—Eleanor Parker—Doubleday, Doran and Co., New York, 1932

MANUEL OF LACE—Jeannette E. Pethebridge—Cassell and Co. Ltd.—London, 1931

MODES AND MANNERS OF THE XIX CENTURY—Dr. Oscar Fischel and Max Von Boehn—4 vols.—J. M. Dent and Co., London—E. P. Dutton Co., New York—1909–1909–1909–1927

PAGEANT OF HATS ANCIENT AND MODERN—Ruth Edgar Kilgour—Robert M. McBride and Co., New York, 1958

POCKET TEXTILE DICTIONARY—Kogos Publications Co., New York, 1962

REMEMBER WHEN—Allen Churchill—Golden Press, Inc., New York, 1967

SHORT HISTORY OF COSTUME AND ARMOUR—Kelley and Schwabe—B. T. Batsford Ltd., London, 1931

TASTE AND FASHION—James Laver—George G. Harrap and Co. Ltd., London, 1948

TASTE IN AMERICA—Ishbel Ross—Thomas Y. Crowell Company, New York, 1967

THE ART OF ENGLISH COSTUME—C. Willet Cunnington—Collins, London, 1948

THE BEAUTIFUL PEOPLE—Marylin Bender—Coward—McCann, Inc., New York, 1967

THE DANDY—BRUMMELL TO BEERBOHM—Ellen Moers—Viking Press, Inc., New York, 1960

THE REGIONAL COSTUMES OF SPAIN—Isabel de Palencia—Madrid, 1926

THE ROMANCE OF LACE—Mary Eirwen Jones—Spring Books, London

THE STORY OF LACE AND EMBROIDERY—David E. Schwab—Fairchild Publications, Inc., New York, 1951

THE STORY OF LINEN—WILLIAM F. LEGGETT—Chemical Publishing Co., New York, 1945

THE WONDERFUL WORLD OF CLOTHES—U.S. Committee for Unicef—Robert Hall Clothes, Inc., 1965

THE WORLD AND ITS PEOPLES—Greystone Press, New York—1960's

THIS IS FASHION—Elizabeth Burris-Meyers—Harper and Brothers, New York, 1943

TOOLS AND TOYS OF STITCHERY—Gertrude Whiting—Columbia University Press, New York, 1928

TWO CENTURIES OF COSTUME IN AMERICA—Alice Morse Earle—The Macmillan Co., New York, 1903

WEBSTER'S NEW INTERNATIONAL DICTIONARY—G. and C. Merriam Co., Springfield, Mass., 1937

WEBSTER'S BIOGRAPHICAL DICTIONARY—C. and G. Merriam Co., Springfield, Mass., 1953

PERIODICALS—

CIBA REVIEW—Basle, Switzerland

FAIRCHILD PUBLICATIONS, Inc., New York

GENTLEMEN'S QUARTERLY, Esquire, Inc., New York

HARPER'S BAZAAR, New York

THE METROPOLITAN MUSEUM OF ART—Bulletins—New York

THE NATIONAL GEOGRAPHIC MAGAZINE—Washington, D.C.

THE NEW YORK TIMES, New York

TIME MAGAZINE Inc., New York

VOGUE MAGAZINE, New York